An Emerging Digital Wall

C. Y. Cyrus Chu

An Emerging Digital Wall

palgrave
macmillan

C. Y. Cyrus Chu
Academia Sinica
Taipei, Taiwan

ISBN 978-981-95-3576-7 ISBN 978-981-95-3577-4 (eBook)
https://doi.org/10.1007/978-981-95-3577-4

This Palgrave Macmillan imprint is published by the registered company Springer Nature Singapore Pte Ltd.
The registered company address is: 152 Beach Road, #21-01/04 Gateway East, Singapore 189721, Singapore

Preface

My motivation to write this monograph originated in 2016 when I served as the Head of Delegation of Taiwan's Permanent Mission at the World Trade Organization (WTO). As an economist, I understand that the traditional trade barriers analyzed in the literature are measures such as tariffs and quotas. However, according to WTO practices, new types of trade barriers often arise discreetly. A salient example is internet blocking: when a country makes it difficult for its domestic citizens to browse foreign e-commerce websites (or even worse, the citizens may not even be aware of the existence of such websites), then these local citizens can hardly be cognizant of the fact that such foreign commodities and sellers actually exist. As a result, certain forms of international e-commerce trade are completely out of the question. If we think of traditional trade barriers as a physical wall built around the customs checkpoints of the importing country, then the trade barrier caused by prohibiting the flow of internet information may be referred to as a "cyberspace trade barrier," which is essentially a wall "in the digital space."

When thinking about the issue from a broader perspective, one may find that the wall in the digital space exists in many different scenarios. The export control and entity list regulations enforced by the U.S. over the past several years have essentially attempted to build a wall inhibiting the outflow of technology from various U.S. digital industries. Digital platform regulations such as the legislation enshrined in PAFACA (the Protecting Americans from Foreign Adversary Controlled Applications

Act) have sought to prevent unfriendly foreign countries from collecting the digital data of U.S. citizens, resulting in the formation of a digital wall that blocks the flow of data. The profuse monitoring measures implemented by authoritarian rulers result in all kinds of digital fences, which serve to trap potentially disobedient citizens in authoritarian countries in a panopticon, where every move they make is monitored. After Russia invaded Ukraine, a number of democratic countries ousted Russia from the SWIFT system. This was when we observed that service networking such as SWIFT can be used as a digital wall to block unpopular users. Putting together all the dimensions mentioned above, we have suddenly come to the realization that building walls in cyberspace as opposed to the physical space has become increasingly easy. While digital services provide us with much convenience, when such convenience is removed, the digital barriers become walls.

In international politics, the formation of these digital walls often needs a coalition of several states. As these coalitions are established, they take on the appearance of various "camps," the major ones being centered around either democratic or authoritarian countries. In digital industries, the supply chains are decoupled and are developed in parallel. As for social media platforms, the users are divided into two groups. In infrastructure deployments, there is hardly any sharing of facilities between camps. In research and development endeavors, the joint efforts are clustered. Finally, because neither camp trusts the other, there exist strong incentives to consolidate the cooperation within each camp, thereby gradually making the digital walls higher, thicker, and wider.

The above observations are both empirical and theoretical. As for the empirical part, because digital barricades can be observed, their hypothetical patterns can be identified and tested. With regard to the theoretical part, conceptual frameworks can be built to help us understand the causes and consequences of these digital walls. From mulling over the ideas for this book and its preparation, more than five years have passed. During this period, I have benefited greatly from my colleagues at Academia Sinica and have acknowledged their joint efforts in some of the chapters. I owe all of them my most sincere appreciation.

Finally, I would like to thank Professor Andrew Nathan (Columbia University) for his helpful criticism, the professional assistance of the staff of Springer-Nature, the persistent understanding and tolerance of my family, and the psychological encouragement provided by my lovely granddaughters. Such help and support always make such endeavors worthwhile, in both physical and digital spaces.

Taipei, Taiwan
October 2025

C. Y. Cyrus Chu

Contents

Abbreviations

ADS	Automated Driving System
AI	Artificial Intelligence
AIIB	Asian Infrastructure Investment Bank
ASML	Advanced Semiconductor Materials Lithography
BIS	Bureau of Industry and Security
BRI	Belt and Road Initiative
BSN	Blockchain-based Service Network
CCP	Chinese Communist Party
CDO	Collateralized Debt Obligation
CFIUS	Committee on Foreign Investment in the United States
CHIPS and Science Act	Creating Helpful Incentives to Produce Semiconductors and Science Act
CIPS	Cross-border Inter-bank Payments System
CLARITY	Creating Legal Accountability for Rogue Innovations and Technology
CNI	Clean Network Initiative
CoCom	Coordinating Committee for Multilateral Export Control
CoWoS	Chip on Wafer on Substrate
CPC	Central Product Classification
CPTPP	Comprehensive and Progressive Agreement for Trans-Pacific Partnership
CSIS	Center for Strategic and International Studies
CTB	Cyberspace Trade Barrier
DRAM	Dynamic Random-Access Memory

DSB	Dispute Settlement Body
DSP	Digital Society Projects
EAA	Export Administration Act
EAR	Export Administration Regulation
ECCN	Export Control Classification Number
ECRA	Export Control Reform Act
EIU	Economic Intelligence Unit
EUV	Extreme Ultraviolet
FDA	Food and Drug Administration
FDI	Foreign Direct Investment
GATS	General Agreement on Trade in Services
GATT	General Agreement on Tariffs and Trade
GDPR	General Data Protection Regulation
GEO	Geosynchronous
GFW	Great Firewall
GPS	Global Positioning System
GPSS	Global Patent Search System
GPT	Generative Pretrained Transformer
GPU	Graphic Processing Unit
HFCE	Household Final Consumption Expenditure
ICH	International Council for Harmonization of Technical Requirements for Pharmaceuticals for Human Use
ICTs	Information and Communication Technologies
IEEPA	International Emergency Economic Power Act
IOT	Internet of Things
LEO	Low Earth Orbit
MFN	Most-favored-nation
MTCG	Missile Technology Control Group
NATO	North Atlantic Treaty Organization
NDAA	National Defense Authorization Act
PAFACAA	Protecting Americans from Foreign Adversary Controlled Application Act
PPF	Production Possibility Frontier
REEs	Rare Earth Elements
SMEs	Small and Medium Enterprises
SOEs	State-owned Enterprises
SWIFT	Society for Worldwide Interbank Financial Telecommunication
TSMC	Taiwan Semiconductor Manufacturing Company
UCRG	Universal Credit Rating Group
UEL	Unreliable Entity List
USICA	United States Innovation and Competition Act

USMCA	United States-Mexico-Canada Agreement
USTR	United States Trade Representative
VCS	Vehicle Connectivity System
VPN	Virtual Private Network
WA	Wassenaar Arrangement
WTO	World Trade Organization

List of Figures

List of Tables

CHAPTER 1

Introduction: From Geographic Space to Cyberspace

Over thousands of years of human history, "geopolitics" has arguably been the dominant keyword in international conflicts. A review of major historical conflicts—such as the Peloponnesian War between Athens and Sparta in 431 BC, Alexander's invasion of India in 331 BC, the wars between the Roman Empire and surrounding nomadic groups, the Mongol invasion of Europe in 1236 AD, the nineteenth-century conflict between the U.S. and Spain in the Caribbean, and the containment coalition among Western European countries against the Soviet Union—reveals that most conflicts occurred among geographically proximate countries or groups with common interests in nearby areas. For most of human history, interactions were largely local; long-distance relations were rare and developed only gradually along geographic lines. Although advances in transportation technology over the past century have made long-distance travel more efficient, they have not fundamentally altered geographic constraints.

In recent decades, however, drastic changes have taken place. The rise of cyberspace has given birth to entirely new kinds of conflicts that are not bound by geographic dimensions. The most concise description of the above-mentioned changes was made by Professor Nicholas Negroponte (1994), who claimed that in the digital era, the traditionally inefficient transportation of atoms will be replaced by the efficient transmission of bits. Negroponte called this phenomenon the *atom/bit transformation.*

C. Y. C. Chu, *An Emerging Digital Wall*,
https://doi.org/10.1007/978-981-95-3577-4_1

We will show in this monograph that this transformation has not only changed our daily lives, but also reshaped the interactions and conflicts of international politics.

The cyberspace conflicts to be discussed in this book primarily concern, though are not limited to, those between the U.S. and China. Although there are still geographic conflicts—such as disputes over the first island chain in the Western Pacific—the competition in cyberspace (in areas such as artificial intelligence (AI), quantum computing, high-end chips, and satellite deployments) is equally, if not more, critical. It may be fair to say that a country unable to succeed in cyberspace is likely to suffer losses in the geographic domain as well.

With these background changes in mind, this monograph discusses several themes. We examine how trends in the global division of labor and the emergence of cyberspace have led to interstate conflicts that no longer adhere to traditional geographic boundaries. Conflicts between countries may not manifest themselves within geographic borders; rather, they often originate in cyberspace. Cyber hostilities can accompany geopolitical tensions, yet they frequently occur independently. In some instances, a targeted country remains unaware that cyberattacks have already inflicted significant harm on its national sovereignty and interests. We will describe the characteristics of cyberspace, explain how these features have altered traditional international interactions, and explore the new strategies opponents are adopting.

The primary focus of this book is on the emerging battlegrounds in cyberspace, including predictions about possible conflicts. Looking at the strategy dimension, we analyze and explain the decoupling and networking policies adopted by both the democratic camp (led by the U.S.) and the authoritarian camp (led by China). Looking at the equilibrium, we predict that eventually there will be a "digital wall" dividing the two above-mentioned camps. Focusing on the dynamic transition, we argue that AI will stabilize the authoritarian control and make its regime transition into democracy (the so-called democratization) less likely. We also discuss the intrinsic advantages and disadvantages of both camps in the context of digital competition and confrontation.

As documented in the literature, China is perhaps the most typical Leninist regime in the world. According to Dickson (2022), the Chinese Communist Party (CCP) traditionally adheres to an aggressive doctrine of dominating all aspects of society. Although information and communication technologies (ICTs) can improve the CCP's capacity to monitor, control, and discipline dissent throughout society, the Leninist doctrine also has a weak spot: because the algorithms and software behind screens are opaque to outsiders, "trust" becomes essential in cyberspace interactions. We argue that an aggressive political entity often struggles to earn trust from international counterparts in cyberspace operations.

In the remainder of this chapter, we present an overview of U.S.-China conflicts in international politics and gradually outline the narratives that will unfold in later chapters.

1.1 Two Decades of a Unified Global Supply Chain: 1995–2015

It is widely understood that globalization encompasses various dimensions. In this monograph, our focus is on the increasingly refined global division of labor and the interdependence of international supply chains.

Almost all globalization studies cite the rapid advances in transportation and communication technologies as a key factor.[1] These technological changes have dramatically reduced the costs of transportation, travel, and interpersonal communication. An equally important factor, noted by Zeihan (2022), is the so-called Pax Americana, which ensured the safety of global transportation under U.S. hegemony after WWII. This safety enabled the global division of labor, allowing intermediate and final goods to be produced anywhere in the world and then transported safely to their destinations.

1.1.1 Globalization Disciplined by the WTO.

Advances in transportation and communication technologies are only the physical enablers. Organizational and institutional frameworks, such as the General Agreement on Tariffs and Trade (GATT) of 1948, the General Agreement on Trade in Services (GATS) of 1995, and the establishment of the World Trade Organization (WTO) in 1995, are equally important. The GATT, GATS, and the WTO share the goal of eliminating trade barriers so that international competition is based primarily on comparative advantages. These comparative advantages stem from various local

[1] See for instance https://www.piie.com/commentary/speeches-papers/globalization-concept-causes-and-consequences, written by John Williamson.

factors (such as the work ethic, female labor force participation, and bureaucratic procedures) that are not necessarily tied to geography. As we will show, the final division of labor may follow a pattern very different from traditional geographic expectations.

There are three main designs of the WTO that facilitated globalization. First, the *most-favored-nation* (MFN) principle requires that WTO members not discriminate between their trading partners and should treat them all alike. Second, the national treatment principle states that imported goods should be given equal treatment, at least after the foreign goods have entered the local market, to the locally produced goods. Both of these principles encroach upon a country's domestic sovereignty by preventing differential tariffs or internal regulations and effectively suppress any intention to establish trade barriers. Third, the WTO has a judicial mechanism—the Dispute Settlement Body (DSB)—that enforces its regulations. In ordinary circumstances, violators face retaliation or disciplinary measures from other WTO members.

After decades of operation under the WTO's free-trade framework, international competition has intensified, the division of labor has become more refined, and global supply chains are being shaped by comparative advantages rather than mere geographic proximity. The well-known book *The World Is Flat* by Thomas Friedman (2007) illustrated a scenario of low trade barriers. Over the past three decades, countries have become accustomed to complex supply chains, manufacturing outsourcing and insourcing, and a robust interdependence for both intermediate and final products. For instance, there is no inherent geographic reason why nearly 90% of high-end chips are produced by Taiwan Semiconductor Manufacturing Company (TSMC); it is the result of long-term competition, learning by doing, efficient yields, and decades of stable international transportation.

It was not until the COVID-19 pandemic (2019–2022), the Russian invasion of Ukraine (2022), and concerns over a potential Chinese invasion of Taiwan that many countries began to recognize the risks inherent in global supply chain interdependence. For example, during the COVID-19 crisis, major automobile companies worldwide experienced chip shortages due to shipping delays and limited alternative supplies. A unified global supply chain originally being praised as efficient began to show its vulnerability. As such, the unified global supply chain started to unravel. In addition, the dual (military and commercial) uses of some electronic products also compelled some countries to resort to more "secure" supplies of products or parts. This (military and national) security concern serves as another force facilitating the bifurcation of some sectors within the global supply chain.

1.1.2 The "Unfair" WTO Rules.

The globalization framework under the WTO also has flaws, and these shortcomings can give rise to new forms of competitive conflict, mainly between democratic and authoritarian countries. For example, internet censorship in authoritarian countries creates disparities in e-commerce market access, resulting in unfair competition. Similarly, differential government subsidies to high-tech industries have led to uneven international competition. Simply put, WTO rules—most of which were established before 1995—were designed for traditional trade interactions among liberal market economies. They are often ill-equipped to address new forms of cyber-enabled economic practices (such as e-commerce) and the prevalent state-owned enterprises in Leninist regimes (typically China). Consequently, starting from 2016, these outdated rules have led to conflicts, retaliatory measures, and counteractions between China and the U.S. Since amending WTO rules requires consensus, changes are practically impossible when certain countries benefit from the status quo.[2] The United States Trade Representative (USTR) reports in various years have revealed the U.S.'s frustration from facing such ill-equipped but unchangeable WTO multilateral rules, and this might have led the U.S. to depart from the unified WTO rules, and seek unilateral measures.[3] These unilateral measures, as one can imagine, often result in changes in the global supply chain. Since Donald Trump's first Presidential term, the unilateral measures implemented by the U.S. have increased significantly, with most of them concentrated in ICT areas, the main target having been, and subsequently always being, China. When Trump commenced his second term as U.S. President in 2025, the U.S. began to impose bilateral tariffs on various countries, and the WTO's multilateral system is now essentially passé.

[2] For more details, see Chu et al. (2022).

[3] The most typical example may be the "reciprocal tariff" unilaterally announced by the U.S. in April 2025. This reciprocal tariff essentially destroys the MFN principle of the WTO.

To understand why China has become a key competitor of the U.S. in ICT technologies, we have to understand that the momentum of economic growth is always the key force behind the R&D of ICTs. China's stellar economic growth has undeniably benefited from three decades of globalization. By absorbing manufacturing sectors that rely on cost reduction and then exporting the products globally, China has enjoyed extremely low trade barriers—especially following its accession to the WTO in 2001. For many products, China has long been either the largest manufacturing base or the largest market. Chapter 2 of this monograph will examine China's expansion over the past three decades, which is reflected in both its growing influence on world politics and its ICT competitiveness.

China's economic ascent has also fueled its ambition to become a leader in several industries. A critical turning point occurred in 2015 when National Chairman Xi Jinping announced the *Made in China 2025* initiative.[4] While much debate has centered on how this initiative has increased U.S. concerns and accelerated countermeasures, it is important to note that much of its content pertains to ICTs in cyberspace. The year 2015 marked the evolution of ICT competition into full-fledged cyber battles.

1.2 ICT Aspects of the *Made in China 2025* Initiative

According to the Pew Research Center, the attitude of U.S. citizens toward China gradually began to change from favorable to unfavorable in 2012, the year in which Xi came to power. The percentage of unfavorable views reached an unprecedented high of more than 80% in 2022–2024.[5] However, since many Asian and European countries have been very much tied to China in the global supply chain in the past decades, the U.S. has found it difficult to find allies who are willing to confront China and sacrifice their vested economic interests. Indeed, the process of globalization

[4] See https://en.wikipedia.org/wiki/Made_in_China_2025 for an introduction to the content, and https://ustr.gov/about-us/policy-offices/press-office/press-releases/2018/june/ustr-issues-tariffs-chinese-products for US responses.

[5] This might be partly due to China's wolf-warrior allegation that the U.S. Army should be blamed for the spread of COVID-19. See https://www.the-scientist.com/chinese-officials-blame-us-army-for-coronavirus-67267, and https://www.pewresearch.org/global/2024/05/01/americans-remain-critical-of-china/

has strengthened the ties between China and most countries in the world, and disentangling this interdependence is like a *de-globalization* process.

The situation can be better understood using the following simple illustration: globalization is a process whereby many countries in the world have begun to become "addicted to" the principle of comparative advantage and efficiency competition, whereas de-globalization may be thought of as a process of "rehabilitation" from the previous addiction, which is costly, slow, and painful. The difficulty faced in attempting to de-globalize has forced the U.S. to try to find other confrontational strategies, which the U.S. can control (almost) unilaterally, to contain the rising Leninist China. It turns out that some of the new measures can be found in cyberspace, and this is particularly true in areas where the U.S. is ahead of China.

Following the paralysis of the WTO's DSB,[6] the rule-based globalization mechanism has been severely impaired, and the global supply chain has begun to disintegrate. Over the past several years, the U.S. has been less constrained in exercising unilateral measures to counteract China, and a collateral consequence has been the acceleration of supply chain bifurcation. These measures include the rapid expansion of export controls on ICT-related products, the international coalition of telecommunications infrastructure, the blockage of foreign digital platforms, the subsidies on ICT industries and R&D in democratic countries, and of course Trump's reciprocal tariff impositions on almost all countries around the world in 2025.

1.2.1 What Is so Special About Cyberspace?

The reason for the rise of cyberspace over the past several decades has been the extraordinarily rapid development of ICTs. These technological breakthroughs have themselves been related to the widespread dissemination of cables that have served as the backbone of internet communications, the rapid increase in both high and low Earth orbit satellites, the advances in the speed of calculation along with Moore's

[6] Since 2019, the DSB has been more or less paralyzed, partly because of the U.S. boycott. See https://www.bloomberg.com/news/newsletters/2023-08-30/supply-chains-latest-paralysis-at-wto-appellate-body-hurts-global-trade

Law, and the prevalence of smart devices in recent years.[7] In Chapter 3 of this book, we will describe the key areas of ICT progress over the past few decades, and explain how they have gradually replaced the importance of the physical space.

On the user side, advances in ICTs imply convenience and efficiency, which attract more and more internet adoption. According to statistica.com,[8] as of November 2024, there were 5.52 billion internet users globally, which account for about 67.5% of the world's population. In China, there were roughly 1.1 billion users, or about 78% of the Chinese population. The corresponding statistic for the U.S. was 97.1% in December 2024. The prevalent use of the Internet by the majority of people and the frequent information uploads and downloads by billions of terminal users highlight the prosperity of cyberspace activities, and thereby the importance of the related policies, manipulations, regulations, and strategies. As a result, many conflicts may arise in cyberspace.

Furthermore, by building on the prevalent use of the Internet and the advancement of ICTs, there have been tremendous developments in e-commerce, big data, AI, social media, various electronic payment mechanisms, virtual currency, and the availability of widespread digital monitoring and surveillance. Faced with such new technologies and the flourishing internet platforms with their related activities, all governments may respond to such developments by setting up corresponding regulations and legislation, although various checks and balances mechanisms often constrain the adaptation flexibility of liberal democratic regimes.

1.2.2 China's Ambition in ICTs.

Authoritarian governments are evidently less constrained in adapting to the digital era, and they may make the best use of these new cyberspace technologies to strengthen their authoritarian control domestically and to engage in unrestrained competition and aggression with foreign countries. China's *Made in China 2025* initiative is a salient example: there

[7] Moore's Law, proposed by Gordon E. Moore, states that the number of transistors on a microchip doubles every 18–24 months with a very small cost increase. While not actual science, it was an observation and extrapolation that has steadily prevailed since 1965. For references, see https://www.investopedia.com/terms/m/mooreslaw.asp

[8] See https://www.statistica.com, various pages. Logged on December 15, 2024.

are 10 priority industries listed in the project: (1) New advanced information technology; (2) Automated machine tools & robotics; (3) Aerospace and aeronautical equipment; (4) Maritime equipment and high-tech shipping; (5) Modern rail transport equipment; (6) New-energy vehicles and equipment; (7) Power equipment; (8) Agricultural equipment; (9) New materials; and (10) Biopharma and advanced medical products.

In the above list, items (1), (2), (3), (5), and (7) are directly related to ICTs. Item (6) also encompasses future autonomous driving, which relies on ICTs. Item (10), pharmaceuticals, appears to be in the biomedicine area. However, if one understands that future preclinical and clinical trials will heavily rely on bioinformatics, then one also recognizes its dependence on computing power. In the process of discovering new drugs, supercomputers and AI can help us figure out the possible antibiotic, understand the metabolic consequences through computer simulation, facilitate the dosage optimization, speed up the clinical trials, increase the probability of successful drug development, and hence increase the likelihood that the drug will be the first to receive FDA approval.

In short, if we consider the extensive network influenced by ICTs, then we see that the network spans almost all areas of modern industries. This is why competition in ICTs is so important. It is fair to say that the *Made in China 2025* Initiative is essentially an *ICT initiative*, which involves extensive Chinese government subsidies. This initiative has revealed China's ambition but, as one can imagine, has also provoked the countermeasures by the U.S.

1.3 Technology-Denial: Decoupling the ICT Manufacturing

Facing China's ambitious initiative in ICTs, what could the U.S. do? A great story narrated by Miller (2022) and echoed by many others is the competition in the design and manufacture of chips. Because chips are used in almost all kinds of modern products that are related to electronics (cell phones, cars, system engineering, computers, and missiles), things that are related to chip design, manufacturing, optical lithography, and so on are all targets in international competition. Of course, chips are just one part of the ICTs, and we should try to understand the U.S. countermeasures from a broader perspective.

1.3.1 Dual-Use Technologies.

As we mentioned, a key reason for the fierce competition in relation to chips concerns the *dual* (military/commercial) *uses* of some technologies. The global positioning system (GPS) used in cars is qualitatively the same as the guiding system deployed in missiles, and the competition in regard to the latter is related to national security. Another example has to do with the future of autonomous self-driving cars, which hinges upon 5th- and 6th-generation (5G and 6G) telecommunications. Because 6G is particularly important in wars when base station facilities are destroyed in the first strike, the competition related to 6G communications will also be extremely fierce. These kinds of dual uses also generate extra incentives for R&D competition between countries. On the one hand, dual uses imply a double bonus for the winning side. On the other hand, national defense is something that cannot be compromised, not only for the incumbent power, but also for any challengers.

1.3.2 From Competition to Battles.

Because cyberspace activities may be related to national security, all governments may want to disrupt the cyber operations conducted by opponent countries. This also makes cyberspace a possible battleground. In response, threatened countries may adopt various countermeasures. Perhaps the most well-known battles between the U.S. and China relate to the implementation of *export controls* and the *entity list*. This is a topic to be examined in Chapter 4.

In 2018, the U.S. enacted the Export Control Reform Act (ECRA). On the surface, it is literally an export control act. In essence, however, it is entirely different from the traditional export control of weapons. In particular, it is worth pointing out that this ECRA is not about mercantilism. The export control measures derived from ECRA have allowed the U.S. to impose various export restrictions related to the development of some ICT technologies, to which we refer as *technology access denial.* The execution of ECRA cannot be implemented by the U.S. unilaterally, and some of the forms of cooperation by foreign companies are forged by certain clauses within ECRA.

We should note that traditional trade barriers are about some *existing* products, whereas technology barriers embodied in ECRA may refer to the research and development of some products that may possibly appear *in the future*. As a matter of fact, ECRA may not even be related to trade per se, but potentially it may decouple the supply chain and technologies of future high-tech industries. Furthermore, because the general public is less sensitive to future industries, export control strategies will usually face less of a backlash from the society than, say, imposing high tariffs, which may directly affect the domestic price level of existing commodities. As such, export controls may be more welcomed by politicians who face regular voting pressures.

The Export Control Classification Number (ECCN) is a numeric designation that is part of a list of production-related items (hardware or software or equipment or IPs or individuals' knowledge) drawn up by the U.S. Commerce Department that are subject to scrutiny, before these items can be transported to, or used in the production process of, certain companies in the target country. The number of items on the ECCN list has increased very quickly over the past several years, and the content has also been broadened. The essence of the export control is to prevent a target country from obtaining certain final or intermediate commodities or inputs, so that the target country's production cannot be accomplished, or at least will be delayed.

1.3.3 A Comprehensive Web of Technology-Denial.

Other than the ECCN regulations on export *items*, there are also the entity list regulations on export *recipients*. It is fair to say that U.S. export controls and the entity list imposed in parallel have started to decouple the ICT supply chains and have laid the foundation for building a *digital wall* between authoritarian countries and democratic ones. While at present it is not known how wide, thick, and tall this digital wall will become, the wall has so far been built by the U.S. jointly with other liberal democratic countries, mainly because the ICTs on the side of the U.S. and its allies are ahead of those on the other side of the wall. The digital wall is simply a new phenomenon which one can only barely imagine today.

1.4 Platform Denial: Restricting Data Collection

The discussion above illustrates that the ICT revolution and deepening globalization have not only altered the objective environment but have also increased the potential for international conflicts that are independent of geographic distance. However, such environmental changes do not guarantee conflict; a subjective factor also plays a role: the inherently aggressive ideology of certain authoritarian regimes.

1.4.1 Aggressive Ideologies.

As Doshi (2021) pointed out, international politics after WWII operated under Western rules established by liberal democracies, with the U.S. as the leader. After the 2008 financial crisis, China argued that Western capitalism had become distorted and sought to promote a "multipolar" world order with one pole representing liberal democracy and the other embodying the Chinese model. A key difference is that economic activities in liberal democracies are rarely driven by a top-down agenda, whereas Leninist regimes often impose one.

Given the Leninist doctrine that "the Party leads all," Xi Jinping's efforts to establish a multipolar world order implied that the CCP's ideology might sometimes be imposed abroad. However, many operational practices in liberal capitalist societies are in conflict with the doctrine of "the Party leads all." The TikTok case serves as an illustrative example. The U.S. government suspected that the algorithm behind the TikTok platform may be controlled or influenced by the CCP. The question is: Can the government's suspicion justify a regulatory measure to ban a social media platform?

1.4.2 Social Media Platforms' National Security Threats.

Chapter 5 examines the U.S. government's attempts to block the data collection by platforms controlled by foreign adversaries. This is a highly controversial issue in the U.S. due to its overlap with the fundamental constitutional value of the freedom of expression. Since TikTok collects extensive user data (including the user's personal information, what videos they watched, for how long, and which ones they skipped), it amasses a large dataset that can be used to profile users and influence video distribution. If TikTok's algorithm is indeed influenced by a political agenda from, say, the CCP, then the platform's distribution could be biased toward that agenda, providing the U.S. with justification for regulatory action—whether via an executive order or legislation. The challenge, however, is that proving such a political agenda behind the algorithm is extremely difficult, and the platform can easily refute all accusations in the absence of clear evidence.

When the U.S. government fined TikTok in 2019 and later demanded that the company clarify its ownership, TikTok escalated the matter to the U.S. judicial system. In the U.S. and many other liberal democracies, the judicial system is largely independent and serves as the final arbiter. A voice opposing the White House's executive order to ban TikTok advocates more tolerant regulatory policies regarding ICT software. As such, the platform-denial measure of the U.S. faces challenges. After a long tug of war, in 2024 the U.S. Congress passed an Act which essentially says that TikTok should either exit the U.S. market or be sold to a company which cannot be influenced by China. On January 17, 2025, the U.S. Supreme Court ruled in favor of the regulatory Act targeting TikTok.

Chapter 5 provides a detailed analysis of this ruling and the rationale behind the U.S.'s regulation of foreign internet platforms. In general, internet platforms differ from traditional media in several key respects. The most important difference is that traditional media generally do not collect extensive viewer data, whereas many internet platforms do. The Supreme Court's ruling on TikTok follows the doctrine of judicial minimalism (Sunstein 2008), whereas we will point out in Chapter 5 that big data naturally involves the idea of information complementarity, which may shake the legitimacy of judicial minimalism.

Regarding the critical issue of whether there is a political agenda embedded in the algorithm of a platform controlled by a foreign state, we propose a methodology to investigate this issue. The methodology requires: (1) a large number of clean devices, (2) a well-designed experimental group and control group, and (3) carefully articulated stimuli. We show that there is statistical evidence showing the existence of content manipulation in the algorithm of TikTok.

1.5 Cyberspace Trade Barriers and Application Networking

In discussions of U.S.-China conflicts over the past decade, many commentators have described the situation as a "trade war."[9] However, this description may be inadequate in the digital era, where many trade barriers differ significantly from traditional ones.

1.5.1 Cyberspace Trade Barriers.

Traditionally, trade wars have involved imposing tariffs, quotas, and other measures to increase the cost of transportation and logistics, with a view to boosting exports and reducing imports. By contrast, the digital era has introduced another type of barrier: the information-acquiring trade barrier. This barrier prevents potential buyers from accessing information about a foreign seller, or even learning of the foreign seller's existence. For example, if 1.4 billion Chinese citizens cannot easily access a Japanese store's website, they simply remain unaware of the opportunity to purchase its products, effectively impeding trade.

Broadly speaking, e-commerce refers to any business transactions that use the Internet. In this sense, almost all economic activities today involve e-commerce. As such, this information barrier in cyberspace is as significant as a tariff applied uniformly to all economic transactions. In Chapter 6, we explain why it is difficult to deal with this trade barrier in the WTO, and we also estimate the impact of China's cyberspace trade barrier (CTB) on the trade volume and GDP of both China and the U.S.

1.5.2 China's Application Networking in BRI Countries.

In response to the above-mentioned technology denial and data collection denial strategies, China has pursued various ICT deployments in Central and West Asian countries, particularly in relation to the Belt and Road

[9] On March 22, 2018, the Trump administration released the Section 301 investigation report, suggesting the imposition of tariffs on 60 billion dollars of Chinese products imported into the U.S. This action then spiraled into an overall trade war between the two countries. In his second term as President, the U.S.'s tariff on China's imports escalated to 245% in April 2025.

Initiative (BRI). A prominent example is the extensive use of blockchain applications. We refer to this strategy as *application networking*.

The blockchain is perhaps the only ICT technology in which China has been dominant in terms of worldwide patents. While democratic countries have emphasized cryptocurrency as a blockchain application, China has taken a different route by integrating blockchain with the Internet of Things (IoT) to extend its application platforms across BRI countries. Through these deployments, China has successfully shaped the landscape on the "other side of the cyberspace wall." This networking effort, as we will explain in Chapter 7, does not necessarily involve advanced technologies, but improves the resilience of participating countries against possible embargoes from the democratic camp.

On the U.S. side, President Trump announced before his 2nd term inauguration that the U.S. will accumulate a large number of Bitcoins as part of its Federal Reserve. Knowing that Bitcoin is a special application of the blockchain technology, in Chapter 7 we will also provide a comprehensive analysis of the problems of Bitcoins, and explain why it is not a wise strategy to make Bitcoins part of any country's monetary reserves. This Bitcoin example demonstrates the importance of understanding the cyberspace correctly, before adopting any policies.

1.6 Dynamic Changes Caused by the Digital Wall

As we argued, the future digital wall may divide the world into two camps, one being the democratic camp and the other the authoritarian. There are several kinds of cross-wall interactions: one is like East Germany in 1990, when the country tried to "transform" itself into a different regime. Even though the digital wall cannot be torn down as in the case of the Berlin Wall in 1989, there may still be similar transformation analogies. The second kind of interaction is more hostile: both sides penetrate antagonistic countries on the other side of the wall, just as in regular espionage activities. We will explore how such interactions differ in the digital era.

1.6.1 ICT Consolidates the Autocrats.

We have observed in the past few decades that some countries have transitioned from the authoritarian to the democratic camp, and some have transitioned in the other direction. The fall of the Berlin Wall in 1989 is a typical example, where within a couple of years many members of the authoritarian camp transitioned to the democratic camp. How would the recent advances in ICTs change the above transition?

Chapter 8 argues that certain ICTs are not "neutral" in that their benefits are unevenly distributed. Specifically, AI and related technologies tend to favor those who own large datasets. In China, for example, the CCP benefits from access to vast amounts of individual data collected from domestic platforms such as Alibaba, WeChat, Baidu, and Alipay. This data advantage reinforces the authoritarian regime and reduces the possibility of democratization, as suggested by Acemoglu and Robinson (2019) and Chu et al. (2025). We argue that countries in the democratic camp tend to increase their cybersecurity facilities, whereas countries in the authoritarian camp increase their capacity to monitor and exercise control. Chapter 8 provides both an empirical and theoretical analysis of this issue. Our conclusion is that ICTs are likely to stabilize the authoritarian domestic controls, making authoritarian countries less likely to transition to the democratic regime.

1.6.2 New Forms of Cyberspace Penetration.

Some invasive activities in cyberspace can totally eliminate the limitation of geographic distance. In 1988, Robert Morris Jr., then just a teenager from New Jersey, invented the first computer "worm," which penetrated and paralyzed a vast number of computers and operating systems all over the U.S. Indeed, worms can penetrate any geographic space. In 2016, the Fancy Bear, which was the nickname for a group of hackers in Russia, successfully penetrated the operating system of the campaign headquarters of Hillary Clinton. It turned out that this penetration might have led to the change in the result of the 2016 U.S. Presidential election. In both of these two examples, the attackers were thousands of miles away from the targets being attacked.[10] A salient feature of the cyberspace penetration is that it can be exercised without extensive resource input, so that even relatively weak countries may successfully bring down a giant opponent. This would be unlikely to happen in most physical space confrontations. Furthermore, very often cyberattacks do not cause observable casualties, so that the attacking side can easily deny any involvement.

[10] Both these stories were described in detail in Shapiro (2023).

Cyberspace penetration can take place in accordance with various scenarios. It may be between competing businesses, where one side steals business secrets or technological proprietary information by hacking into the opponent's computer system. It may occur where an authoritarian ruler uses censorship chips or GPS positioning or other monitoring techniques to know the moves and traces of disobedient civilians. It may refer to one group of people systematically sending fake information to disturb the general public's perceptions about some public issues, or a social media company which uses the data it collects from users to send marketing messages to maximize its revenue. One can think of hundreds of different penetration scenarios.

Other than regular internet hacking, Chapter 9 will also discuss more subtle penetrations—the ones that use big data. These penetrations always begin with the collection of huge amounts of data. The big data collected, together with the help of AI, can result in more accurate penetration.

We understand that cyberspace penetrations are often covert operations, and even the attacking side does not want to admit that there has been a cyberattack. This particular property makes it difficult to form any "engagement rules" of cyberspace confrontation. Related issues will also be discussed in Chapter 9.

1.6.3 International Politics in the Digital Era.

A more aggressive scenario is one in which domestic citizens are mobilized by the authoritarian government to foster strong nationalist sentiments against another country, thereby strengthening the autocrat's negotiating position in international conflicts. In this case, the domestic platforms are orchestrated and become a supporting force behind a country's foreign aggressions.

Since Xi Jinping assumed leadership of the CCP, significant changes have occurred, including domestic reforms (such as anti-corruption measures), international initiatives (such as the Belt and Road Initiative and the Asian Infrastructure Investment Bank), and military expansions (including increased spending, submarine and carrier development, and aggressive maneuvers in the South China Sea). Other than the above aggression in the physical world, ideological aggressions and challenges to multipolar values are equally unsettling, with their effects being felt across geographic boundaries. Typical examples include the various expressions of wolf warrior diplomacy. In democratic countries, right-wing politicians often regard foreign countries and immigrants as being responsible for the domestic economic failure. This tendency to put the blame on foreign countries has been more prevalent in recent years.

In Chapter 10, we examine the changes in international relations in the Internet era. Specifically, we examine three hypotheses: (1) Do smaller countries tend to be more tolerant of the larger ones' aggressions? This phenomenon is described as the power-difference effect.[11] (2) Do countries' behaviors reveal "herd behavior"? That is, large displays of group behavior may be triggered by an incidental event. This is called the demonstration effect. (3) Since past tough responses by other countries are public knowledge, are incumbent politicians (particularly those facing imminent re-election) under pressure to adopt similarly firm stances? This is called the amplification effect. We also show that European countries' generally negative attitude toward China in the late 2010s had facilitated the U.S. success in digital infrastructure coalition.

1.7 Previous Literature

1.7.1 The Internet and the Leninist Regime.

The distinctive features of China's Leninist regime have been well documented by Schurmann (1973), who analyzed how the CCP created a pervasive network of organizations throughout society. Subsequent works by Doshi (2021), Gore (2021, 2023), and others have extensively explored the revival of Leninist doctrines under Xi Jinping's leadership.

What this line of the literature has largely overlooked is the increasing role of cyberspace in the past three decades. In the Leninist regime of China, the CCP naturally takes the center stage. However, what has been less examined is the changing environment, the stage upon which the CCP wields its influence, both domestically and internationally. This monograph emphasizes an important point: in the twenty-first century, the stage is increasingly being dominated by cyberspace. We argue that cyberspace plays a critical role in shaping China's strategies and the corresponding international responses. Further analysis along these lines will enhance our understanding of the 2.0 version of the Leninist regime, contemporary international conflicts, and the strategic maneuvering of nations.

[11] See https://www.pewresearch.org/global/2023/07/27/views-of-china/

1.7.2 Competition Among Regulatory Regime.

Regarding digital-era international interactions, Anu Bradford (2023) offers an intriguing analysis of the competition for digital supremacy. She describes three distinct models by the second decade of the twenty-first century: the U.S. regime as market-driven, the China regime as state-driven, and the EU regime as rights-driven. These entities compete both horizontally—to extend their development models—and vertically—to manage internal pressures from their respective business and public sectors.

Of particular note, while most internet giants in the democratic world are U.S. companies (thus requiring the U.S. government to balance domestic tech interests with external challenges), the EU—armed with robust privacy regulations like the General Data Protection Regulation (GDPR)—must nonetheless confront foreign companies operating within its jurisdiction. China, on the other hand, maintains stringent control over its internet; although its domestic development is well-protected by the Great Firewall, it remains mistrusted by both the U.S. and the EU. Bradford's comprehensive discussion of these competing regulatory models is complementary to our focus on international political conflicts.

The U.S. model and the EU model can basically be compromised: the market-driven approach can be adjusted to include more regulations on privacy protection, and the rights-based model can also allow some market orientations. However, there appears to be a big gap between models in democratic countries and those in authoritarian regimes such as China. In this monograph, we explain why Leninist China is less inclined to compromise on internet regulations and why such inflexibility inevitably leads to conflicts in some digital arenas. In the context of international politics, the struggle for digital supremacy involves many nasty measures: trade embargoes, spyware deployment, cyberattacks, hacking, industrial espionage, and various forms of infrastructure networking. These measures together with the regulatory rules facilitate our understanding of the fight for digital supremacy.

1.7.3 ICT Containment in Chip Manufacturing and Other Areas.

Chris Miller's best-selling book *Chip War* (2022) examines a crucial dimension of the U.S.-China technology confrontation—chip design and manufacturing. Miller's work laid the theoretical foundation for the

CHIPS and Science Act in the U.S. during the Biden administration. Other aspects of technology competition have been less explored, partly due to the technical complexities involved for social science researchers. This monograph aims to provide a comprehensive policy analysis across the spectrum of ICT competition.

As we show in this monograph, measures related to chips can be understood as a special form of the *technology-denial* strategy: the U.S. and its democratic allies jointly try to block China's access to various frontier technologies of chip manufacturing. While the democratic camp currently leads in chip manufacturing and pursues a technology-denial strategy, China holds advantages in areas such as internet platform operations, often prompting liberal democracies to adopt platform-denial measures. Throughout various chapters, we classify ICT confrontational strategies into several categories: *technology-denial*, *platform-denial* (or data collection denial), *infrastructure networking*, *application networking*, and standard *cyberspace penetration*. Simply put, the "denial" strategy is similar to the *Containment* during the Cold War period, whereas the "networking" strategy is pursued to consolidate the allies. Our analysis provides readers with a full picture of the U.S.-China technology confrontations.

The purpose of this book is not to exhaust the U.S.-China confrontational measures in ICTs, but to exercise a theory-building endeavor, which helps us conceptualize and explain the rationale behind technology confrontations between China and the U.S. In this theory-building process, it is important to understand the institutional differences between Leninist China and democratic countries such as the U.S. For instance, China has its unique Great Firewall, which makes massive data collection by democratic countries practically impossible. As such, the Great Firewall makes platform denial a default status in China.

In the remaining chapters, we introduce seven dimensions of cyberspace conflicts between the U.S. and China. Some of these conflicts manifest themselves as direct competition (e.g., in high-end chip manufacturing), while others are embedded in the ideological and constitutional values that differentiate democratic and Leninist regimes. Our theory-building effort should help readers understand the rationale behind various policy measures and also more accurately predict the possible outcomes.

1.7.4 *Other Political Implications in the Digital Era.*

Chadwick (2006) examined the impact of internet communications on domestic political parties, elections, pressure groups, social movements, local democracy, public bureaucracies, and political governance, but he placed less emphasis on international political interactions. This monograph focuses on the international confrontations between China and the U.S.

Heeks et al. (2025) summarized the literature on China's digital expansions in the "global south," including many countries in Latin America and those targeted by the BRI. These expansions are mainly concerned with deploying surveillance technologies and e-commerce platforms in southern countries where ICT infrastructure is lacking. These deployments are different from the technological confrontation between China and the U.S., which is the focus of this monograph. Conceptually, deploying e-commerce platforms and surveillance facilities in the global south is similar to the infrastructure networking that we discuss in Chapter 7, but is very different from the chip war studied in Miller (2022).

1.7.5 *Analysis of Technologies.*

Of course, there are many books focusing on the engineering/technical features of ICTs. For instance, there are books emphasizing the engineering dimensions of blockchains and artificial intelligence (e.g., Sherman et al. 2019). In this book, we analyze various social science aspects of the U.S.-China ICT confrontations. The technical parts of ICTs are presented in a generally accessible way, so that the knowledge barrier for social science researchers (law, economics, political science, or international politics) is low.

There has also been some analysis (see, e.g., Takach 2024) that has taken stock of the status quo of various technologies between China and the U.S. Takach described the ICT competition scenario as a Cold War 2.0, where the corresponding Cold War 1.0 may be characterized by the Berlin Wall. Toward the end of this book, we suggest that a digital wall is emerging: on one side is the democratic camp, and on the other side is the authoritarian regime. The Berlin Wall and the digital wall may not be comparable, but all walls play the same role, namely, that of dividing the space.

1.7.6 *The Future of Technologies: Humanistic or Materialistic?*

Recent debates have raised concerns about the future development of AI—chief among them being the risk that an unguided or undisciplined AI might produce outcomes that conflict with humanistic objectives, as argued by many U.S. scientists (e.g., Tegmark 2018; Li 2023). While AI is a major focus, other ICTs also raise humanistic concerns. For instance, high-tech ICT devices used in contexts such as the Uyghur concentration (or re-education) camps would be unacceptable to liberal democracies and might even face international censure. This human-centered perspective sharply contrasts with Leninism's materialist doctrine. In Western debates, the emphasis is on moral consequences rather than merely winning or losing in the geopolitical arena.

Tegmark (2018) described the AI era as "life 3.0," suggesting that our future may be profoundly enriched by AI applications. Natural scientists like Tegmark (2018) and Li (2023) have often stressed a human-centered approach to technology. This narrative appears to be like the *Terminator* movie, where human beings constitute a unified group and "evil machines" the other group. Most social scientists, however, stress the diversity of human ideologies and values, noting that ICTs and AI can be wielded in ways where some groups of people harm others. An "inhuman" outcome may occur not because ICT/AI betrays humanity, but because individuals or regimes use these technologies in antagonistic and inhumane ways against certain other individuals. The cyberspace confrontations discussed in later chapters of this monograph will highlight the interplay between heterogeneous groups, both domestically and internationally.

Given the role of ICT in international politics, the ultimate outcome of the cyberspace "dance" will determine not only the rise and fall of industries and nations, but also whether humanistic ideologies will prevail in future centuries.

References

Acemoglu, D. & J.A. Robinson, 2019, The narrow corridor: States, societies, and the fate of liberty. New York, Penguin Press.

Bradford, A. (2023). *Digital empires: The global Battle to regulate technologies.* Oxford University Press.

Chadwick, A. (2006). *Internet politics, states.* Oxford University Press.

Chu, C. Y. C., Chang, J. J., & Lin, C. C. (2025). Why does artificial intelligence hinder democratization. *Proceedings of the National Academy of Sciences, 122*(19), e2423266122.

Chu, C. Y. C., Lee, P. C., Lin, C. C., & Lo, C. F. (2022). *Ultimate economic conflicts between China and democratic countries*. Routledge.

Dickson, Bruce J. (2022) The Party Leads All: The Leninist Revival in China, in *The Party Leads All: The Evolving Role of the Chinese Communist Party*, eds. by Jacques deLisle and Guobin Yang. Brookings Institution Press.

Doshi, R. (2021). *The long game: China's grand strategy to displace American order*. Oxford University Press.

Friedman, Thomas (2007) The world is flat: The globalized world in the twenty-first century. St. Martin's Thomas Dunne Books.

Gore, L. P. (Ed.). (2021). *The Chinese Communist Party in transformation*. World Scientific.

Gore, L. P. (2023). Leninism for the 21st century: Xi Jinping's ideological party-building. *China: An International Journal, 21*(2), 8–25.

Heeks, R., Foster, C., Gao, P., Han, X., Jepson, N., Schindler, S., & Zhou, Q. (Eds.). (2025). *China's digital expansion in the global south*. Routledge.

Li, Fei-Fei (2023) *Curiosity, Exploration and Discovery at the Dawn of AI*. Macmillan.

Miller, C. (2022). *Chip war: The fight for the world's Most critical technology*. Simon & Schuster.

Negroponte, Nicholas (1994) *Being Digital*. New York: Knopf.

Schurmann, F. (1973). *Ideology and Organization in Communist China* (2nd ed.). University of California Press.

Shapiro, Scott J. (2023) *Fancy Bear Goes Fishing: The Dark History of the Information Age, in Five Extraordinary Hacks*. Macmillan Publisher.

Sherman, A. T., Javani, F., Zhang, H., & Golaszewski, E. (2019). On the origins and variations of blockchain technologies. *IEEE Security Privacy, 17*(1), 72–77.

Sunstein, C. R. (2008). *Beyond judicial minimalism*. University of Chicago Law School working paper.

Takach, George S. (2024) *Cold War 2.0: Artificial Intelligence in the New Battle Between China, Russia, and America*. Simon and Schuster.

Tegmark, Max (2018) Life 3.0: Being human in the age of artificial intelligence. Knopf.

Zeihan, Peter (2022) The end of the world is just the beginning: Mapping the collapse of globalization. HarperCollins.

CHAPTER 2

China's Economic Growth and Aggressions: 1994–2024

Let us begin our discussion in this chapter by presenting a summary table of the annual GDP amounts and growth rates of China, together with the corresponding figures for the U.S., the U.K., and Taiwan as a comparison. The GDPs listed in Table 2.1 are in year-2000 constant dollars. As one can see from Table 2.1, the overall economic performance of China appears to be excellent during this 30-year period, especially before 2020, when COVID-19 started to impact the world. Although the focus of this monograph is on cyberspace interactions, we should keep in mind that economic capability is a key factor behind the cyberspace competition. We will therefore discuss China's economic development process during 1994–2024, and its corresponding international aggressions. The latter will set the stage for the future backlashes in international politics. Let us provide a basic analysis of the numbers revealed in Table 2.1.

2.1 The Unprecedented Economic Growth

Leaving aside the few who always optimistically boasted about China's economic miracles or those who always predicted that China's economy would crash as a pattern of badmouthing,[1] most people would not deny

[1] For a recent optimistic view, see for instance Justin Yifu Lin's comments on March 8, 2024, Global Times, https://www.globaltimes.cn/page/202403/1308456.shtml. For recent pessimistic views, see https://time.com/6835935/china-debt-housing-bubble/.

C. Y. C. Chu, *An Emerging Digital Wall*,
https://doi.org/10.1007/978-981-95-3577-4_2

Table 2.1 GDP and Its Growth Rate: Taiwan, China, USA, and UK: 1994–2024

Year	*TW*	$\widehat{GDP}$ (%)	*CN*	$\widehat{GDP}$ (%)	*USA*	$\widehat{GDP}$ (%)	*UK*	$\widehat{GDP}$ (%)
1994	275.34		690.06		8082.84		1494.77	
1995	292.91		790.09		8299.80		1451.71	
1996	299.97		873.21		8612.94		1473.46	
1997	304.33		956.71		8995.96		1621.15	
1998	272.09		1032.09		9399.27		1695.74	
1999	301.07		1110.80		9849.35		1707.56	
2000	330.68		1205.53		10,250.95		1688.69	
2001	301.18		1306.90		10,348.90		1625.78	
2002	310.67		1427.83		10,524.87		1725.40	
2003	325.27		1573.05		10,819.12		1937.33	
2004	358.24	2.03	1730.43	8.16	11,235.40	3.08	2224.19	4.36
2005	392.15		1956.37		11,626.80		2270.85	
2006	410.27		2263.98		11,950.57		2353.51	
2007	434.24		2712.62		12,190.05		2623.66	
2008	455.86		3239.49		12,203.86		2429.55	
2009	427.85		3609.21		11,889.43		1950.39	
2010	492.69		4003.79		12,209.89		1972.66	
2011	548.56		4600.02		12,400.89		2067.58	
2012	557.95		5123.64		12,684.75		2068.99	
2013	568.83		5652.55		12,953.41		2085.29	
2014	583.96	4.06	6117.62	12.08	13,280.32	1.34	2264.70	−0.03
2015	563.98		6460.35		13,671.49		2148.76	
2016	568.71		6435.69		13,920.24		1942.23	
2017	623.85		6745.44		14,262.36		1895.03	
2018	647.21		7355.04		14,685.46		1992.82	
2019	650.60		7523.27		15,047.75		1936.63	
2020	703.13		7758.89		14,714.66		1743.89	
2021	791.40		8882.83		15,568.17		2032.19	
2022	763.39		8689.72		15,869.47		1906.80	
2023	740.47		8453.42		16,271.14		1920.53	
2024	753.65	2.94	9101.20	3.49	17,273.33	2.37	2362.34	0.95

Notes 1. Unit: U.S. billion dollars. 2. The GDP data are adjusted to year-2000 constant prices. 3. *Sources* Taiwan—Gross domestic product (GDP) 1987–2029 (dgbas.gov.tw), China: GDP at current prices 1985–2029 | Statistica, United States | Data (worldbank.org), United Kingdom | Data (worldbank.org). 3. $\widehat{GDP}$ is the annual growth rate of GDP

China's impressive growth numbers before the outbreak of COVID-19. Indeed, the 30-year-long continuous growth in China is unprecedented in human history. A simple mathematical calculation gives us the so called "70% principle": if we put 70% as the numerator and a country's annual GDP growth rate as the denominator, then the calculated quotient will be close to "the number of years the country needs to double its GDP".[2] For example, if China's annual growth rate is 7%, then it takes 10 years (70%/7%) to double its GDP. Similarly, if the annual growth rate is 5%, then it takes 14 years (70%/5%) to double the GDP, and a 28-year span will quadruple the GDP. For the case of China, the average annual growth rate between 1994 and 2024 is 8.98%, and its GDP has been growing 13.19 times during this three-decade period. This is indeed a remarkable achievement.

Although China's reform and opening started toward the end of 1979, its initial pace was not at all rapid and the reform was hampered by conservative forces. In the 1980s, many reforms proposed by Deng Xiaoping faced resistance of various kinds. It was not until Deng Xiaoping gave the Southern Tour Speeches (in 1992) that the persistent opposition was (gradually) silenced. In addition, since the economic changes in many Eastern European countries began to take place in 1991 when the Soviet Union started to disintegrate, it would be convenient to compare China's economy after the early 1990s with other transitional economies in Eastern Europe. Therefore, 1994 is used as a starting point, and the ending year is 2024, which is the last year with a complete growth calculation at the time of writing this book. This 30-year period appears to form a fair basis of comparison.

Based on Table 2.1, in 1994, if one adds up the GDPs of China and the U.S., and normalizes the sum to be 100%, then the U.S. had 92.13% of the total, while China only had 7.87%. In the year 2010 using a similar comparison, the U.S. GDP accounted for 75.30% of the same pie, and China's share increased to 24.70%. In 2021, the U.S.'s GDP share fell to 63.67% of the total, and China's share became 36.33%. The year 2021 was the year when China's GDP had the largest percentage share of the sum

[2] Let y_t be the GDP of year t, and g be the GDP annual growth rate. Given that $y_t = (1+g)^t y_0$ and that $y_t/y_0 = 2$ (meaning that the GDP doubles from year 0 to year t), we have $t \cdot \ln(1+g) = \ln 2$. For small g, it is well known using a Taylor expansion that $\ln(1+g) \approx g$, and we also know that $\ln 2 \approx 0.7$. Thus, we have the 70% principle in the text.

of China and U.S. GDP; after that, for various reasons such as U.S. sanctions in relation to ICT products, China's real estate market crash, Xi's domestic policies, and the outflow of foreign capital, China's economy began to shrink, and the U.S. accounted for a larger share of the 100% pie.[3]

The above is a comparative analysis of the China/U.S. GDP growth, and one can similarly perform a three-economy comparison. For example, if we add up the GDPs of the U.S., China, and Taiwan and let the sum be 100%, we can also calculate the percentage changes among these three places. As one can see, in 1994, the U.S./China/Taiwan percentages were 90.3%, 7.6% and 3.0%, and China's GDP was only 250% that of Taiwan. By that time, we can imagine that Taiwan played quite an important role in the first island chain. However, when the share of Taiwan in the GDP total became smaller and smaller, the original U.S./China/Taiwan "triangular" relationship essentially became a bilateral one, mainly between the U.S. and China. This is exactly what has happened in the Taiwan Strait, where the tension is now mainly between the U.S. and China, and Taiwan's active role has decreased.

China's outstanding economic growth in the past several decades has eliminated the poverty of hundreds of millions of people, has boosted China's international influence, and has significantly changed China's leverage in international confrontations and negotiations. Most Chinese are also proud of this economic growth, and thereby echo the slogan "the great rejuvenation of the Chinese nation" voiced by the CCP leaders. These echoes have helped the CCP maintain internal stability and also cause the CCP to believe that its "socialist market economy" can perform equally well as, or even better than, Western capitalism. They proudly claim that they have a social democratic system with "Chinese characteristics."[4]

[3] Paul Krugman had a different calculation method. He used current prices to calculate the U.S.'s and China's GDP, and then adjusted the results by the current exchange rate between these two countries. This method generates a higher China/U.S. GDP ratio: 71% in 2022. While Krugman's approach may be more accurate for static comparisons; for dynamic comparisons between countries, our approach presents a more consistent pattern of economic growth over a 30-year period. See https://cn.nytimes.com/opinion/20230815/china-us-economy/zh-hant/.

[4] See http://theory.people.com.cn/BIG5/n1/2022/0401/c40531-32389641.html.

2.2 Factors Contributing to China's Rapid Growth

To predict whether or for how long China's rapid economic growth in 1994–2024 can persist, the timeframe should be extended, and 10 or 20 or even 30 years may not be long enough. To understand the economic growth path over a longer timeframe, the pattern of economic development summarized by Acs et al. (2000) may be helpful. In economic terms, China's rapid economic growth between 1994 and 2024, at least partly, may be due to the fact that China was in the *factor-driven* and *efficiency-driven* phases of economic development. The economic growth in these phases was like moving from inside the production possibility frontier (PPF) toward the frontier,[5] which often occurs rapidly. For example, agricultural products can increase at a fast pace when the land cultivation changes from being labor-intensive to machine-intensive; this is a typical example of efficiency-driven growth.

When the economy is already on or close to the PPF, any further growth must be driven by innovations (see Fig. 2.1). It is essentially impossible to have rapid innovation-driven growth, simply because valuable innovations do not occur at such a fast pace.[6] If we believe that China is already on or close to the PPF in 2024, then its nearly 10% growth rate per year in the past is unlikely to persist.

2.2.1 From Input-Driven and Efficiency-Driven to Innovation-Driven Growth

All countries in the world started their economic growth at the factor-driven and efficiency-driven stages, but many of them did not experience a growth rate as high as that of China. Why was that?

First of all, it is not difficult to imagine why China's economic growth in the 1990s was rapid: the base period number was so low, and the economy was well below the PPF. Between 1966 and 1976, China went through the Cultural Revolution, which destroyed the social order in

[5] The PPF refers to the theoretical output combinations a country can possibly produce, if it is producing them in an efficient way. Improving efficiency can help a country move from the interior of the PPF toward its boundary, whereas innovations can help push the PPF outwards.

[6] See https://aaas.confex.com/aaas/2013/webprogram/Session6519.html.

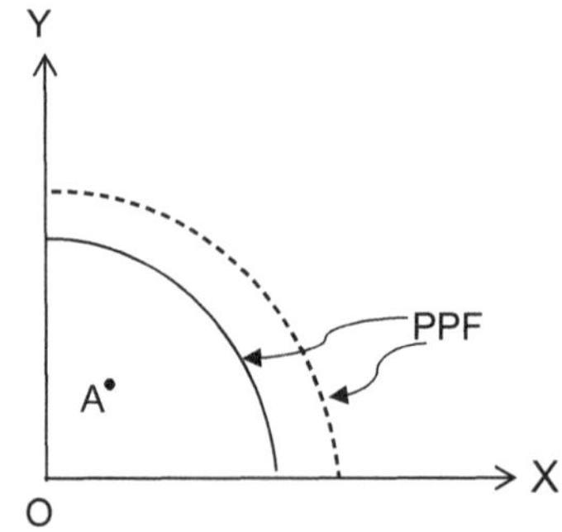

Fig. 2.1 Illustration of China's Economic Growth. *Notes* (1) A production possibility frontier (PPF) is the output combination (x,y) that can be efficiently produced in an economy. (2) In the early period of economic development, the economy has production factors that are either unused, or inefficiently used, and therefore ends up in the interior of the PPF, say, at point A. (3) In the innovation-driven stage, the economy is already on the PPF, and an innovation will push the PPF outward, from the solid line to the dash line. (4) If point A is very much inside the PPF originally, then the initial stage of growth may be very rapid, which indeed happened in China

an unprecedented way. Before the Cultural Revolution, there was Mao's Great Famine (1958–1962), the Great Leap Forward, (1957–1960), the Three-anti and Five-anti campaigns (1951–1952), and the violent Land Reform (1949–1953). In short, before the Reform and Opening in 1979, the whole country was exhausted and was far below the PPF. Given the extremely low GDP to start with, initiating a market opening would certainly result in very rapid economic growth.

After several decades of speedy development, by the time Xi Jinping took power in 2012, the Chinese economy was already close to the PPF, and further growth depended increasingly on innovation. Once the economy was in this innovation-driven stage, the growth rate started to decrease.

The three stages of development mentioned by Acs et al. (2000) were similarly observed in the "four little dragons" of Southeast Asia, namely, South Korea, Taiwan, Hong Kong, and Singapore. After the Korean War (1950–1953), there had been very rapid GDP growth in these four economies for three decades, and the corresponding numbers can be easily found in various databases. Around the start of the new millennium, the growth rates in these four economies started to decrease. Again, this was because these four little dragons had all passed the stage of being input-driven and efficiency-driven, and had started to enter the innovation-driven stage by the year 2000. This is why Paul Krugman has described the growth of the four little dragons as being "fragile."[7] The input-driven and efficiency-driven stages are described by Krugman as "working harder," and the innovation-driven stage is described as "working smarter."[8] The growth driven by working harder cannot persist, indicating that growth driven solely by increased input is unsustainable.

There have been dozens of articles discussing the reasons why China's economy has grown so rapidly over the past few decades. A representative view can be found in an IMF paper by Hu and Khan (1997), where the authors argue that the reason behind China's rapid economic growth is that China adopted a market-oriented economic reform policy beginning in 1979.

China's "reform and opening" was indeed formally approved as a policy toward the end of 1978, when Deng Xiaoping expelled "the Gang of Four" and took power. While there is nothing wrong with identifying the market-oriented reform as a pattern, as an explanation it is over-simplified and misses several other important elements, which will be briefly described below. At the outset, it is important to note the difference between China's economic growth and that of Russia and many Eastern European countries. The term "reform and opening" lacks precision; there are different ways in which reform and opening take place, and each ends up with different results.

2.2.2 *The Failure of the Shock Therapy Approach*

The first question to be addressed is: Are there any "wise strategies" that have contributed to China's exceptional performance compared with other "reform and opening" countries in the same period? The answer to this question is both yes and no. For the yes part, China has indeed performed much better than Russia and many Eastern European countries during the period 1989–2000. 1989 was the year when the Berlin

[7] See https://english.cw.com.tw/article/article.action?id=755.

[8] See https://www.nytimes.com/2018/02/12/smarter-living/just-working-harder-wont-get-you-ahead-working-smarter-will.html.

Wall fell, and many European countries one by one started to break away from the Soviet Union and became independent. 1992 was the year in which Deng Xiaoping accelerated China's economic reform. From data compiled by the World Bank, we observe that China's GDP *grew* by 258.1% during this 12-year (1989–2000) time period, whereas Russia's GDP *declined* by 40%. If we transform this into an annual growth rate over this 12-year period, China's growth rate was 9.94% in each year, whereas Russia's growth rate was −4.99% in each year over the same period.[9] So, why was there such a large difference?

In the 1990s, Russia and many Eastern European countries adopted the "shock therapy" approach to economic development, which essentially dictates that a country originally led by a communist regime should "quickly and dramatically change into a free-market economy." This was often referred to as part of the *Washington Consensus*.[10] This shock therapy approach was later seriously criticized by Nobel Laureate Joseph Stiglitz,[11] and the data also showed that the economic performance of Russia and Eastern Europe was considerably inferior to that of China, at least during the period between 1989 and 2000. This indicates that the term "reform and opening" is too vague and imprecise to explain China's salient performance in terms of economic growth.

2.2.3 *Crossing the River by Feeling the Stones*

Instead of impetuously following the shock therapy approach, China adopted the strategy of "crossing the river by feeling the stones," a well-known statement used by Deng Xiaoping. Because crossing a river is dangerous, feeling the stones would warrant a gradual progress, thus minimizing the risk of a systemic collapse. In terms of policies, China adopted a step-by-step approach referred to as "pilot testing," that is, reforms should be tried in some particular cities or areas first, and would

[9] The numbers are calculated from the free data source published by the World Bank. For Russia, see https://data.worldbank.org/indicator/NY.GDP.MKTP.KD.ZG?locations=RU, and for China, see https://data.worldbank.org/indicator/NY.GDP.MKTP.KD.ZG?locations=CN.

[10] The term was mainly used because the consensus was promoted by several Washington-based institutions, such as the World Bank and the International Monetary Fund. See https://en.wikipedia.org/wiki/Washington_Consensus.

[11] See https://tsd.naomiklein.org/shock-doctrine/reviews/bleakonomics.html.

only be expanded and extended to other areas or dimensions if success and smoothness had been observed at the pilot point. This pilot testing strategy reduced the resistance of the CCP conservatives and also avoided the risk of an economic crash, such as that in Russia. In general, the pilot tests started in the southeast coastal provinces such as Guangdong and Fujian, and then gradually expanded toward other coastal provinces, and only later to inland areas.

In retrospect, China in the late 1980s still faced strong resistance to market-oriented reforms, and the atmosphere then made any large-scale reform, such as shock therapy, practically impossible.[12] Furthermore, the earlier experiences in Eastern European countries also revealed a threat to the CCP: the turmoil following shock therapy might also undermine the CCP's hold on power and the authoritarian regime, and result in a split in the country. From its observation of Russia and Eastern Europe, the CCP hesitated to implement the shock therapy treatment. Was it wisdom (i.e., choosing to cross the river by feeling the stones) or luck (i.e., as a result of observing the earlier failure of the Soviet Union)? Perhaps it was a little bit of both.

2.3 Helps from Taiwanese Businessmen and Chinese Officials

Compared with the poor performances in Russia and Eastern Europe, the "crossing the river by feeling the stones" policy has proved to be superior, especially with the help of some exogenous factors. A group of particularly important helpers, according to Wu (2022), were the Taiwanese businessmen. Thanks to their common language and common cultural background, Taiwanese businessmen adapted swiftly to the Chinese economy and society. In the early 1990s, many laws and regulations in China were still loose, and hence whether a business venture would be successful or not depended on the agility and flexibility of the businessmen. As such, the common cultural background made it easier for Taiwanese businessmen to understand whether some regulatory ambiguities could or could not be pursued, with the subtle help of local officials. This of course increased their operational agility.

[12] More details about the resistance against Deng Xiaoping's reform and opening in the 1980s can be found in Vogel (2011).

2.3.1 *Migrant Labor as a Cheap Workforce*

The second factor that contributed to the early success of China, as mentioned by Roberts (2020), was the "hukou" (household registration) system. According to this system, all immigrant workers living in a coastal city with promising employment opportunities, say, Shenzhen, did not have the right to reside in that city, unless they had a legal household registration issued by the Shenzhen authorities. However, since this registration was not open to the public, the hukou system essentially made millions of rural migrant workers "illegal."

Since most of the immigrant labor from rural farms had very low living standards back home, they were willing to tolerate poor working terms and conditions, and rarely complained. As Wu (2022) mentioned, this gave the factory owners a golden opportunity to suppress workers' terms, thereby reducing the manufacturing costs. Furthermore, because most immigrant workers were working illegally, even when the working conditions were harsh, they would only very rarely file complaints. As such, the scenario was biased in favor of the capitalists. In some rare cases when the workers filed complaints about their unfair or illegal treatment, the local officials were always on the side of the firm owner, possibly accompanied by behind-the-scenes bribery.

In traditional competitive markets, along with the development of the economy, labor costs typically rise with the increase in labor demand. The rising wage will then shrink the firms' profit margins, and more or less curb the economic expansion. However, for China in the 1990s, this did not happen, at least partly because the terms of the immigrant labor supply were very much suppressed under the hukou system. In regard to bilateral bargaining games, the implicit bargaining that took place between the businessmen and the workers was disadvantageous to the latter, thanks to the hukou system.

2.3.2 *A Rent-Seeking Scenario*

A third factor that may have contributed to China's rapid economic progress in the 1990s has also been mentioned, namely, the rent-seeking maneuvering of various levels of officials (Wu, 2022). In the 1990s, there were many kinds of lax regulations. To actually set up and operate a firm, a businessman needed a zoning permit in terms of the plant's location, a factory construction permit from the city bureau, an emission permit from the environmental agency, and a sanitary check certificate from local health agencies, etc. All these had gray areas which could end up resulting in either an approval or a denial. For each firm, an approval suggests a corresponding profit inflow, and this approval depends on the extent to which the officials are willing to bless the businessmen; a less stringent enforcement of rules leads to lower costs, resulting in higher profits for the business.

For instance, when a businessman puts pressure on the workers and the latter complain, the official can use the household registration rules as leverage. The harsher the execution of the household registration rule, the higher the profit that the business will earn. In economics, the profits thereby generated are referred to as "rents," which will be divided between the businessmen and corrupt officials. For the businessmen and corrupt officials, their maneuvering of various lax regulations actually constitutes rent-seeking activities. Of course, the rent is often obtained at the cost of the weak, such as the migrant labor, the civilians whose farmland was expropriated with a low reimbursement, or the poor villagers who were located in areas affected by pollution. In general, the higher the rank of the official, the larger the rent that is expected. Shen (2021) explained how China's rent-seeking operates even at the level of the prime minister.

The reform and opening up started in 1979. As discussed above, the inflow of an abundant supply of Taiwanese businessmen and their capital, the lax regulations as opportunities, and the rent-seeking maneuvering of corrupt officials collectively contributed to the early success of pilot firms. One question naturally arises: Is this rent-seeking model sustainable when the economy enters the innovation-driven scenario? We will provide more discussion on this in later sections.

2.4 Benefits from Joining the WTO

Many scholars have also emphasized the importance of China's accession to the WTO as an explanatory factor of its rapid economic growth at the beginning of the twenty-first century. China joined the WTO in December 2001, and at that time its accession was very much welcomed by the U.S. After 17 years, however, the Trump administration said in 2018 that allowing China to enter the World Trade Organization (WTO) was a strategic error.[13] However, what is meant by saying that the U.S. government made a mistake? Is there any scientific evidence as to whether the Chinese economy actually benefited from joining the WTO?

2.4.1 MFN and the "Flat" World

Theoretically, why would any country's joining the WTO bring about an economic benefit? In addition, through which mechanism does the benefit arise? Here we will briefly explain the crux. First, joining the WTO means that the MFN (most-favored nation) principle must apply, and therefore since 2002 China has faced uniformly low tariffs from all other WTO members. Furthermore, China also promised to remove various trade barriers in its WTO Accession Agreement. With these lower trade barriers, global markets became more accessible to China, for both imports and exports.

The second change as a result of joining the WTO was also brought about by China's Accession Agreement, in which China agreed to remove many domestic regulations that had become obsolete. That would improve a foreign country's willingness to invest in China.[14]

The MFN and the Accession Agreement indeed forced China to move closer to the doctrine of free capitalism, and thus contributed to China's opening up to the world market. In retrospect, of course there were areas where China did not follow its original accession commitments, but overall joining the WTO reinforced its reform and opening-up strategy.

Table 2.1 also provides us with some preliminary evidence of how China performed both before and after its WTO accession. One can simply compare China's GDP before and after 2002; however, this plain comparison does not provide us with any scientific proof for two reasons: (1) we do not know how China's economy would have performed if it had not joined the WTO in 2001, and (2) we do not know to what extent China's economic performance can be attributed to the WTO accession. In terms of scientific experiments, we need to have rigorously defined "control" group data, before we can say anything about the "experimental" group (i.e., China) data.

[13] See Donnan, S. "US says China WTO membership was a mistake". *Financial Times*, available at https://www.ft.com/content/edb346ec-fd3a-11e7-9b32-d7d59aace167.

[14] For more discussion about how China benefited from joining the WTO, see Fewsmith (2001).

2.4.2 *Empirical Assessment of the Joining-the-WTO Effect*

For this purpose, Li et al. (2023) have provided a solid analysis of the contribution of WTO accession to China's economic growth. They created two reference groups of countries for comparison. The first group (group A) of countries joined the WTO at least five years *later* than China (they all joined between 2007 and 2015), and the second group (group B) joined the WTO at *roughly the same time* as China (they all joined between 1999 and 2004). By comparing the growth rate of China with the growth rates of the countries in group A, one can infer whether there exists any advantage of China's *earlier* WTO accession, relative to later joiners. By comparing the growth rate of China with those countries in group B, one can check whether China benefits from joining WTO *more than* other similar-time joiners.

The analysis of Li et al. (2023) revealed the following. First, regarding the GDP growth rate between 2002 and 2006, the first five years after China's accession, China outperformed the group A members. China's GDP increased by 61%, whereas that for group A members increased by 41%. This 20% (61%–41%) difference seems to be the contribution of the WTO accession. Second, China's GDP growth during 2002–2006 was roughly the same as that of the members in group B, which indicates that the benefit that China derived from WTO accession was not an outlier case, compared to other members joining the WTO at roughly the same time. Third, after 2008, China's GDP growth outperformed most other member countries in both groups A and B. This suggests that China was largely insulated from the 2008 financial tsunami. This point will be discussed in more detail in the next section.

2.4.3 *The Market Size Effect*

Although the assessment of Li et al. (2023) tries to control everything in the background, it still has one missing part. Almost by definition, the growth effect of joining the WTO depends on how large the economy was originally. If a country has only 500 low-cost workers who were originally working on rural farms, then removing the trade barriers and joining the WTO would at most attract the inflow of foreign direct investment (FDI) that would absorb these 500 farmers. Even worse, large foreign firms would not even bother considering engaging in FDI in this case, because a labor force of only 500 workers would be too small in scale. However, if a country has 500 million low-cost workers, then the scale, intensity, and ability to sustain FDI would be entirely different.

In the case of China, these 500 million low-cost workers were only released gradually, starting from the southeast coastal areas to the north-west inland areas. This large reserve of excess labor has evidently extended the period during which market liberalization could yield benefits in China.

2.5 A New Chapter After the 2008 Financial Tsunami

In summarizing the previous discussion, it can be seen that several factors have contributed to China's rapid economic growth over the past three to four decades: the previous turmoil before 1979, which created a low base period and a starting point very much inside the PPF; the prudent strategy of "crossing the river by feeling the stones"; the restrained migrant workers who could not fight for their terms and rights given their illegal status; the rent-seeking officials who benefited the capitalists by undermining the rights and welfare of the environment, labor and other weak groups; the accession to the WTO in 2001; and the large economic capacity that could digest the benefits of the market-oriented opening up over a long period of time.

In 2008, the world suddenly faced the financial tsunami, an ensuing crisis. How would this impact the China economy and China's role in international politics?

2.5.1 *China's Immunity to the Financial Tsunami*

Researchers such as Doshi (2021) have mentioned that 2008 was a turning point for several Chinese policies, and one critical reason was that the financial tsunami seriously hurt the economies of many Western countries, but barely affected China's economy. According to research by Vitaliy Novik,[15] among 198 countries in the world, when the percentage changes in GDP between 2007 and 2009 are compared, the financial tsunami was found to have impacted Eastern European countries and

[15] For the details, see https://bigeconomics.org/the-countries-most-and-least-affected-by-the-2008-financial-crisis/.

trade-dependent advanced economies the most seriously. The three countries most affected were Estonia (#1), Latvia (#2), and Ukraine (#3), and the least affected area was Africa. Advanced economies like the U.S. (#46) and Germany (#28) only recovered by 2010. China was one of the least affected countries (#189).

It is well-known that the key reason behind the occurrence of the 2008 financial crisis was the lack of healthy regulations in the U.S. banking system (especially investment banks). Wall Street proposed to issue CDOs (collateral debt obligations) to "wrap up" subprime mortgages, and many flawed CDOs were somehow ranked AAA by credit-rating agencies (such as S&P, Fitch, and Moody's). As such, quite a few international institutional investors were misled by such credit ratings and bought large quantities of CDOs, thereby facilitating the global spread of these instruments. Furthermore, commercial banks (which provided such subprime loans) were less worried about the default risk of subprime loans, because the risk could be passed through using CDOs so that the buyers of such CDOs would bear part of the burden of potential defaults.[16] The consequence was a prevalence of subprime loans and an impending financial crisis.

In short, at the micro level, those who were affected the most were those who had bought many CDOs. At the macro level, those countries which were more integrated with or connected to Wall Street generally bought more CDOs, and hence the more they were affected when the financial crisis struck. This explains why advanced economies like the U.S., the U.K., and Germany were among the countries more affected. Chinese banks and Chinese citizens in particular were less connected to Wall Street in 2008, and therefore they were less adversely impacted by the financial tsunami.

Most scholars, including those in the U.S., agreed that there was a serious problem with respect to the U.S. regulations on investment banks. These flaws in the U.S. regulations (which led the U.S. into trouble) and the U.S. financial connections with Germany and the United Kingdom (which led the latter into trouble), however, do not suggest the superiority of those less integrated with Wall Street, in particular the Chinese

[16] More detailed analysis regarding the issues of CDOs can be found in Chu (2010).

banking system or the CCP regime.[17] Ironically, this was exactly the main interpretation of the leaders of the CCP: CCP leaders believed that the flaws in the Western system had caused the financial tsunami, and that China's socialist capitalism might be a better alternative.[18]

2.5.2 *China's Strong Domestic Demand*

Other than the limited economic impact of the financial crisis itself, China also showed its strength by recovering swiftly after the financial tsunami. The typical government strategies to get out of the 2008 recession, thanks to the traditional Keynesian economics and the lessons from the 1929 Great Depression, were to increase government expenditure and encourage private spending. Furthermore, since a large part of many countries' effective demand came from exports, the seriously depressed economies around the world significantly decreased the purchasing capability of many countries. Hence, the most reliable way for any country to recover from the 2008 crisis was to increase its effective *domestic* demand.

For developed economies, there were not too many domestic targets on which to focus fiscal policy and to spend the government budget, as most government expenditures such as those for constructing roads, bridges, and highways had already been incurred for developed economies. China, however, had a wide spectrum of spending targets: modernizing the northwest inland areas which, as mentioned in the previous discussion in this chapter, was pretty much underdeveloped in 2008. Indeed, this large capacity to absorb government expenditure helped China get out of the mess relatively faster than the Western countries. To be fair, even if democratic countries did have many channels through which to increase their government spending, their budgetary efficiency in general was inferior to that of authoritarian countries. In China, increasing government spending to develop the northwest inland is just a one-man decision, and can be executed almost immediately.

Table 2.1 shows that, after 2009, China was notably distinct in maintaining its rapid pace of economic growth, compared with other developed countries. The analysis by Li et al. (2023) also showed that,

[17] In fact, China faced its own real-estate financial crisis in 2024. For more discussion, see https://www.theglobaltreasurer.com/2024/04/29/understanding-chinas-real-estate-crisis/.

[18] More discussion along these lines can be found in Doshi (2021) Chapter 7.

compared with group B countries (which joined the WTO at roughly the same time as China), China significantly outperformed all of them after the 2008 financial tsunami; before 2008, China and group B members performed roughly the same.

2.6 Marching on a Proactive Drum

According to Doshi (2021) and the many documents cited therein, the 2008 financial crisis did make Chinese officials believe that Western capitalism faced systemic problems, and that China might be able to challenge the U.S. The then CCP chairman Hu Jintao started to modify the original development doctrine set up by Deng Xiaoping of "keeping a low profile and waiting patiently." Since it was believed that the balance of international power had drastically changed after 2009, Hu proposed adopting a more proactive approach. This change of strategy was later followed and pushed further after Xi Jinping took power in 2012. Doshi (2021) has summarized several dimensions of the strategic changes, and some of them will be discussed in this section.

2.6.1 Navy Expansion and Reclamation in the South China Sea

First, China implemented its plan to construct aircraft carriers in 2009. The strategic target in deploying aircraft carriers was to "defend the sovereignty of the South China Sea, peacefully unify Taiwan, and protect ocean rights, which all need carriers" (Doshi p.168). Together with the carrier construction initiative, there was also a swift buildup of battleships, naval mines, and amphibious forces.

In addition, according to the Guardian, a Pentagon report stated that China had reclaimed over 3200 acres of land in the south-eastern part of the South China Sea.[19] China's focus has thus started to be directed toward developing and weaponizing those constructed islands so that it will have greater control over the maritime region without resorting to armed conflict. In its assessment of China's island-building program, the

[19] See https://www.theguardian.com/world/2016/may/13/pentagon-report-china-reclaimed-3200-acres-south-china-sea.

U.S. defense department said that the Spratly Islands had nearly 10,000-foot runways and large ports in various stages of construction by 2015.[20] Furthermore, on these islands China has excavated deep tunnels, created and dredged harbors, and constructed communications, logistics, and intelligence gathering facilities.

Although the accelerated building effort does not give China any new territorial rights, the airfields, ship facilities, surveillance, and equipment have enabled China to significantly enhance its long-term presence in the South China Sea. The reclamation of land enables China to deploy land-based weapons to challenge U.S. Navy ships. This deployment was drastically different from that before 2009, and it indicated that China was possibly preparing to construct an area denial force to confront interference by the U.S. military. Judging from the timeline, it is only logical to infer that such a strategic change was at least partly boosted by the occurrence of the 2008 financial tsunami.

2.6.2 BRI and AIIB

Secondly, in 2013, one year after Xi Jinping assumed the CCP chairmanship, China started its Belt and Road Initiative (BRI), which is a global infrastructure development strategy to invest in more than 150 countries and international organizations. This project involves billions of dollars of investment in roads, railways, and other infrastructure across the Eurasian region and Africa, mainly financed by China. China claimed that the BRI had created 420,000 jobs and lifted 40 million people out of poverty. As pointed out by *The Economist* magazine, however, many politicians in the West think that the real purpose of the BRI is to construct a Chinese-led world order in which China plays a dominant role.[21]

Together with the BRI, there was also the financial counterpart, the AIIB (Asian Infrastructure Investment Bank), also initiated in October

[20] See https://www.newsweek.com/china-close-completion-10000-foot-runway-disputed-south-china-sea-349499.

[21] Seehttps://www.economist.com/the-economist-explains/2023/10/17/how-chinas-belt-and-road-initiative-is-changing?utm_medium=cpc.adword.pd&utm_source=google&ppccampaignID=21,228,634,515&ppcadID=&utm_campaign=a.22brand_pmax&utm_content=conversion.direct-response.anonymous&gad_source=1&gclid=CjwKCAjwhIS0BhBqEiwADA.Uhc1O1wI-mRwU6yeAwSoFKmDpGUeso1StCmq9pgbEVsXW57KxQ5wKnBoCcrsQAvD_BwE&gclsrc=aw.ds.

2013. The starting capital of the bank was $100 billion, equivalent to two thirds of the capital of the Asian Development Bank and about half that of the World Bank.[22] Since its inception, the AIIB has been viewed as a potential rival and alternative to the World Bank and the International Monetary Fund, both of which were founded and supported by the U.S. Again, this demonstrates China's more aggressive strategies after Xi took power.

2.6.3 De-dollarization

China's third effort in challenging the U.S. influence was to establish a financial system independent of the Western-dominated one. The first step was to initiate a UCRG (Universal Credit Rating Group) in 2012, evidently targeted at the then notorious U.S. credit-rating companies that were partly responsible for the 2008 financial crisis. However, the UCRG was not successful and ceased operating in 2018.[23]

In 2015, China initiated another "de-dollarization" mechanism referred to as the CIPS (Cross-Border Inter-Bank Payments System), which works like a system parallel to SWIFT.[24] Witnessing the fact that the U.S. had sanctioned several countries using the SWIFT system as a weapon (just like the more recent sanctions on Russia, after its invasion of Ukraine), China made concerted efforts to consolidate the CIPS regime. In addition, China also tried to expand the use of the Renminbi to settle foreign exchange, intending to alter the originally almost monopolistic position of the U.S. dollar in international clearance. By October 2024, CIPS had 1573 participating banks, of which 560 banks were in China, 491 in other areas of Asia, and 244 in Europe.[25] Its influences were still limited.

[22] See https://en.wikipedia.org/wiki/Asian_Infrastructure_Investment_Bank.

[23] See https://publications.parliament.uk/pa/ld5801/ldselect/ldeconaf/105/105.pdf.

[24] See https://en.wikipedia.org/wiki/Cross-Border_Interbank_Payment_System.

[25] More details can be found in https://zh.wikipedia.org/zh-tw/%E4%BA%BA%E6%B0%91%E5%B9%A3%E8%B7%A8%E5%A2%83%E6%94%AF%E4%BB%98%E7%B3%BB%E7%B5%B1.

2.6.4 Wolf Warrior Diplomacy

Wolf warrior diplomacy is a confrontational form of public diplomacy adopted by Chinese diplomats in the late 2010s, although components of it had already been incorporated into Chinese diplomacy before that time. The assertive diplomatic posture that characterizes wolf warrior diplomacy had its roots in the 2008 financial tsunami, with an acceleration of wolf warrior diplomacy following Xi Jinping's ascension into office in 2012.[26] The emergence of wolf warrior diplomacy has followed Xi Jinping's political ambitions and foreign policy inclinations, especially his "Major Country Diplomacy" (Da Guo Wai Jiao) theory, which has legitimized a more active role for China on the world stage, including engaging in an open ideological struggle with the West.

CCP officials say wolf warrior diplomacy is a "necessary" response to Western diplomats' social media presence. More specifically, China's foreign vice-minister Le Yucheng has said he believes that foreign countries "are coming to our doorstep, interfering in our family affairs, constantly nagging at us, insulting and discrediting us, [so] we have no choice but to firmly defend our national interests and dignity."[27] Perhaps the most representative case was that in relation to China's ambassador to France, Lu Shaye, who was summoned twice by the French foreign ministry, first for posts and tweets by the embassy defending Beijing's response to the COVID-19 pandemic and criticizing the West's handling of it, then for "insults and threats" over new economic sanctions placed on China for its crackdown against the Uyghur minority in Xinjiang.

The general perception is that Wolf Warrior diplomacy refers to a style of coercive diplomacy, which is in contrast to the traditional diplomatic practices of cooperative rhetoric and the avoidance of controversy. The country being "coerced" tends to feel bullied, and its decision as to whether or not to protest against this coercion will be analyzed in more detail in a later chapter.

[26] See https://www.nbr.org/publication/understanding-chinese-wolf-warrior-diplomacy/ for more discussion.

[27] See the *South China Morning Post* archived from the original on 12 December 2020.

2.6.5 *Setting Up Confucius Institutes Worldwide*

Other than the economic, military, and diplomatic aggressions, China has also tried to penetrate the cultural dimension. Since 2004, China has gradually established roughly 550 Confucius Institutes and more than 1190 tutoring classes around the world,[28] which are all supported by the Chinese government. On the face of it, Confucius Institutes are public educational and cultural promotion programs funded and arranged by a non-governmental organization (NGO). However, this NGO is merely a façade; it is actually indirectly under the Ministry of Education of the People's Republic of China.

Confucius Institutes have been accused of being used as a form of "soft power" by the Chinese government, which spends approximately $10 billion a year on related programs to exercise these initiatives. There have been concerns about potential censorship regarding certain content, including discussions on individual freedoms and democracy, the 1989 Tiananmen Square protests and massacre, Taiwan independence, human rights in Tibet, Falun Gong, and the persecution of Uyghurs in China. Because such cultural and educational institutes have often been found to have collective national agendas, many countries in the world have begun to restrict or ban their activities.[29] When cultural and educational activities are supported by a political entity under the CCP ideology, it is not surprising that some democratic governments may have counteractive moves.

2.6.6 *Other Aggressions*

Over the past few decades, China has leveraged trade as a coercive tool against targets such as Australia. As a punishment for the then Australian Prime Minister Scott Morrison's call for an inquiry into the origins of COVID-19, China imposed unofficial embargoes on the importation of Australian coal, along with prohibitive tariffs on Australian barley and wine.[30] Another target of coercion was the NBA. In 2019, China suspended broadcasts of Houston Rockets games, because the

[28] Gary Sands, Are Confucius Institutes in the U.S. Really Necessary? The Diplomat https://thediplomat.com/2021/02/are-confucius-institutes-in-the-us-really-necessary/.

[29] More details can be found in https://en.wikipedia.org/wiki/Confucius_Institute.

[30] See the article "A view from Australia," *The Asian Forum*. 27 December 2021.

Rockets' then General Manager Daryl Morey had tweeted his support for the pro-democracy movements during the 2019–2020 Hong Kong protests.[31]

Yuan (2023) noted that tourism also serves as a strategic economic lever for China to influence other nations. The substantial economic impact of Chinese tourists makes a potential tourism boycott a powerful form of pressure. For instance, following South Korea's decision to implement the U.S. THAAD missile defense system, China informally prohibited group tours to South Korea. This action led to a significant decline in tourism and adversely affected the South Korean economy.

In 2021, some businesses started to prohibit the use of Xinjiang cotton, the purpose being to protest against the "re-education camps" for the Uyghurs in Xinjiang, which many democratic countries believe to be against the Uyghur ethnic group. Many international boycotts similar to the one against Xinjiang Cotton have occurred before, and there was even a movie "Blood Diamond" that was widely publicized. In retaliation to the business protest in 2021, the Chinese government identified several businesses and banned their operations in China. The Swedish fast-fashion company H&M was identified as a target, and subsequently its garments became unavailable on most of China's e-commerce websites, while its physical stores have "disappeared" from smartphone maps.[32]

Fong et al. (2021) also summarized China's aggressions in its periphery area: undermining Hong Kong's democratic institutions, influencing the election of Taiwan, mitigating anti-China sentiments in Central Asia, and interfering with the sectors of the media, entertainment, and religion of foreign countries. These activities all surged after 2009, in parallel with the above-mentioned aggressions, following the 2008 financial tsunami.

[31] See "China suspends business ties with NBA's Houston Rockets over Hong Kong tweet." CNN October 7, 2019.

[32] See the 2001 April 3–9 issue of *The Economist*. This also shows that apps attached to smartphones are also complying with the CCP instructions, otherwise how could physically existing "stores" all disappear in the map apps at the same time?

2.7 Why Did China Not Democratize?

Other than the above-mentioned international aggressions, China's domestic oppression of the Uyghurs, civil rights lawyers, human rights advocates, news reporters, etc., has raised concerns among democratic nations. As such, many Western scholars sometimes cast doubt on the "democratization hypothesis." Indeed, as regards the relationship between economic development and the political regime changes, orthodox views when China joined the WTO were that bringing China into the global market-economy system would eventually change its political institutions, and that it might help China to move toward democracy. In fact, this was what President Bill Clinton openly suggested: "Now of course, bringing China into the WTO doesn't guarantee that it will choose political reform. But accelerating the progress—the process of economic change will force China to confront that choice sooner, and it will make the imperative for the right choice stronger."[33]

The above-mentioned "democratization" hypothesis was pioneered by Lipset (1959) and followed by Diamond and Linz (1989) and many others. The reason why economic development may lead to democracy is because the former produces certain socio-cultural changes that influence political attitudes. The possible channels mentioned in the literature include increasing literacy, an expansion of educational opportunities, the rise of the middle class and related social organizations, and more intensive interactions with people in traditional democratic countries. These all facilitate human rights perceptions and the promotion of democratic ideas. However, researchers such as Inglehart and Welzel (2010) have provided numerous counterexamples that economic development has not led to democracy.

The prediction that economic development leads to democratization, in fact, rests on the implicit assumption that political institutions are malleable. Nevertheless, in China, with its Leninist regime, the communist party–state is the ultimate decision maker for almost every conceivable aspect of the society. In fact, China's constitution explicitly vests this privilege in the party–state apparatus. Under a Leninist regime, therefore, it is the political institution that determines the malleability of the market mechanism, and not the other way round. This is exactly the

[33] Cited in Fong et al. (2021) p. 3, with its original reference therein.

message delivered in deLisle and Yang (2022). As a result, in the globalization era, China's Leninist regime tends to reshape international market mechanisms and economic activities into its "socialist" version.

Understandably, every political system, be it democratic or not, affects or modifies the operation of an economy to some extent, which is why we have antitrust laws, appropriation laws, and zoning laws, among other things. Nonetheless, the situation in Leninist China is entirely different. In democracies, political forces tend to modify the market system from time to time, with the intention of facilitating business competition and preventing market failures. By contrast, the political system in China firmly controls and comprehensively monitors the operations of its domestic economy, and sometimes even the global economy.

Indeed, the CCP's party cells have become deeply rooted in all major government agencies, big companies, universities, schools, factories, and many NGOs. When there are so many party cells everywhere, the usual civil society forces are actually branches of political forces, and it is unlikely that China can democratize under the CCP's strict authoritarian rule. Later in Chapter 8, we will analyze how a Leninist autocrat can even use modern technologies to help the government exercise control.

The case of Jack Ma may be a good example. According to the *New York Times*,[34] in September 2020 Ma was trying to push the IPO of the Ant Group, China's biggest fintech conglomerate. Financial analysts then predicted that it would raise$34 billion, the largest offering in history. However, Chinese regulators had been criticized by Mr. Ma; in a speech, Ma described Chinese regulators as too cautious and pilloried state-owned banks for their "pawnshop" mentality of providing loans only to borrowers who could post collateral. This open critique evidently annoyed the CCP leader. A few months after his speech, Ma announced his retirement.

In liberal democratic regimes, criticisms and harsh feedback are part of the "social forces," which according to the democratization hypothesis are important to push political reforms. However, if Jack Ma, by 2020 the richest and most influential tycoon in China, had to self-exile after his offending statement, other civil society voices must surely have been deterred from speaking up.

[34] See https://www.nytimes.com/2021/04/28/opinion/jack-ma-china-ant.html.

2.8 Will There Be a Multi-Pole World Order?

As Doshi (2021) pointed out, China has been trying to establish a "multipolar" world order, replacing the original single-pole system backed and led by the U.S. Indeed, the world order of marine transportation after WWII was very much dominated by the U.S. Without the maintenance of ocean transportation safety by the U.S. Navy, as we mentioned in Chapter 1, the worldwide refined division of labor and the globalization in the past 80 years would not have been possible. Furthermore, the Marrakech Agreement enacted in 1994, based on which the WTO was established, was also promoted and initiated by the U.S. It would be fair to say that, before the year 2000, the single-pole world order backed by the U.S. never faced any serious challenge.

2.8.1 Unprecedented Strong Challenge Against the U.S.

The Soviet Union did try to challenge the U.S. in the Cold War period, and Japan's economic power also became a threat to the U.S. in the 1980s. However, Doshi (2021) correctly pointed out that in the past several decades, neither the Soviet Union, nor Japan, nor any other country that tried to challenge the U.S. had a GDP that exceeded half that of the U.S. From Table 2.1, however, one can see that China's GDP surpassed one half of the GDP of the U.S. in 2019. By 2021, the ratio (China GDP/U.S. GDP) even increased to 57%. If we think of the U.S./China conflict as a Thucydides scenario,[35] then China certainly has become a powerful challenger to the incumbent power, the U.S. We can think of China's challenge in the second decade of the twenty-first century as being a combination of the Soviet Union and Japan of the 1980s: it has the military industrial capability of the then Soviet Union, and also the consumer industry capability of the then Japan.

China has clearly recognized its growing economic might mentioned above, and this is why the CCP proposed a multipolar world order, challenging the original U.S. single pole. The various aggressions referred to in the previous sections actually reveal China's strong intentions. In fact,

[35] A Thucydides Trap is a term used by American political scientist Graham T. Allison to describe an apparent tendency towards war when an emerging power threatens to displace an existing great power. See https://en.wikipedia.org/wiki/Thucydides_Trap.

China wanted to challenge the U.S. in almost all dimensions, and the aspects we have discussed in this chapter can hardly exhaust all of them.

Will this multipolar effort be successful? It depends on three factors: (1) whether China can gain the upper hand in the innovation-driven economy, relative to that of the U.S.; (2) whether there are other new arenas in which China can dance better than the U.S.; and (3) whether the isolationism under Trump's second term (after January 2025) will undermine the support of other democratic countries. At the time of writing, we do not have sufficient observations regarding factor (3). The new arenas referred to in (2) include "cyberspace" which is the core of this book, and they will be discussed one by one in later chapters. Now we will briefly discuss factor (1): Will China's economic capacity surpass that of the U.S.?

We all know that the final outcome of the technological competition between the U.S. and China may hinge upon their respective economic capacities: the side that has a stronger economic caliber is likely to win. In the era when economic growth is driven by innovation, it needs to be asked which regime is more efficient in driving its innovation engine, the U.S. or China? According to Acemoglu and Robinson (2012 Chapter 3) and also echoed in our discussion in previous sections, despite China's economic growth rate having been high over the past thirty years, it is believed that this was due to the fact that China was in its early stage of economic development. Once the economy is in this innovation-driven stage, China's economic growth will slow down. However, the critical question is: Will China grow faster than the U.S., or vice versa?

2.9 Facing the Era of Innovation-Driven Growth

The question raised toward the end of the previous section almost boils down to a simple binary choice: between the U.S. and China, which society is more conducive to an innovation-driven economy?

2.9.1 Several Factors Behind the Innovation-Driven Growth Engine

This may be a question where it is very difficult to provide a clear answer. There are, however, three aspects that we should keep in mind. First, innovations are usually novel ideas, and very different from the original orthodox doctrines. It is fair to say that a free society with less authoritarian oppression is more likely to generate new and sometimes even wild ideas contradicting the unorthodox ones. Second, compared to an extractive authoritarian regime, an inclusive democratic society, as claimed by Acemoglu and Robinson, would be more likely to be more conducive to fostering innovation, because most people in the society would be less worried about the new resource reallocation and even deprivation that may come along with the innovation.

The above two factors constitute the negative side of an extractive authoritarian state in an innovation-driven economy. There is, nevertheless, a third factor in relation to which an authoritarian society may have an advantage: when an innovation needs some large-scale field tests to evaluate its feasibility and to improve or refine its setups, an authoritarian regime can easily perform the test and make progress.

For instance, China has identified Suzhou as the city for conducting an experiment involving 5G, and it has set up more than 10,000 base stations, requiring citizens to use specific applications, and testing whether certain communications and operations run well.[36] This kind of large-scale co-ordination is absolutely impossible in any democratic country. As we will explain shortly, the case of COVID-19 may be a good example to understand this advantage of the authoritarian state. In short, effective co-ordination may sometimes help innovations succeed.

Another possible benefit of an authoritarian regime in innovation was well described in Beraja et al., (2023a, 2023b). In regard to the relationship between authoritarian regimes and AI innovation, Beraja et al. identified an interesting channel that shows that the relationship between the authoritarian regime and innovation may be mutually reinforcing. On the one hand, the authoritarian government can use the big data it owns as tools to help the training of better AI. On the other hand, private AI firms which sign contracts with the government can use these big data to train the AI, and improve their AI innovation. Because many AI products (such as facial recognition) can be used by both the public and private sectors, in equilibrium we may have a prosperous private AI sector and a stable autocracy. Beraja et al. showed that this self-reinforcing mechanism does exist in China, and it serves as another reason to support the positive correlation between AI advancement and the stability of autocracy.

[36] See https://www.huawei.com/en/media-center/our-value/suzhou-5g-lab, where China's leading 5G company, Huawei, claims the successful use of 5G.

2.9.2 Why Did China Fail and Succeed During COVID-19?

For scholars who have argued about the disadvantages of an authoritarian regime, an often-quoted example is the case of Li Wenliang, who was a famous doctor and a whistleblower before the spread of the COVID-19 pandemic. Because of the Leninist authoritarian control and the severe internet censoring by the CCP, Li's warning of a possible new virus was quickly picked out and his warning was soon removed from the social media. Li was later called in by the authorities, warned, threatened, and obviously coerced to sign a document signifying repentance.[37] This oppression of internet information turned out to delay the response of the government and finally led to the spread of the virus all over the world. The cost in terms of human lives and economic activities was evidently overwhelming. It is clear from this example that information screening and censoring is a disadvantage faced by an authoritarian regime. As pointed out by Repnikova (2022) and many other Western reports, this is the cost that has to be borne in an authoritarian regime when the autocrat's centralized control limits information feedback, which may result in policy rigidity and adjustment inertia.

Most Western critics, however, have overlooked the *advantage* of an authoritarian regime, which became evident in the latter phase of the COVID-19 crisis. The control of a pandemic disease requires two public health measures: the widespread implementation of vaccines, and the effective quarantine of possibly contagious patients. It goes without saying that China's authoritarian regime accomplished these two things much more efficiently than democratic countries. For the vaccines, injections in China were mandatory, unlike the situation in many democratic countries, where even rumors were spread regarding the possible damage caused by vaccines, not to mention the legal right to refuse the vaccine injection. As for quarantine, China could easily lock down a 10-million people city, and this is a scale of forced quarantine that can hardly be found in any democratic country.

The implementation of a mass lockdown in China was actually related to the ICTs. Almost all Chinese in large cities have smartphones, which are often equipped with GPS tracking and electronic payment kits. During the quarantine period, the cell phone became a must for citizens, because

[37] See "Li Wenliang: Coronavirus Death of Wuhan Doctor Sparks Anger," BBC News, February 7, 2020.

without it one could hardly buy anything or move anywhere. The smartphones can measure the temperature and heartbeats of individuals, which can predict whether they are infected and potentially contagious. All stores and public gathering places in China have their respective QR codes, which only allow individuals to enter when their smartphones' QR codes' screening feeds back with positive information about their health condition. When individuals are not allowed to enter any place or pass any roadblock, their cellphone will trigger a red light and the guards will stop them. The quarantine exercised in the physical space is actually executed in cyberspace, with sophisticated monitoring, censoring, calculation, and screening in the background. This is the advantage of cyberspace authoritarianism: the efficiency of co-ordination and control.

2.9.3 *The Authoritarian Regime's Quarantine Success*

The fact that China efficiently dealt with COVID-19, especially in effectively implementing quarantine, was one form of propaganda that the CCP used to brag about, both domestically and abroad. In containing COVID-19, the authoritarian Chinese regime performed much better than the U.S. and other democratic countries, as evidenced by the extremely low number of new infection cases in the later period of COVID-19, when most democratic countries still had thousands of new cases every day. This quarantine success, with the help of ICTs in the background, has to some extent boosted Chinese confidence in their "Great Rejuvenation of the Chinese Nation," which has also strengthened and toughened the position of Chinese leaders toward the democratic countries. Indeed, the CCP was able to lead all aspects of China mainly because it was also able to control the information in cyberspace. This tight control in China has shown that the information technology in the background forms a powerful apparatus, even though such an apparatus is not appreciated in democratic societies.

2.9.4 *Expecting the U.S./China Dance in Cyberspace*

In addition to the above-mentioned abstract comparison between the U.S.'s and China's advantages in innovation-driven economies, many recent reports have also mentioned the imminent problems that China faces. These include an extremely rapid decline in the labor force due to the earlier one-child policy, the dramatic drop in foreign direct investment, the defaults of several major property developers and the related impacts on the financial market, the outflow of financial assets, the increasing tension with the U.S., the forthcoming population aging and the corresponding social welfare burden, the lack of confidence in the party-state under Xi's leadership, and the increasingly harsh U.S. sanctions on hi-tech products and machines.[38] These have cast shadows on the Chinese economy. If China's economy cannot be as strong as it was in the past decades, then the outlook for it to compete with the U.S. in cyberspace does not look optimistic.

Of course, one should not ignore the uncertainty on the U.S. side after Donald Trump began his second term as President in 2025. Diplomatically, the U.S. is expected to have a tense relationship with its allies in Europe, Japan, Canada, and Mexico, to say the least. Economically, the high tariff imposed by the U.S. is going to disturb the world economy in an uncertain way. Both these factors will weaken the economic capability of the U.S., which will in turn be to the advantage of China.

As has been mentioned, when China's GDP reached 50% of U.S. GDP, the CCP leaders felt that China was ready for more aggressive moves and would challenge the incumbent hegemony, the U.S. However, readers should also be reminded about the changes that will take place in future battlefields. In most periods of human history, one would expect to see geopolitical conflicts, but in the twenty-first century, the nature of the conflicts is shifting. How cyberspace enters the scene will be the focus of the next chapter.

References

Acemoglu, D., & Robinson, J. (2012). *Why Nations Fail: The Origins of Power, Prosperity and Poverty*. Crown Business.

Acs, Z. J., Desai, S., & Hessels, J. (2000). Regional Innovation. In Z. J. Acs (Ed.), *Regional Innovation, Knowledge, and Global Change*. Open access on Springerlink.com.

Beraja, M., Kao, A., Yang, D., & Yuchtman, N. (2023a). AI-Tocracy. *Quarterly Journal of Economics, 138*(3), 1349–1402.

[38] See the analysis by AEI, https://www.aei.org/economics/chinas-economy-is-in-deep-trouble/.

Beraja, M., Kao, A., Yang, D., & Yuchtman, N. (2023b). Data-intensive Innovation and the State: Evidence from AI Firms in China. *Review of Economic Studies, 90*(4), 1701–1723.

Chu, C. Y. C. (2010). The Regulation of Structured Debts: Why? What? And How? *Southern California Interdisciplinary Law Journal, 3*, 443–472.

DeLisle, J., & Yang, G. (2022). *The Party Leads All: The Evolving Role of the Chinese Communist Party*. Brookings Institution Press.

Diamond, L., & Linz, J. (1989). Introduction: Politics, Society and Democracy in Latin America. In L. Diamond, J. Linz & S. M. Lipset (Eds.), *Democracy in Developing Countries, Vol. Four -- Latin America*.

Doshi, R. (2021). *The Long Game: China's Grand Strategy to Displace American Order*. Oxford University Press.

Fewsmith, J. (2001). The Political and Social Implications of China's Accession to the WTO. *China Quarterly, 5*, 573–591.

Fong, B. C. H., Wu, J.-M., & Nathan, A. J. (2021). *China's Influence and the Center-periphery Tug of War in Hong Kong*. Routledge.

Hu, Z., & Khan, M. S. (1997). Why is China growing so fast? *International Monetary Fund Economic Issues, 8*.

Inglehart, R., & Welzel, C. (2010). Changing Mass Priorities: The Link between Modernization and Democracy. *Perspectives on Politics, 8*(2), 551–567.

Li, J., Liu, Y., & Zhou, Y. (2023). Assessing the Impact of WTO Accession on China's Economic Growth. In H. Gao, D. Raess & K. Zeng (Eds.), *China and the WTO: A Twenty-Year Assessment*. Cambridge University Press.

Lipset, S. M. (1959). Some Social Requisites of Democracy: Economic Development and Political Legitimacy. *American Political Science Review, 53*(March), 69–105.

Repnikova, M. (2022). *Chinese Soft Power*. Cambridge University Press.

Roberts, D. (2020). *The Myth of Chinese Capitalism: The Worker, the Factory, and the Future of the World*. Macmillan.

Shen, D. (2021). *Red Roulette: An Insider's Story of Wealth, Power, Corruption, and Vengeance in Today's China*. Scribner.

Vogel, E. (2011). *Deng Xiaoping and the Transformation of China*. Harvard University Press.

Wu J-M. (2022). *Rival Partners: How Taiwanese Entrepreneurs and Guangdong Officials Forged the China Development Model*. Harvard University Press.

Yuan, S. (2023). Tracing China's Diplomatic Transition to Wolf Warrior Diplomacy and Its Implications. *Humanities and Social Sciences Communications, 10*(1). https://doi.org/10.1057/s41599-023-02367-6. ISSN 2662-9992.

CHAPTER 3

The Rise of Cyberspace

Three decades ago, Professor Nicolas Negroponte (1994) of the MIT Media Lab described the digital revolution as consisting of two major transformations: the atom/bits transformation and the static/mobile transformation. As to the former, it was noted that atoms are the basic units of the physical space, whereas bits are the basic units of cyberspace. Because the movement of atoms is very inefficient compared with the extremely rapid transmission of bits, in the digital era, many activities in the physical space will shift to the digital realm. For example, the traditional shipping of printed magazines (atoms) will be replaced by the transmission of PDF files (bits) through the Internet, and the printing will take place in the destination location.

As to the static/mobile switch, young readers may need to be informed of what the world looked like in the 1990s. In those days, most devices (such as the big televisions and the bulky desk computers, both of which had a thick screen because the cathode ray tube needed to be projected over a longer distance) were difficult to move, which was described by Negroponte as "static." By contrast, three decades ago signals were mainly transmitted through the air from senders to terminal devices, which were described as "mobile." Today, the roles of static and mobile have essentially been swapped, as predicted by the static/mobile transformation: the terminal devices are mostly cellphones, iPads, and laptops, which are light and can easily be moved. The digital data are transmitted

C. Y. C. Chu, *An Emerging Digital Wall*,
https://doi.org/10.1007/978-981-95-3577-4_3

and relayed efficiently by cables buried underground or under the sea, by thousands of base stations installed on the ground, and by dense Wi-Fi routers deployed around human gatherings. These transmission facilities are described as "static."

Note that the year (1994) in which Negroponte published his prediction of the above two transformations was also the year when the Marrakesh Agreement was enacted (based on which the WTO was established). After Chapter 2's discussion regarding how China has benefited from joining the WTO, this chapter will examine the transformative impact of the digital revolution, especially in the context of international politics and conflicts.

3.1 The Expansion of Information Collection

As was explained in the above discussion, the Negroponte switch predicted the static/mobile transformation, and hence the widespread use of mobile devices. Regardless of location, these devices can be used to upload and download information. Furthermore, given the fast speed of uploading and downloading (which will be explained later in Sect. 3.4), the Internet is filled with all kinds of user-generated content from every corner of the world. Exactly how prosperous is the flow of information on the Internet? A good index is the annual increases in the numbers and penetration rates of smartphones across countries.

3.1.1 The Prevalence of Terminal Devices

Table 3.1 provides statistics for 16 countries or areas, including the numbers of smartphone users and the percentages of these users relative to the corresponding populations in those countries. Here, a smartphone refers to a mobile phone that has a touchscreen interface, can access the Internet, has an operating system capable of running downloaded apps, and can perform the basic functions of a computer. In essence, smartphones are ubiquitous endpoint devices that have the function of uploading and downloading information.

From Table 3.1, one can see the growth and prevalence of global smartphone users. The country that has the largest number of smartphone users is China: by the end of 2023, there were 1.081 billion users. The country that has the highest penetration rate is Singapore: the penetration rate had reached 95.41% by 2023, with 5.72 million smartphone

Table 3.1 Smartphone Prevalence, by Country and Year

Year	*22020*		*2021*		*2022*		*2023*	
Country	#	%	#	%	#	%	#	%
China	943.2	65.5	993.1	68.8	1,039.10	71.8	1081.2*	74.5
Japan	77.25	69.3	80.65	74.3	83.79	77.3	86.55	78.9
Philippines	19.93	37.7	36.41	60.7	43.26	67.12	50.94	73.7
UK	54.18	93.7	57.81	97.0	58.55	97.0	59.25	97.0
France	47.18*	86.66	47.95*	92.2	48.63*	95.63	49.24*	97.0
Germany	74.13*	97.0	74.8*	97.0	75.23*	97.0	75.47*	97.0
U.S	296.8	85.73	302	86.11	307	86.43	311.8	86.69
Turkey	49.13	66.68	57.18	68.9	63.06	70.79	69.99	72.38
Mexico	42.34	54.4	51.27	60.1	55.81	61.5	64.54	66.96
India	241.03	54.23	389.84	60.63	637.11	66.21	883.5	70.95
Singapore	5.26	89.95	5.42	91.87	5.57	93.74	5.72	95.41
Australia	21.77*	85.4	22.11*	85.7	22.43*	86	22.74*	86.3
Israel	7.49	97.0	7.66	97.0	7.98	97.0	8.29	97.0
Saudi Arabia	30.44*	97.0	31.88*	97.0	33.14*	97.0	34.27*	97.0
South Korea	35.61	76.5	37.68	79.75	38.57	81.66	40.0	84.08
Hong Kong	6.61	97.0	6.67	97.0	6.86	97.0	6.96	97.0

Notes Numbers of smartphone users are in millions; * means values are estimates
Source Various country websites

users. The country that has the highest growth rate of penetration is the Philippines: it has grown from 37.7% in 2020 to 73.7% in 2023. By 2023 the U.S. had 311.8 million smartphone users, and the penetration rate was 86.69%. Of course, there are other types of terminal devices that can interact with the Internet, but Table 3.1 should provide a clear picture of device and user prevalence worldwide.

Given the prevalence of mobile devices and users, there is no doubt that the data in cyberspace have been growing exponentially. To understand what kinds of data are uploaded into the Internet, it may be useful to classify the data into two categories: the data voluntarily or accidentally provided by individuals through their internet activities, and the data collected by surveillance cameras, GPS, or Wi-Fi routers (often without users' knowledge). In what follows, the discussion proceeds based on this classification.

3.1.2 Data Collected from Individual Activities

The first kind of data collected arises when users intentionally access websites, and therefore those websites know the activities that one is pursuing. In recent years, individuals using platforms in many democratic countries have often been notified that their personal information is being collected, and they are given the option to consent to or opt out of such information collection. In earlier years, website users were never notified of such data collection. With regard to such activities, the following are the major kinds.

E-commerce and E-payment

Other than a few bulky commodities such as cars and airplanes, major e-commerce platforms such as Amazon and Alibaba sell almost everything. Many consumers today rarely go to traditional supermarkets or department stores and simply purchase various things from e-commerce platforms. These platforms often have their own logistic facilities and provide delivery to buyers much more efficiently than traditional stores. Because of these advantages, as pointed out by Galloway (2017), many consumers have moved away from brick-and-mortar shopping to e-commerce platforms such as Amazon, causing corresponding changes in the revenues and rise and fall of various companies. This pattern can be found in most countries around the world.

A main feature of e-commerce platforms is that they have all records of one's previous purchases, the pages one had browsed, the amount of time one stayed on certain pages, the comparisons one made across various pages, the last page being browsed before one left the website, the addresses to which one requested the deliveries, the complaints one made, the method of one's payment, the lapse of time since one's last visit, how frequently one reads other customers' reviews, and many other features that one often fails to notice. As pointed out by Stephens-Davidowitz (2017), people's browsing and buying activities reveal their *true preferences*, which they probably have never revealed to anyone else; in fact, in physical contacts they may even want to hide such preferences due to the social norm pressure. After a long time of tracing, the e-commerce platform may know us even better than our closest friends. In addition, e-commerce platforms also have comments from other previous buyers. This "consumer evaluation" information is not available in most conventional brick-and-mortar purchasing channels.

Corresponding to an e-commerce purchase, there is usually an e-payment. The e-payment system must involve an authentication process verifying that the payment is supported by a financial institution or has an e-commerce platform account balance. While e-payment is a must for online transactions, in some places such as China, e-payment has become popular even in face-to-face transactions, so that it has very much replaced cash or credit-card payments. When one frequently uses e-payments, one's records of transactions, balances in bank accounts, and default records are all data collected by the e-payment agencies.

Social Media

Social media usually refer to technology platforms that facilitate the creation and sharing of content, ideas, and queries. These interactive platforms allow individuals, organizations, and legal entities to share, create, discuss, participate in, and modify user-generated or self-curated content. As far as information dissemination is concerned, the major difference between social media and traditional media is that the former operate in a transmission system with many sources to many receivers, whereas traditional media operate in a transmission model with one source to many receivers. The traditional media has an editor, and therefore extreme opinions may be deleted or modified, so that extreme information is rarely seen by others. Social media do not have regular editorial screening, and therefore even extreme opinions may generate attention and interactions. As such, the information spectrum shown in social media has a heavy-tail phenomenon.

The starting point for delineating social connections is to identify the group that one classifies as "friends," to count the "likes" one shares with others, and to measure the intensity with which one positively or negatively interacts with others. More intense interactions include the time one spends on certain content uploaded by certain people, the "likes" one shows regarding certain content, and the frequency with which one shares others' opinions. Social media platforms collect all the data from people's interactions.

People's interactions with others reveal their underlying emotional trends. These emotional aspects complement their preferences regarding physical commodity purchases, which they reveal on e-commerce platforms. People's emotional tendencies are particularly evident in political campaigns, policy subjects that have antagonistic views (such as abortion rights and evolution/creationism in school teaching), religions (such as Catholic vs. Muslim), and the attitude toward immigrants.

Sometimes one uploads videos or pictures to a social media website, which may also disclose the location background or information about the surrounding environment more than one intends. A navy soldier's picture may include his "dog tag" number, as well as the battleship on which he serves in the background. This information is sometimes sufficient to predict the location and movement of the entire fleet.

Search Engine

A search engine is a software system which provides links to web pages and other relevant information, in response to one's query. One uses a search engine to seek unknown information, or what one wants to know more about, or whether or not some hypothetical pattern exists. People's searches may be the previous step of their shopping, purchasing, reading, or other activities. Because search engines keep the records of one's previous searches, the amount of time that one stays on a web page, and the sequence of one's consecutive searches, the platform knows pretty much what one is "up to." On search websites, as also pointed out by Stephens-Davidowitz (2017), one usually tells the truth, and hence reveals one's true character.

Collectively, people's search records can be easily aggregated into macro predictions, as in the famous Google Flu Trends (GFT) reports. GFT was a web service operated by Google. It provided estimates of influenza activity for more than 25 countries. By aggregating Google Search queries (such as asking about the symptoms of a flu, or the difference between symptoms of a flu and a cold), GFT attempted to make accurate predictions about flu activity. Similarly, if a lot of people in a certain country have recently searched for "migration to Canada," then it indicates that they are not satisfied with their current situation. In short, a pure aggregation of searches may reveal a social trend.

3.1.3 Data Collected from Surveillance

The second kind of data may be gathered without user awareness, and there are several broad categories.

Global Positioning System (GPS) or Wi-Fi Router
Most cars manufactured today have a built-in GPS, which helps people find routes to reach their destinations. Sometimes the GPS is built into a cell phone, and the function is the same. The GPS sends the outdoor coordinate data of different people's positions to satellites, and the satellites calculate and inform people of the directions that they should take. As one implements the GPS function, in theory one's detailed movement patterns can be captured. Although GPS data are blocked by the building when people stay indoors, their positions can still be collected through the connection between the mobile phone and the indoor Wi-Fi routers that they use. Because these footprints are not erased immediately, people's locations over a certain period of time can be traced.

Other than the above-mentioned micro guidance, the GPS data also have their aggregate implications. They are often used to warn of traffic congestion, which results when a lot of cars are simultaneously located on the road without much moving. Furthermore, during a pandemic, GPS can be used to trace contagious patients' footprint records, based on which the health authorities can release warnings to people whose moving patterns intersect with those of the patients. Finally, the government can issue warnings to people located in a place where a natural disaster (such as a tsunami) is imminent.

Surveillance Cameras and Satellite Pictures
The government and building management units often have large numbers of surveillance cameras installed in elevators, transportation cabins, building entrance halls, places for public gatherings, on street corners, at school gates, etc. Most of these cameras are for security or safety reasons, but they do capture our pictures at specific times and in specific places.

There are also thousands of satellites in the sky, which may take all kinds of pictures. Low and medium-resolution satellite images feature pixel resolutions from 10 meters to several kilometers (km), and high-resolution satellite images have a pixel size between 1 and 10 meters and provide detailed information about individual building features on the ground. Very high-resolution satellite images can have a pixel size of less than 1 meter, even down to 30 cm per pixel, and are capable of capturing individual trees, vehicles, or other relatively small objects.

With the help of refined facial recognition techniques, future satellites could be able to identify individuals on streets. Footprints shown by GPS may just be machine signals, whereas footprints shown by facial recognition can verify individual identities. In general, satellite pictures complement other means of information collection because they provide a viewing angle orthogonal to the earth's surface. This is particularly useful when identifying changes in geographical outlooks, so that one can trace landscape dynamics and predict the activities that have taken place.

3.2 Refined Uses of Data Collected

Some readers may doubt whether knowing seemingly trivial data such as "Mr. A buying brand-X dog food" from an e-commerce platform has any empirical significance. In this section, by reviewing a famous case in the U.S. Supreme Court, the possible use of big data collection will become clear.

3.2.1 Mosaic Profiling and Infringement

In the U.S. v. Jones,[1] Justice Alito and Justice Sotomayor proposed the following mosaic theory as their concurring opinion. The mosaic theory suggests that seemingly insignificant data points, "though individually of limited or no utility to their possessor, can take on added significance when combined with other items of information" (Kerr, 2012; Pozen, 2005; Schlabach, 2015). The key idea was that "each individual piece of intelligence information, much like a piece of jigsaw puzzle, may aid in piecing together other bits of information even when the individual piece is not of obvious importance in itself."[2]

In the context of informational privacy, the mosaic theory suggests that even though some non-sensitive data, such as one's favorite dog food brand, does not reveal much on its own, the collection of many pieces may provide a full profile of each individual and constitutes a violation of privacy. In fact, "putting together mosaic pieces" is an idea highly related to AI. In the era of generative AI, it is only a matter of time when the judicial system will further apply the mosaic theory in this domain. Readers should also note that privacy is just one type of damage to which the

[1] United States v. Jones, 565 U.S. 400 (2012).

[2] Halperin v. Central Intelligence Agency, 629 F.2d 144 (D.C. Cir. 1980).

mosaic information theory may be applicable; other types of damage will become clear as we proceed.

In general, AI can help perform more precise mosaic profiling, not only with regard to individuals, but also by including many aggregate metrics. In Zuckerman (2019), the author analyzed how Jim Simmons' fund uses cryptographic techniques to identify (otherwise negligible) patterns of various economic activities, and these patterns can help the Simmons' fund generate significant profits. Indeed, neither Jim Simmons nor his team members had any background knowledge of finance or economics, nor did they have any prior theoretical framework explaining each "pattern"; the patterns were merely the outcome of computational profiling.

As to the issue of mosaic information, a related report was issued in 2014 by the U.S. President's Council of Advisors on Science and Technology. This report mentioned the term "data fusion," which "occurs when data from different sources are brought into contact and new facts emerge." As a result, data fusion could easily result in comprehensive profiling that enables the government or the data processor to identify any target or pattern. As pointed out by Sheer (2016), the overwhelming surveillance exercised by the government itself is likely to encroach upon privacy; now with the help of AI, the extent of the intrusion is evidently more severe.

Because of the possibility that a big secret may be identified by putting together various pieces of individually trivial data, several concerns immediately arise, depending on the owner of the secret. First, the privacy of that identified person would be infringed upon. Second, business secrets could be probed, potentially leading to millions of dollars of losses. Finally, in the case where the person being identified is a high-ranking government official, national security might even be compromised.

3.2.2 More Efficient Business Decisions

Businesses may not be interested in individual privacy per se, but they may wish to use the profiled information to engage in targeted marketing strategies. By accurately knowing individual preferences and behavioral patterns, businesses can send advertisements that are more likely to be welcomed by individuals, thereby increasing expected sales. Or, in the case of fund managers such as Simmons, more accurate profiling and predictions could facilitate higher investment returns, which would generate more profit for their funds.

According to Vance (2023), the Planet Labs company has used the counted number of cars parked outside Walmart, together with other information, to forecast retail performance. In addition, the company has used the pictures surrounding oil wells to predict their annual production, and has added them up to forecast the total oil output of an area. While one does not know how useful and accurate these predicted numbers generated from satellite cameras can be, the fact that such data are welcomed by Wall Street futures brokerage companies suggests that the mosaic pictures put together are quite similar to the real ones. As for more macro aspects, the company has also used a series of satellite pictures taken over Xinjiang to tell how many additional buildings have been constructed, which are likely to be "re-education camps." An accurate prediction like that may help the business in an indirect way: it helps enhance the reputation of the Planet Lab company.

3.2.3 Profiling for the Purpose of Intensifying Control

It is useful to draw an analogy between an authoritarian country and a business: the autocrat is the business CEO, the citizens in the country are the employees that the autocrat wants to control or to send information to, and foreign countries are companies which the autocrat sees as threats or at least competitors.

It has been mentioned in the previous discussion that big data allow the data owner to do better profiling. In authoritarian countries, the data owner is of course the autocrat, who can use such refined information to shape citizen behavior. As a natural use of the profiling results, the autocrat can "educate" the citizens in a way that is more likely to be welcomed by individuals. This may improve the stability of the autocrat's ruling. On the more negative side, the autocrat can use the profiled information to know the weakness of each citizen, and to identify and suppress dissent by targeting individual vulnerabilities. This may quickly put a stop to any possible opposition and challenges. On the event side, the autocrat can foresee a possible opposition gathering and implement corresponding preemptive countermeasures (such as blocking the road that connects with the gathering place). On the international side, the interference by "Fancy Bear," a Russian hacking group, has already been mentioned in

Chapter 1. This penetration allegedly affected the 2016 U.S. election result. We will have more discussion on this later in Chapter 9.

To sum up, mobile devices can help with the collection of big data, AI can help sort and profile the information, and it is purely the intention of the user that determines the impact. To really implement such data collection and profiling, however, the computation speed is the key prerequisite; a long waiting time will kill the appetite of any device users. The next section will review how the advances in ICTs have improved the speed of various operations.

3.3 Advances in Computation Speed

In 1961, a company in San Francisco proudly announced a new chip named Micrologic, on which 4 transistors were embedded. Today, the chip used in many cellphones has more than 10-billion transistors embedded. Each transistor is a semiconductor device used to amplify or switch electrical signals. All electronic computations are composed of 0 s and 1 s that are controlled by the transistors. The more transistors that are contained in a chip, the more complicated the computations that can be performed. Furthermore, a shorter route within each concise and condensed transistor also implies less use of electricity. This is why engineers try to squeeze billions of transistors into a 1 cm-by-1 cm chip.

We usually classify chips into three types. The first type is "logic," which refers to the processors that run computers, smartphones, and servers. The second type contains DRAM (dynamic random access memory) and NAND (flash memory), which are used to memorize short-term and long-term data, respectively. The third category is more varied, but not the subject of our later discussion, mainly because it is less related to Moore's Law (which is to be explained soon). The memory chips are mostly standardized products, whereas the logic chips involve more sophisticated designs.

3.3.1 Sustaining Moore's Law

Given that one wants to make smaller logic and memory chips, what is the limit of miniaturization? This leads us to the commonly known Moore's law (1968): it was Gordon Moore's prediction (rather than a truly scientific "law") that the number of transistors on a single chip would double every 18–24 months, without much increase in costs. In the past half a century or so, the empirical developments have been pretty much consistent with the "law." In short, Moore's law predicts an exponential growth of computation power in cyberspace consisting of "bits"; by contrast, we have never observed an exponential growth in the physical space consisting of "atoms."

The realization of Moore's law has encountered significant obstacles in the past 50 plus years. The more transistors on a single chip, the smaller the distance between any nearby transistors, and this creates two problems: (1) electric interferences and leakages between transistors,[3] and (2) heat dissipation. These two problems were, to some extent, solved or at least lessened by the design of FinFET and GAAFET.[4] However, it is not the design itself that can resolve the problem; usually there are numerous patents and know-hows associated with each design. As far as the latest GAAFET patents are concerned, TSMC (Taiwan Semiconductor Manufacturing Company) owns the largest number of related patents.[5] In addition, TSMC has developed a unique CoWoS packaging technology that can enable three-dimensional chip stacking in order to minimize data transmission delays between chips.[6] The above advantages explain why TSMC leads the industry in manufacturing high-end chips.

To practically manufacture smaller and smaller chips, engineers face other obstacles. The most advanced chip in 2024 is the 2 nm technology, where each nanometer (nm) is 10^{-9} meters, which is about 1/10 of the size of a virus. On each chip, there may be several billions of transistors. The problem is: How does one "fabricate" so many small circuits onto one small chip with a size of only 1 cm by 1 cm?

Leaving aside the details, the technology involved is called EUV (extreme ultraviolet) lithography. In 2024, this process can be implemented by only one firm, ASML (Advanced Semiconductor Materials

[3] As regards the electric interference, the major ones include the short-channel effects, the drain-induced barrier lowering, and the saturation velocity. The explanation of these effects involves technical knowledge, and interested readers can do their own preliminary reading from various search engines.

[4] FET refers to "field effect transistor," and GAA means "gate-all-around." The FinFET chip design is named "fin" because it has a vertical part orthogonal to the horizontal one, which looks like a tail fin.

[5] See https://www.cw.com.tw/article/5125326.

[6] See https://3dfabric.tsmc.com/english/dedicatedFoundry/technology/cowos.htm. CoWoS refers to Chip on Wafer on Substrate, which is a packaging technology used in the manufacture of chips.

Table 3.2 The chip manufacturing technology, by years

Year	*Process Node*	*Year*	*Process Node*
1971	10 μm	2003	90 nm
1974	6 μm	2005	65 nm
1977	3 μm	2007	45 nm
1981	1.5 μm	2009	32 nm
1984	1 μm	2012	22 nm
1987	800 nm	2014	14 nm
1990	600 nm	2016	10 nm
1993	350 nm	2018	7 nm
1996	250 nm	2020	5 nm
1999	180 nm	2022	3 nm
2001	130 nm	2024	2 nm

Note 1 μm = 1000nm
Source see https://www.hitachi-hightech.com/global/en/knowledge/semiconductor/room/about/history.html

Lithography), which is a Dutch company. Furthermore, to implement the lithography process, the engineer needs to find a very pure light source of this extreme ultraviolet. It turns out that only a couple of companies in the world can produce this unique light source. As such, the competition for the manufacturing of high-end chips at least partly becomes a competition for acquiring such light sources and lithography machines.

For readers to have a fuller visual understanding of the advances in chip technology, Table 3.2 presents a timeline summarizing the key advances in chip technology.

3.3.2 *Why Is the Computing Speed Important?*

As has been explained, more advanced chips result in faster and more efficient computations. It is understood that faster is better than slower, but why do such mini-second differences in computation speed matter?

For regular computer users, a mini-second delay in speed is not much of a concern; but there are areas where computation speed matters a great deal. For missiles, efficient computation is a dominant factor in deciding whether the missile will hit the target or be intercepted by an antimissile system. In August 2024, a Ukrainian drone shot down another Russian drone, which reveals the advantage of a faster computing speed in predicting the movement of a flying object.[7] Indeed, in war there is no substitute for victory.[8] For military uses, a mini-second is the time unit that matters.

For AI, computation speed determines how fast and accurately the machine can learn, and thereby which AI operation performs better. If this AI is used in wartime, then it may determine the final outcome of the war. In the case of cipher code decryption, the computation speed is crucial in order to understand the opponent's tactics. Furthermore, computation speed also determines the pace of other forms of technical progress that rely on AI, and hence the success or failure of various industrial competitions.

Indeed, many of the recent ICT breakthroughs are related to the speed of computation. In June 2024, the market value of the up-and-coming company Nvidia surpassed that of Microsoft and became the leading global technology company. Nvidia's product is the GPU (graphics processing unit), and it is the most effective accelerator when engaging in "parallel computing."

Parallel computing is a process in which many computations and processes are carried out separately and simultaneously, and then integrated at a later stage. This parallel computing concept has existed for decades, but has been more effectively realized only in recent years, thanks to the development of the GPU. Together with the GPU, there is also the NPU (neural processing unit), which mimics the logic of neural networks. It is generally believed that the computation speed will be increased further by these new processors and new packaging technologies.

3.3.3 Export Controls and Entity List as Confrontation Weapons

Given that the competition for computing speed in particular and ICTs in general is unavoidable and critical, and given that there are some crucial elements (such as technologies, patents, chips, engineers, and other inputs) that are important to this competition, the technology leading side will have strong incentives to prevent or delay competitor access to such essential elements. Since the U.S. and its democratic allies

[7] See https://mil.in.ua/en/news/russian-zala-drone-shot-down-by-upgraded-ukrainian-fpv-drone/#google_vignette.

[8] See https://www.americanrhetoric.com/speeches/douglasmacarthurfarewelladdress.htm. That was a famous quote by Douglas MacArthur.

as of 2024 are evidently in front of China in terms of ICTs, the U.S. government is therefore motivated to use the Export Control Act and the Entity List (which are to be explained in detail in Chapter 4) to ban the export or outflow of many such items. As such, the competition for computing speed is evolving from technological innovation into a battle between country groups. Note that this battle is about the dominance in some *future* industries, which is entirely different from the traditional trade wars, which in most cases focus on *existing* industries.

Banning the outflow and export of critical elements (of chip manufacturing) is an embargo in a broad sense, and essentially the practical target of these strategies is China. As with all economic embargoes, applying the export control has its downsides. The first possible negative impact is that it may serve as an incentive for China to develop its own domestic production line. The often-mentioned example may be that of Qian Xuesen,[9] who was exiled by the U.S. in the 1950s and then returned to China and single-handedly helped China establish its own guided missile system. The case of chip design and manufacturing, however, is more complicated and delicate than the case of manufacturing missiles. For the U.S., even if China does successfully develop its own chip industry, as long as it is delayed for several years due to export control measures, then these policies will still seem to be worth implementing.

The second negative comment regarding the traditional economic embargo is its secondary impact on civilians. For example, banning the export of oil to a particular country may hurt its energy supply in winter, and hence hurt civilians. Again, this does not seem to constitute a problem in the case of high-end chips, because they are not highly related to livelihood necessities. The above analysis facilitates the conclusion that, at least politically, the export control and entity list policies appear to be effective instruments for the U.S.

So far, it has been explained that the world has millions of smart devices with advanced computational capabilities, thanks to the advances in chip design and manufacturing technologies. However, to effectively access or transmit various data, we also need a fast speed of uploading and downloading. This is related to the progress being made in the telecommunications industry. We will get to that in the following section.

[9] For details, see https://www.bbc.com/news/stories-54695598.

Table 3.3 Transmission speed of telecommunications, by generations

Generation	*Data Transfer Rate*
1G	2.4 KB/s
2G	64 KB/s
3G	2 MB/s
4G	100 MB/s
5G	10 GB/s

Note 1GB = 1000MB = 1,000,000KB
Source Decision Telecom. (2023). How 1G, 2G, 3G, 4G, and 5G communication standards evolved. https://decisiontele.com/news/1g-5g-evolution-telecommunication-networks.html

3.4 Transmission Speed and the Role of AI

Starting from 2018, we entered the 5G phase. In what follows, we will explain the distinctions among different telecommunication generations.

3.4.1 Speed of Uploading and Downloading

Theoretically, a 5G network can achieve download speeds of up to 20 GB/s and upload speeds of up to 10 GB/s. In comparison, 4G can only reach speeds far below 1 GB/s for both uploading and downloading (see Table 3.3 for a detailed comparison). Of course, the actual speed that users experience may vary depending on the type of spectrum, the number of devices simultaneously connected, the distance between users and the base station, and the interference from obstacles such as buildings. However, in general, uploading and downloading a short video using 5G will take only a few seconds. This enables billions of users to upload a broad variety of content to the Internet.

At the beginning of this Chapter, the importance of Negroponte's atom/bit transformation was mentioned, with the underlying factor being the speed of transmitting bits. Using the data compiled by Decision Telecom, the transmission speeds of various telecommunication generations are summarized in Table 3.3.

3.4.2 Analyzing the Big Data

Some registry and administrative data have always been available, and the advances in ICT can enable the creation, transmission, storage, and retrieval of new content. Because of the advances in the speed of transmission, nowadays most data are stored in the cloud, and one can retrieve them only when one needs to use them. However, could ICTs help us analyze these big data in more diverse ways? Here comes the role of AI.

One typical way of seeing the importance of big data is to understand the concept underlying AI. Traditionally, one wrote programs for the computer, and the computer provided feedback based on the program-generated data. This is the "program-in-data-out" pattern. AI operates in reverse: one feeds the computer with big data, and the computer provides feedback in the form of programs.[10] This is the "data-in-program-out" pattern. In the past, the role of programmers was significant in that the computer mainly provided computational assistance. In the era of AI, the computer can perform deep learning, thereby reducing the role of the programmer.

For instance, if we provide the computer with a large dataset of historical Go game moves, AI then generates for us a playing program such as AlphaGo, which can outperform all human professionals. The key parameters to be defined in the training of AI are: how "pieces being surrounded are killed," and what defines a "win" in the Go game. In addition, we also need to tell the AI to "replace captured pieces with empty intersections." Given the above specifications of the game, the AI takes care of the rest. Thus, the key parameters in AI design are the game rules and the objective function that we feed into the computer. In short, we provide the big data and the game specifications that we have in mind, and then AI feeds back with the dynamic suggested moves.

A crucial factor in making a success of AlphaGo is that the dataset must be enormous, or at least consisting of millions of examples, covering all great players of the Go game in human history. The larger the amount of fed-in data, the greater the likelihood that the AI will produce efficient strategies. The reasons why computers can nowadays digest such big data, as has been mentioned, are due to the advances in computation speed and the implementation of parallel computing. In the AlphaGo game, for instance, in a 19X19 game board, what happened or will happen in the northwest corner of the plate most likely has nothing to do with the subgame in the southeast corner of the plate, and therefore the computation in these two areas can be implemented in parallel.

[10] See https://www.facebook.com/cateinbigcity/videos/3961569707191616/.

This also tells us why the GPU frequently used in computer games has played a leading role in AI. Computer games need to modify screens immediately in response to players' actions. As long as players' actions affect only part of the screen, it is more efficient to do the area-specific pixel computation rather than the traditional global computation. In short, as long as interdependencies between data (which means that the data in one area of computation are correlated with the data in another area) are minimal, then parallel computation will be much more efficient than the traditional aggregate computation. Since the GPU has been adapted for parallel computation in video games for a long period of time, it can be revised relatively quickly, and thereby help with the massive amount of computation that AI requires.

To sum up, without the super speed of computation, the computer cannot drive the big data; and without the big data, there is insufficient training material for the AI to learn from. When both are available, the AI becomes super powerful.

The description by Fei-Fei Li (2023), a professor of computer science at Stanford University, also helps us understand the mutual dependency of big data and AI. Professor Li established a large image database, called ImageNet, which contains more than 14 million pictures. Then, scientists from ImageNet organized an annual competition inviting global participants to develop algorithms. They soon realized two things: the pictures have to be numerous in order for the computer to generate meaningful and useful results, and that the real breakthrough was achieved by an algorithm design called AlexNet, which uses neural network learning algorithms. This pretty much describes the tight connection between big data sets, the GPU, and the NPU.

3.4.3 General Purpose AI

AlphaGo is a single-purpose AI; it can only play the Go game. Starting in 2020, we witnessed rapid progress in general purpose AI. A typical example is ChatGPT. This is an interactive software which can respond to all kinds of questions that we raise. The training of GPT needs the inputs of billions of scripts and sentences, and the AI figures out the grammar, rules, and contexts of all such sentences. Then, when we type our questions, GPT can generate quite reasonable responses. Heuristically, GPT's learning of language is like that of babies: parents never teach grammar to the babies; babies hear millions of sentences that adults say, and figure out the grammar and sentence rules all by themselves.

Because the above-mentioned responsive software can cover areas such as script, music, and pictures, it is categorized as a "general purpose" AI. Very often a general-purpose AI can easily pass the Turing test,[11] and we say that the AI appears to have "wisdom."

3.5 Infrastructure Deployment

Let us pause to assess the situation. As a result of the static/mobile transformation, most data are now generated and collected by individual devices. The amount and variety of data are both increasing at a very fast speed. The premise of the static/mobile switch is the speed of transmission and computation, and the amount of computer memory. So far, nothing has been said about the infrastructure for telecommunications transmission. In what follows, we first go through the undersea cable network and then the spread of base stations.

3.5.1 Undersea Cables and Base Stations

The first undersea (or submarine) cable was deployed in 1858, and the transmission speed was very slow: it took roughly 18 hours for a trans-Atlantic transmission.[12] Today, the same transmission would take only seconds. According to the Naval Research Institute, by 2024 there were about 750,000 miles of undersea cables spanning the world's oceans.[13] Regarding cable networks, there are more than 400 main lines, and the U.S. was already densely connected to the global network via over 100 cable systems by 2024. A report by Michael Sechrist (2023) indicates that China has invested $1.1 billion in the construction of 16,777 miles of

[11] In a Turing test, a human evaluator judges a text transcript of a natural-language conversation between a human and a machine. Passing the test means that the evaluator cannot tell which one is the machine. See https://en.wikipedia.org/wiki/Turing_test.

[12] See https://en.wikipedia.org/wiki/Transatlantic_telegraph_cable.

[13] See https://www.usni.org/magazines/proceedings/2023/may/information-warfare-depths-analysis-global-undersea-cable-networks.

cables.[14] The submarine cables carry more than 97% of intercontinental communications each day, with a transaction value of approximately $10 trillion.

The Naval Research Institute estimated that these cables are mostly (roughly 59%) controlled and maintained by private companies, but 19% of them are state-owned. The maintenance of cables often relies on autonomous underwater vehicles and remote-control systems, with relatively little protection. There are two major kinds of security threats associated with these cables. The first is: when the ownership or management of cables is affiliated with an authoritarian government, then there are often concerns that there are "backdoors" embedded within them. These backdoors can either monitor regular transmissions or compromise important information transmission, thereby disrupting critical communications. The second threat is that some party may try to damage the cable line itself, especially in a war or during a crisis period.

Submarine cable lines are mainly for the transmission of data across oceans. On land, information sent by a mobile device in the form of electromagnetic waves needs to be relayed through base stations to reach the target. Each base station can send these waves over a distance of between 1.25 and 18.5 miles, therefore, relays are necessary for most communications. In any city with a large population, more base stations are needed to mitigate network congestion. By 2023, the U.S. had roughly 100,000 5G base stations, Japan had 146,000, South Korea 217,000, Europe 356,000, and China had an astonishing 2,970,000 base stations, partly because a Chinese company named Huawei manufactures the least expensive base station facilities.[15]

As in the case of submarine cables, base stations can also have "backdoor" programs or chips. The challenge in detecting such backdoors lies in the fact that, regardless of mounting suspicions, the existence of backdoors can hardly be proved. These forms of spyware, if they exist, can be remotely activated or deactivated by their originator, and therefore whenever detection is ongoing, it is expected that the backdoors will be in the "shut down" mode, so that nothing can be found.

[14] A detailed submarine cable map can be easily found from the search engines. The map is worldwide, in which connections with large countries such as China and the U.S. are particularly clear.

[15] The numbers vary in various data sources. We ignore the minor discrepancies here.

3.5.2 International Coalitions of Decoupled Deployments

The essence of the "backdoor" suspicion reveals a profound lack of mutual trust, especially between the democratic countries and authoritarian ones. This makes it easier for each side to build its own telecommunications infrastructure, in spite of the infrastructure being just like highways and railroads, the use of which in theory is capable of being shared. A typical example of such mutual distrust may be the *Clean Network Initiative* (CNI) launched in 2017. The background to this initiative was that several European countries planned to procure 5G facilities manufactured by Huawei.[16] The CNI was a U.S. government-led effort to mitigate potential backdoor threats to data privacy, human rights, and national security, in cases where the infrastructure is made by firms from an authoritarian state. It was intended to implement internationally accepted digital trust standards across a coalition of partners, with trustable telecommunications equipment suppliers. As we can imagine, the CNI must involve a restructuring of the supply chain of telecommunications facilities.

In December 2020, the U.S. announced that more than 60 nations, representing more than two-thirds of the world's GDP, joined the CNI, and 180 telecom companies publicly committed to the principles of the CNI. This alliance included 27 of the 30 NATO members; 26 of the 27 EU members; 31 of the 37 OECD nations; 11 of the 12 Three Seas nations as well as Japan, Israel, Australia, Singapore, Taiwan, Canada, India, New Zealand, and Vietnam. Evidently, the result of a successful CNI would facilitate the formation of two infrastructure camps for telecommunications.

As was claimed, the targets of the CNI are to ensure three things: (1) at the individual level, privacy is well respected; (2) at the business level, intellectual property rights and know-how are well-protected; and (3) at the country level, national security is adequately safeguarded. Other coalitions unrelated to infrastructure will be discussed in later chapters.

[16] Michael R. Pompeo, "The Clean Network," *U.S. Department of State*, https://2017-2021.state.gov/the-clean-network/index.html.

3.5.3 LEOs and the 6G

In the above discussion, the terms "4G" and "5G" have been mentioned, which refer to the fourth and fifth generations of telecommunications. The difference between generations is the corresponding maximum download speed. In 1946, when telecommunications first emerged, speeds were extremely limited. Starting in 1979, the first analog generation was launched, and no meaningful communication could occur. In 1991, the second-generation (2G) telecommunications became digital, and thereafter the theoretical maximum speed began to increase rapidly. 3G was launched in 2001, 4G started in 2017, and 5G was launched in 2018.[17]

6G is expected to be launched by 2030, but we do not yet know its exact capacity. One thing we are quite sure of is the role that low Earth orbit satellites (LEOs) will play in 6G. According to NASA,[18] a LEO satellite is a satellite that circles around the earth at lower altitudes than geosynchronous (GEO) satellites. An LEO satellite orbit lies between 200 and 2000 km above the earth, whereas the GEO satellite is 35,786 km above the earth. GEO satellites move at the same speed as the Earth, so that if there is a GEO satellite on top of us in the sky, it will always be on top of us roughly in the same position. However, because a lower altitude implies a stronger gravitational pull, LEOs must move very fast in their orbit (roughly 7.8 km per second), otherwise they will be attracted by gravity and fall to the Earth. Because they all move so fast, each satellite can cover a given area for only a few minutes. To have a comprehensive coverage of LEO satellites for communications, we have to launch and deploy many LEOs. And this is exactly what Starlink has been doing. By September 2024, Starlink had deployed more than 7000 LEOs into orbit. The follower, Jeff Bezos' Project Kuiper, plans to deploy 3236 LEOs by the year 2029. The European OneWeb company already had 648 LEO satellites in March 2025.

[17] For references, see https://en.wikipedia.org/wiki/List_of_wireless_network_technologies, and https://www.thalesgroup.com/en/markets/digital-identity-and-security/inspired/basics-of-mobile-networking/milestones. Different sources have slightly different numbers for download speeds.

[18] https://www.nasa.gov/humans-in-space/leo-economy-frequently-asked-questions/.

There are two advantages of LEOs. The first is their truly universal coverage, including oceans and deserts. This makes global communications much more comprehensive. In areas lacking terrestrial infrastructure (such as oceans which cover 70% of the Earth's surface, and deserts where base station deployment is extremely inefficient), telecommunications using 6G will be possible in the future.

The second advantage is even more important for international politics: LEOs change the strategic approach of military aggressors. A good example was the Russian invasion of Ukraine in 2022. The traditional first strike before an army invasion or marine landing is to disrupt critical ground communication and defense infrastructure, including base stations and airplane runways, so that the country being invaded becomes deaf, blind, and immobile. With the help of Starlink, however, Ukraine was able to use LEOs to sustain its telecommunications even after Russia's first strike. Indeed, that made the Russian invasion more difficult, because Ukraine was neither blind nor deaf after Russia's air strike. The national security importance of LEOs is very obvious in this example. If it is necessary to have secure cables and base stations, it is certainly necessary to have secure LEOs.

3.6 New Playing Fields and Battlegrounds

Some people think of the export control and entity list regulations as forms of trade embargoes. People have seen many embargo cases initiated by the U.S. in the past—against Cuba, North Korea, Iran, etc. There were also embargoes implemented by multiple countries against South Africa during the apartheid period.[19] However, all such embargoes are targeted at existing products (such as oil) and are not about future products. The only comparable historical case is the Manhattan Project. In that case, however, most of the effort was concerned with preserving the confidentiality of the nuclear bomb development plan and status, and preventing critical knowledge pertaining to the Manhattan Project from being leaked to the axis powers.

The contemporary export control list related to chips covers an unprecedented range of items that encompasses the chip manufacturing machine, the lithography machine, the light source, the software, and

[19] See Levy (1999).

even extends to scientists who are resident aliens and do not have citizenship affiliation. Such an unprecedented coverage of restrictions underscores the strategic significance of cyberspace warfare.

It has been mentioned in the previous discussion that the rise of ICTs has fundamentally changed the strategies, tactics, tools, and forms of the game of international competition, but in fact its impact goes even further. The rise of cyberspace and its accompanying ICTs has actually created many new games, new weapons, and new battlefields. Even in traditional games, cyberspace very often changes the game rules. This is illustrated by the following examples.

3.6.1 SWIFT

Perhaps the most well-known cyberspace embargo weapon was the removal of certain Russian banks from the SWIFT network in 2022. The full name of SWIFT is the Society for Worldwide Interbank Financial Telecommunication, which is a cooperative that was established in 1973 in Belgium. This cooperative is owned by the banks and other member firms that use its service. SWIFT provides the primary messaging network through which international payments are initiated and related sides are informed. Roughly speaking, for each payment, SWIFT sends an internet message notifying the target banks of this payment. In 2022, after the Russian invasion of Ukraine and in response to the requests by the European Union and other Western countries, a SWIFT ban against some Russian banks was put in place, with the aim of weakening Russia's economy in the hope of ending the invasion.

As one can see, SWIFT, as many other internet mechanisms, was originally created to facilitate financial transactions and to improve efficiency. But now it has become a critical vulnerability in cyberspace. In ordinary transactions, SWIFT transmits bits between banks using fiber lines, which have replaced the traditional telegrams; however, in critical moments, especially when people are used to the efficient bit transmission, stripping away this mechanism creates enormous disruption. In essence, removing the cyberspace convenience has become a weapon.

3.6.2 ICT Patents and Knowledge

Because the coverage of the U.S. export control list is so broad, the battle front is equally extensive. For example, the U.S. banned ASML from selling their EUV machine to China, even though ASML is a Dutch firm. The reason why the U.S. can exercise this banning order is because many of the patents embodied in the ASML machine are owned by U.S. citizens.[20] Because the EUV machine has very sophisticated technology content, one sees a natural extension of a trade embargo: from tangible commodities to patents and technical knowledge.

In chip manufacturing, any wafer process at 7 nanometers or below requires an EUV machine, and ASML is the only company in the world that can produce it. To compete in cyberspace, chip manufacturing machines have become key targets in the battle front. In upstream markets, the cyberspace competition may also be extended to various other resource dimensions, including rare earth elements such as Ga, Ge, and Nd, etc. All these can be covered by export control measures.

3.6.3 Data Collection

The U.S. move to ban TikTok is another unprecedented example. TikTok is a platform composed of hundreds of software components in its background system, none of which are owned by U.S. citizens. The key purpose in sanctioning TikTok is to prevent China from collecting (big) data from U.S. citizens, knowing that big data are very powerful resources, if not potent weapons. It seems that the U.S. is trying to establish a "data wall" between the U.S. and China, and possibly even between democratic allies and authoritarian ones (the latter possibly include Russia, China, and North Korea). The scenario is something like: on our side of the wall, we collect and compile data as usual; on the other side of the wall, we don't care; however, as for data collection or transmission across the wall, it is strictly prohibited.

People generally understand that Alibaba also collects U.S. buyers' information every time they visit the Alibaba website. If shopping information is as important as videos uploaded to TikTok, then the same logic behind banning TikTok may also be applicable to banning Alibaba's information collection. However, one should understand that, in the case of Alibaba, for every piece of data transmitted through the Internet, there is often a physical commodity being purchased in the background. Restricting Alibaba's data collection would effectively halt e-commerce

[20] See https://today.line.me/tw/v2/article/1D8ojNB for details.

activities. It may turn out that the data wall is actually a very thick trade wall.

3.6.4 *Cyberspace Trade Barriers*

It is also important to understand that much unfair trade may arise due to man-made digital barriers in cyberspace. For instance, the famous firewall of China makes it very difficult for 1.4 billion Chinese to access all foreign e-commerce platforms, resulting in only a limited number of Chinese consumers being able to access the Cdiscount website in France. However, since France does not block the Internet, all French people can access Alibaba to buy Chinese commodities. Thus, the cyberspace trade barrier created by China, in the form of an internet firewall, can lead to significant trade imbalances that may surpass those caused by traditional tariffs and quotas.

3.6.5 *Human Rights Intrusions*

In July 2020, the U.S. Department of Finance imposed sanctions on Chen Quanguo and three other Chinese officials for human rights abuses in Xinjiang.[21] Mr. Chen was a retired politician, who previously served as the party secretary of Xinjiang, where millions of Uyghurs were held in the "re-education" camps. Mr. Chen is regarded as a key architect of Beijing's surveillance policies against minorities, and he was previously in charge in Tibet. The sanctions include freezing these four persons' assets in the U.S., and prohibiting them as well as their relatives from entering the U.S.

What Mr. Chen did in Xinjiang was essentially physical and cyberspace surveillance. From the website *Inside China's Digital Gulag* one can see details of how the Chinese government is employing advanced technological surveillance in its quest to establish the most comprehensive surveillance state in human history. Xinjiang's Integrated Joint Operations Platform gathers data on residents using iris scanners, CCTV cameras with facial and voice recognition, and even DNA sampling. This platform links the collected data with residents' online activity, banking information,

[21] See https://www.bbc.com/news/world-us-canada-53355697.

phone calls, and text messages to identify behavior that the government regards as "problematic."

Furthermore, Chinese companies aggressively export such surveillance techniques to other authoritarian countries, perhaps in an effort to dominate some application branches of the AI industry, which was valued at a billion dollars in 2018 and is rapidly growing. Chinese tech companies have already provided artificial intelligence–based mass surveillance systems to at least 18 countries mostly having poor human rights records.[22] In short, the ICTs have become powerful surveillance weapons for autocrats.

3.7 Final Remarks

The above discussion has explained when, why, and how cyberspace has risen in the past several decades. It has been argued that in many international and domestic interactions, the importance of cyberspace has been neglected or ignored, compared with that of physical space. There are new games in cyberspace, there are new cyberspace weapons in the old games, and there are new scenarios that people accustomed to traditional ways of thinking cannot even imagine.

Against the background of a rising cyberspace, however, it should be emphasized that traditional geopolitics may still play an important role. In the case of Taiwan, for instance, the U.S. has conflicts with China in the Taiwan Strait both due to the first island chain—a geopolitical concern—and chip production security, which impacts cyberspace. The point is not to argue which concern is more important, but to serve as a reminder that geopolitics is not the only issue involved.

From our discussion of the export control and entity list, readers may feel that the democratic camp appears to play a passive role: it strives to prevent its data, IPs, and engineering techniques from being used by authoritarian regimes. However, sometimes the development of ICTs may also have implications that undermine the authoritarian regimes.

For example, it has been mentioned that LEO satellites resemble thousands of base stations suspended in the sky. Would LEO satellites threaten China's Great Firewall (GFW)? The GFW was built by monitoring information going through base stations and websites, which are all within the

[22] See https://www.cbc.ca/passionateeye/features/in-xinjiang-china-surveillance-technology-is-used-to-help-the-state-control.

geographic space. However, in the future, LEO satellites may be operated by democratic countries and all kinds of information transmission are allowed. As such, if Chinese citizens connect themselves to these "democratic" LEO satellites and use them as base stations, their communications would be far more difficult for the CCP to intercept, because their transmissions do not go through any facilities on the earth's surface. It appears that this may create a loophole in the GFW. Is it possible for the CCP to block Chinese citizens from connecting "upward to the sky"? Or, more simply: Could 6G potentially destroy or at least disturb the GFW, thereby undermining the CCP's internal control? The answer is not known yet.

References

Galloway, S. (2017). *The Four: The Hidden DNA of Amazon, Apple*. Penguin.

Kerr, O. S. (2012). The Mosaic Theory of the Fourth Amendment. *Michigan Law Review, 111*(3), 311–354.

Levy, P. I. (1999). *Sanctions on South Africa: What Did They Do?* (Economic Growth Center Discussion Paper No. 796). Yale University.

Li, F.-F. (2023). *The Worlds I See: Curiosity, Exploration, and Discovery at the Dawn of AI*. Macmillan.

Negroponte, N. (1994). *Being Digital*. Knopf.

Pozen, D. E. (2005). The Mosaic Theory, National Security, and the Freedom of Information Act. *Yale Law Journal, 115*, 628–679.

Schlabach, G. R. (2015). Privacy in the Cloud: The Mosaic Theory and the Stored Communications Act. *Stanford Law Review, 67*, 677–721.

Sechrist, M. (2023). *Cyberspace in Deep Water: Protecting Undersea Communications Cables by Creating an International Public-Private Partnership*. Mimeo, Harvard Kennedy School.

Sheer, R. (2016). *They Know Everything About You*. Bold Type Books.

Stephens-Davidowitz, S. (2017). *Everybody Lies: What the Internet Can Tell Us About Who We Really Are*. Bloomsbury Publishing.

Vance, A. (2023). *When the Heavens Went on Sale: The Misfits and Geniuses Racing to Put Space Within Reach*. HarperCollins.

Zuckerman, G. (2019). *The Man Who Solved the Market: How Jim Simmons Launched the Quant Revolution*. Penguin.

CHAPTER 4

Technology-Denial: Decoupling the ICT Industries

We explained in Chapter 2 that the General Agreement on Tariffs and Trade (GATT), the General Agreement on Trade in Services (GATS), and the Marrakesh Agreement have very much lowered trade barriers, and even established a judicial system, namely, the Dispute Settlement Body of WTO, to enforce WTO regulations. However, as pointed out by Chu and Lee (2019), when the Marrakesh Agreement was passed in 1994, the digital era had not begun, and most WTO members then had liberal market economies. When the digital economy gradually grew and when some state-controlled economies joined the WTO in the early twenty-first century, it became evident that WTO rules enacted in 1994 contained numerous loopholes. Whenever some countries want to engage in de-globalization, they can readily exploit these loopholes to justify their actions. One of the most significant loopholes in WTO regulations concerns national security, which we will explain below.

We should first understand that trade barriers may not necessarily decrease in the digital era. Intuitively, barriers persist simply because certain countries desire them. Indeed, international trade is just like interpersonal trade: there are often parties that simply prefer not to engage in transactions with others, and they can always find justifications to avoid such engagements. Saying "I do not want to trade with you" represents the passive stance; a more aggressive perspective might be: "I do not want to see you succeed." In that case, the strategies involved are not just trade

C. Y. C. Chu, *An Emerging Digital Wall*,
https://doi.org/10.1007/978-981-95-3577-4_4

barriers; they may include the deliberate disruption of supply chains, such as cutting off the supply of some necessary components in the production process. This is the focus of our discussion in this chapter.

From our discussion in previous chapters, we have identified numerous disruptive factors associated with the digital era. In particular, when a digital product has dual-use applications, national security concerns invariably take precedence, and the competition in cyberspace increasingly resembles a battle by fair means or foul. Against this backdrop, the tendency toward de-globalization has become more pronounced.

4.1 What Are the Purposes of Export Controls?

In regard to export controls, one may argue that similar policies have been observed in the conventional trade literature. For example, because many log-related materials are important inputs in making synthetic wood board, sometimes a country (such as Indonesia) which exports logs may want to restrict its exports so as to cause the producers of synthetic board in a foreign country (such as Taiwan) to face shortages of the material for manufacturing wood board, thereby making them unable to compete with the producers in Indonesia, even though the Taiwanese board producers may be more efficient. Some analysis can be found in Tachibana (2000). The above-mentioned example, however, is a very rare exception in traditional trade practices; we will explain shortly that most export controls after WWII are about military weapons.

Article XXI of the GATT is about the Security Exceptions. It says the following: Nothing in this Agreement shall be construed (a) to require any contracting party to furnish any information the disclosure of which it considers contrary to its essential security interests; or (b) to prevent any contracting party from taking any action which it considers necessary for the protection of its essential security interests (i) relating to fissionable materials or the materials from which they are derived; (ii) relating to the traffic in arms, ammunition and implements of war and to such traffic in other goods and materials as is carried on directly or indirectly for the purpose of supplying a military establishment; (iii) taken in time of war or other emergency in international relations; or (c) to prevent any contracting party from taking any action in pursuance of its obligations under the United Nations Charter for the maintenance of international peace and security. A key takeaway from Article XXI is the primacy of national security concerns. In general, a country alone has the authority to determine what constitutes a national security interest, and no other entity can challenge that judgment.[1]

In practice, the above clauses enable WTO members to maintain measures that would otherwise be inconsistent with WTO rules—such as discriminatory tariffs, import quotas, or outright bans on grounds of national security. Research has shown that there has been a growing use of economic sanctions by numerous countries in recent years.[2] The major measure that we are about to discuss in this chapter is that related to export restrictions, which are frequently justified on national security grounds.

4.1.1 *Export Control Laws: Historical Development*

The earliest U.S. export control law can be traced back to 1917, when the Trading with the Enemy Act was passed. However, a similar law in Continental Europe was enacted much earlier—in 1806 by Napoleon.[3] These laws granted national leaders the authority to monitor and restrict the export of goods to adversarial nations. Typically, the restricted goods consisted of weapons, munitions, and other logistics supplies deemed critical to wartime efforts. In essence, with regard to those laws, the timing was wartime, the commodities were limited to military uses, the target countries were wartime opponents, and the main concern then was indeed national security.

After World War II, export restrictions persisted even in peacetime. On the U.S. side, for instance, the Atomic Energy Act (enacted in 1954), the Arms Export Control Law (enacted in 1976), and the Export Administration Act (enacted in 1979) were typical practices (Whang, 2019). Because unilateral export controls can create a free-rider problem, export restrictions on arms and weapons were typically co-ordinated among multiple allied countries. Indeed, the practices of previous export restrictions on arms and weapons were all pluri-lateral co-ordinated moves.

In response to the aggressions of the Soviet Union, in 1949 the U.S., UK, France, Italy, and the Benelux nations negotiated the creation of

[1] See https://www.wto.org/english/tratop_e/safeg_e/safeg_e.htm.

[2] See https://eastasiaforum.org/2023/06/14/testing-the-limits-of-security-exceptions/.

[3] See https://en.wikipedia.org/wiki/Trading_with_the_Enemy_Act.

the Coordinating Committee for Multilateral Export Controls (CoCom), which was officially established in 1950. All NATO members except Iceland joined CoCom. It should be noted that CoCom did not have any formal treaty, and the content of this committee agreement was up to the honor of each country's domestic law enactment. Over time, similar multilateral frameworks emerged such as the Nuclear Suppliers Group (formed in 1974), the Australian Group (formed in 1985), and the Missile Technology Control Group (MTCG, formed in 1987). For example, the MTCG is an informal, non-treaty association of governments sharing common interests in the nonproliferation of missiles, unmanned drones, and related technologies.

The export control agreements usually had several commodity lists; some contained items that were subject to a complete embargo, and some (mostly dual-use technologies) were subject to review and approval.[4] To strengthen the collaboration among members, changes to the lists were subject to a consensus being reached by the participating pluri-lateral members. As one can imagine, since dual-use technologies involve business interests of various countries, reaching a consensus is difficult, even among like-minded countries.

After the collapse of the Soviet Union and the end of the Cold War in the early 1990s, CoCom transitioned into the Wassenaar Arrangement (WA). As stated on the WA webpage, "Participating States seek, through their national policies, to ensure that transfers of these items do not contribute to the development or enhancement of military capabilities which undermine these goals and are not diverted to support such capabilities."

4.2 Conflicts of Interest Among Alliance Countries

As in the case of all forms of international co-ordination, there have been conflicts of interest among participating members of CoCom and the WA. On the one hand, leading countries such as the U.S. have sought

[4] See https://www.govinfo.gov/content/pkg/GPO-CRPT-105hrpt851/html/ch9bod.html.

to broaden the embargo list.[5] This is natural, because the U.S. occupies the confrontation line (with the Soviet Union then and with China now), and it does not want to lose its hegemony competition. Evidently, broader export controls serve to weaken the opponent's capabilities and thereby increase the likelihood of the U.S. prevailing. On the other hand, other countries are more concerned about the industrial benefits for their domestic firms; they may want to shorten the embargo list, so that they can benefit more from their comparative advantages and trade. The conflict, therefore, hinges upon whether the U.S. can sustain its hegemony by proposing a legitimate criterion that is accepted and shared by other countries.

Another aspect of the extension of the export control list concerns the proposal by the European Commission to revamp the export control system in order to embody human rights concerns. This would happen, for instance, when some of the surveillance facilities are used by authoritarian rulers to monitor their citizens, and thereby constitute a violation of human rights. The European Commission's proposal has sparked debate among EU members; naturally, the resulting conflicts include the interests of manufacturers of surveillance equipment. The argument from EU members that were against the embargo was: that surveillance facilities can be used in good or bad ways, and extending export controls to such end-use scrutiny would give rise to equal concerns for domestic users.[6]

So far, we have seen two different purpose statements for the export controls acts: the first is to suppress the military capability of antagonistic countries, and the second is to exercise a "moral embargo" on a country involved in immoral actions (such as using surveillance facilities to monitor its citizens). A more recent development has been to extend the policy purpose to include areas where "emerging and foundational technologies" are involved.[7] This was brought up by the U.S., but was opposed by some European countries. This will be the focus of the following discussion.

[5] Details can be found in Whang (2019) and Wu (2021).

[6] See European Commission "Proposal for a Regulation of the European Parliament and of the Council setting up a Union regime for the control of exports, transfer, brokering, technical assistance and transit of dual-use items (recast)," 28 September 2016, 2016/0295 (COD) 5–6.

[7] See the National Defense Authorization Act of the U.S. for the fiscal year 2019, Section 1758.

The general idea is that in all international co-ordinations, there are always conflicts of interest, and the discussions, compromises, and negotiations are always costly. The more serious and complex these international co-ordinations become, the more likely it is that a particular country may resort to unilateral solutions and leave the original coalition. This is precisely what has occurred over the past decade or two: the U.S. has shifted from the "Magnificent Seven" approach toward solo actions akin to those portrayed in Jason Bourne.

4.3 Recent Developments in U.S. Export Control Acts

Before 1994, the legal foundation for the U.S. to implement export controls was the Export Administration Act (EAA) of 1979, which controlled the export of dual-use goods and technologies (that had been agreed upon by the CoCoM or WA committee), as well as some unilaterally applied export control measures based on national security concerns. It is noted that all unilateral measures had clear termination dates.[8] These termination dates restricted the U.S.'s unilateral freedom to apply export control measures that were not aligned with international standards, such as those set by the Wassenaar Arrangement. In other words, periodic renewal reviews constitute a constraint on the implementation of export controls by the White House.

When the Cold War ended, and in view of the disintegration of the Soviet Union, the above-mentioned export control regime needed to be revised, mainly because the largest enemy (the Soviet Union) had vanished. Originally, the EAA granted the U.S. President the power to determine what was to be included in the export controls list.[9] The U.S. President then delegated the power to the Bureau of Industry and Security (BIS) of the Department of Commerce (DOC) to implement such export controls through the enactment of the Export Administration Regulations (EAR). The EAA required constant congressional renewal approval; however, a consensus could not be reached in Congress in 1994, which resulted in the lapse of the EAA.

[8] See the Export Administration Act (1979) §20, 50 U.S.C. Section 4622.

[9] See the Export Administration Act (1979) 50 U.S.C. Sections 4601–4623.

In August 2001, President George W. Bush issued an executive order that continued the operation of the EAR under the authority granted to him by the International Emergency Economic Powers Act (IEEPA).[10] After 2002, U.S. presidents issued annual continuations of the EAR through the IEEPA to maintain the function of the U.S. export control system, until 2010. During this 16-year period (1994–2010), the problem of tedious annual renewal was always postponed but never resolved, so that export controls were just an executive order, without a solid legal foundation. However, after the 9–11 event in 2001, the executive power of the White House expanded in general, and consequently little attention was paid to the implementation of export controls.

In 2010, President Barack Obama introduced the Export Control Reform Initiative which proposed concentrating enforcement of export controls on the most critical technologies while lifting controls on other items. The purpose of the reform was to make U.S. industries more competitive on a global scale. In addition, Obama's reform aimed to consolidate the U.S. export control system by unifying the system of licensing agencies, control list preparation, enforcement structure, and information updating. After several years of legislative negotiation, a new export control statute, the Export Control Reform Act (ECRA), was finally signed into law in 2018 by President Trump.[11]

There are some important points that we should note about this ECRA of 2018. First of all, the law does not have a termination date, and so the previous requirement for periodic renewal or negotiation between the U.S. executive branch and Congress is no longer necessary. In short, U.S. export control became the power of the executive branch after 2018. Secondly, the scope of technologies subject to export controls was expanded to include an "emerging and foundational technologies" category. According to the ECRA, the emerging and foundational technologies will be determined by the U.S. Secretary of Commerce, Secretary of Energy, Secretary of Defense, Secretary of State, and other heads of federal agencies. Together, they determine which technologies

[10] See Executive Order No. 13222, as amended by Executive Order No. 136372 in 2001.

[11] As regards the rationale behind pushing for this export control reform, see the address by President Obama, https://obamawhitehouse.archives.gov/the-press-office/remarks-president-export-import-banks-annual-conferencehite.

are essential to U.S. national security and should be subject to export controls.

The above-mentioned inclusion of the vaguely defined "emerging and foundational technologies" in the U.S. export control statute suggests additional considerations beyond strictly military-oriented strategic concerns. Since the policy purpose of the ECRA is for the U.S. to maintain its leadership in science, technology, engineering, and manufacturing, it can hardly be aligned with other international allies. Essentially, through the enactment of the ECRA, the U.S. has decoupled itself from the original international co-ordination framework for export controls. This has thus become the beginning of the "unilateral" era of export controls. Objectively, the U.S.'s definition of "emerging and foundational technologies" is unlikely to be consistent with those defined by other countries.

In 2018, the Bureau of Industry and Security (BIS) provided advance notice of proposed rules concerning emerging technologies. The list of these emerging technologies included biotechnology, artificial intelligence, navigation technology, micro-processing technology, advanced computing technology, data analytics technology, quantum information and sensing technology, logistics technology, additive manufacturing such as 3D printing, robotics, brain-computer interfaces, hypersonics, advanced materials, and advanced surveillance technologies. Because the scope of coverage was so broad, this advance notice gave rise to a huge amount of negative feedback and criticism, mainly because export controls are tightly related to vested interests.[12] In addition, the list showed similarities to the items in *Made in China 2025*, and hence suggests the nature of international industrial competition. Note that this is very different from the original purpose of export controls under the Wassenaar Arrangement, where the primary concern was reducing military capability.

[12] See Comments on Review for Controls for Certain Technologies, BIS-2018-0024, https://www.regulations.gov/docketBrowser?rpp=25&po=0&dct=PS&D=BIS-2018-0024&refD=BIS-2018-0024-0001.

4.4 The Weaponization of the ECRA

On August 13, 2018, President Trump signed the National Defense Authorization Act (NDAA), of which a major part was the ECRA. The ECRA requires the DOC to establish a comprehensive list of new and foundational technologies, according to which regulations can be formulated. The DOC then delegates authority to the BIS to draw up the detailed regulations. From that point on, the control lists are frequently updated, and the changes in the list reveal the dynamics of export control.[13] Below, we discuss the content and progress of such regulations.

4.4.1 *Export Controls Based on Items and Destinations*

According to the Export Administration Regulations (EARs), export controls can be classified into three types: (1) exports, (2) re-exports, and (3) deemed exports. The definition of type (1) is clear; and type (2) means that something is exported from the U.S. to country X, and then from country X to a destination Y. If there is a regulation prohibiting certain exports from the U.S. to Y, then the same regulation applies even though it is the U.S. exporting to X and then X to Y. Type (3) attempts to block alternative methods of bypassing the EAR. For instance, if a U.S. company licenses a technology X on U.S. soil (and therefore the technology is literally not "exported") to individual K, and then K uses that technology to produce in K's subsidiary factory in country Y, the transaction is still deemed an export, subject to the EAR, as long as exporting to Y is under export controls.

According to the EAR part 734.3, the items being regulated include the following five categories. (1) All items in the U.S., including in a U.S. Foreign Trade Zone or moving in-transit through the U.S. from one foreign country to another; (2) All items originating in the U.S. wherever located; (3) Foreign-made commodities that incorporate controlled items originating in the U.S., foreign-made commodities that are "bundled" with controlled software originating in the U.S., foreign-made software that is co-mingled with controlled software originating in the U.S., and foreign-made technology that is co-mingled with controlled technology originating in the U.S. in quantities exceeding *de minimis* thresholds, which vary according to the products, and are specified in other parts;

[13] See https://www.bis.doc.gov/index.php/8-bis/33-export-control-reform-ecr.

(4) Certain foreign-produced direct products of specified technology and software, as described in other parts of the EAR; and (5) Certain foreign-produced products of a complete plant or any major component of a plant that is a "direct product" of specified technology or software as described in other parts of the EAR.[14]

One should note that the above-mentioned control list has to be combined with the "country chart" to determine whether an export license is required. For example, for many items it is not necessary to apply for permission to export if the destination is the U.K. However, if the destination is North Korea or Cuba or China, then they may be regulated, and one has to obtain permission in order to export.[15] Of course, exports to the U.K. are still subject to the re-export or deemed export regulations mentioned above. In short, the above-mentioned export controls are commodity- and destination-specific.[16]

4.4.2 *A Comprehensive Control List*

The actual export control list is specified according to the Export Control Classification Numbers (ECCNs), which consist of five digits. It is important to review the content of these five codes, because they reveal the comprehensiveness of the coverage.

The first code is a digit specifying the commodity type, such as nuclear equipment and facilities, electronics, computers, etc. The second code is an English character, which specifies whether the item refers to material or software or technology, etc. The third code identifies the reason why the commodity is being regulated, and the reasons include national security, missile technology, or antiterrorism, etc. The fourth code refers to whether an international multilateral regulation or a U.S. unilateral

[14] See https://www.ecfr.gov/current/title-15/subtitle-B/chapter-VII/subchapter-C/part-734/section-734.3.

[15] See https://www.bis.doc.gov/index.php/documents/regulations-docs/federal-register-notices/federal-register-2014/1033-738-supp-1/file.

[16] Of course, this commodity-plus-destination regulation may create loopholes. In February 2025, the U.S. was investigating whether some of Nvidia's GPU chips were being exported to China through Singapore. Conceptually, if a company has thousands of foreign customers, it would be difficult to check whether there are some items being re-exported by a couple of these customers. See https://www.techpowerup.com/331912/us-investigates-possible-singapore-loophole-in-chinas-access-to-nvidia-gpus.

regulation is involved. And the fifth code is a serial number, with each representing a specific item.

The two most important codes are the first and the second, for together they form a comprehensive coverage of the commodity that is to be regulated. For example, if the first code refers to electronics (which includes high-end chips), then the material, components, software, technologies, and testing equipment are all encompassed by the control regime, as indicated by the second code. Thus, in the case of chips, for example, the export control does not just forbid exports of high-end chips, but also includes preventing the target country from manufacturing such chips using any inputs or technologies or machines that are under the control of the U.S. If the control target is high-end chips, then the purpose of the ECCNs is to make sure that the target country definitely cannot get those chips, one way or another.

4.4.3 Export Controls on Recipients

Other than the above-mentioned export controls on commodities and countries of destination, according to Sections 744 and 746 of the EAR, the export license review may also be applied to entities (recipients) acting, or at significant risk of acting, contrary to U.S. national security or foreign policy interests. The entity in question may be an individual, business, research institute, or government. The list, based on its seriousness, may be separated into several types: (1) The denied person list, of which the export of regulated items is prohibited outright. (2) The entity list, of which the export of regulated items is prohibited by default, unless it is approved by the DOC. (3) The unverified list, for which a red flag is added, resulting in the export in question being scrutinized, which increases the probability of a denial. (4) The military end user list, for which the regulation is mostly about possible weapon manufacturing.

With respect to the entity list, the BIS may impose licensing requirements related to foreign policy exports, re-exports, and transfers, as well as limitations on the availability of license exceptions, and formulate its license application review policy based on the criteria set forth in the regulation. Such requirements, limitations, and policies are *in addition to* those set forth elsewhere in the EAR. Thus, by combining the entity list and the commodity list for the ECCNs, we see a comprehensive web of export regulation coverage.

On May 9, 2024, for instance, the BIS of the U.S. DOC added 37 entities to the Entity List under the EAR.[17] The BIS announced that with these 37 additions, the Commerce Department had increased China's entries on the Entity List by 355—more than any prior Administration. This announcement suggests that the target country is mainly China. Because the entity list has been revised very frequently, it is difficult to count or verify the exact total number of Chinese entities included.[18]

Content-wise, using the BIS news release in May 2024 as an example, we can also observe the broad spectrum: among the new entities added to the Entity List, 22 institutes and firms were added for their participation in the People's Republic of China's (PRC) quantum technology advancements and for acquiring or attempting to acquire items originating in the U.S. to enhance the PRC's quantum capabilities. Four items were added for acquiring or attempting to acquire items originating in the U.S. to be used by the PRC's military for its unmanned aerial systems (UAS). Eleven items were added due to their involvement in China's High Altitude Balloon program, which poses significant national security concerns. Later, we will have more discussion on the coverage of the entity list targeted at China.

4.4.4 *The CHIPS and Science Act*

In August 2022, President Joe Biden signed the CHIPS and Science Act (where CHIPS stands for "Creating Helpful Incentives to Produce Semiconductors"). This Act provides approximately $280 billion in government subsidies, of which $200 billion would be used in subsidizing science and technology research focusing on AI, robotics, quantum calculation, etc., $52.7 billion would be used in subsidizing chip manufacturing firms on U.S. soil, and $7 billion would be used on chips innovation-related funds. In addition, there would be $24 billion of

[17] See https://www.bis.gov/press-release/commerce-adds-37-prc-entities-entity-list-enabling-prc-quantum-and-aerospace-programs.

[18] Wikipedia suggests that the total number of China's entities exceeds 600, but it needs to be verified. See https://en.wikipedia.org/wiki/Entity_List.

tax-equivalent expenditure due to tax incentives provided to chip manufacturers.[19]

Along with the announcement of the CHIPS and Science Act, a notable "guardrail" rule was also announced.[20] The final rule implementing the national security guardrails contains two core provisions of the statute. The first prohibits CHIPS funds recipients from expanding their material semiconductor manufacturing capacity in *foreign countries of concern* for ten years, while the second restricts these recipients from engaging in certain joint research or technology licensing efforts with *foreign entities of concern*. The rule will help ensure that CHIPS investments enhance global supply chain resilience in co-ordination with U.S. allies and partners. Despite there being no specific reference to China, given that China is the only country that may contend with the U.S.-led coalition, everyone knows that the "countries of concern" refer to China.

The immediate significance of this guardrail clause is not about the "future 10 years," but about the ongoing yet unfinished investment or R&D projects. Because the wording used in the clause is "expanding material semiconductor manufacturing capacity," it makes companies such as Samsung worry about the fate of facilities like the NAND Flash factory they have been building in Xian, China. Similarly, roughly one fourth of Intel's revenue had come from China by 2022, and thus the company has also had to carefully consider its expansion pace in China, if it plans to make use of the subsidy provided by the CHIPS Act.[21]

As such, the guardrail clause forces almost all semiconductor companies in the world to "take sides." If a company wants to benefit from U.S. subsidies, it must be prepared to comply with U.S. national security requirements. Moreover, although the investment is prohibited for just 10 years, because the technology specifications may be very much settled in this 10-year period, it would be hard to imagine how any company would renew its investment in "countries of concern" after 10 years of such a prohibition. The guardrail rule appears to play the role

[19] See https://www.whitehouse.gov/briefing-room/statements-releases/2022/08/09/fact-sheet-chips-and-science-act-will-lower-costs-create-jobs-strengthen-supply-chains-and-counter-china/.

[20] See https://www.nist.gov/news-events/news/2023/09/biden-harris-administration-announces-final-national-security-guardrails.

[21] See https://www.taipeitimes.com/News/taiwan/archives/2022/10/27/2003787811.

of increasing the height and thickness of the technology wall. Simply put, the guardrail rule forces the decoupling of many sectors of chip-related industries.

4.4.5 *The Penalties for Not Complying*

Violations of the EAR may be subject to both criminal and administrative penalties. Under the ECRA of 2018 (50 U.S.C. §§ 4801–4852), criminal penalties can include up to 20 years of imprisonment and up to $1 million in fines per violation, or both. Administrative monetary penalties can reach up to $300,000 per violation or twice the value of the transaction, whichever is greater. In general, the administrative monetary penalty maximum is adjusted for inflation each year.

Violators may also be subject to the denial of their export privileges: a violation prohibits a person from participating in any transaction subject to the EAR. Furthermore, the reputation of the business may be in jeopardy, its ability to compete internationally questioned, and sometimes it may be denied by the U.S. banking system, which may potentially result in severe financial difficulties.[22]

The above-mentioned penalties may affect U.S. as well as non-U.S. companies or citizens. For instance, the *de minimis* rule allows the U.S. to implement a long-arm regulation in relation to many foreign companies, in spite of the U.S. having only, say, 25% of the technology of software patents. If a foreign company owner violates the export regulation, it nearly implies a formal severance of its business and financial ties with the U.S., not to mention the lifetime risk of being arrested by either the U.S., or the countries that have extradition treaties with the U.S. Indeed, the deterrence effect of the ECRA is extremely strong.

After President Trump commenced his second term in 2025, he pressured foreign companies such as TSMC to build more production lines in the U.S.[23] He said that semiconductor companies would come back without any U.S. budget spending of the CHIPS and Science Act. Even if Trump is right about his "cost-saving" comments, it does not change the

[22] See https://www.bis.doc.gov/index.php/enforcement/oee/penalties.

[23] See https://www.reuters.com/technology/tsmc-ceo-meet-with-trump-tout-investment-plans-2025-03-03/.

ECRA regulations or the guardrail clause of the CHIPS Act; the tendency that the worldwide ICT industries are decoupling is hardly avoidable.

4.4.6 *Chronological Changes in Export Control Content*

In this section we summarize the chronological order of two lines of events, one being the U.S. restrictions on technology (or software or talents) exports to China, and the other items in the entity list. The export content is revised fairly frequently; we only include the more recent revisions (at the time of writing). As for the entity list, we summarize the items annually, starting from 2018, the year when the ECRA was enacted. We manually compile the list from a page-to-page survey of the U.S. Register website, although we may miss some items that are announced irregularly. However, readers should see the main point, which is that the U.S./China technology war has been aggravated over the past several years. All sources are from the U.S. Register and DOC official websites, and we skip the citation details.

4.4.7 *The Content of Export Controls*

August 2022:

The BIS added the following to the list of controlled items: (1) EDA (electronic design automation) software tools; (2) 3 nm GAA and EDA software tools controls; (3) Semiconductor devices and high-performance logic chips for China.

October 2022:

The BIS added export controls regarding advanced computing chips and supercomputers, including (1) Single-chip performance exceeding 4800 TOPS (Tera Operations Per Second); (2) Interconnection bandwidth exceeding 600 GB/s; (3) Supercomputing systems exceeding 100 PFLOPS (PetaFLOPS, or 1000 trillion operations per second).

The BIS also added U.S. talent restrictions: (1) Limitations on U.S. persons involved in technology and equipment development in China; (2) Restrictions on Chinese nationals holding U.S. citizenship or residency from working in related sectors.

August 2023:

(1) The BIS added restrictions on investments in sensitive Chinese technologies; (2) The BIS banned investments in three key Chinese technology areas: quantum computing, semiconductors, and AI.

October 2023:

The BIS expanded the scope of export controls to include advanced computing chips and AI chips.

March 2024:

The BIS implemented more comprehensive export controls, including (1) A total ban on exports to certain Chinese entities; (2) Specific restrictions on components used in notebook computers and handheld devices.

4.4.8 The Changes in the Entity List

2018

Forty-four entries in China were added to the entity list. They are mainly technology companies and their related accessories.

2019

Sixty-three Chinese entries were added to the Entity List, most of them related to surveillance facilities for the Uyghurs in Xinjiang.

2020

Fifty-nine Chinese entries were added to the entity list. Besides some companies, many high-tech research institutes were also included.

2021

Thirty-one Chinese entries were added to the entity list, including 12 entries for China's Academy of Military Medical Sciences.

2022

Thirty-five entries were added to the entity list, most of them being high-tech companies.

2023

Forty-one Chinese entries were added to the entity list, most of them being high-tech companies.

2024 (as of July 3rd)

Thirty-nine Chinese entries were added to the entity list, most of them being high-tech companies.

As we have mentioned, for export controls, in order to know the "target" of technology and software exports, the content of the control has to be combined with the country map. For the entity list, however, because companies are always registered in specific countries, the "target" is very clear. By scanning through the list since 2018, especially in more recent years, we see that roughly 90% of the entries are Chinese companies or institutions. The target of the export controls and entity list is undoubtably clear: China. In addition, we note that only one item pertains to human rights (the Uyghurs in Xinjiang); all others are targeted at restricting the competition capability of China's industries. In short, the U.S. intention to decouple with China in certain high-tech industries is unequivocal.

4.5 The Good Old Times Before *Made in China 2025*

From the above discussion, we have seen an obvious trend. Democratic countries led (or dragged) by the U.S. are imposing stronger and stronger restrictions on exports of ICT products destined to "countries of concern," in particular China. Very often, the U.S. has taken the lead unilaterally and has persuaded other allied countries to do the same. These allied countries, bound by their existing economic ties with China, sometimes exhibit reluctance or resistance. Occasionally, it appears that the diplomatic pressure from international politics plays a role in making some allied countries comply with the U.S. initiative. There have been many criticisms regarding the U.S.'s unilateral export control measures; we will discuss them one by one in this section.

James Andrew Lewis, a senior VP of CSIS has said that "export controls are not a panacea, they are a relic."[24] Lewis mentioned several examples in the 1980s, 1990s, and even early 2000s of U.S. export control strategies which resulted in adverse consequences. In those cases, they either inspired the target countries to nurture their own technology, or some U.S. companies to exit the market owing to declining sales, or because U.S. market shares were eroded by foreign competitors. In all these cases, the backfiring consequences proved that the original export controls failed to justify their efficacy. The natural question (or doubt) raised by Lewis is: Would the export controls on high-tech items nowadays fare differently?

4.5.1 Subsidizing the Increasing Return Industries

The above argument, however, overlooks an important feature of contemporary technology competition, compared with that of several decades ago. It is helpful to take a detailed look at the 10 industries described in the *Made in China 2025* initiative. As one can see, a key feature of this huge industrial initiative of China is that the ten industries targeted are all high-tech ones. As we all know, there is hardly any advantage in being a frontrunner in the traditional sectors such as retailing, apparel manufacturing, or agriculture. Due to the law of diminishing returns, the latecomers are likely to eventually catch up with the frontrunners. Thus, for traditional industries, it does not pay trying to stop the unstoppable latecomers.

As *Made in China 2025* is designed to help Chinese businesses establish themselves as frontrunners in these ten high-tech industries, one question that obviously springs to mind is: What is the key difference between subsidizing the agricultural sector (which many countries are doing) and subsidizing high-tech industries? The answer to this question is simple: increasing returns. For industries characterized by increasing returns, the frontrunner's advantage may be sustained and may even be enhanced. In other words, there is a greater chance of the strong ones today becoming even stronger tomorrow, thus making the efforts needed

[24] See https://www.csis.org/analysis/end-export-controls.

to secure that leading position much more worthwhile. Indeed, if high-tech industries have the property of increasing returns, then it does pay to slow down the competitors' pace. In the traditional manufacturing industries or agriculture with diminishing returns, even being the frontrunner or having a large market share is unlikely to yield substantial dividends.[25]

4.5.2 *Why Do High-tech Industries Have Increasing Returns?*

It is important to note that the increasing returns advantage of the high-tech industries is not just due to the property of decreasing average cost that is often associated with the output scale.[26] According to Brian Arthur (1989, 1996), several features of the high-tech industries explain why they tend to generate increasing returns.

Firstly, high-tech manufacturing or production often involves substantial up-front research and development (R&D) costs. Once the manufacturer becomes a frontrunner and grabs a large market share, the average cost of providing goods is low. For later challengers, however, the up-front R&D expenses are still unavoidable. This makes it difficult for latecomers to compete with the frontrunner, thereby helping the incumbent leader to sustain its position. In short, this refers to the increasing returns resulting from large R&D expenditure. Second, due to reasons such as learning-by-doing, the marginal costs of making additional improvements may be lower for frontrunners. The only way a latecomer may possibly compete with the frontrunner is to receive sizeable subsidies from the government, which was indeed the essence of China's *Made in China 2025* initiative.

Third, there is the network effect in general, and the compatibility effect in particular in many ICT platforms. For instance, if success is achieved with the Huawei 5G network, then it prompts many facility

[25] Readers should be reminded that the distinction between traditional industries and high-tech industries may be blurred in some cases. For future electric cars with autonomous driving, for example, the car manufacturing part is quite traditional, whereas the autonomous driving part involves very advanced telecommunications technologies. China may be more efficient in the manufacturing part, but the U.S. is capable of developing an automated driving system (ADS). It would be difficult to tell the nature of this industry.

[26] For public utilities, for instance, the more customers a company has, the lower the average facility maintenance cost for each customer (because the same facility is shared by more customers), and hence the company faces a lower average cost.

providers to produce equipment compatible with Huawei. When Huawei has more facilities and users, it is easier to find bugs and therefore make changes that can further improve their operational efficiency with 5G. This in turn makes it more attractive to invest in the improvement of the Huawei-related facilities, which in turn attracts more users to adopt the Huawei system. This network effect refers to the demand-side increasing returns, meaning that successful frontrunners have larger customer bases and are more attractive to other factors in the product ecosystem. As such, the ecosystem improves, and the demand curve of the frontrunner faces upward shifts.

Fourth, according to Arthur (1989), there is also the customer lock-in effect that benefits the frontrunner. For instance, if switching to another system means a dramatic change in many other associated periphery facilities, then people are likely to retain the system that they had in the past. This makes it difficult for latecomers to compete with the frontrunner.

One should also note that a company does not have to be operationally efficient to be a frontrunner in the high-tech industries. As Arthur (1989 p. 119) points out, frontrunners may well be inefficient. Some companies became frontrunners merely by chance or because they happened to be an early entrant in the market. What is evident, though, is that competing from the front is more advantageous, even without substantive efficiency gains. In short, in high-tech industries, the target of government subsidies is not to help a firm to cut its costs or to lower its prices, but to help it gain a frontrunner's position in the market.

Another typical means of achieving frontrunner success in the high-tech competition is to win the "standard" competition. Whoever wins this standard competition will reap huge industrial profits. In pharmaceuticals, which is one of the 10 industries included in *Made in China 2025*, the government's regulation and approval (such as by the United States Food and Drug Administration (FDA), or the International Council for Harmonization of Technical Requirements for Pharmaceuticals for Human Use (ICH)) has also become the "standard," which precludes other unapproved competitors from competing in the drug market. New drugs that are approved earlier may be used by millions of patients, which generates more feedback data, with the result that there are more opportunities to adjust dosages for different patient groups. High-tech industries with the feature of the "standard" therefore have an even greater incentive to become frontrunners.

In the ECRA, the administration has specifically emphasized the importance of competition in "emerging technologies," which is a point neglected by James Lewis of CSIS. Indeed, both *Made in China 2025* and the *CHIPS and Science Act* are government subsidy programs; they both aim to subsidize R&D expenses so as to establish a frontrunner position for future technologies. The traditional concerns of market substitution or of firms exiting the market, which Lewis noted, are relatively unimportant.

4.5.3 *Science and Technology Subsidies: Institutional Differences*

Since both China and the U.S. are subsidizing or helping their high-tech industries, a question that one may ask is: What is the difference between the *Made in China 2025* project and the U.S. Science projects? We should first note that, before the *CHIPS and Science Act* of 2022, most of the U.S. national research programs were science-based, and not technology-based. The Human Genome Project includes gene sequencing, genomics, proteomics, etc., and is designed to explore scientific knowledge not directly related to immediate commercial gains. Similarly, the U.S. BRAIN initiative aims to enhance our understanding of memory and learning.[27] At some point in the future the BRAIN initiative may be related to cures for autism, amnesia, and Parkinson's disease, but the research initiative today has little to do with any specific industrial values or business revenues.

Another example would be the Industrie 4.0 project, which Germany describes as being more application- and engineering-oriented than just pure scientific research. However, it still only outlines concepts, such as ICT itself, ICT-based manufacturing, smart factories, individualized product specifications, computerized manufacturing, the Internet of Things, the Internet of Persons, self-diagnosis, self-configuration, self-optimization, and so on. It is more like a description of future roadmaps of technology/production which German scientists and engineers need to explore jointly, rather than any specific industrial subsidy project that

[27] National Human Genome Research Institute, *An Overview of the Human Genome Project*, https://www.genome.gov/12011238/an-overview-of-the-human-genome-project/. See also the BRAIN Initiative Mission, http://www.braininitiative.org/mission/.

has direct revenue flows.[28] By pointing to these future directions as being keys to the fourth industrial revolution, the German government seems to be lighting the way for their own (and other EU countries') R&D orientations. In fact, the Industrie 4.0 project has been much criticized as being too diffuse and somewhat impractical to implement.

By contrast, the *Made in China 2025* project has some very specific and concrete industrial targets. It encompasses ten high-tech industries. These are specific beneficiary industries or even companies (for instance Huawei as a leading Chinese telecommunications company), as opposed to the more abstract description of the U.S.'s BRAIN or Human Genome science initiatives. For each of the ten *Made in China 2025* industries, there may be a technology breakthrough that is critical to its development. Facilitating such technology breakthroughs is a key element of *Made in China 2025*, with the ultimate aim being to have a Chinese company as a global frontrunner in these industries.

4.5.4 Competition Involving Government Subsidies

As we mentioned above, according to the CHIPS and Science Act, the U.S. government will provide $52 billion to fund the semiconductor manufacturing programs. An essential part under Section 9902 of the National Defense Authorization Act (NDAA) is that it plans to provide "financial assistance to covered entities to incentivize investment in facilities and equipment in the United States for semiconductor fabrication, assembly, testing, advanced packaging, or research and development." The United States Innovation and Competition Act (USICA) also includes $1.5 billion for the Public Wireless Supply Chain Innovation Fund to spur mobile broadband technologies. These are indeed blunt government subsidies possibly moving into businesses' pockets, very similar to those in *Made in China 2025*.

Although we hold the view that the inherent checks and balances under the democratic system could significantly restrain the market distorting effects of USICA-like subsidization (for example, it could never directly allocate all state resources to a few enterprises), we still see the concern. The USICA has been drafted with the express purpose of competing

[28] Federal Ministry for Economic Affairs and Energy of Germany, What Is Industrie 4.0?, https://www.plattform-i40.de/I40/Navigation/EN/Industrie40/WhatIsIndustrie40/what-is-industrie40.html.

with China. As such, it may be seen as a sign of a downward spiral, in that liberal democracies are adopting state capitalism's way of fighting to counter state-capitalism. This results in market competition in the international arena being transformed into competition between states. This downward spiral is not a direction we would like to see.

4.6 China's Reactions

4.6.1 China's Earlier Response

In response to the U.S. ECRA sanctions, the Chinese government announced in May 2019 that it would establish an "unreliable entities" list (UEL).[29] It would allow China to respond to activities that endanger its national sovereignty, security, or development interests as well as practices such as banning or discriminating against a Chinese entity in violation of "normal market transaction principles" thereby causing serious damage. The regulation went into effect in September 2020 after the Trump administration attempted to ban some Chinese apps. The Chinese government even warned Dell, Microsoft, Apple, and Boeing not to join the bans on the sale of American technology to Chinese companies. However, the lobbying was not successful. The reason is not difficult to imagine: most American companies do not want to face the penalty of the ECRA. In 2023, Lockheed Martin and Raytheon became the first two companies on the UEL.

Here, it is important to note a major difference between export controls and traditional trade barriers such as tariffs and quotas. First, if Country A imposes any of these traditional trade barriers on Country B, B can easily retaliate by imposing an equivalent or even higher tariff. The result would be very much like the trade war which occurred between the U.S. and China when Trump was in his first term as President (2017–2020). This kind of trade war usually ends up with a lose-lose outcome, and most politicians know this. Thus, traditional trade barriers are often more like political gestures than real fights.

The export controls on high-end technologies and software are entirely different in that only the leading side in the technology race can launch an effective export control; the trailing side usually lacks any retaliatory weapon or measure. In the case of ICT, evidently the leading side, so far,

[29] See https://en.wikipedia.org/wiki/Entity_List.

is the U.S. and its allies, and not much retaliation can be exercised on the China side.

Secondly, in a traditional trade embargo or a game of raising tariffs, the overall economy (including price levels, employment, and supply chain stability) is affected. Because the vested interests of the industry under the embargo may be strong, sometimes the negative economic impact may eventually backfire on the political leader, which in turn causes the leader to hesitate to persistently pursue such a course of action. The imposition of export controls on high-end technologies is different: very often it is about the possible success of some *future* technologies or industries; the present vested interests are insignificant, and the welfare impact is limited. Politicians are therefore not worried about the project not being accepted by the society.

Finally, traditional trade coalitions involve only economic consequences, hence sometimes the target country can engage in a prisoner's dilemma scenario and persuade some companies to deviate from the coalition. As we mentioned in the previous discussion, however, a violation of the export controls is subject to a criminal penalty of up to 20 years in prison, which has a huge deterrent effect. It is doubtful that any multinational companies will dare to risk such penalties of the U.S. jurisdictions and deviate from the coalition, not to mention companies on U.S. soil.

4.6.2 China's Recent Export Controls on Rare Earths

Facing the above-mentioned export control measures imposed by the U.S., China recently resorted to a new leverage: rare earth elements (REEs). In April 2025, in response to President Trump's threat to levy high tariffs on China's imports, China announced that it would restrict the export of rare earths to the U.S. The restriction applies to seven out of seventeen REEs—samarium, gadolinium, terbium, dysprosium, lutetium, scandium, and yttrium—and it requires companies to secure special export licenses to export the minerals and magnets.

The REEs are not just mines to be dug from their reserves. The seventeen REEs are all chemical elements with extremely similar characteristics, and they often mingle with each other; the technological difficulty is the separating and purifying of these REEs. For example, rare earth magnets are crucial components in various military applications due to their high strength and resistance to demagnetization. These magnets are found in guided missiles, smart bombs, and advanced aircraft like fighter jets, unmanned aerial vehicles, and submarines. The purer the rare earth is, the more accurate the missiles and bombs will be. Led by a Chinese legend Xu Guangxian, China's technology for refining REEs is superior to that of the U.S.[30]

Note that China's export restrictions only apply to seven medium and heavy rare earths (not the light ones), of which the supply chain is particularly important to the U.S. For light rare earths, a more diverse set of countries can undertake the purifying process. According to CSIS's research, until 2023, China accounted for 99 percent of global heavy REEs processing, with only minimal output from a refinery in Vietnam. This gives China a definite monopoly position in REEs supply.[31]

The CSIS report summarizes the prevalent use of REEs in modern weapons, which include F-35 fighter jets, Virginia- and Columbia-class submarines, Tomahawk missiles, radar systems, Predator unmanned aerial vehicles, and the Joint Direct Attack Munition series of smart bombs. These modern weapons often need hundreds and thousands of pounds of REEs. Even before the latest REE restrictions, the U.S. defense industrial base struggled with limited capacity and lacked the ability to scale up production to meet defense technology demands. The export controls on REEs make the U.S. face a more difficult situation.

4.7 Final Remarks and Related Literature

4.7.1 Related Literature

There have been few academic discussions regarding the U.S. export controls, especially the impact of the ECRA after 2018. In his book, Achilleas (2017) wrote that export controls can be viewed as an interplay between trade and international security. This role of interplaying has been diluted following the enactment of the ECRA in 2018. The developments after 2018 have also indicated that export controls have become an active weapon to suppress or hinder the technology industries of antagonist countries. To say the least, the ECRA's content regarding the international security of "emerging and foundational technologies"

[30] See https://www.apexmagnets.com/news-how-tos/military-weapons-rare-earth-magnets-used-in-defense-applications/.

[31] See https://www.csis.org/analysis/consequences-chinas-new-rare-earths-export-restrictions.

has become too broad and too vague to render Achilleas's notion of "international security" practically irrelevant.

There is also a handbook by Aubin and Arnaud (2016), which serves primarily as a practical guide for export businesses, and has little relevance to the strategic aspects of current export control practices. In view of the developments since 2018, a very large part of that handbook may need to be rewritten.

Regarding the issue of an entity list, Bu (2020) examined the dilemma faced by multinational companies, which maintain investments in both China and the U.S. This appears to be the only study related to the entity list that has been published in an international journal. The authors admitted that there was no easy solution in the foreseeable future.

4.7.2 *Previous Export Controls by China*

The export controls we have discussed in this chapter may be interpreted more broadly; in this broad sense, China has exercised its own export controls in the past. In 2021, a famous Swedish company named H&M tried to boycott Xinjiang cotton to protest the practices of re-education camps for Uyghurs. That move irritated the CCP, and immediately all of H&M's commodities were removed from Taobao, and all H&M's physical stores disappeared from Chinese mapping services.[32]

We can interpret the H&M business operation in two steps. The first step is that Taobao "exports" its App to a Swedish company named H&M, and the second step is that this Swedish company uses its App to sell products in China. Of course, without the Taobao App, H&M cannot sell its products through this Chinese platform. When China forbade the export of the Taobao App to H&M, it was indeed an implementation of its export controls and entity list, even though H&M sells products in China. By viewing it in this manner, one may examine other cases and discover that numerous export control practices have been employed in the past.

[32] See https://www.bbc.com/news/world-asia-china-56519411.

4.7.3 *An Unscrupulous Game?*

As Whang (2019) pointed out, the traditional export control agreements possessed four key features: (1) They were based on the consensus reached by the participating members, and hence any country restrained itself from implementing unilateral measures. (2) They were list-based, meaning that only the listed items were subject to the control of export controls. (3) They were predominantly related to weapons and military capacities rather than encompassing national security in the broad sense or emerging and foundational technologies. (4) Although a country might implement unilateral export control measures, such measures typically had expiration dates and required periodic renewal.

After the enactment of the ECRA in 2018, all of the four features mentioned above changed. In short, the U.S., evidently the leading country in ICTs, could decide which commodities, parts, technologies, software, or talents were critical to the emerging technologies, and impose export controls unilaterally. Moreover, these measures have a long-arm jurisdiction, thanks to the *de minimis* calculation, so that almost all major high-tech companies in democratic countries are influenced by (or forced to align themselves with) the U.S.'s unilateral export control measures.

As such, the ECRA very much does away with the previously rule-based (list-based) international practices regarding export controls, and the unilateral measure of the U.S. also eliminates the consensus decision-making mechanism of international co-ordination. This is very similar to the situation where the U.S. paralyzed the dispute settlement system of the WTO by not joining the consensus for the appointment of new appellate body members.[33] As Miller (2022) pointed out, the U.S. was engaging in a throat-blocking measure against the Chinese chip manufacturing industry. Miller focused on the chip industry, whereas we have discussed the serious competition taking place in all ICT industries in the previous sections. Indeed, any scenario in which one side overturns the chessboard would suggest that players are unscrupulous. Now we are witnessing the unscrupulous competition taking place within the ICT industries.

Looking at the issue following the ECRA's enactment in 2018, the above comments are indeed reasonable. However, what if we push the

[33] See https://pism.pl/publications/members-seek-to-mitigate-appellate-body-paralysis-in-wto-dispute-settlement.

timeline one step backward and look at the *Made in China 2025* initiative proposed in 2015? In that initiative, the entire Chinese establishment (or CCP) supported the 10 emerging industries in question, and the measures proposed in the initiative included all kinds of government subsidies and supports. The purpose of the initiative was to make China the leader of the 10 listed industries. Because China's subsidies (including monetary and in-kind) are overwhelming, one may also argue that the *Made in China 2025* initiative is already unscrupulous.

Chinese might treat the *Made in China 2025* initiative as normal, for two reasons. (1) The CCP is accustomed to the doctrine of "the party leads all," and does not recognize the line between politics and economics that liberal democratic countries do not want to cross. Indeed, before the *CHIPS and Science Act*, neither the U.S. nor EU members had ever provided any direct government subsidies to specific industries. (2) In China, state-owned enterprises or businesses over which the government exerts direct influence remain widespread. Thus, it is difficult to tell whether a "private" company named Huawei is truly private. If an entire country backs a Chinese company, then its competition with a purely private company such as Qualcomm would also be unscrupulous.

In this sense, the messy and unscrupulous strategies that we observe today are the result of institutional differences between an authoritarian regime and a democratic regime. As pointed out by Chu et al. (2022), the U.S. has claimed that the consensus and rule-based operation of the WTO have been disrupted by China, and its boycott of the WTO appellate body is merely a response. Similarly, enacting ECRA is just a weapon in response to *Made in China 2025*.

4.7.4 *Consequences of the ECRA and Entity List*

As we have mentioned in the above discussion, the spectrum of U.S. export controls over ICT items (machines, technologies, talents, IP, software) is extremely broad, and the entries in the entity list also include companies, upstream research institutes, universities, and various sub-branches. In regard to these export control measures, the term originally used by U.S. officials was "decoupling," but later some U.S. officials downplayed it with the term "de-risking." Literally, de-risking is motivated by a desire to reduce reliance on a single supplier or to protect against potential economic or geopolitical events. Unlike decoupling, de-risking seeks to continue basic trade and investment activities; once the risks have been dealt with, the policy should be deactivated.[34]

The real impact of the export control and entity list, however, appears to resemble decoupling more than de-risking. For example, we saw that the guardrail clause of the *CHIPS and Science Act* specifies a 10-year period during which investment is banned. This restriction is unlikely to be the result of a rational risk calculation.

Is there any sign that in the future the U.S. and China can somehow "couple" themselves in cyberspace and the ICT industries? Recent evidence does not suggest an optimistic prediction. The differences between the U.S.-led democratic countries and China are deeply embedded in values: the former consist of liberal democratic regimes, and the latter is an authoritarian Leninist regime; there exists little trust between these two camps. Because ICTs are related to very broad national military and industrial benefits, the lack of trust and the divergence of values are likely to keep these two sides apart. The institutional differences make the U.S. and China like oil and water. Even if we mix oil and water in the same tank, they are still oil and water, and only coexist in a decoupled way.

4.7.5 Caveats Regarding the Encouragement Comments

Some scholars recently criticized the U.S. as being too short-sighted to have blocked the development of Chinese ICT industries. Some said that this blocking would stimulate China to develop its own ICT parallels.[35] This criticism, however, might overlook the fact that the export control and entity list were only to *delay* China's development. For high-tech industries with increasing returns, delay is all the U.S. wants.

There were also news reports suggesting the success of China's *Made in China 2025* program, saying that China has scored successes on many fronts, despite foreign boycotts. These kinds of reports are mostly based on on-site observations, which attest to the "success" of certain projects. However, that is also misleading, because the purpose of *Made in China*

[34] https://www.hinrichfoundation.com/research/article/trade-and-geopolitics/china-decoupling-vs-de-risking/.

[35] See https://www.storm.mg/article/5255941.

2025 was to make China a leading player in related industries worldwide, which is entirely different from simply "being able to manufacture a product." For instance, several countries can indeed manufacture 3 nm chips, and possibly so could China. However, it is the yield rate that matters, which can be seen only through international comparisons. We should always keep this in mind as we read related reports.

References

Achilleas, P. (2017). *Theory and Practice of Export Control: Balancing International Security and International Economic Relations*. Springer.

Arthur, W. B. (1989). Competing Technologies, Increasing Returns, and Lock-In by Historical Events. *The Economic Journal, 99*, 116–131.

Arthur, W. B. (1996). Increasing Returns and the New World of Business. *Harvard Business Review, 74*(4), 100–109.

Aubin, Y., & Arnaud I. (2016). *Export Control Law and Regulations Handbook: A Practical Guide to Military and Dual-use Goods Trade Restrictions and Compliance*. Wolter Kluwer.

Bu, Q. (2020). China's Blocking Mechanism: The Unreliable Entity List. *Journal of International Trade Law and Policy, 19*(3), 159–180.

Chu, C. Y. C., & Lee, P.-C. (2019). Three Changes Not Foreseen by WTO Rules Framers Twenty-Five Years Ago. *Journal of World Trade, 53*(6), 895–922.

Chu, C. Y. C., Lee, P.-C., Lin, C.-C., & Lo, C.-F. (2022). *Ultimate Economic Conflict between China and Democratic Countries—An Institutional Analysis*. Routledge. https://www.routledge.com/search?author=C.Y.C.%20Chu

Miller, C. (2022). *Chip War: The Quest to Dominate the World's Most Critical Technology*. Simon & Schuster Audio. https://www.amazon.com/-/zh_TW/s?ie=UTF8&search-alias=audible&field-keywords=Simon+%26+Schuster+Audio&ref=adbl_dp_pd_publ

Tachibana, S. (2000). Impacts of Log Export Restrictions in Southeast Asia on the Japanese Plywood Market: An Econometric Analysis. *Journal of Forest Research, 5*(2), 51–57.

Whang, C. (2019). Undermining the Consensus-Building and List-Based Standards in Export Controls: What the US Export Controls Act Means to the Global Export Control Regime. *Journal of International Economic Law, 22*(4), 579–599.

Wu, C-H. (2021). *Law and Politics on Export Control Restrictions: WTO and Beyond*. Cambridge University Press.

CHAPTER 5

Data Collection Denial: Segregating the Platform Industries

Given that big data collection serves as a fundamental prerequisite for implementing AI, some authoritarian governments have started to use platforms to gather data from individuals, whether domestic or foreign. Later in Chapter 8, we will discuss how authoritarian rulers can use the collected big data to improve their domestic monitoring and control. In this chapter, we focus on the collection of citizens' information by platforms, either owned or controlled by a foreign adversary. In general, any internet platforms owned or controlled by a foreign adversary involve a national security risk: the extent and purpose of data usage by foreign governments remain uncertain. This concern regarding social order or national security has resulted in several governments imposing restrictions or outright bans on foreign-controlled platforms.

A notable example occurred in 2024: after a long tug of war, U.S. President Joe Biden signed the "exit or sell" Act (of which the detail will be introduced shortly) mainly targeted at TikTok, a widely popular social media platform originating from China that was suspected of being under the control of the Chinese Communist Party (CCP).[1] Earlier, during his first term as U.S. President, Donald Trump had issued similar executive orders. These orders, along with the "exit or sell" option, were subsequently challenged by TikTok through various judicial channels. The

[1] See https://www.nytimes.com/article/tiktok-ban.html.

C. Y. C. Chu, *An Emerging Digital Wall*,
https://doi.org/10.1007/978-981-95-3577-4_5

controversy was finally settled after the U.S. Supreme Court ruling on January 17, 2025. To facilitate our discussion, in this chapter we will separate the potential harm into two types: D-day penetration and everyday penetration.

5.1 Banning TikTok: Earlier Concerns Vary Across Countries

The earliest ban on TikTok occurred in India in April 2019, and the cited reason was that it "encouraged pornography" and showed "inappropriate content." Indeed, some uploaded videos featured dangerous or disturbing behavior, which might have encouraged young viewers to mimic them.[2] This of course constituted a social problem. The Indian banning order, however, only lasted 8 days and was abolished after TikTok quickly agreed to recruit 20 more people to scrutinize the uploaded content in the future.

After the ban in India, TikTok was also banned by Pakistan (2020–2021, intermittently), Afghanistan (April 2022), Nepal (2023–2024), and Kyrgyzstan (April 2024), with most of them similarly providing reasons related to the possible influence of some content on "social order." As one can see, many of these nations have specific religious backgrounds or relatively strict social norms, and therefore they have more stringent criteria with regard to content. While we will skip the various citations in relation to the above country-specific banning, they can be easily found using search engines.

Beyond content concerns, the primary justification for banning TikTok has been national security. Below we will list key entities and the timeline for the most prevalent form of restriction in many countries—prohibiting use by government officials and the military. By once again skipping the detailed references, they include the U.S. Navy (2019), U.S. Army (2020), U.S. Federal Government and 39 State Governments (various times), Taiwan (2022), Canada, Japan, the European Commission, the European Parliament, the EU Council, Belgium, Latvia, the UK, Estonia, Finland, the Netherlands, Norway, New Zealand, and Austria (the above were all in 2023), France, Kosovo (both in 2024), and the military of

[2] See https://en.wikipedia.org/wiki/Censorship_of_TikTok.

many countries.[3] Evidently, the banning of official uses was to prevent the possible leakage of information from civil servants or the collection of public-sector information by TikTok.

Of particular note, these official-sector bans applied exclusively to TikTok—not to similar platforms like YouTube—due to concerns over TikTok's alleged ties to the Chinese government. For example, India changed its banning of TikTok and WeChat from the original social order reason to "prejudicial to the sovereignty and integrity of India, defense of India, security of state and public order."[4]

From a technical standpoint, banning TikTok within government networks is straightforward—blocking access to its servers or software suffices. As of January 2025 (the time when the U.S. Supreme Court decided the case of TikTok), very few countries (such as Indonesia and Nepal) in the world had a complete ban of TikTok. Regarding the case of the U.S., we will provide a comprehensive analysis in the following sections.

5.2 Banning TikTok in the U.S.: A Five-year Timeline

The TikTok banning scenario in the U.S. is distinctive in its "sell or exit" format. Moreover, the case progressed through multiple legal and governmental stages, including an executive order, congressional legislation, and a Supreme Court ruling. In the following sections, we will outline and analyze each of these key events in detail.

On August 6, 2020, during his first presidential term, U.S. President Donald Trump signed an Executive Order, imposing comprehensive sanctions on TikTok, unless it was sold by ByteDance, the parent company of TikTok, within 45 days (Executive Office of the President, Executive Order 13,942, 2020). In the following discussion, we will refer to this as the "sell or exit" requirement. The executive order alleged that TikTok posed potential national security risks, including the possibility that it could enable the Chinese government to track the locations of federal employees and contractors, compile personal information for blackmail,

[3] See https://www.pbs.org/newshour/world/these-countries-have-already-banned-tiktok.

[4] India bans TikTok, WeChat and dozens more Chinese apps. (2020, June 29). *BBC News*. https://www.bbc.com/news/technology-53225720.

and conduct corporate espionage. Furthermore, the order claimed that TikTok "reportedly censors content that the Chinese Communist Party (CCP) deems politically sensitive, such as content concerning protests in Hong Kong and China's treatment of Uyghurs and other Muslim minorities."

5.2.1 *Failed Selling Attempts*

On August 14 in that same year, President Donald Trump issued a new executive order, extending the divestiture deadline to 90 days. The order stated that credible evidence suggested that ByteDance could take actions that threatened U.S. national security. It should be noted that Trump's executive order was based on the International Emergency Economic Powers Act (IEEPA) and the National Emergencies Act, which allowed the U.S. President to prohibit certain "transactions" involving ByteDance. Later, however, when TikTok brought the case to the court, the court ruled that Trump's executive order exceeded the authority under IEEPA.

In response to the "sell or exit" ultimatum, TikTok pursued a partnership with Oracle in early September 2020, a deal that would make Oracle a "trusted technology partner" rather than the owner of TikTok. Even if the agreement had been finalized, ByteDance would have retained majority ownership. The terms of the proposal allowed Oracle full access to TikTok's source code and updates to ensure that no backdoor programs existed. However, as long as ByteDance maintained control over TikTok, national security concerns persisted. At the same time, the Chinese government strongly opposed the deal. The Global Times, a state-backed media outlet in China, asserted that "China is prepared to prevent Chinese firm TikTok and its advanced technologies from falling into U.S. hands at all costs."

Despite TikTok's repeated assurances that it has never provided user data to Chinese authorities, its parent company, ByteDance, ultimately agreed to divest TikTok's U.S. operations completely. Several potential buyers emerged, with Microsoft initially expressing interest, followed by other U.S. tech companies, including Twitter and Oracle. Meanwhile, TikTok sued the U.S. government, arguing that the Trump administration's actions violated due process and infringed on freedom of expression.

5.2.2 *Court Ruling Against the Executive Order*

On September 27, 2020, a federal judge issued an injunction blocking Trump's executive order to ban TikTok, ruling that the ban might exceed the President's legal authority. Indeed, Trump's executive order lacked concrete, evidence-based justification. There might have been confidential intelligence that Trump received, but that might not have been sustained in court scrutiny. Meanwhile, TikTok appealed to the U.S. Court of Appeals, requesting a review of the government's national security claims and the legality of the executive order to divest.

On December 14, 2020, the Court of Appeals in Washington D.C. held a hearing, in which two out of three judges disagreed with the executive order to ban TikTok. As a result of these judicial rulings, Trump's TikTok ban never took effect.

5.2.3 *The Biden Administration's Turn*

Following the 2020 power transition, the Biden administration revoked Trump's TikTok ban on June 10, 2021.[5] Instead of enforcing the ban, President Biden issued a new executive order, requiring a rigorous, evidence-based review of TikTok's potential security risks" and to "address any unacceptable or undue risks consistent with overall national security, foreign policy, and economic objectives, including the preservation and demonstration of America's core values and fundamental freedoms."[6] Specifically, the executive order mandated the submission of two reports by the Secretary of Commerce and other relevant agencies.

The first report, which was scheduled to be submitted within 120 days, was intended to address the harm from the unrestricted sale of, transfer of, or access to U.S. persons' sensitive data. The second, which was scheduled to be submitted within 180 days, was to recommend executive and legislative actions to address the risk associated with connected software applications that were designed, developed, manufactured, or supplied by persons owned or controlled by, or subject to the jurisdiction or direction

[5] BBC, Donald Trump-era ban on TikTok dropped by Joe Biden (2021, June 9), https://www.bbc.com/news/technology-57413227.

[6] White House, Executive Order on Protecting Americans' Sensitive Data from Foreign Adversaries, (2021, June 9) https://www.whitehouse.gov/briefing-room/presidential-actions/2021/06/09/executive-order-on-protecting-americans-sensitive-data-from-foreign-adversaries/.

of, a foreign adversary. Meanwhile, the Biden administration sought to negotiate with ByteDance to explore the possibility of divesting TikTok's U.S. operations. However, no agreement was reached.

5.2.4 *Legislation and Court Fights*

On October 29, 2020, Senator Marco Rubio introduced the Adversarial Platform Prevention Act, aiming to "[i]ntroduce a set of data protection and censorship related standards and restrictions that must be met by high-risk foreign software." It defined "high-risk foreign software" as "any software owned by an entity organized under the laws of, headquartered in, or whose principal operations are in China, Russia, Venezuela, Cuba, or a country designated as a state sponsor of terrorism, or any software that stores U.S. consumer data in one of those nations."[7] Following the introduction of this bill, several legislative revisions sought to restrict TikTok's operations, with bans sometimes limited to university campuses and other specific locations.[8] In short, the above-mentioned moves had shifted the banning from executive orders to legislation proposals.

Ultimately, Congress passed the Protecting Americans from Foreign Adversary Controlled Applications Act (PAFACAA). On April 23, 2024, President Biden signed this bill, which forces a sale of the video app or a banning of it.[9] More precisely, PAFACAA prohibits any entity from distributing, maintaining, or updating an application controlled by a foreign adversary in the U.S. This prohibition makes device companies, such as Apple, unable to update any of TikTok's apps, thereby practically disabling the app. The law also cited national security concerns because of TikTok's Chinese ties. Both lawmakers and security experts have said that there are risks that the Chinese government could lean on ByteDance for access to sensitive data belonging to its 170 million U.S. users or to spread propaganda. The law would allow TikTok to continue to operate in the U.S. if ByteDance sold it within 270 days, a timeframe that the U.S. President could extend to a year. Again, the measures are essentially the

[7] See https://www.rubio.senate.gov/public/index.cfm/press-releases?ID=6BBDD1FB-9A04-4A52-976D-2AD71A508E60.

[8] https://time.com/6249522/public-universities-banning-tiktok/.

[9] https://www.nytimes.com/2024/04/23/technology/bytedance-tiktok-ban-bill.html.

same as the "sell or exit" requirement mentioned in the previous discussion. However, despite PAFACAA's enactment, TikTok retained the right to challenge the law in court.

TikTok filed a petition with the D.C. Circuit Court, challenging PAFACAA's constitutionality, in particular alleging a violation of the First Amendment. The D.C. Circuit court denied the petitions on December 6, 2024, mainly saying that ByteDance was a Chinese company regarding which the First Amendment was not applicable.[10] Then TikTok brought the case to the U.S. Supreme Court, and again the petition was denied (and finalized) on January 17, 2025. Following Donald Trump's second inauguration, he expressed sympathy for TikTok's position and extended PAFACAA's enforcement several times. At the time of writing (July 2025), TikTok is still operating in the U.S., and PAFACAA is not yet enforced.

5.2.5 *Banning WeChat*

At roughly the same time as Trump's first executive order, the Trump administration also banned WeChat on August 6, 2020, on the grounds of "national emergency with respect to the information and communications technology and services supply chain" (Executive Office of the President, Executive Order 13,943, 2020). In that executive order, Trump said that "Like TikTok, WeChat automatically captures vast swathes of information from its users. This data collection threatens to allow the CCP access to Americans' personal and proprietary information."

Owned by another Chinese tech giant, Tencent, WeChat is a multi-functional super-app integrating messaging, social media, and digital payment services, making it indispensable in China's digital ecosystem. In 2020, the year of the said Executive Order, it had more than 1 billion users in the world, including an average of 19 million daily active users in the U.S. Compared to TikTok, it is less popular in the U.S., but it is still widely used among American Chinese or Americans that do business in China. In what follows, we will focus only on the case of TikTok and shorten the discussion on WeChat.

[10] See https://www.reuters.com/article/technology/u-s-appeals-court-rejects-immediate-wechat-ban-idUSL1N2HH2SJ/.

5.2.6 *PAFACAA Regulatory Criteria*

We should first note that PAFACAA regulates companies that operate an application that "enables users to generate, share, and view content and has more than 1,000,000 monthly active users" (§2(g)(2)(A)). However, the Act excludes companies whose primary purpose is to allow users to post "product reviews, business reviews, or travel information and reviews" (§2(g)(2)(B)). In essence, these reviews are not deemed a national security risk.

It is important to note that PAFACAA specifically targets content-sharing platforms, such as YouTube, TikTok, and Facebook, while excluding search engines and e-commerce platforms from direct regulation. As discussed in Chapter 3, both e-commerce and search engines collect large volumes of user data, but they do not function primarily as content-sharing platforms. However, PAFACAA also establishes a broad designation framework, which allows the U.S. President to classify any application as a potential national security threat, provided it meets two conditions: (1) It is operated by a company controlled by a foreign adversary, and (2) It is deemed to present a significant security risk to the U.S. (§2(g)(3)(B)). This discretionary authority means that even platforms beyond social media—such as search engines, cloud storage providers, and e-commerce platforms—could be subject to future regulatory action if designated as threats by the U.S. President.

5.3 Threats and Complications Related to TikTok

TikTok has gained widespread popularity among both civilians and members of the U.S. armed forces. By 2019, TikTok's downloads had surpassed those of Instagram,[11] (owned by Facebook), and YouTube (owned by Google). As of May 2024, 170 million people in the U.S. had downloaded the TikTok app. However, in 2024, user preferences began to shift: Instagram expanded its user base across a broader age demographic, while TikTok remained the dominant platform among younger audiences.[12] Given the sheer volume of daily video uploads,

[11] Isobel Asher Hamilton (February 27, 2019), TikTok was bigger than Instagram last year after passing the 1 billion download mark, *Insider*, https://www.businessinsider.com/tiktok-hit-1-billion-downloads-surpassing-instagram-in-2018-2019-2.

[12] See https://shift.com/blog/apps-hub/tiktok-vs-instagram/.

TikTok's algorithm-driven content curation has had a profound influence on American digital habits, consumer trends, and social discourse.

The legal battle over TikTok's future is ongoing, with President Trump holding final discretion over the platform's fate. However, this has led to a critical question: Have concerns over TikTok's data practices been exaggerated? Why have tech companies affiliated with other countries not received similar challenges? These questions become more puzzling given that the data collection and sharing practices of TikTok are quite standard in the industry. Major social media and e-commerce platforms—such as Facebook, Instagram, and Amazon—use similar machine-learning algorithms to recommend content, products, and advertisements based on user behavior. In traditional media such as the New York Times, the Editor does the screening and decides what content is to be published and circulated. Despite these similarities, why has TikTok faced disproportionate scrutiny compared to its U.S.-based counterparts? Along the lines of the U.S. Supreme Court ruling, in what follows we will summarize four factors that highlight the uniqueness of the issue here.

5.3.1 *Factor 1: The "Inferred" Threats*

According to the Supreme Court Ruling (2025 Nos. 24–656 and 24–657 p. 13), TikTok's data collecting practices include obtaining the user's age, phone number, precise location, internet address, device used, phone contacts, social network connections, the content of private messages sent through the application, and the videos watched which include keystroke patterns and rhythms.

If users allow TikTok to access their phone contact list to connect with others on the platform, then TikTok can access any data stored in the users' contact list, including names, contact information, contact photos, job titles, and notes. The U.S. government worries that China may use such data to track Federal employees. Because Chinese laws enable China to require companies to surrender data to the government or the CCP, these data may become China's espionage tool. For instance, if the CCP knows the private IP addresses of high-ranking government officials, it would be much easier for it to engage in cyberspace penetration.

The U.S. Supreme Court also asserted that it does not matter whether China actually acquired such data or whether China was involved in any espionage. Neither does the probability of these events matter, because (p. 14) "sound policymaking often requires legislators to forecast future events and to anticipate the likely impact of these events based on deductions and inferences for which the complete empirical support may be unavailable." As such, as long as the D-day national security threats can be "inferred," then a regulatory law may be justified.

5.3.2 Factor 2: The Difference Between TikTok and YouTube

The key worry behind all the debates is the *objective function* of the tech companies in question. For any algorithm to be operative, the programmer must feed in an objective function. Using China as an example: given an authoritarian government's access to the data and that the big tech companies have been effectively controlled by the CCP, the CCP has the authority to determine what drives the algorithm. TikTok states in its terms of service that it can share data with its parent company, ByteDance, and ultimately, the Chinese government. Even if TikTok or ByteDance is purely profit-oriented, ultimately, the U.S. must inquire what the objective function of the CCP is, if it is able to access the data collected from the TikTok platform indirectly. With the assistance and development of the AI algorithm, a foreign adversary may of course be able to use the big data to manipulate political winds or influence the U.S. election, and therefore threaten the national security of the U.S. This is the main argument of the U.S. Supreme Court.

In short, the U.S. government may not like the algorithms behind most Western AI companies, such as Facebook and YouTube, which maximize their profits, but usually it does not feel any national security threat, because it is unlikely to have a systematic force which can twist the arms of these private platform giants. Or, if TikTok is owned by, say, the UK, the threat may also be lighter. Platforms owned by a foreign state may not be a problem; the term "adversary" is the key. According to PAFACAA, the judgment of what constitutes an adversary is left to the U.S. President.

TikTok officials have always insisted that TikTok stores its data in the U.S., and that TikTok does not send such data to the Chinese government. However, this argument is not plausible because the CCP effectively controls all tech giants (including ByteDance) in China both internally and externally. In practice, whether some datasets have been shared with the CCP is hardly verifiable. Foreseeing this monitoring difficulty *ex post*, the U.S. Supreme Court (p, 19) agreed with the government's assessment and allowed PAFACAA to be enacted *ex ante*.

5.3.3 *Factor 3: Can the CCP Effectively Control TikTok?*

There are various national security and data laws in China that regulate Chinese companies. Undoubtedly, ByteDance will also be bound by these laws, because it is a Chinese company. TikTok may not be directly under the jurisdiction of these laws, because TikTok is not available in China. Nevertheless, it is not difficult to imagine a chain of command from the CCP to ByteDance, and then from ByteDance to TikTok. Indeed, Zhang Yiming, the founder of ByteDance, has admitted that his company is willing to cater to the CCP's propaganda and monitor any content that crosses the party's red line.[13]

Even though TikTok is separate from its Chinese counterpart (Douyin) in terms of being a legal entity, research shows that its algorithm is still developed by ByteDance's China-based engineering teams.[14] As a consequence, there is little difference between TikTok and Douyin in this regard. Admittedly, TikTok has hired many engineers from the U.S., but they have had to comply with the requests from superiors in China. In fact, TikTok has already been accused in California of sending user data to China.[15]

To sum up, the CCP can effectively control these tech giants both internally and externally. Because of these internal and external controls, it is implausible, according to the U.S. Supreme Court, to claim that China does not have the ability to control or manipulate the data possessed by TikTok.

5.3.4 *Factor 4: Limited American Technology Inputs*

In Chapter 4, we mentioned that the U.S. could use its export controls or entity list as weapons to chokehold a Chinese tech company. For instance, if there is a significant portion of U.S. patents or software in TikTok's operation, then an export ban or including ByteDance in the entity list would effectively block TikTok's operation in the U.S. These "export"

[13] See https://www.npr.org/2020/09/26/917134452/new-doj-filing-tiktoks-owner-is-a-mouthpiece-of-chinese-communist-party.

[14] See Australian Strategic Policy Institute, 2020.

[15] Paul, K. (2019, December 3). TikTok accused in California lawsuit of sending user data to China. *Reuters*. https://in.reuters.com/article/us-usa-tiktok-lawsuit-idINKBN1Y708.

control measures still apply, despite the fact that TikTok's operation is on U.S. soil.

The case of TikTok, however, is very different. The technologies and know-hows of TikTok are mostly, if not entirely, developed by the Chinese. Although there are some U.S. citizens working for the TikTok service branch in the U.S., they do not constitute a significant element of the business operation, and hence a U.S. technology transfer embargo could not work in this case. Thus, if the U.S. really wants to boycott the TikTok service, there does not exist any means on the administrative arm that can achieve the goal. The enactment of a law seems unavoidable.

5.3.5 *Previous Battles of the First Amendment*

In the past 5 years, TikTok has already had a strong record in similar First Amendment battles. When President Trump tried to force a sale or ban of the app in 2020, federal judges blocked the effort with the reason that it would have had the effect of shutting down a "platform for expressive activity." In 2023, Montana tried to ban TikTok in the state because of the app's Chinese ownership, but a federal judge ruled against the state law for similar reasons.[16]

Only one narrower TikTok restriction has survived a court challenge. The governor of Texas announced a ban of the app on state government devices and networks in 2022, because of its Chinese ownership and related data privacy concerns. A federal judge upheld the state ban in December, finding it was a "reasonable restriction" in light of Texas's concerns and the narrow scope affecting only state employees.[17]

Note that the above-mentioned judicial wins were all against Federal- or State-level executive orders. After PAFACAA was enacted, TikTok lost both the D.C. circuit appeal trial and the Supreme Court trial.

5.3.6 *Divestment Complication*

Even if TikTok moves forward with a sale, the process of separating TikTok from ByteDance is likely to be complex. The legislation prohibits

[16] See https://www.npr.org/2023/11/30/1205735647/montana-tiktok-ban-blocked-state.

[17] See https://www.npr.org/2024/04/24/1246663779/biden-ban-tiktok-us.

any connection between ByteDance and TikTok after a sale. TikTok employees, however, are used to the ByteDance software and network in their communications. This forced separation, as one can imagine, is not easy.

Another option is to break off just the U.S. portion of TikTok. However, that is also challenging. The TikTok algorithm, which figures out what users like and provides content accordingly, is the key to the success of the app. That algorithm is owned by ByteDance. During President Trump's attempt to force a sale in 2020, the Chinese government issued export restrictions that required its regulators to grant permission before ByteDance algorithms could be sold or licensed to outsiders. In 2023 and 2024, China's commerce ministry said it would "firmly oppose" a sale of the app by ByteDance.[18] In essence, China threatened to exercise its own "export control" (of ByteDance software). If the divestiture ultimately severs TikTok's access to ByteDance's algorithm, the app may no longer function as it did before.

5.4 Debates Regarding the First Amendment

The First Amendment of the U.S. Constitution states the following: "Congress shall make no law respecting an establishment of religion, or prohibiting the free exercise thereof; or abridging the freedom of speech, or of the press; or the right of the people peaceably to assemble, and to petition the Government for a redress of grievances." With respect to the issue of TikTok, the violated freedoms claimed by the petitioners are mainly the freedom of speech and the freedom of the press. For the sake of conciseness, we will refer to these collectively as "freedom of information." Our discussion here is to consider a series of scenario changes which may help us understand the key differences between TikTok and the traditional discussion of the freedom of information in the U.S.

Following the structure of the Supreme Court ruling, we will divide our subsequent discussion into two parts. First, we discuss the ends, and then the means.

[18] See https://www.bbc.com/news/articles/c289n8m4j19o.

5.4.1 *Are the Ends of PAFACAA Justified?*

Let us first consider a traditional freedom of information scenario. There are well-known "position differences" associated with traditional media such as the *New York Times* (NYT), *Wall Street Journal* (WSJ), *Guardian*, and the *Economist*. Suppose the Editor of the NYT or WSJ plays the role of an "algorithm," that decides through "brain deliberation" what articles or reports should be published (or released on the webpage), and from what angles they should be analyzed. This is definitely the freedom of information protected by the First Amendment. The opinion of the NYT/WSJ may be "biased," but that is the Editors' freedom of expression. Viewers have multiple sources available, allowing them to exercise their right to access diverse viewpoints.

In addition to the above discussion, suppose that there is sufficient evidence that the Editor of the NYT/WSJ is influenced by, or even asks for advice from, the Labour Party of the UK, and therefore the "algorithm" in the Editor's brain is actually manipulated by the Labour Party. It can be inferred that this scenario is still protected by the First Amendment. The Editor's ideology may come from his/her previous college education, which may well be in the UK. The strong influence of a certain ideology does not constitute a legitimate reason for infringing the freedom of information.

Now, suppose there is evidence that the editor of the NYT or WSJ is not taking orders from the Labour Party, but rather from the CCP. Consequently, the "algorithm" in the editor's mind is now manipulated by the CCP. What distinguishes this case from the previous one? The key difference lies in the fact that there is substantial evidence (see Chapter 9 for the details) indicating that the CCP has been involved in espionage, cyberattacks, and intellectual property (IP) theft against the U.S. By contrast, the British Labour Party has no such record. Here we see the significant role of the term "foreign adversary." The UK is not treated as a foreign adversary, whereas China is treated as an adversary. As such, the U.S. Supreme Court says that, regarding the freedom of information, the legislation can have different positions in relation to different countries.

Beyond the issue of TikTok's potential control by a foreign adversary (the CCP), there is another critical aspect that has not been a major focus in traditional First Amendment discussions: the collection and utilization of big data. TikTok is a platform that is able to collect the big data of individuals, which we have explained in our previous discussion. Given that there are 170 million U.S. users who have downloaded TikTok, and assuming that very young and very old people may not be able to use TikTok apps, then this suggests that TikTok has been able to collect the data of more than 60% of U.S. adults. This has not included the data contained in the contact lists of TikTok users. Indeed, it is this intensive data collection issue that dominates the reasoning of the Supreme Court ruling, not that of the freedom of information per se.

In its ruling, the U.S. Supreme Court put quite some effort into determining the difference between "strict scrutiny"[19] and "intermediate scrutiny."[20] Generally speaking, whenever a law is "content-based" (that is, the law prohibits the expression or sharing of certain kinds of content), then it is presumably unconstitutional and may be justified only if the government proves that the prohibition is "narrowly tailored to serve compelling state interests" (Supreme Court of the United states, 2025, p. 9). However, if the laws are not targeting specific content, then they are subject to an intermediate level of scrutiny, because "in most cases they pose a less substantial risk of exercising certain ideas or viewpoints from the public dialogue." In this case, TikTok's data collection practices and the potential misuse of big data are not content-specific. As a result, the Supreme Court classified PAFACAA as "content-neutral" and therefore applied the intermediate scrutiny standard.

5.4.2 *Are the Means of PAFACAA Justified?*

The U.S. Supreme Court has acknowledged that the big data collected by TikTok and their possible use by the CCP constitutes a potential risk to U.S. national security. Although TikTok argued that China has more effective and more efficient ways to collect such data (instead of using the platform as a device for data collection), the Supreme Court disagreed with this argument, asserting that the risk was based on reasonable "deductions and inferences" of the legislator (p. 14). In addition, for

[19] Strict scrutiny is the highest standard of review that a court will use to evaluate the constitutionality of government action. See Spece Jr. and Yokum (2015) and Gerstmann and Shortell (2011).

[20] Intermediate scrutiny is a test courts often use in the field of Constitutional Law to determine a statute's constitutionality. Intermediate scrutiny is only invoked when a state or the federal government passes an act which discriminates against, negatively affects, or creates some kind of classification affecting certain protected classes (this is described in further detail in the next section). See Bhagwat (2007) and Holoszyc-Pimentel (2015).

the government to implement *ex post* monitoring as to whether there is such an abuse of big data on the TikTok side is rather difficult (p. 19). It suggests that other policy means are not sufficiently effective to reduce the national security risk, and therefore an *ex ante* forced divestiture is a legitimate means.

Other policy means referred to above may include promoting "more speech," to let the marketplace of ideas decide what is right and what is wrong; or "issuing explicit warnings to TikTok users about the potential risks that their data may be used by foreign adversary entities." In his concurring opinion, Justice Gorsuch (p. 4) explained why these measures are insufficient. In addition, Gorsuch argued that even if these means were to be adopted, they "could not eliminate the risk that some big data have already been collected and may have already been abused by a foreign adversary."

5.4.3 D-day Interference vs. Everyday Interference

Suppose there are strong interconnections between TikTok, ByteDance and the CCP, and suppose the CCP does try to influence the U.S. in a detrimental way. There is one issue not explicitly addressed in the Supreme Court ruling. In general, there are two kinds of activities that a foreign adversary can pursue. The first is a D-day interference, such as influencing the U.S. presidential election, or delaying the U.S. decision to help Ukraine. These D-day interferences may potentially significantly impact critical decision-making moments, and the corresponding consequences are often irreversible. The second kind of interference refers to everyday interference, such as suppressing videos related to China's human rights abuses in Tibet, Xinjiang, and Hong Kong, thereby reducing U.S. public awareness of these issues. Everyday interference is subtle and accumulates over time, and there may not be corresponding critical governmental decisions that are the targets of influence.

In his Executive Order issued on August 6, 2020, President Trump said: "TikTok also reportedly censors content that the Chinese Communist Party deems politically sensitive, such as content concerning protests in Hong Kong and China's treatment of Uyghurs and other Muslim minorities." This accusation pertains to everyday interference and differs from the D-day national security threat highlighted in the Supreme Court ruling. Since China maintains serious controls on the press and Internet, the Chinese government or the CCP becomes the only channel that reports on Uyghurs or Tibet. Using economic terminology, the CCP essentially monopolizes news related to China from the perspective of U.S. viewers. Thus, if 170 million U.S. citizens are allowed to access TikTok and watch the censored videos, it appears that the U.S. government is helping a foreign monopoly (of news) to exercise its dissemination of a one-sided view, while simultaneously diminishing the already limited competing narratives.

As articulated in the preceding paragraph, the TikTok case raises concerns over the freedom of information in general. The Supreme Court's intermediate scrutiny approach is content neutral, and hence avoids this problem. However, if a strict scrutiny standard were applied while leaving aside the D-day national security threat for a moment, what kind of evidence would be required to justify the enactment of a law? In the concurring opinion of Justice Gorsuch, it was pointed out that the Supreme Court did not consider the classified evidence provided by the government, which may be consistent with the content of Trump's executive order on August 6, 2020. Conceptually, what level of proof would be necessary for the court to conclude that TikTok's algorithm did give rise to everyday interference, as Trump described? This is what we will explain in the next section.

5.4.4 *What About Other Internet Platforms Owned by Foreign Adversaries?*

Beyond TikTok, other Chinese internet platforms, such as Alibaba, WeChat, and Alipay, also engage in large-scale data collection from U.S. citizens. Given that the CCP exercises centralized control over Chinese enterprises, and that Chinese laws governing data access and transfer apply uniformly across these platforms, it is reasonable to infer that Alibaba's collection of U.S. customer data similarly raises national security concerns.

E-commerce platforms gather a broader spectrum of personal data compared to video-sharing services. Other than one's name, age, sex, phone number, precise location, email address, and device used, e-commerce platforms also have one's previous purchase records, credit-card information, default records, and the frequency of viewing and writing customer responses. These data are very different from video sharing and viewing, but contain even more information about customers' preferences, financial balances, and daily consumption habits. The only difference between an e-commerce platform and a video-sharing platform is that, other than commodity advertisements, the former rarely distribute information to consumers, and hence they cannot directly, for example, disturb the U.S. election. Although there is customer feedback based on the purchases made, it consists of "product reviews" which are ruled out by PAFACAA, as we mentioned before. The product reviews are usually retrieved by potential customers and are not actively sent by the platform.

In short, because most commodities are not politically sensitive, e-commerce customers do not receive information related to Uyghurs or Tibet or Taiwan, so that the risk of everyday penetration is limited. Although e-commerce platforms lack direct political influence, the use of artificial intelligence (AI) and predictive profiling could still facilitate a form of D-day penetration. False narratives could be easily curated and delivered to specific audiences with tailored variations for different interest groups. This would be a "curated D-day penetration," and it might cause more serious damage to national security than social media platforms.

Beyond e-commerce platforms, the U.S. Department of Commerce's Bureau of Industry and Security (BIS) issued a final rule on January 15, 2025, prohibiting Chinese and Russian connected vehicle technology in the U.S. Under this rule, hardware and software integrated in the vehicle connectivity system (VCS) and software integrated in the automated driving system (ADS) for new passenger vehicles from the two countries will be banned. Software-related prohibitions will take effect for units with the model year 2027 and hardware-related prohibitions will take effect for units with the model year 2030, or 2029 for units without a model year, according to a press release.[21]

The rationale behind this regulation is that modern cars function as mobile data collection hubs; they have cameras, microphones, GPS tracking, and other technologies that are connected to the Internet. Equipped with cameras, microphones, GPS tracking, and internet connectivity, vehicles constantly gather sensitive data about their drivers, passengers, and surroundings. Because it is difficult to detect whether such information collected by VCS and ADS is leaked to adversary entities, the U.S. DOC decided to ban the vehicle altogether. Again, cars cannot share information like social media, and hence it is the pure data collection that causes national security concerns. The platform role of VCS and

[21] See https://www.repairerdrivennews.com/2025/01/15/department-of-commerce-publishes-final-rule-banning-chinese-and-russian-vehicle-technology/.

ADS is even weaker than the e-commerce platform, but VCS and ADS are banned anyway.[22]

The purpose of the above discussion is to provide a framework that can help our thinking about the general issue of banning platforms of different forms. In addition, we should note that big data are often compiled by a combination of several otherwise independent data sources. Setting regulatory rules targeting specific platforms (as was the case in PAFACAA) may not be the right approach.

Other than the above discussion on the legal aspects, there is one question that needs to be clarified. For regulations that are related to content-based everyday penetrations (such as decreasing the circulation of content on Uyghur re-education camps), do we really have solid and indisputable evidence which indicates that the CCP is behind the algorithm? In the next section, we will summarize what has been mentioned and discussed so far.

5.5 Content Distortion—Previous Accusations

According to a report in the Guardian (2019),[23] a former employee of TikTok revealed an internal guidance for moderators to determine the content that was to be removed or flagged. The guidelines divide banned material into two categories: some content is completely deleted from the platform, with potential account bans for repeat offenders, which would be deleted from the site entirely, and can also lead to users being banned from the service. The lesser infringements are not deleted, but algorithmically suppressed, which leaves the content reachable by search, but its distribution is restricted by the algorithm. In the latter case, the users are usually not sure about the reason for the low circulation. In any event, if a piece of content is suppressed for whatever reason, this suppression is content-based.

[22] In the era of autonomous driving, however, cars are all elements of the IoT (Internet of Things), and they do need to interact with each other while moving.

[23] See https://www.theguardian.com/technology/2019/sep/25/revealed-how-tiktok-censors-videos-that-do-not-please-beijing.

5.5.1 *Early Evidence Revealed by the Guardian*

In its investigation, the Guardian found that rules regarding China-related content were often framed within broader, seemingly neutral categories. For example, in a section governing "hate speech and religion," it would be very convenient to treat harsh criticism as hate speech. Criticism of China's socialist system was banned under a rule against "attacks on the policies or social structures of any country, such as a constitutional monarchy, monarchy, parliamentary system, separation of powers, socialist system, etc." Mentions of sensitive historical events—such as the Tiananmen Square massacre, the Cambodian genocide, or the May 1998 riots in Indonesia—were flagged as "demonization or distortion of history." Another example is the ban on "highly controversial" topics, such as separatism, religious conflicts, and conflicts between ethnic groups, for instance by exaggerating the conflicts between Islamic sects, promoting the independence of Northern Ireland, the Republic of Chechnya, Tibet, and Taiwan and overstating the ethnic conflict between black and white people.

The above-mentioned cases are all in the "visible by self" list. Content that promotes Falun Gong is marked as a "violation," because the organization is categorized as a "group promoting suicide." Note that the criteria mentioned are all vague and only superficially justified, because we certainly should not allow a platform to promote suicide. Furthermore, there appears to be nothing wrong with reducing the circulation of "highly controversial topics." The problem is that these criteria hide the theme that the CCP may want to ban under a broader but seemingly neutral umbrella. Is criticizing the brutality of the CCP's oppression in Tibet a "demonization" of Chinese history?

The leaked documents also revealed that at least 20 global leaders and "sensitive figures" were automatically flagged as "visible to self," meaning that any TikTok content referencing them would receive algorithmic suppression. The list includes Kim Jong-il, Kim Il-sung, Mahatma Gandhi, Vladimir Putin, Donald Trump, Barack Obama, Kim Jong-un, Shinzo Abe, Park Geun-Hee, Joko Widodo, and Narendra Modi. In essence, therefore, anything related to these leaders will be less circulated. The inclusion of democratic leaders like Obama, Trump, and Modi alongside authoritarian figures like Kim Jong-un and Putin raised concerns about whether TikTok's censorship criteria were politically motivated. If content about former U.S. presidents is restricted, would not this violate

First Amendment rights by limiting American users' access to political content?

Following the Guardian's exposé, TikTok did not deny the existence of such censorship guidelines. However, TikTok said that the information the Guardian retrieved was an old version. "The old guidelines in question are outdated and no longer in use. Today we take localized approaches, including local moderators, local content and moderation policies, local refinement of global policies, and more."[24] TikTok essentially acknowledged past censorship practices but insisted that they had since been reformed. The company framed the issue as a past mistake, suggesting that the "smoking gun" found by the Guardian was just a relic of the past.

5.5.2 More Recent Accusations

Wikipedia has also summarized many incidents or complaints in which accusations were leveled at the content-based censoring of TikTok.[25] They consist mostly of individual experiences such as (1) uploading sensitive information (on Xinjiang) and then the account was suspended; (2) uploading videos (of Xinjiang's re-education camp) and then the content was banned or restricted; (3) uploading speeches that harm the "national honor" or broadcasts of streams about "state organs such as the police" and then the content was banned; (4) uploading videos related to the Sino-Indian border dispute and the China–India skirmishes and then the videos were shadow banned; (5) the Acton Institute's TikTok account was suspended after it promoted videos about the imprisonment of Jimmy Lai and the Chinese government's crackdown on the pro-democracy camp in Hong Kong; (6) pro-Palestinian content was suppressed (due to accusations by Malaysia's Minister of Communications); and (7) researchers claiming that there was a strong possibility that content on TikTok was either amplified or suppressed based on its alignment with the interests of the Chinese government. There were other screening criteria regarding LGBTQ and other moral concerns, which are skipped here because they are less related to international conflicts.

[24] See https://www.businessinsider.com/internal-guidelines-show-tiktok-censors-videos-that-would-anger-china-2019-9.

[25] See https://en.wikipedia.org/wiki/Censorship_by_TikTok.

With regard to the above criticisms, TikTok seemed to have smooth responses; it either reinstated the banned account, or provided modified approaches, or explained why some content fit into a broad but seemingly neutral category, or promised to do better in the future. Sometimes it even invited retired U.S. congressmen or UK lawyers to provide advice for their future operation.[26]

5.5.3 *Lack of Hard Evidence*

Despite numerous allegations of content suppression, TikTok has largely managed to deflect accusations. The primary challenge in proving TikTok's systematic bias lies in the lack of hard evidence. The general accusation is that "TikTok has a distribution algorithm or criteria that fulfills the interest of the CCP." The "visible to self" option suggests that uploaded videos are rarely deleted; the only possible way to fulfill the CCP's interests is to reduce the circulation of the video. The next question is: How can we identify the down-touch pattern? Specifically, how are we sure that the down-touches are related to CCP interests?

Indeed, the methodological flaws in previous accusations have been raised in some recent reports. Regarding the videos with themes that China may deem sensitive, people have found that the number of such videos on TikTok is evidently lower than that on Instagram. That comparison has been correctly pointed out by Paul Matzko as an example of flawed methodology.[27] It is difficult, if not impossible, to compare two platforms with different user specificities and different operating histories. A similar mistake was made by Alicia Clanton and Aisha Counts,[28] who claimed in a report that anti-China videos are more difficult to find on TikTok than other media. Again, the comparison is not scientific, because the algorithms behind each platform are based on platform users, and hence different distribution results may well be due to the user pool difference, rather than the algorithm bias.

In general, the accusation that a user's videos had a low circulation does not constitute solid scientific evidence for two reasons. First, we

[26] See https://www.washingtonexaminer.com/news/1779002/inside-tiktoks-army-of-lobbyists-of-ex-senators-congressmen-and-staffers/.

[27] See https://matzko.substack.com/p/lies-damned-lies-and-statistics-a.

[28] See https://vapingunderground.com/threads/tiktok-shows-less-%E2%80%98anti-china%E2%80%99-content-than-rivals-study-finds.3049636/.

do not know whether the user in question *should have* or *could have* had a higher circulation, as in the case where there is no content-based screening. Technically, we need an identification test: we should have some controlled observations to be paired with experimental observations to sustain a valid conclusion. Across different platforms, we simply cannot establish satisfactory statistical controls. Second, we should have a large number of observations that suffice for a statistical test. A statistically significant result will sustain a "pattern" of distortion, so that TikTok cannot use "exceptional cases" as a defensive excuse. We do not know how many observations are associated with the above accusations, but evidently they did not provide test statistics for us to verify. If we are to take care of the above two obstacles, then we are very close to obtaining some hard evidence.

5.6 Evidence from a Scientific Experiment

To implement a rigorous test of whether there is political influence behind the algorithm which affects the distribution of videos, Chu et al. (2025) suggest the following experimental design.

5.6.1 Acquiring "Clean" Devices

First, the researcher must obtain brand-new smartphones (or other mobile devices). These new phones ensure that no prior browsing history, cached data, or communication logs exist, and hence they do not have other search or communication backgrounds which may compromise the later comparisons.[29] The number of cellphones should be chosen with some statistical inference in mind, so that researchers will have sufficient observations to perform various statistical tests. Secondly, these new smartphones must support 4G or 5G connectivity, so that they can facilitate seamless video uploads, downloads, and interactions.

The cellphones are then distributed to research assistants (RAs), and they are instructed to perform the daily operations. The RAs are not allowed to use these cellphones for purposes other than this research, so that the cellphones remain "clean" during the experimental period. These cellphones are then randomly assigned to two groups, with each

[29] For example, a device which has been banned before because of hate speech may be marked and is more likely to be banned in the future.

group of equal size: one group is the control group and the other is the experimental group.

The RAs first download the TikTok app and register accordingly. Their registrations are staggered over time, and their user names are randomly selected from a curated list. For each RA, the names of these accounts are designed to ensure that each registered account appears as a legitimate user, and technically each registered name is authentically owned by this RA.

5.6.2 *Establishing Regular Patterns and Sending Stimuli*

The cellphones used in the experiments then simulate real user behavior, and each phone user is engaged with TikTok by watching recommended videos for several minutes per day. Each cell phone is also required to complete the watching of at least one video, to establish a typical user profile. In addition, each cellphone is required to follow several others, so that they will be fed with some videos uploaded by these "friends" that they follow.

The RAs are required to compile worksheets every day, which are like laboratory notes for future checking and verification. If this experiment is implemented outside the U.S., then the cellphones should be separated, with roughly half of them using local telecommunications to upload and download, and the other half using a virtual private network (VPN) to connect, where the VPN channel is designated as the U.S. Such an arrangement may allow us to observe the possible differences between the U.S. and other countries.

After some weeks of regular exercises, the researcher can create two otherwise similar groups: they are similar in their frequencies and time span of browsing each day, the number of followers, the "likes" they have given to others, and the frequencies of uploading videos, etc. The two groups are randomly chosen, and hence we do not have any a priori guide to differentiate them. At this stage, videos with different stimuli are created and uploaded, where the experimental group has content that is presumably more sensitive to the CCP, whereas the control group has correspondingly modified content. Note that other than the slightly modified content, the videos in these two groups are otherwise the same.

5.6.3 *Empirical Findings*

The time when Chu's team performed their experiment was during the grace period granted by President Trump, and hence it is expected that the platform would be cautious when engaging in possible screening. Chu et al. (2025) therefore designed an experiment purely for the algorithm. Specifically, the research team used a graph/emoji in the TikTok app to hide the text when creating the posts. For example, in a post the experimental group's text "Free Tibet" in white was completely hidden by the white ghost graph (with "Free America" in the control group). By doing so, the real viewers were unable to notice the content of the text, and hence the content difference should not have driven the viewers' different responses. On the other hand, since the text was added through typing in the TikTok app, this enabled the content to be clearly identified by TikTok's algorithm. Thus, only the algorithm in TikTok was able to apply discrimination based on the text content.

Chu et al. obtained the following results: (1) Keywords such as East Turkistan, Wuhan Pneumonia (in Chinese), and Falun Gong (in Chinese) were indeed shadow banned. Because the text in either the experimental group or the corresponding control groups (i.e., Xinjiang, COVID-19 pneumonia, and Taichi) could not be seen by human viewers, the circulation differences must have been due to the algorithm. (2) TikTok's algorithm appears to be based on keywords, not sentences that are context dependent. For instance, the algorithm cannot distinguish between "Taiwan independence will prevail" and "Taiwan independence is a dead end." As such, only in the case of keywords with unequivocally negative implications (such as Wuhan pneumonia, which directly suggests the origin of the pandemic) will the algorithm exercise shadow banning. Details can be found in Chu et al. (2025) and will not be repeated here.

In summary, in regard to the threats of a platform owned or controlled by a foreign adversary, the U.S. Supreme Court ruling on January 17, 2025, has upheld the theoretical foundation of regulating the D-day threats, and the research by Chu et al. (2025) has validated the existence of everyday content manipulation. Putting together the above-mentioned two threats, legislators in democratic countries may be persuaded to establish regulations. A bigger question is: How does one regulate the platform businesses? This is the focus of the discussion in the next section.

5.7 Remarks on Regulatory Models

Due to the controversy over TikTok's ban by the Trump administration and the subsequent judicial rulings against the White House during 2021–2023, scholars have explored the possible regulatory models that may be applied to the TikTok case. The summary provided in recent papers by Ghosh (2019) and Sitaraman (2022) may be a good start.

5.7.1 Is an Internet Platform Compatible with a Public Utility?

The fundamental perspective of the above-mentioned papers is to classify internet platforms alongside natural monopolies, network industries, and public utilities that have historically been subject to specialized regulations because of their unique dynamics in the economy. Typical examples include banking, communications, power supply, and transportation. If we think of the economy as our body, then these industries function as the aorta network, critical to national security and economic stability. As one can imagine, if some of the aorta industries are controlled by adversary entities, then national security will certainly be compromised. If we believe that the internet platforms belong to the aorta industry, then, almost by definition, they should be regulated by a special set of laws and rules.

The above proposal to treat the internet platform as a special infrastructure industry is a response to some alternative views that were prevalent. The first is termed "tech neoliberal," which proposes the deregulation, privatization, and liberalization of most market sectors, including internet-related platforms.[30] The most critical claim is that "nation-states have no sovereignty in cyberspace." They therefore opposed the banning of TikTok. Sitaraman (2022), however, forcefully objected to this line of reasoning.

The second line of regulatory logic of the platform is referred to as the "national security technocrats." A typical example of such a regulation is related to the Committee on Foreign Investment in the United States (CFIUS). For all foreign direct investments, CFIUS in the U.S. has the power to review whether they should be allowed, or whether additional conditions should be imposed. A key criticism of this approach is

[30] A typical view can be found in Barlow (1996). For a brief history of neoliberalism, see Gerstle (2022).

its case-by-case review process, which gives rise to the following potential harm: (1) The review is firm-based rather than industry-based. Because firms have so many specificities, it is difficult to find general principles from CIFIUS rulings. (2) When the case being reviewed has complicated downstream consequences, it is difficult for the CFIUS board to comprehensively examine it due to each case being considered separately. (3) The review only applies to foreign *investments* and is not applicable to TikTok. The video-sharing platform mainly consists of software and does not involve much investment.

The contribution of Sitaraman (2022) is to propose a paradigm of regulation for internet platforms, where the platforms are treated like an infrastructure industry or a public utility industry, similar to the traditional transportation or banking industries, so that traditional regulatory theories of these industries can be conveniently applied. This proposed paradigm avoids the case-by-case review of the CFIUS and can also embody more specific regulatory measures such as the possible separation of control and ownership, and various reciprocity conditions related to entry approval.

Although the paradigm proposed by Sitaraman is convenient, we note that there are some special features associated with modern internet platforms which are quite different from traditional infrastructures.

5.7.2 *Unique Features of the Internet Platforms*

First, most traditional infrastructure industries typically do not intersect with the freedom of information, whereas many internet platforms do. The regulation of the banking industry does not involve the First Amendment, but regulating TikTok or WeChat does involve curbing the freedom of information. Second, most traditional industries do not collect big data from customers, but internet platforms do. In essence, the possible national security threat of internet platforms originates from the collection of big data, which is different from the "aorta control" threat of the traditional infrastructure. Third, because internet platforms collect users' big data and may use AI to analyze such big data, we see the risk of profiling and individualized penetration. For traditional infrastructures such as transportation, the connection between privacy and national security may be farfetched. The special features of the internet platform industry referred to above make us wonder whether it is really helpful if we try to design regulations to treat the internet platforms as an infrastructure industry.

In addition, internet platforms have a variety of forms, and some traditional regulatory means may not be applicable to some platforms. For instance, consider the e-commerce platforms. The proposed regulatory measure (by Sitaraman, 2022) such as the "separation of ownership and control" poses significant practical challenges. The e-commerce platform itself only involves the information transmission part, but in the background there are complicated issues such as the supply chain management, logistics, franchised production, international shipping, and risk hedging of exchange rate fluctuations, etc. For example, logistics may be related to custom profiles, and the latter are only available from the information databank of the platform. As such, for e-commerce platforms, it is simply impossible to separate the information platform from its physical counterparts.

Finally, we should refresh our understanding of the "mosaic theory of information profiling" referred to in Chapter 3 of this book: each internet platform collects fragmented user data from its users, but if there is an entity capable of aggregating data across various platforms, then this organization will be extremely powerful. In China, in particular, this organization is called the CCP, and it can easily put together information collected from Alibaba, WeChat, TikTok, Alipay, and Baidu, etc. The risk of information fusion across several platforms may not be a threat in democratic countries, but it is a more realistic threat in authoritarian regimes. As such, the regulation of foreign platforms should be considered in a more integrated manner.

5.7.3 Response Strategies on the China Side

A final remark we should make is that the data collection denial is a strategy to be considered only by democratic countries. For authoritarian regimes such as China, it is extremely difficult for Western platforms to establish their business branches. Both Amazon and Google tried, but decided to exit the market due to various obstacles, and we will discuss some cases later in Chapter 6. A general problem faced by Western platforms is indeed internet censoring and the Great Firewall. If Western platforms compromise and agree with China's censoring, they may be criticized by Western media and users. If they do not compromise, then their algorithm will have to go through other hurdles of screening and checking, which seriously decreases the efficiency. If setting up a platform in an authoritarian regime is practically impossible, then big data collection is out of the question.

Furthermore, even if Western platforms can operate in China, do collect the data of millions of Chinese and do implement profiling, it is quite unlikely that these platforms can use such profiled data to engage in D-day or everyday penetration. Again, this is due to the prevalent internet firewalls in China. Uploaded posts that contain "harmful" information will automatically be screened and censored, and in general the penetration success rate will be low. In short, because of the Great Firewall, China does not have to worry about information penetration from liberal democratic countries.

References

Bhagwat, A. (2007). The Test That Ate Everything: Intermediate Scrutiny in First Amendment Jurisprudence. *Illinois Law Review, 3*, 783–838.

Gerstle, G. (2022). *The Rise and Fall of the Neoliberal Order: America and the World in the Free Market Era*. Oxford University Press.

Gerstmann, E., & Shortell, C. (2011). The Many Faces of Strict Scrutiny: How the Supreme Court Changes the Rules in Race Cases. *University of Pittsburg Law Review, 72*(1), 1–52.

Ghosh, D. (2019, May 30). Don't Break Up Big Facebook—Treat It Like a Utility. *Harvard Business Review*. https://hbr.org/2019/05/dont-break-up-facebook-treat-it-like-a-utility

Holoszyc-Pimentel, R. (2015). Reconciling Rational Basis Review: When Does Rational Basis Bite?". *New York University Law Review, 90*, 2071–2117.

Lai, C.-Y., Chen, K.-M., Chen, Y.-C. , Sheen, G. C.-H., Lin, M.-J., Chen, M.-C., Wang, C.-H., & Chu, C. Y. C. (2025). Identifying the Political Manipulation Behind TikTok's Algorithm. mimeo.

Sitaraman, G. (2022). The Regulation of Foreign Platforms. *Stanford Law Review, 74*, 1073–1152.

Spece, Jr. R. G., & Yokum, D. (2015). Scrutinizing Strict Scrutiny. *Vermont Law Review 40*, 285–351.

Supreme Court of the United States. (2025). No. 24–656 (TikTok Inc et al. vs. Merrick B. Garland, Attorney General), and No. 24–657 (Brian Firebaugh vs. Merrick B. Garland, Attorney General) on Applications for the Injunction Pending Review to the United States Court of Appeals for the District of Columbia Circuit.

CHAPTER 6

Cyberspace Trade Barriers

As cited in Chapter 1, Bradford (2023) emphasized the competition between the regulatory models of the U.S., China, and the EU. The battle that Bradford referred to is related to the regulatory aspects of various internet platforms, and the issues involved are mostly privacy, national security, and the possible lack of consumer choices due to platform monopoly by tech giants.

There are, however, several major differences between e-commerce platforms (such as Amazon and Alibaba) and other information-flow platforms (such as Google, Baidu, Facebook, and TikTok). Such differences, as we will show in this chapter, introduce distinct regulatory challenges. First, in the case of e-commerce platforms, there are usually physical commodity purchases, shipments, and payments associated with the platform communications, whereas other information-flow platforms do not have those physical counterparts. Users of such e-commerce platforms can evaluate the services provided and decide whether they want to use these platforms in the future. As such, Paul Romer's (2021) criticism regarding the distortion of the advertisement-based business model may apply to search engine and social media platforms, but does not apply to e-commerce.[1]

[1] See https://news.uchicago.edu/story/nobel-laureate-paul-romer-how-curb-big-techs-power.

C. Y. C. Chu, *An Emerging Digital Wall*,
https://doi.org/10.1007/978-981-95-3577-4_6

Second, for information-flow platforms, it is often the case that citizens in various regulatory domains operate independently. For instance, U.S. and Chinese citizens use Google and Baidu to search in their own respective countries, and in principle, perhaps due to language differences, there are few interactions between users and platforms located in different countries. However, e-commerce platforms often involve cross-country interactions: many citizens of country A may log onto e-commerce platforms in country B and buy goods there, and this constitutes a major part of trade globalization.

Third, when cross-country interactions are involved, "symmetry" becomes important. As Goldfarb and Tucker (2019) pointed out, the crux of the digital economy is the cost reduction (for instance, of acquiring information). However, in the international context, if one country lowers the information cost whereas another country does not do the same, then the asymmetric cost faced by citizens of these two countries will cause serious problems. If U.S. citizens use the Taobao platform very often whereas Chinese are not allowed to use the Amazon platform conveniently, then it is likely to be the case that more goods will be imported from China to the U.S. than in the other direction, and hence a trade deficit (surplus) will result on the U.S. (China) side. This information asymmetry, often termed "cyberspace trade barriers," will be explored in detail in this chapter.

Fourth, while a democratic country such as the U.S. can easily ban a social media platform controlled by a foreign adversary, this platform-denial strategy would be more difficult in the case of e-commerce platforms, mainly because these platforms are rightly related to international trade; denial of the e-commerce platform would be equivalent to outright trade blocking, and its impact is much more complicated.

We start the discussion in this chapter by introducing the general impact of internet blocking on the digital economy.

6.1 China's Economic Benefit from Blocking the Internet

The Internet has created a whole new market for the digital economy, but it has also brought with it a whole new set of challenges related to unfair international competition. The boom in the digital economy already witnessed and anticipated in the future may well propel a mercantilist mindset for some policymakers. A government may thus be incentivized to shield its digital economy from foreign competition, while allowing its own platforms to prey on the more liberal digital market access of foreign countries at the same time. Unlike traditional trade barriers, which are generally applied directly to the object of the transaction (goods or services), the protectionist measures used in the digital economy scenario often come in the form of the imposition of internet censorship or cross-border data flow restrictions.

China is the leading proponent of this (what is often termed) *digital mercantilism*. Indeed, as observed by The *Economist* magazine (August 6, 2016) almost a decade ago:

> *China is a sort of technological Galapagos Islands; a distinct and isolated environment in which local firms flourish. Chinese firms are protected from external competition by government regulation and the Great Firewall. And that protection means that they need not innovate but can thrive by copying business models developed in the West.*

For example, Alibaba was founded in 1999, five years after Amazon; and Baidu was founded in 2000, two years after Google. Despite their earlier establishment, those Western platforms were systematically barred from entering China for the service market therein, thereby creating an environment conducive to the growth of China to nurture its domestic counterparts. The same scenario occurred in regard to search engines, social media, and many other forms of platforms. For a long time, China has been a prime case study in research on digital economic protectionism (Aaronson, 2019; Wu, 2006).

In the above-mentioned story of "copying business models from the West," the key role of the GFW is to make the Chinese version immune to the competition from already-existing foreign platforms, so that the Chinese-version businesses can grow and prosper. In spite of Alibaba being a latecomer relative to Amazon, which is usually detrimental for businesses with a network economy, thanks to the GFW, Amazon was never a threat to Alibaba. When Alibaba gradually grabbed China's domestic market and gained the momentum, the network effect of the platform economy began to consolidate Alibaba's market share in China, and Amazon would no longer be a threat. We understand that the original purpose of the GFW was to block the Chinese people from accessing foreign information, but the collateral consequence was the protectionism that was extended to all kinds of internet platforms. It turns out that this collateral benefit has been a huge surprising reward to the CCP.

Instead of providing a comprehensive analysis of the full range of China's digital mercantilist policies, this chapter will focus on one particularly influential barrier that deters e-commerce access—internet censorship and connection latency. Conceptually and for the purpose of the discussion in this chapter, internet screening or censoring may result in a longer waiting time for each (mouth) click, whereas an internet block refers to the case where the connection waiting time is infinitely long.

There is no doubt that prolonged page load times significantly increase visitor attrition, reducing potential customer engagement. For example, according to a Google survey, 53% of visits are abandoned if a platform site takes more than 3 seconds (hereafter 3 s in short) for readers to see the loaded screen (Google, 2016). Other data show that when the page loading time goes up from 1 to 10 s, the probability of a mobile site visitor "bouncing" (leaving the site being visited) increases by 123% (An, 2017).

Before going further, it might be useful to clarify in advance some of the terminology that we use in this chapter. The terms "e-commerce" and "digital trade" are used interchangeably; both terms refer to their broadest meaning, "any transaction occurring online," and their scope includes transactions in goods, services, and digital content. Similarly, the terms "information" and "data" are also used interchangeably in this chapter, although some researchers tend to treat them as different concepts (Aaronson, 2019).

As pointed out by Chu and Lee (2020), as a general phenomenon, Chinese consumers need to wait a much longer time to connect to foreign websites (if the connections are not bluntly blocked) than foreign consumers to connect to Chinese websites from abroad. These two-way asymmetrical internet speeds are caused by China's censorship of cross-border data flows, known as the GFW. In the literature, there has been very little discussion on the subject of how the GFW affects trade. We will see shortly that this "per-click waiting time" provides us with unique information to calculate the trade distortion brought about by the GFW.

6.2 E-Commerce Advantage Brought About by the GFW

We begin with some market data to provide an overview of the global landscape of e-commerce. The gross domestic product (GDP) and the growth rate figures are from the open database provided by the International Monetary Fund. The figures on household final consumption expenditure (HFCE) are from the World Bank. The e-commerce retail sales data shown here are collected and compiled by Statistica.com, an open-data source containing country-wide e-commerce sales amounts and predicted growth rates. Given the fact that various data become available at different times, the e-commerce and GDP numbers are based on data collected in 2018, whereas the HFCE data are from 2017.

The e-commerce data after 2019 are more varied, mainly because COVID-19 affected transportation as well as the supply chain. During the COVID-19 period, since many crews (of ships and docks) were infected, international transportation was very much disrupted. As international transportation became increasingly risky during the pandemic, people decided to switch from buying and importing from foreign platforms to ordering from domestic e-commerce platforms. This kind of switching may have a long-term effect, because people who are used to certain platform operations and logistics may have become used to this approach, and may not want to switch back after the pandemic. It may therefore take some years before we see what the new equilibrium will look like; for now, we only use the data before 2018, which are summarized in Table 6.1.

6.2.1 The Disproportionate Prosperity of China's E-commerce

As shown in Table 6.1, in the e-commerce business-to-consumer (B2C) retailing sector, it appears that China is the big winner in terms of e-commerce revenue and prosperity. For each country, we have also calculated the corresponding percentage numbers: we have added up the e-commerce amounts of these 10 countries and put the total in the denominator, and the numerator is the corresponding e-commerce revenue of each country. In 2018, China accounted for 40.57% of the total revenue of the top ten e-commerce operating countries, a much bigger share than that of the No. 2 country, the U.S., which accounted for 32.18%.

Table 6.1 Country-wise E-commerce, GDP and HFCE Data

	E-commerce retail revenue ($billion) [a]			*GDP ($billion)* [b]		*HFCE ($billion)* [c]
	2018 (% of 10)	*2023* (% of 10)	*Growth (%)*	*2018* (% of 10)	*Growth (%)*	*2017* (% of 10)
China	636.1 *(40.57)*	1,086.1 *(45.38)*	70.7	13,407.4 *(24.44)*	6.6	4,704.44 *(16.17)*
U.S	504.6 *(32.18)*	735.4 *(30.73)*	45.7	20,494.1 *(37.36)*	2.9	13,321.41 *(45.80)*
Japan	81.7 *(5.21)*	103.6 *(4.38)*	26.8	4,971.9 *(9.06)*	0.8	2,696.81 *(9.27)*
Germany	70.3 (4.48)	95.3 (3.98)	35.6	4,000.4 *(7.29)*	1.5	1,951.97 *(6.71)*
UK	86.5 *(5.52)*	113.6 *(4.75)*	31.3	2,828.6 *(5.16)*	1.4	1,733.55 *(5.96)*
France	49.4 *(3.15)*	71.9 *(3.00)*	45.6	2,775.3 *(5.06)*	1.5	1,396.80 *(4.80)*
Canada	39.9 *(2.54)*	55.4 *(2.31)*	38.8	1,711.4 *(3.12)*	1.8	958.55 *(3.30)*
Russia	17.2 *(1.10)*	24.8 *(1.04)*	44.2	1,630.7 *(2.97)*	2.3	831.57 *(2.86)*
Korea	63.7 *(4.06)*	80.2 *(3.35)*	25.9	1,619.4 *(2.95)*	2.7	736.21 *(2.53)*
Australia	18.6 *(1.19)*	26.9 *(1.12)*	44.6	1,418.3 *(2.59)*	2.8	755.11 *(2.60)*

Notes [a]Statistica, as cited in Orendorff, 2019 at www.shopify.com/enterprise/global-ecommerce-statistics#2. The 2023 data were predicted by Statistica in 2018. [b]The International Monetary Fund DataMapper, *World Economic Outlook, Gross Domestic Product* at: www.imf.org/external/datamapper/datasets/WEO/1. [c]World Bank, *Households and NPISHs Final Consumption Expenditure*, at https://data.worldbank.org/indicator/NE.CON.PRVT.CD

To see whether China's advantage in e-commerce is compatible with its economic capacity, we use some other indexes for the purposes of comparison. As Table 6.1 shows, China's GDP in 2018 accounted for just 24.44% of the above-mentioned ten-country group, a much smaller share of the group total than that of its e-commerce. Given that GDP contains the value-added of all sectors whereas e-commerce mostly consists of household consumption, we also compared the e-commerce figures with the HFCE numbers (i.e., the consumer market sizes). We found that the disproportion is even more obvious, with China's HFCE share accounting for only 16.17% of the group total in 2018. One may suspect that this disproportion may be partly explained by the fact that Chinese consumers shop online more often than they do offline, but the huge discrepancies mentioned above appear to go well beyond what might be expected in response to simple differences in consumer behavior. These figures seem to echo the Galapagos advantage described by the *Economist*, which we cited in the first section of this chapter.

Note that GDP and HFCE include both the goods sector and the services sector. In general, developed economies, such as the U.S. and Japan, have relatively larger services sectors compared with those of the developing economies, such as China. Some may therefore doubt whether it is fair to compare the GDP and the HFCE with the e-commerce retailing sales revenues. It should be noted, however, that the sales revenues from e-commerce retailing include not only the revenues from the sale of goods, but also the revenues from the provision of associated services, such as logistics and e-payment (which are both services). Therefore, at the B2C level at least, the e-commerce retailing sales revenues should serve as a reasonable reference for estimating the overall e-commerce activities (goods and services) within an economy and be comparable with GDP and HFCE.

For business-to-business (B2B) e-commerce, such as the sales of components or parts with clear technical specifications, internet blocking may not constitute a trade barrier as effectively as that for B2C e-commerce. The reason is that for B2B transactions, foreign businesses are sometimes able to set up a branch in the target country and provide the services directly to limited B2B customers therein. This is referred to as mode-3 services (services through foreign affiliates) in international trade practices. We will have a brief discussion on the mode-3 case of Amazon later in this chapter. This mode-3 choice, however, is not always possible. For instance, services in the "social media" and "search engine" categories have never been allowed to compete freely and fairly in China. Google used to have services in China for a while, but withdrew from the market in 2010. As we mentioned, once China's domestic firm (Baidu) has started to enjoy the network effect of the digital economy, it would be very difficult for foreign companies such as Google to penetrate the market. Further discussion on this will be provided in the next section.

As for forecasts, China's e-commerce businesses are expected to grow at a much higher rate than those of any other countries in the list. According to Chu and Lee (2020), it was estimated that, by 2023, China would account for 45.38% of the total revenue of the top 10 most active e-commerce countries. The realized percentage in 2023 is that China accounted for 43.16%, slightly lower than the prediction, perhaps due to COVID-19, as we explained earlier in this section.

The next question one might ask is as follows: Why has China managed to secure such a commanding position in e-commerce business when its GDP accounts for just over 24% of the total of the same ten countries? Does the GFW play any role? If the GFW does play a role, how does it affect the e-commerce activity? How does the digital mercantilism work?

6.2.2 *How Thick and Wide Is the GFW?*

We argue that China's leading position in B2C e-commerce largely stems from its widespread and strict regulation of the cross-border online data flow, or the GFW. As we mentioned, such a regulation was originally intended for political purposes, i.e., preventing the Chinese people from accessing "harmful information." This prevention is not just related to receiving and disseminating, but also to searching and reviewing, on subjects such as the June 4 Tiananmen Square uprising, the Tibet riots, the Uyghur "re-education" camp, and so on. The purpose has been to oppress voices of democracy and to prevent any incidents like the "Arab Spring" (The *Economist*, April 6, 2013) from occurring. Because CCP leaders cannot pre-screen all website content, they resort to comprehensive blocking. This makes it impossible, or at least very difficult, for Chinese people to access foreign websites and platforms.

To give the reader some idea of how broad the "harmful information" may be, we cite the following regulation. Article 5 of Order No. 33 of the Ministry of Public Security of China is entitled "Measures for Security

Protection Administration of the International Networking of Computer Information Networks," which has the following content[2]:

> *No unit or individual shall use international networking to produce, duplicate, search and disseminate the following information: 1) information that instigates the resistance to and disruption of the implementation of the Constitution, laws and administrative regulations; 2) information that instigates the subversion of the state political power and overthrow of the socialist system; 3) information that instigates the splitting up of the country and sabotage of national unity; 4) information that instigates hatred and discrimination among nationalities and sabotages solidarity among nationalities; 5) information that fabricates or distorts facts, spreads rumors and disrupts social order; 6) information that propagates feudalistic superstitions, obscenity, pornography, gambling, violence, murder and terror and instigates crimes; 7) information that openly insults others or fabricates facts to slander others; 8) information that damages the reputation of state organs; and 9) other information that violates the Constitution, laws and administrative regulations.*

Because the prohibited target is information, it goes without saying that anything possibly printed or carrying such information is not allowed to be distributed. Thus, any T-shirt on which a picture of the "Tank Man" standing in Tiananmen Square is printed cannot be sold in China (perhaps violating item 8 above, damaging the reputation of state organs), not to mention books, videos, and magazines. Again, since checking each article contained in a magazine is so time-consuming if not impossible, the electronic content of all suspicious magazines is blocked.

In addition, item 8) is very vague and broad, and hence the internet content to be screened is also very broad. Furthermore, while logically it might make sense to prohibit the duplication and dissemination of harmful information, it does not make any sense to block "search," for without searching and reading, how could anyone possibly know whether the website contains harmful information? In short, in order to guarantee

[2] See Ministry of Public Security Order No. 33 (16 December 1997), at: http://www.dffyw.com/faguixiazai/xzf/201003/20100325213033.htm. Similar standards are adopted by the Internet Illegal Information Reporting Center under the Office of the Central Cyberspace Affairs Commission of China. Please refer to the Internet Illegal Information Reporting Center, "Guidance on Reporting," at: http://www.12377.cn/txt/2018-02/05/content_40215072.htm.

that all such prohibitions are implemented, the internet checks have to be comprehensive and severe. A frequent consequence is outright blocking.

At the same time, however, foreigners are not prevented from accessing Chinese websites. This naturally results in market access asymmetry: it makes it less likely, if not impossible, for Chinese consumers to buy from the platforms of the rest of the world, although it is very convenient for the rest of the world to buy from Chinese platforms. The playing field is thus skewed to the advantage of Chinese e-commerce operators. In short, the access asymmetry of the Internet results in a whole new kind of trade barrier in the digital era.

6.3 How Does a Cyberspace Trade Barrier Work?

As cyberspace trade barriers (CTBs) differ from traditional trade barriers such as tariffs and quotas, we first present a structured comparison to highlight their distinctions between these two kinds of barriers.

Conceptually, any e-commerce transaction in goods can be divided into a series of different stages, as shown in Fig. 6.1. The first stage is a potential buyer acknowledging that an e-commerce platform X does carry commodity A that he or she may want to buy; in the second stage, this potential buyer compares the target commodity A with another competing commodity A' possibly carried on a competing platform Y; the third stage is that, after comparison, the potential buyer places an order for A carried on platform X; the fourth stage is the shipment of the commodity; the fifth stage is the process in the customs, including tariff imposition, and possible sanitary checks; the sixth stage is domestic (or local) logistics; and finally, in the seventh stage, the buyer receives the commodity, and either enjoys it or returns it while possibly filing a complaint.

In the context of traditional trade in goods, barriers to trade most often exist in stages 4 to 6. These usually take the form of high custom taxes, non-tariff barriers, or other harassments. However, these traditional barriers are becoming less and less prevalent, because most countries in the world have joined the WTO, and the tariffs and non-tariff barriers are very low. Besides, given the national treatment rule, countries cannot

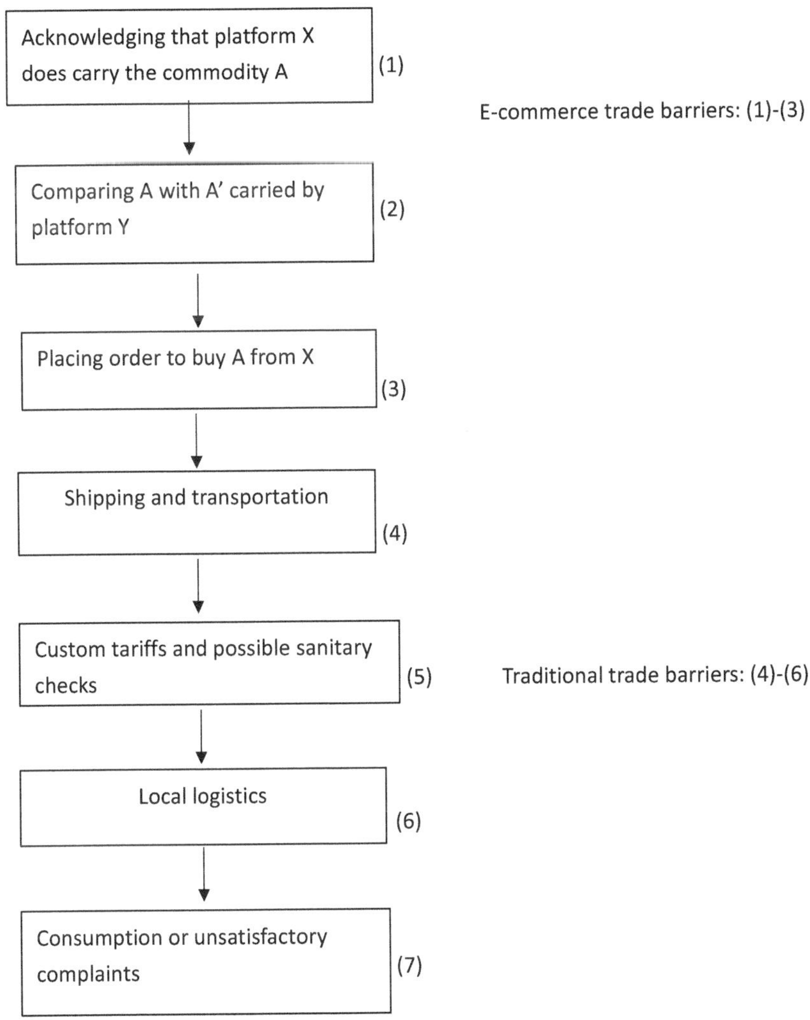

Fig. 6.1 Seven steps to accomplish an e-commerce purchase

discriminate against imported commodities, and hence harassments are nowadays less likely.[3]

In the case of digital trades, however, the barriers are entirely different. Most of these barriers are implemented in the first three stages (1 to 3), and they usually take the form of regulatory measures related to information flow. For example, the Chinese government intervenes in internet traffic, either directly or with the assistance of the internet service providers, to filter online requests and to block access to foreign platforms (which may carry commodities that contain harmful information). Although the same censoring requirements may also apply to domestic platforms, such interventions mostly result in higher marketing, transaction, and administration costs for the foreign e-commerce operators, mainly because Chinese domestic websites are more compliant and are less likely to sell products that violate Chinese laws. Furthermore, it is more difficult for the Chinese government to press charges against foreign websites as opposed to domestic ones. Hence, the access to foreign websites is subject to more censorship and scrutiny. In extreme cases, the foreign operators may face complete exclusion from the Chinese market. Even though Chinese may be able to access foreign websites through VPNs, it is less likely that they will do so simply to purchase goods.

In Fig. 6.1, we identify the first stage of an e-commerce transaction as "acknowledging" the existence of a seller, say, X, which sells commodity A. However, how could this fact "X sells A" be known to any potential buyer? Usually, X either buys an advertisement from a search engine (with the hope that potential buyers may search and then find out the fact that "X sells A"), or X has a social media account which pops up on the page of other users who are also potential buyers. However, if China's domestic potential buyers cannot access the foreign website of X, or cannot access the search engine from which X buys its advertisement (such as Google), there is no way that potential Chinese buyers may acknowledge the existence of X, not to mention knowing whether "X sells commodity A." As such, the potential buyer can never succeed in buying from X. Evidently, this is a very effective trade barrier as not knowing implies not buying.

[3] Of course, things started to change after Trump commenced his second term. On April 2nd, 2025, the White House announced a spectrum of very high "reciprocal tariffs" on imports from almost all countries in the world. References can be found in all media, and hence are skipped here.

Chinese e-commerce businesses, however, face no similar hurdles in most of the foreign markets: citizens in Japan, for instance, can easily access Alibaba's website. Chinese businesses can therefore benefit from the expansion in global e-commerce, and with their protected domestic markets, they will always have an edge on the forthcoming competition.[4] Simply put, the 120 million Japanese citizens can access Alibaba and be potential buyers of Alibaba, whereas the 1.4 billion Chinese citizens cannot access Rakutan.co.jp (because of the internet blocks) and they cannot be potential buyers of Rakutan.

6.3.1 The Broad Spectrum of China's Internet Blocking

China's stringent regulation of the Internet has been a well-known fact, and we are not the first to put forward this argument. According to the reports of the non-governmental organization Freedom House, China has been ranked as the country with the least internet freedom for the tenth consecutive year.[5] According to Freedom House's 2024 report, which cited the watchdog website GreatFire.org, some world-popular news and social media websites (such as Google, Facebook, WhatsApp, YouTube, Flickr, Tumblr, Dropbox, Instagram, SoundCloud, WordPress, and Pinterest) are all blocked by the Chinese government.

As a matter of fact, many small and medium-sized enterprises (SMEs) use some of these social media platforms as their sole connecting window for international sales.[6] Therefore, the blocking of these platforms essentially denies access to such businesses by all of China's 1.4 billion potential consumers. According to the USTR 2020 report to Congress, China has blocked more than 10,000 websites worldwide,[7] and hence the possible

[4] As we showed in Fig. 6.1, in most B2C cases, digital trades start from a potential consumer conducting searches on various platforms or SME websites to find potential suppliers; it is quite unlikely that a potential supplier will conduct searches among billions of potential consumers worldwide to investigate their willingness to buy. For B2B transactions, it is indeed possible for a potential supplier to search among a limited number of potential buyers to initiate a communication for possible transactions. However, in these B2B cases, since potential business buyers are limited, making contact in other ways is always possible, and hence internet blocking has a minor impact. Therefore, in this chapter we focus our discussion on the case of B2C.

[5] See https://freedomhouse.org/country/china/freedom-world/2024.

[6] See Facebook Business case studies at https://www.facebook.com/business/success.

[7] See https://ustr.gov/sites/default/files/2020_National_Trade_Estimate_Report.pdf.

commodity information on these websites is not accessible to people in China.

6.3.2 *Spillover to the Advertisement Industry*

Commercial advertising is another important business-related distortion resulting from the internet blocking. For instance, China's ban on Facebook effectively restricts Chinese consumers from accessing the advertisements published on it. Moreover, because of China's blocking of foreign platforms such as Facebook, foreign businesses seeking exposure in the Chinese market have no choice but to register with the Chinese Facebook-like platforms, such as Weibo. On the other hand, Chinese businesses do not necessarily need to choose to advertise on Facebook to market their goods abroad, because international potential consumers can freely access the Chinese platforms. As such, China's internet blocking provides additional competitive advantages (in advertising revenue) to its local platform businesses compared with foreign ones.

The above concerns have in fact been shared by many WTO members. In 2016, the U.S. first listed China's GFW as a trade barrier (USTR, 2016). In its released trade estimate report, the U.S. places emphasis on the mercantilist dimension of the Chinese internet regulatory regime, accusing China of dominating the domestic market "due in large part to restrictions imposed on foreign companies by the Chinese government" (USTR, 2019). From 2016 to 2024, the USTR repeated this accusation of China's digital trade barrier in each year's annual report.

6.4 Evidence of CTBs: Per-Click Waiting Time

Chu and Lee (2020) conducted a comprehensive field test to see whether connecting from China to the e-commerce platforms in the rest of the world takes about the same time as doing it the other way round, that is, connecting from the rest of the world to China's Taobao. The field test took place in 2018, and the following is a brief summary of the result.

The field tests were conducted using portable computers of similar capacity to ensure that any observed differences were not due to the computers. First, the "per-click waiting time" was defined as "the time lapse since the click until the full webpage is shown on the screen." Three major cities in China (i.e., Shanghai, Shenzhen, and Beijing) were chosen, and the per-click waiting time from China outbound was the average of these three places. There were also 17 countries in the rest of the world that were chosen, including five in Europe (France, Germany, Switzerland, Turkey, and the UK), four in Pan-America (Brazil, Canada, Mexico, and the U.S.) and eight in the Asia-Pacific region (including Australia, Japan, Korea, India, Indonesia, Malaysia, Singapore, and Taiwan).

Chu and Lee (2020) found research assistants worldwide to help them perform the test. In addition, they also conducted remote tests on the websites GreatFire.org, WebSitePulse.com, and WebPageTest.org, where a user can measure the connection speed to a specific URL from China or other locations. The remote test and on-site test outcomes were qualitatively similar, and hence only the on-site test results are reported.

6.4.1 *Test Results of Large Platforms*

As for the comparison of the per-click waiting time for connection, the above-mentioned field tests revealed the following results. First, connecting from large Chinese cities to some of the largest e-commerce retailing platforms in other countries often entails excessively long waiting times, making it impractical for Chinese consumers. For instance, it takes 62 seconds for a click to connect from Beijing to Cdiscount.com of France. If a transaction takes ten clicks to complete (from browsing the home page to check out and payment), 62 seconds per click adds up to a total of 10 minutes and 20 seconds to complete a transaction. This is believed to exceed the tolerance levels of almost all internet users.

Second, despite the fact that the exact numbers of waiting seconds vary across Chinese cities and across destination websites, the long waiting time pattern is the same: in all three cities, it takes a prohibitively long time for Chinese consumers to buy products from e-commerce websites around the world.

Third, if one compares such waiting times with those recorded in New York City, it turns out that the U.S. consumers can buy goods from foreign e-commerce operators much more conveniently than can the Chinese consumers, even though the U.S. is geographically farther away from, say, Malaysia, than is China.

6.4.2 *A Symmetric Reverse Test*

Fourth, some people may suspect that it might be the poor undersea cable capacity which connects China and France that results in the long connection waiting time from China to Cdiscount.com in France, compared with the same access trial from New York to France. To refute such a possible explanation, Chu and Lee also performed a "reverse test": they calculated the waiting time per click from other countries to China's Taobao website, the largest retailing website owned by Alibaba.

Since Internet communications function as two-way highways, systematic disparities in connection speeds between directions should not occur under normal conditions. The field test showed that the waiting times are repetitively longer for connections from China to other countries, than the other way round. This reverse-test evidence shows that the long waiting time for Chinese users is due to China's GFW, and thus the cable capacity conjecture is ruled out.

6.4.3 *Mode-3 Alternative for a Few Large Businesses*

All platforms in foreign countries can hardly avoid China's GFW's blockage, unless it has the capacity to provide a special service solely for Chinese. For example, Amazon once provided a Chinese-version webpage, which could be accessed directly in China, mainly because the webpage had been censored already, and hence the Chinese-access webpage was on "this" side of the firewall. There is no way that one can see the comprehensive and detailed differences between the Chinese Amazon webpage and the worldwide Amazon webpage. However, it was evident that, by 2018, books and T-shirts containing the keyword Tiananmen Square were absent on the Chinese Amazon website, although there are hundreds of items of this type on, say, Amazon.co.uk. Thus, the commodity spectrum limited by the Chinese government still exhibits access asymmetry.

Furthermore, because of the extremely high cost of setting up a special webpage and facilitating its management, most businesses do not have the capacity to access Chinese consumers in this mode-3 way. Hence, other than the rare exception of Amazon, foreign business platforms cannot be seen by the 1.4 billion Chinese. Starting July 16, 2023, Amazon closed its app store service in China anyway.

6.4.4 *A Test of Small and Medium Enterprises (SMEs)*

Finally, to assess whether China's GFW has any impact on the accessibility of SMEs, Chu and Lee referred to Google and the country-specific tour websites to identify the most representative local food items of the country and their corresponding renowned or highly recommended food stores' websites. Of course, it is not usual for cross-border food to be ordered from the website. However, food seems to be a featured product of every country, and hence a comparison is easier to make. The focus is not on ordering a meal from abroad, but on the task of testing the comparative internet accessibility and waiting times. Another advantage of using food as a target of analysis is that food can hardly contain "harmful information"; if it is another general product with some information content that is picked out to perform the comparison, it is possible that the comparison should involve more qualifications.

It turns out that, with only a few exceptions, accessing the websites of foreign SMEs from China is even more difficult than accessing the big e-commerce platforms, and the country-specific waiting time pattern is consistent with the results of the big e-commerce platforms. The general message is clear: Because of the GFW, it is extremely difficult for Chinese to access foreign e-commerce platforms, and the same applies in the case of SMEs.

6.5 Can the WTO Deal with CTBs?

Given the above-mentioned obvious trade barriers, our next question is: Could the WTO deal with this market-access unfairness in e-commerce? Can WTO rules, or the GATS (General Agreement on Trade and Services) rules in particular, address this problem? A quick answer to this question is: No.

6.5.1 *Weak Commitments of the GATS*

Given that the GATS makes no distinction between services supplied online and those supplied offline, theoretically its rules apply to government measures related to e-commerce.[8] However, the structure of the

[8] This is the so-called technical neutrality principle confirmed by WTO Members as well as in a number of cases in the WTO dispute settlement system. See WTO Work Program

GATS limits its ability to provide a systematic solution to the digital mercantilism problem. In the GATS, the provisions related to substantive obligations, such as Articles XVI (Market Access), XVII (National Treatment), and VI (Domestic Regulation), apply only to those service sectors and models under which WTO Members make specific *commitments*. If a WTO Member has not committed itself to payments and money transaction services in its schedule, then the above GATS obligations do not apply. That Member then retains the discretion to impose restrictions on electronic payment services without breaching any WTO obligations.

Most of the existing GATS commitments were the outcome of the Uruguay Round of negotiations during 1986–1993. For countries that joined the WTO after 1995, the commitments were set through individual accession negotiations. In the case of China, e-commerce-related commitments are few. As for the internet blocking and the resulting CTBs, China's defense has been straightforward: internet regulation (including blocking) is a part of state sovereignty, and is not subject to WTO rules.[9]

Note that the earliest platform company Amazon was established in 1994, at which time there was not even the term e-commerce, not to mention related regulations in the WTO. Because a WTO rule amendment needs a consensus of votes, any country which has benefited from the current flawed rules (by imposing a GFW and the CTBs) would not be part of the consensus. So far, the WTO has failed to achieve another round of large-scale services trade negotiations.

Another practical difficulty is the lack of updates of the service classification of the GATS' applicability. As pointed out by Ahmed (2019), almost all WTO Members' Schedules of Commitments under the GATS are based on classifications contained in the provisional version of the United Nations Statistics Division (UNSD)'s Central Product Classification (CPC) system, which was published in 1991.[10] Although the UNSD

on Electronic Commerce—Progress Report to the General Council, S/ L/74 (27 July 1999), para. 4.

[9] See https://advox.globalvoices.org/2011/11/21/china-father-of-gfw-on-internet-sovereignty/.

[10] See WTO, *Services Sectoral* Classification *List*, MTN.GNS/W/120 (10 July 1991).

keeps updating the CPC,[11] most WTO Members have not modified their Schedules accordingly. As a consequence, even some common internet services today, such as search engine services, require special efforts in order to even barely fit into one Member's Schedule, not to mention the newly emerging business models (Wu, 2006). In short, the e-commerce is modern business, whereas the CPC classification still updates at a Stone Age pace.

6.5.2 *Could Other Regulations Apply?*

Another angle from which to see the problem of asymmetry in internet access in China is to raise the following question: Can the market access barriers defined in Article XVI of the GATS be interpreted in a flexible way? Indeed, the overall blockage of a foreign website may be regarded as setting a "zero quota" and thus constitutes the "quota criterion" under Article XVI:2 (a) of the GATS. It is questionable, however, whether a measure causing "very slow" connections (a long waiting time) to foreign websites can be interpreted as violating the quota regulation.

Beyond the GATS, there is little discussion about CTBs under the GATT, which applies only to trade in *goods*, whereas e-commerce is a *service*. In the case where an internet regulatory measure makes it difficult for foreign e-commerce operators to reach domestic consumers and thus to supply the goods, one may be able to interpret it as a prohibition on the importation of goods, thereby violating the GATT.

This argument may have a chance of becoming more viable under the broad interpretation of Article XI of the GATT. In practice, however, a foreseeable challenge for the complainants concerns how to answer some difficult hypothetical questions. For instance, what would the trade volume be if there were no such internet blocking? Logically, answering such "what if" questions is needed to establish a comparison between the trade volume differences with and without the internet blocking. The evidentiary threshold associated with the above "what if" questions is likely to be very high, because it would be difficult to estimate the trade volume that "would have happened." So far, no WTO member has even

[11] The latest version of the CPC (version 2.1) was published in 2015, and is available at: https://unstats.un.org/unsd/classifications/unsdclassifications/cpcv21.pdf (Accessed 29 July 2019).

tried to bring up a complaint along these lines. In the 6th and 7th sections of this chapter, we will try to provide an indirect estimate.

6.5.3 *Could Other Countries Counteract?*

Given China's implementation of the CTBs that it created itself, and given that existing WTO rules do not explicitly prohibit its practices, a pertinent question arises: Can other democratic countries retaliate? The answer is that it is "very unlikely." It is not difficult to understand that the most serious CTBs, such as internet blocking and control, are only possible under an authoritarian regime. Government interventions by restricting information flow are at odds with liberal democratic values, and very likely unconstitutional. Technically speaking, to effectively regulate within the borderless cyberspace, a government needs a big internet policy tool-kit and supreme, even unlimited, power.

Indeed, internet blocking requires the extensive cooperation of all kinds of service providers. For instance, to be able to block some websites' access successfully, the servers must be controlled by operators that are willing to follow government orders. To screen out sensitive word-searches, the search engines must comply with the required search algorithm design. Furthermore, to avoid any risk of the public challenging the government, social media operators must monitor sites regularly and shut down the network as instructed by the government whenever necessary. This scale of compliance is possible only under an authoritarian regime. In terms of Bradford's (2023) classification, neither the market-driven system of the U.S. nor the rights-based EU system could possibly implement such retaliations.

To encourage internet operators to cooperate with the regulator, an authoritarian government often grants network-related privilege status to those that comply. Such grants are reviewed and renewed periodically to ensure the continuous compliance of the operators. This periodic review of franchises constitutes an incentive plan to motivate business cooperation. Thus, the government's franchise review and the business' cooperation form a symbiotic system of internet control. In democratic countries, internet facilities and platform businesses are usually not franchised by the government. Furthermore, even if they are franchised, the periodic review system in democratic countries can hardly be manipulated by officials.

6.5.4 What Kinds of E-commerce Rules Are Acceptable?

It is well understood that every country has sovereignty when it comes to regulating data flows. However, the problem is that if all governments allow their sovereignty to expand to be as broad as that of China, then we are back to the Stone Age of mercantilism, and there is hardly any level playing field for e-commerce. Are there some rules that can be accommodated to effectively remove the CTBs? Here we provide some articles in modern free-trade agreements as reference.

To mitigate CTBs, a global standard that prohibits unjustified restrictive measures on cross-border online data flows should be established. Certain FTAs in recent years, such as the CPTPP and the USMCA, have already incorporated rules to this effect.

For example, Article 14.11 of the CPTPP provides that:

> *1) The Parties recognize that each Party may have its own regulatory requirements concerning the transfer of information by electronic means. 2) Each Party shall allow the cross-border transfer of information by electronic means, including personal information, when this activity is for the conduct of the business of a covered person. 3) Nothing in this Article shall prevent a Party from adopting or maintaining measures inconsistent with paragraph 2 to achieve a legitimate public policy objective, provided that the measure:*
> *- is not applied in a manner which would constitute a means of arbitrary or unjustifiable discrimination or a disguised restriction on trade; and*
> *- does not impose restrictions on transfers of information greater than are required to achieve the objective.*[12]

Item 2) of this article clearly states that no country can block an information flow when the activity is for the conduct of business. In addition, item 3) states that no measure should be more than necessary so that it effectively restricts the trade. Unfortunately, the above article is unlikely to be accepted by authoritarian countries. For authoritarian regimes, as we have mentioned, internet censoring is mainly for political purposes: to sustain control and to prevent threats of harmful information. The e-commerce mercantilism is just a collateral consequence. The political decision regarding internet blocking is made first, and business operations can only be adjusted accordingly.

[12] The comprehensive contents are available at: https://www.mfat.govt.nz/assets/Trans-Pacific-Partnership/Text/14.-Electronic-Commerce-Chapter.pdf.

6.6 The Empirical Impact of CTBs: An Assessment Framework

We mentioned in the previous discussion that quantifying the impact on the trade amount with and without the CTBs is difficult. The primary available metric for evaluation is an international comparison of per-click waiting times, which serves as a proxy for digital accessibility and information-flow efficiency. How can we use this information to come up with a trade volume impact assessment? For example, if the per-click waiting time from the U.S. to China is 2 s, and that from China to the U.S. is 15 s, can we estimate how much of the trade amount has been reduced by this 13 s difference? In this section, we try to implement this assessment based on an economic model and some generally accepted assumptions in the literature.

The model we are to use for our empirical assessment builds upon Krugman (1979). We extend Krugman's model to encompass a trade environment that explicitly addresses the complexities introduced by e-commerce.

6.6.1 *Essence of the Model*[13]

For demonstration purposes, here we present a scenario in which there are only two countries in the world, the U.S. and China. Within each country, production is categorized into two distinct modes, either a brick-and-mortar mode or an e-commerce mode. Note that we need at least two countries to conduct the international trade, and we need at least two modes to assess the impact of trade barriers on e-commerce; that is, when one mode faces trade barriers, the other mode can play the role of a substitute. As such, this is the simplest framework for a meaningful assessment.

In each country, we assume for simplicity that the labor force constitutes the primary input for production activities. This labor endowment is distributed across the various producers in both the brick-and-mortar and e-commerce sectors, and labor is freely mobile across modes of production, but immobile across countries. The marginal cost of producing a specific variety by a producer is proportional to the wage rate, and the proportions are parameters to be estimated.

[13] Part of this subsection is excerpted from a working paper of mine, Chu et al. (2025).

Transporting goods between countries involves additional costs, modeled here as iceberg trade costs. That is, goods transported abroad are like icebergs, which melt a little in the transportation process, so that the unit cost of the commodity may become slightly inflated. Specific modeling is provided in a technical appendix toward the end of this book.

6.6.2 *Trade Frictions*

Beyond conventional transportation costs, there are also the trade frictions, which include regulatory, institutional, and technological barriers. The friction between country i and country n for goods produced in mode m, denoted $d_n^{m,i}$, is decomposed into three key components:

$$d_n^{m,i} = G_n^i \times P_n^m \times T_n^{m,i}$$

In the above setting, first, G_n^i represents costs related to geographic constraints that impact the flow of goods between countries i and n. Second, P_n^m denotes production-mode-specific friction. For example, in the context of e-commerce, this might include longer or shorter delivery times and the associated waiting costs, which differ from those encountered in traditional brick-and-mortar transactions.

Neither G_n^i nor P_n^m is our focus; we just need these two parameters to capture the realistic environment. Our focus is on the last term, where $T_n^{m,i}$ signifies institutional barriers, which are regulatory and policy-driven constraints imposed by country n on imports from country i depending on the mode of production m. The term $T_n^{m,i}$ includes regulations, red tape and, in particular, the CTBs for the e-commerce mode. CTBs make the connection to e-commerce platforms very difficult and increase the cost of buying. Specifically, when n refers to China, i refers to the U.S. and m refers to e-commerce, $T_n^{m,i}$ should be particularly high. Together, these components comprehensively model the multifaceted nature of trade frictions that influence international economic interactions.

6.6.3 *Equilibrium and Calibration*

Given the above setting, the invisible hand will allocate labor resources to various production modes and commodities, and an equilibrium is achieved when the labor market is cleared. The full equilibrium conditions are specified in the Technical Appendices toward the end of this monograph.

For our analysis, particular attention is given to China and the U.S.. To conduct robust counterfactuals, we require specific data that capture the economic interactions between these two countries under different trade modes. Essential data points include the expenditure shares of each country on different countries and modes, accounting for a total of eight distinct moments (2 modes, brick-and-mortar and e-commerce; two countries, the U.S. and China; and two directions of imports/exports).

To calculate these data moments, we need to amalgamate various data sources. Key datasets include global e-commerce revenue by countries for 2022, detailed retail e-commerce sales projections in the U.S. from 2014 to 2025, and revenue statistics for the U.S. e-commerce industry extending to 2027. For China, we utilize data on the proportion of e-commerce in total retail sales from 2014 to 2022 and forecasts for the B2B cross-border e-commerce market size through 2025. Furthermore, we consider the distribution of domestic and cross-border e-commerce revenues by country for 2023. Complementing these e-commerce-specific datasets, the OECD input–output table from 2018 onwards provides foundational economic variables that help in understanding cross-country economic flows and incomes.

In our counterfactual analysis of removing institutional frictions affecting foreign e-commerce in China, we adopt some simplifying assumptions. First, we assume symmetry in geographic barriers, indicating that the obstacles to trade in terms of distance, transportation costs, and related geographic factors are roughly the same in both directions. Second, we assume that there are no mode-specific frictions for brick-and-mortar products in either country, and that no country imposes institutional burdens on its own domestic production. Third, we assume that the U.S. as a democratic country does not impose any institutional burdens on imports regardless of their origin or mode of production ($T^{m,i}_{\text{USA}} = 1$), where the mode m can be either brick-and-mortar or e-commerce. Conversely, China does not apply institutional burdens to brick-and-mortar imports ($T^{b,i}_{\text{CHN}} = 1$); however, there is indeed a CTB ($T^{e,i}_{\text{CHN}} > 1$). Using the above simple specification, we are able to estimate the impact of cyberspace trade barriers. Note that these assumptions are not restrictive; they only affect the interpretation. For instance, the estimated e-commerce trade friction is *relative* to that in the brick-and-mortar sector.

6.6.4 Assessing the Numerical Index of CTBs

The empirical assessment that we are to calculate is as follows. If China's CTBs were to be removed, to what extent would the equilibrium change? A key element in our analysis is to use the "per-click waiting time" data to infer the percentage of e-commerce that has vanished because of the bouncing of potential customers.

From Chu and Lee (2020), the average waiting time for Chinese internet users to visit Chinese websites is 0.87 seconds, and the average waiting time for Chinese users to visit US websites is 14.57 seconds. Given the above setting, we show in the Appendix that.

$$T_{\mathrm{CHN}}^{e,\mathrm{USA}} = \log(396.7) \times (P_{\mathrm{CHN}}^{e} - 1) = 2.636\,.$$

This value of 1.636 (=2.636–1) is analogous to China imposing a 163.6% tariff on all U.S. e-commerce. This implies a substantial barrier to market entry for U.S. e-commerce platforms, making it significantly more expensive and less competitive for them to operate in China.

6.6.5 Effect of Removing the CTBs

The counterfactual scenario is to calculate the potential changes in the trade flow and market dynamics if China were to eliminate its institutional barriers against U.S. e-commerce. The quantified measure of friction allows us to simulate the economic outcomes.

To assess the economic impact of removing China's institutional frictions on foreign e-commerce, we first assume constant productivity across all modes of production, ensuring that any changes observed in the economic equilibrium are attributable solely to variations in institutional trade barriers rather than shifts in productivity levels.

Recall that for e-commerce directed toward China from the U.S., the original trade friction is given by $d_{\mathrm{CHN}}^{e,\mathrm{USA}} = G_n^i \times P_n^m \times T_n^{m,i}$. In this counterfactual experiment, we assume that $G_{\mathrm{CHN}}^{\mathrm{USA}}$ and P_{CHN}^{e} remain as in the baseline, while $T_{\mathrm{CHN}}^{e,\mathrm{USA}}$ is reduced from its original value of 2.636 to 1. This reduction indicates that the waiting time for connecting to U.S. websites from China is the same as the waiting time for connecting to Chinese websites from the U.S., simulating an environment in which China imposes no additional institutional barriers on foreign e-commerce.

The relative change in e-commerce trade friction from the U.S. to China is therefore given by:

$$\frac{\left(G_{\mathrm{CHN}}^{\mathrm{USA}}\right)\left(P_{\mathrm{CHN}}^{e}\right)\bullet 1}{\left(G_{\mathrm{CHN}}^{\mathrm{USA}}\right)\left(P_{\mathrm{CHN}}^{e}\right)\left(T_{\mathrm{CHN}}^{e,\mathrm{USA}}\right)} = \frac{1}{T_{\mathrm{CHN}}^{e,\mathrm{USA}}}.$$

For domestic e-commerce within China, the trade friction remains unchanged. This adjustment effectively normalizes trade conditions for e-commerce, reflecting an environment of more open digital trade. Using these assumptions, we recalculated the necessary equilibrium wage adjustments that would maintain all model equilibrium conditions in this scenario of reduced trade frictions.

6.7 Empirical Results

As we will see shortly, our findings clearly demonstrate that both the U.S. and China stand to gain economically from the removal of China's e-commerce barriers, with China experiencing a slightly greater relative benefit. This suggests that policy liberalization in the realm of e-commerce can serve as significant leverage for economic growth, enhancing consumer welfare and stimulating business activities in the digital sector. This prediction is very much consistent with the traditional positive effect of removing trade barriers.

The impact of removing the barriers of the GFW on Chinese e-commerce is illustrated in Table 6.2. The results reveal a remarkable increase of 1518.873% in the trade share of U.S. e-commerce exports to China, indicating a substantial effect of market opening. The removal of institutional barriers on U.S. e-commerce has granted U.S. digital platforms and sellers better access to Chinese consumers, potentially driving a boost in U.S. revenues. By contrast, the brick-and-mortar sector shows a different trend: U.S. brick-and-mortar exports to China have declined by 66.465%. This decline suggests that Chinese consumers are shifting their spending toward the relatively cheaper and more accessible options provided by e-commerce, a shift largely influenced by the reduced barriers that have enhanced e-commerce's appeal over traditional brick-and-mortar purchases.

Table 6.2 Changes in Trade Shares after the Removal of Chinese CTBs

Exporter	*E-Commerce*		*Brick-and-Mortar*	
	USA (%)	*CHN*	*USA*	*CHN*
$100 \times \left(\hat{\pi}^{m,i}_{\text{USA}} - 1\right)$	− 6.116	+ 146.016	− 6.116	+ 146.016
$100 \times \left(\hat{\pi}^{m,i}_{\text{CHN}} - 1\right)$	+ 1518.873	− 12.123	− 66.465	− 12.123

The barrier removal has also triggered general equilibrium effects that are reshaping the relative nominal wages between the U.S. and China. In equilibrium, U.S. nominal wages have increased by 27.231% relative to those in China. This wage increase has made U.S.-produced goods relatively more expensive for consumers, directly impacting expenditure patterns. For U.S. consumers, whose trade costs remain unaffected by the changes in purchasing modes, this wage rise has shifted expenditure shares toward goods produced in China, as U.S. goods become costlier in comparison. In addition, the wage change is also giving rise to welfare changes. It turns out that the welfare in the U.S. increased by 1.59%, which translates into an economic gain of approximately $404.95 billion based on the 2022 GDP figures. In China, the welfare improvement has been even more substantial at 3.28%, which is equivalent to an economic benefit of about $589.84 billion. The overall welfare gain across both countries totals approximately $994.78 billion.

In China's market, heightened competition from e-commerce has generally reduced expenditure shares on brick-and-mortar purchases. Within the brick-and-mortar sector, the higher relative U.S. wage has exacerbated the effect, making U.S. brick-and-mortar goods even more costly than their Chinese counterparts. Consequently, the decline in expenditure shares is more pronounced for U.S. brick-and-mortar imports (−66.465%) compared to Chinese brick-and-mortar products (−12.123%). Overall, the interaction between reduced e-commerce barriers, shifts in wage dynamics, and the relative cost competitiveness of each mode significantly influences the evolving trade patterns between the U.S. and China.

The summarized data in Table 8.2 provide a concise quantitative foundation for analyzing the broader impacts of such regulatory changes on global trade dynamics, offering insights into the immediate financial and strategic outcomes of policy liberalization in China. Despite the above economic gains, we should repeat a caveat: in China, the policy calculus is primarily driven by political considerations rather than economic efficiency; it is the political impact on the CCP's decision-making framework that prioritizes control over digital information flows. It may be inferred that a 3.28% increase in welfare must be lower than the CCP's expected political cost of lifting the GFW.

6.8 A Trilemma of the World Economy

Our analysis of removing cyberspace trade barriers (CTBs) highlights the substantial economic implications of China's digital restrictions. However, the prospect of China dismantling its cyberspace regulations remains highly improbable. According to Acemoglu and Robinson (2017), authoritarian elites inherently resist reforms that threaten their entrenched privileges; they prioritize regime stability over economic efficiency. Furthermore, the notion that political institutions are adaptable is fundamentally incompatible in Leninist party-state systems such as China. In these regimes, political structures dictate the permissible scope of market mechanisms, rather than market forces shaping institutional flexibility. Indeed, when China asserts that it has a "socialist market economy," it means that the CCP has transformed the Western market economy into a different species.

Our analysis in this chapter yields three critical insights from the above discussions: (1) China is unlikely to dismantle its cyberspace trade barriers, as the Great Firewall (GFW) remains essential for maintaining Leninist political control. (2) The cyberspace trade barriers distort global competition by disadvantaging democratic countries (which do not have internet blocks) and have significant empirical consequences. (3) The current WTO rules are ill-equipped to address these digital trade distortions, and democratic countries face structural limitations in formulating effective countermeasures.

In summary, the GFW as a trade barrier has consolidated the digital economy in China, making most Chinese more accustomed to their domestic platforms such as Baidu, Weibo, WeChat, and Alibaba. Once they are used to the convenience of such domestic platforms, they are essentially locked in, and less likely to switch to Western alternatives. The related digital economic activities are therefore dichotomized.

This scenario closely aligns with a "trilemma of the world economy" as mentioned by Dani Rodrik,[14] which posits that democracy, national sovereignty, and global economic integration are mutually incompatible. Societies can uphold any two of these three principles, but achieving all three simultaneously remains elusive. Our e-commerce discussion in this chapter seems to be a typical interpretation of this trilemma.

References

Aaronson, S. A. (2019). What Are We Talking About When We Talk About Digital Protectionism? *World Trade Review, 18*(4), 541–577.

Acemoglu, D., & Robinson, J. A. (2017). *The Emergence of Weak, Despotic and Inclusive States*. NBER Working Paper 23657.

Ahmed, U. (2019). The Importance of Cross-border Regulatory Cooperation in an Era of Digital Trade. *World Trade Review, 18*(S1), S99–S120.

An, D. (2017). *Find out how you stack up to new industry benchmarks for mobile page speed*. Think with Google. www.thinkwithgoogle.com/marketing-resources/data-measurement/mobile-page-speed-new-industry-benchmarks/

Bradford, A. (2023). *Digital Empires: The Global Battle to Regulate Technologies*. Oxford University Press.

Chu, C. Y. C., & Lee, P.-C. (2020). E-commerce Mercantilism: Practices and Causes. *Journal of International Trade Law and Policy, 19*(1), 51–66.

Chu, C. Y. C., Yang, H., & Chang, J.-J. (2025). *Cyberspace Trade Barriers*. Academia Sinica working paper.

Goldfarb, A., & Tucker, C. (2019). Digital Economics. *Journal of Economic Literature, 57*(1), 3–43.

Google. (2016). *Mobile site load time statistics*. www.thinkwithgoogle.com/data/mobile-site-load-time-statistics/

Krugman, P. R. (1979). Increasing Returns, Monopolistic Competition, and International Trade. *Journal of International Economics, 9*(4), 469–479.

USTR. (2016). *The 2016 National Trade Estimate Report*. https://ustr.gov/sites/default/fiav/2016-NTE-Report-FINAL.pdf.

USTR. (2019). *The 2019 National Trade Estimate Report on Foreign Trade Barriers*. https://ustr.gov/sites/default/files/2019_National_Trade_Estimate_Report.pdf.

Wu, T. (2006). The World Trade Law of Censorship and Internet Filtering. *Chicago Journal of International Law, 7*(1), 263–287.

[14] See https://rodrik.typepad.com/dani_rodriks_weblog/2007/06/the-inescapable.html.

CHAPTER 7

Blockchain Applications as Digital Networking

Prior to the November 6, 2024, U.S. Presidential election, then-candidate Donald Trump announced his plan to establish a "bitcoin reserve for the U.S."[1] According to the *Newsweek* report, before Trump's 2025 inauguration the U.S. government already held an estimated 200,000 Bitcoins (BTCs), valued at approximately $19 billion by the end of 2024. This reserve primarily originated from Bitcoin assets confiscated in criminal investigations. Trump's plan aimed to acquire up to 200,000 BTC annually over 5 years, potentially accumulating 1 million BTCs—equivalent to approximately 5% of Bitcoin's total supply, which will be 21 million, estimated to be achieved by the year 2140 (to be explained shortly). These BTC holdings would be integrated into the U.S. Federal Reserve and managed by the U.S. Department of the Treasury.

Several years earlier, in October 2019, Chinese President Xi Jinping emphasized the strategic significance of blockchain technology, stating: "We must take the blockchain as an important breakthrough for independent innovation of core technologies, define the primary development direction, increase investment, and accelerate the development of blockchain technology." Xi's speech delivered a strong signal that the Chinese government will support and devote more resources to this area.

[1] See https://www.newsweek.com/what-donald-trumps-strategic-bitcoin-reserve-could-look-like-1986360.

C. Y. C. Chu, *An Emerging Digital Wall*,
https://doi.org/10.1007/978-981-95-3577-4_7

According to Forbes,[2] a cornerstone of China's blockchain strategy is the Blockchain-based Service Network (BSN) launched in 2020. The BSN provides a government-regulated infrastructure for blockchain developers, enabling multi-chain application development under state supervision. The news report said that the Chinese system will have two versions: one for users inside China and another for international developers.

The same reference also noted that in March 2021, the Chinese government formally incorporated blockchain development into its national strategy with the approval of the "14th Five-Year Plan" (2021–2025). This official plan includes blockchain industry development initiatives for 29 provinces and cities across the country, which also showed China's ambition to increase its global competitiveness in this area.

As blockchain technology serves as the foundation for most cryptocurrencies, both the U.S. and China have prioritized blockchain innovation: blockchain technologies in general and cryptocurrencies as an application in particular. In addition, since China plans to establish its technology-leading role for international developers, it raises the natural question of how China's blockchain technology may affect the U.S.'s response policies. This chapter will explain the content of the blockchain technology and discuss the deployment differences between China and the U.S.

7.1 What Is the Blockchain and the Bitcoin?

A blockchain is a sequential chain of blocks; each block is composed of several transaction or activity records. Conceptually, these blocks function as decentralized ledgers. These ledgers are usually shared by multiple entities, and they are often called diversified ledgers. After these records are verified through some process (to be explained shortly), they are encrypted by a hash number and broadcasted to all peers. When there are thousands of entities owning and viewing the same records, one can perceive that these records can hardly be manipulated.

[2] See https://www.forbes.com/sites/digital-assets/2024/10/08/china-bets-on-massive-blockchain-infrastructure/.

7.1.1 *Encrypted Transaction Records*

The hash numbers mentioned above are generated by a hash function.[3] This mathematical function has the following property: When a transaction record is fed in, the hash function will generate a fixed-length alphanumeric output. Generally speaking, such a hash function generates an encrypted version of the transaction record. Intuitively, one can think of the hash function as a fruit blender, and different fruit inputs generate distinct juices. The Bitcoin, for instance, uses the SHA-256 hash function, which can generate outputs with 2^{256} combinations. This number is super big ($2^{256} \approx 1.15 \times 10^{77}$), and any record going through the hash function would have a one-to-one hash number as the corresponding output.

Once a pack of records are ready to be verified, they will be broadcasted to peers. The peers are potential validators, and in the case of Bitcoins they are called "miners," who are responsible for the operation of the platform. For blockchain applications such as Bitcoins, there is a competition process to become a validator, and the process may be different for different blockchains. The mechanism for Bitcoins is called "proof of work," and some other blockchains use a "proof of stake" mechanism.

The Proof of Work (PoW) mechanism operates as follows. Miners compete to solve a complex cryptographic puzzle, a process that demands significant computational power and energy consumption. The miner that is the fastest at solving the puzzle will be authorized to do the verification of the records in the block, and obtain some Bitcoins in return as a reward. The transaction record after being verified will be added to the originally existing blockchain and form a new chain. This is like what we do in emails: reply, re-reply, re–re-reply, and so on, with increasing data length. This new chain will be broadcasted to all the miners, and each one will have a revised version of the encrypted records. For proof of stake, the mechanism chooses validators based on the number of staked cryptocurrencies that they have. Our later discussion will focus more on Bitcoins, and hence skip much of the discussion on proof of stake.

[3] One can conduct a search on "online hash calculator" to find how such hash numbers are generated.

7.1.2 *Diversified and Unalterable Ledgers*

As of November 2024, according to the statistics, there were about 200,000 Bitcoin miners in the world,[4] and each maintains a copy of the distributed ledger. Because there are so many peers who have the same copy of the records, it is almost impossible to change the records. Furthermore, since for Bitcoins new records are added to the old one without deleting the old one, the length of the chain grows with time. This makes it even more difficult to change the records, because changing a single block at any time t must also change the subsequent series after time t. Since the records are held, verified, revised, and broadcasted by a large number of diversified operators or miners, the block chain is often referred to as a *decentralized* ledger system. This is in contrast to the centralized record system, such as the physical banking system we are familiar with. In the traditional banking system, the bank manager plays the centralized role who coordinates (and of course may also delegate) the various jobs of holding, revising, and verifying our records.

Once the records are encrypted, how do stakeholders access their own transaction data? In essence, they can decrypt the encrypted codes using their private keys. Blockchain security methods include the use of cryptography. There are two keys in the system: a *public key* is a long and random-looking string of numbers, which serves as the address on the blockchain. A *private key* is like a password that gives the account owners access to their digital records and to interact with the various activities (such as transactions) that the blockchain platform supports. Bitcoin is a popular coin used in blockchain transactions, and the second most popular one is Ether, which works with its corresponding blockchain named Ethereum.

The first decentralized blockchain was conceptualized in 2008 by an individual (or group) Satoshi Nakamoto in 2008, whose real identity, however, was never confirmed. Nakamoto enhanced blockchain architecture by implementing cryptographic hash functions, and by introducing a difficulty adjustment mechanism to stabilize the rate at which blocks are added to the chain. This mechanism controls the difficulty associated

[4] See https://www.google.com/search?q=bitcoin%2C+number+of+miners&oq=bitcoin%2C+number+of+miners&gs_lcrp=EgZjaHJvbWUyBggAEEUYOTIGCAEQABgeMgoIAhAAGIAEGKIEMgoIAxAAGIAEGKIEMgoIBBAAGIAEGKIEMgoIBRAAGIAEGKIE0gEKMTE1NDNqMGoxNagCCLACAQ&sourceid=chrome&ie=UTF-8.

with solving the puzzle by miners: a more difficult puzzle takes longer to solve, and hence the time taken to generate new Bitcoins is longer. As of the time of writing, it takes about 10 minutes to solve the puzzle and to create a new block, and then to add it to the old blockchain. Because new Bitcoins are created only when a new block is formed, the corresponding increasing rate of Bitcoin creation is also controlled by the above-mentioned mechanism setting. The Nakamoto design began to be implemented by 2009, and he has been a core proponent of the cryptocurrency. This decentralized ledger design was well-received by a large number of people partly because of the 2008–2009 financial tsunami, which was blamed as an outcome of a distorted and centralized banking system. Nakamoto's decentralized design was claimed and believed to be a persuasive alternative.

7.1.3 *Exponentially Growing File Size*

According to Wikipedia, as of August 2014, the Bitcoin blockchain—which maintains a record of all historical transactions—had grown to 20 GB. In January 2015, the size had grown to roughly 30 GB. From January 2016 to January 2017, the Bitcoin blockchain grew from 50 to 100 GB in size. The ledger size had exceeded 200 GB by early 2020. By November 2024, according to Statistica, Bitcoin's blockchain size was close to reaching 5,450 GB, as the database saw exponential growth by nearly one gigabyte every few days. After President Trump's endorsement of the Bitcoin in 2024, the ledger size is expected to grow even faster.

One of the chief characteristics of the Bitcoin is its limited coin supply. Bitcoin's creator, Satoshi Nakamoto, intentionally designed the cryptocurrency with a fixed supply cap of 21 million. At the time of writing, there have been 19,997,837.5 coins circulating outside.[5] Given the total coin cap, its scarcity increases over time, which in turn is believed to cause its price to appreciate. As we mentioned, new Bitcoins are added to the Bitcoin supply approximately every 10 minutes. With the supply cap approaching, the reward to miners is designed to decrease over time, so as to reduce the miners' incentives.[6] Eventually, miners will be rewarded

[5] The number at each moment can be checked at https://bitbo.io/how-many-bitcoin/.

[6] See https://www.investopedia.com/tech/what-happens-bitcoin-after-21-million-mined/.

only by fees, rather than new Bitcoins. The estimated termination date, according to Investopedia,[7] is 2140. It has been suspected that this "coin cap" was designed to prevent the Bitcoin from depreciation. Currency depreciation is often a criticism leveled against a centralized "money-printing authority." Indeed, anything with a supply cap is unlikely to have a steady price depreciation, but limited supply per se does not have anything to do with price fluctuations, as we will explain below.

7.2 Problems with Cryptocurrencies

Despite the fact that the cryptocurrencies emanating from the blockchain technology, especially the Bitcoin and Ether, are popular among many people, mainstream economists have always been skeptical about them. In this section, we introduce some of the major criticisms of Bitcoins. Our purpose here is to explain the differences between the blockchain as a technology of information science and the cryptocurrency as an investment target, before we move on to explain why superpowers are enthusiastic to dominate the games.

7.2.1 Price Fluctuations of Bitcoins

In Fig. 7.1, we depict the historical prices of Bitcoin from 2009 to 2024, covering a period of almost 15 years.[8] Upon its launch, Bitcoin had no initial market value in 2009. By October 2010, its price started to rise, and reached $0.30 by the end of 2010. By 2011, Bitcoin surpassed $1, peaking at $29.60 in June, before experiencing a steep decline to $5 by year-end. Note that this increase from $0.10 to $29.60 represents a staggering 29,500% appreciation. Starting from 2012, its price began to rise, but again experienced a big drop by the middle of 2014. From 2015 onward, the Bitcoin price revealed a generally rising pattern, still with fluctuations, and reached $96,833.37 at the time of writing (November 21, 2024). If we compare its initial price of $0.1 with its current price of around $100,000, then its appreciation rate is almost an astonishing one million times. In 2014, it also experienced a 10 time drop in about 6 months. Whatever scale is used, Bitcoin prices are extremely volatile.

[7] https://www.investopedia.com/tech/how-much-worlds-money-bitcoin/.

[8] https://www.investopedia.com/articles/forex/121815/bitcoins-price-history.asp.

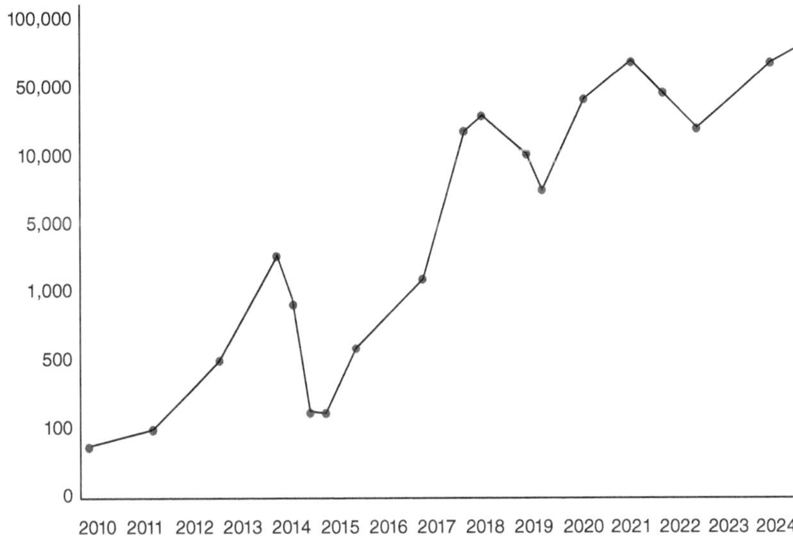

Fig. 7.1 Price History of Bitcoin. *Source*: Investopedia

We understand that all asset prices in a market economy are determined by demand and supply. With Bitcoin's supply remaining stable, both due to its fixed total cap and its predictable issuance rate every 10 minutes (when new blocks are created), its price volatility is primarily driven by demand-side factors. So, what is so special about Bitcoin's demand, compared with, say, the demand for the stock shares of Qualcomm or Apple? We make this comparison because for companies such as Apple, most of the time their total stock shares are also quite stable, unless new shares are issued.

For the stock shares of companies such as Apple, given any price, people are more willing to buy the share if they expect that there will be more profit to be generated by the company. These future profit expectations often have substantive reasons. For instance, Apple may have acquired a new battery plant so that the provision of batteries in its cellphones is expected to be more secure; or an assembly factory in Asia has had serious conflicts with local labor, so that some proportions of future production and sales are expected to be compromised. Factors that are related to such substantive incidents are called *fundamentals*. Other than such fundamentals, of course, there are variations in individual expectations related to various factors, which we call *speculations*. Both these fundamental and speculation factors contribute to the demand for the Apple share in the stock market, and the equilibrium price of Apple stock is jointly determined by these demand and supply forces.

As described in Biais et al. (2023), the fundamentals are to the stock just like the "anchor" is to a ship: they pretty much determine the position range of a ship. Although currents and strong winds can cause the ship to drift here and there on the ocean, the anchor will limit the range of the ship's movements. Technically, Biais et al. (2023) showed that the time-t Bitcoin price, denoted as p_t, is determined by

$$p_t = \frac{1}{1 + r_t} E_t(K_{t+1} \bullet p_{t+1}, F_{t+1}),$$

where (with time-subscript t) r_t is the risk-free interest rate at time t, E_t is the expectation operator at time t, K_{t+1} is a time-dependent parameter, and F_{t+1} is a variable in period-$(t + 1)$. For a company such as Apple, F_{t+1} refers to its fundamentals, which are related to substantive causes, and are independent of the company's stock price. By contrast, for Bitcoins, there are no fundamental factors but only speculations. This results in its price dynamics being solely determined by speculation. Thus, in the case of Bitcoins, it will make the above equation generate a very volatile equilibrium price series of p_t.

Since Bitcoin lacks traditional fundamental value, its demand is largely driven by speculative expectations—meaning that investors' demand for Bitcoins would be higher when they anticipate higher future prices. Robert Shiller (2019), recipient of the 2013 Nobel Prize in Economics, coined the term "narrative economics" to describe markets where asset prices are predominantly driven by speculation rather than intrinsic value. In this case, the role of fundamentals vanishes, and the price is determined solely by "story-telling." In Shiller's terminology, the Bitcoin is just "an interesting experiment."[9]

[9] https://www.weforum.org/stories/2018/01/robert-shiller-bitcoin-is-just-an-interesting-experiment/.

7.2.2 *The Impact of Unstable Prices*

Some may argue that Bitcoins should not be compared to Apple shares, because the former may be used as a medium of payment, akin to traditional currencies. Here we will argue that Bitcoins can hardly be a good choice of "money" either. It is well-known that money has three functions: it is a medium of exchange, a unit of account, and a store of value. However, if Bitcoins encounter huge fluctuations in their prices, they can hardly be a medium of exchange (because they increase the risk between the time of a deal and the time that payment is made), and neither can it be a unit of account (because the numéraire itself is too unstable to play the role of an accounting unit). In addition, stored Bitcoins may end up with an unstable value, and hence may not be a reliable storage item. In short, Bitcoin's price volatility renders it unsuitable as a currency substitute. Broadly speaking, the currency of a country, for instance the U.S. dollar, has some fundamental factors in the background: the country's GDP growth rate, political stability, relationship with foreign countries, etc. As such, although dollars are just pieces of paper, the exchange rates of dollars with the currencies of other countries have been quite stable over the past several decades.

Despite President Trump's announcement that the U.S. government would acquire additional Bitcoin holdings and make them part of the U.S. Federal Reserve assets, he offered no justification for this decision. After all, it does not make much sense to add assets with extremely volatile values to one's wallet, not to mention to the U.S. Federal Reserve. It is also unclear whether the U.S. President can decide the composition of the Fed's assets, given that members of the Federal Reserve Board have term protections. In addition, even if the U.S. government does want to buy 200,000 Bitcoins each year for five consecutive years, announcing the project would make the future buying much more expensive, which only "makes the Bitcoin price great again."

After the announcement by Trump, the price of Bitcoin rose dramatically for several months, also revealing that its price appears to be quite sensitive to the President's "narratives."[10] One conjecture would be that

[10] One month after Trump's endorsement, the Bitcoin price has risen by more than 35%. See https://www.euronews.com/business/2024/11/21/bitcoin-reaches-all-time-high-as-trump-support-for-crypto-gathers-pace. However, its price started to fluctuate after January 2025, ranging from $100,000 to $80,000.

the person or persons who proposed or lobbied the suggestion had owned a lot of Bitcoins, and Trump's announcement just created the capital gains for those Bitcoin holders.

7.2.3 The Problematic Logic of "Decentralization"

As we mentioned above, the whole idea behind the design of the cryptocurrency is decentralization, that is, to avoid the flaws associated with letting one authority determine the rules of the monetary system, such as the circulation amount, the regulation rules, the interest rates, and so on. However, if we read the above discussion carefully, we find that there are also some Bitcoin protocols that are to be determined. For instance, the "21 million cap" on the total Bitcoin number is definitely not a "hard" rule. In fact, knowing that a blockchain is composed of a P2P (peer to peer) computer network, we understand that many operational rules and protocols are determined by the miners and nodes' operators. As we mentioned, by November 2024 there were roughly 200,000 miners. These 200,000 miners and nodes' operators effectively constitute a *centralized* governance structure.

In addition, no one knows how the 21-million coins cap was determined by Nakamoto in the first place. Some email correspondence evidence shows that this cap was just an "educated guess" by Nakamoto. This cap, protected by the incentive and governance model and operated by the process of "halving" the Bitcoin mining reward, will be reached by the year 2140.[11] In theory, the Bitcoin supply cap is not immutable, if a majority consensus among miners and node operators is achieved. However, since the terminal date is still far away from now, the discussion is premature. The nutshell is: no one knows what is going to happen.

Here comes the core question as to whether a cryptocurrency can become a well-received medium of exchange by people in general: Can it foster widespread public trust as a legitimate financial instrument? The drawbacks of a centralized power are well-known in democratic regimes. In democratic countries, the usual way of dealing with this issue is through the division of power and the checks and balances provided by the different authorities. From this point of view, the problem of the 2009 financial tsunami was not an issue of the concentration of power in the

[11] See https://river.com/learn/can-bitcoins-hard-cap-of-21-million-be-changed/.

banking system, but that the banking system (especially in the U.S.) at the time was not well-regulated and the monitoring rules were not efficiently implemented. Decentralization may not be a logical solution.

It has been well documented in macroeconomic theory (see, e.g., Bernholz, 2015) that monetary crises are often related to some failed fundamental factors, such as printing too much money, sustaining too large a government budget, and experiencing too bad an economy. All these reduce the trust people have in the government, which eventually leads to an economic crisis. When people's trust is lost, decentralizing is not the way to cure the system, but is more like an escape away from the system.

In the U.S., the cornerstone of the Federal Reserve system is in fact the Constitution and the legislation, and the preventive mechanism for not overissuing money supply is the budgetary system, the checks and balances of the Congress, and even the media. If economic crises still occur, then the final remedy may be to replace the ruling party by voting. For Bitcoins, however, there are no hard rules that warrant the trustworthiness of the operational protocols, which are determined by miners and nodes' operators. As Shiller put it, "Practically no one outside of computer science departments can explain how cryptocurrencies work."[12] In a democratic regime, government officials often step down if the country's currency deflates by a significant percentage, but for Bitcoins, we do not see anyone being responsible no matter how large the fall is in its price. In fact, we do not even know the true identities of the network peers. We know that the "constitution" of Bitcoins was drafted by Nakamoto, but who is Nakamoto?

Finally, if one really tries to embody cryptocurrencies into the asset holding list of the U.S. government, there is an operational problem. In a democratic system, from time to time the records of the administrative branch need to be verified, monitored, or compared by the Auditor's office or by the Court system. When all such records are encrypted in cyberspace, one can imagine that the verification work would be extremely difficult.

[12] See https://www.investopedia.com/news/why-nobel-economist-robert-shiller-still-bitcoin-skeptic/.

7.2.4 Energy Consuming

We mentioned that the blockchain operation needs the effort of miners. The aim of the miner is to find a "nonce" parameter such that the hash function generates an output with specific features, which are controlled by the protocol. In the Bitcoin network, given the 256-bit cryptographic hash, finding the correct nonce to solve the puzzle needs continuous trying, and the success probability of each trial is very low. Therefore, the mining competition involves a lot of computer-intensive trials. The first miner that solves the puzzle will be rewarded with a block reward of Bitcoins and some transaction fees. As such, competition among miners soon becomes an arms race: everyone tries to improve the computer capacity and calculation speed. Vranken (2017) and Pankovska et al. (2024) have provided a comprehensive analysis of the use of electricity in cryptocurrency mining.

A well-known criticism leveled by Bill Gates is that "Bitcoin consumes more energy per transaction than any other known payment system," according to the *New York Times*.[13] Gates has called himself a "bitcoin skeptic," and said that "it's not a great climate thing." To validate Gates' point, a data scientist estimated that each Bitcoin transaction emits an average 300 kg of carbon dioxide (CO2)—equivalent to the carbon footprint produced by roughly 750,000 Visa swipes. It has been estimated that the mining process produces a total of 36.95 million tons of CO2, the same "carbon footprint" as New Zealand. In addition, in terms of electricity consumption, it is equivalent to that of an entire country such as Chile, Austria, or the Czech Republic.[14] The problem is further compounded by the fact that many mining networks are based in China, where much of the power is generated from coal. As the cryptocurrency has become more popular, it has been estimated that its energy consumption has soared by a factor of 10 since just 2017.[15] Although there are alternative mechanisms for Ether, the essence of competition is the same. In short, peers in the Bitcoin network are incentivized to be the

[13] See https://www.nytimes.com/2021/03/09/business/dealbook/bill-gates-bitcoin.html.

[14] https://www.dallan.com/en/news/bitcoins-energy-consumption-greater-than-chile-austria-and-the-czech-republic/.

[15] See https://www.forbes.com/sites/jonathanponciano/2021/03/09/bill-gates-bitcoin-crypto-climate-change/.

fastest in computing in order to retrieve the reward of the block, and this competition is zero-sum in nature and therefore wasteful in essence.

Bitcoin's Proof-of-Work algorithm is not designed to validate that computational effort or that a computational puzzle was actually solved. Instead, this algorithm is designed to deter the manipulation of data by establishing a large energy hurdle and a high computing capability barricade. Simply put, this algorithm forces all active players engaged in mining to have "skin in the game": all miners devote resources including hardware, electricity, and employees, and they do want to sustain the Bitcoin's operation. On the other hand, people who do not put in equivalent resources are unlikely to compete. Thus, it is in the best interests of current miners to have the proof-of-work algorithm in order to guarantee that their vested interest is not compromised. Environmental and sustainability concerns are not the worry of present blockchain operators.[16]

7.2.5 *Illegal Transactions and the Risk of "Missing Coins"*

As previously discussed, every blockchain operates through a core network, and since there is always a mechanism that regulates the algorithm of the network, whoever controls the governance of this mechanism can be treated as the central controller of the blockchain. In this sense, "decentralization" may be a misleading term to describe the blockchain; instead, de-government may be a more accurate descriptor. Behind the operation of the Bitcoin, there is no governmental monitoring.

This is why many illegal activities are using Bitcoins as payments. According to Teichmann and Falker (2020a, 2020b), around US$2.5 billion was laundered through Bitcoin between 2009 and 2018, and the fraction of cryptocurrency transactions linked to illicit activities has been on the rise since early 2019. Some have estimated that, in 2021, 0.15% of known cryptocurrency transactions conducted were involved in illicit activities like cybercrime, money laundering, and terrorism financing, representing a total of $14 billion.[17] However, the estimate by Statistica is higher: the fraction in 2019 (1.9%) was the highest. The preference for

[16] See https://en.wikipedia.org/wiki/Proof_of_work.

[17] https://finance.yahoo.com/news/only-0-15-total-crypto-174206641.html.

Bitcoin in illicit activities mirrors the pre-internet era, when cash transactions were favored over checks for untraceable financial dealings (Frey & Schneider, 2001).

Another aspect of the Bitcoin is that all the records, including ownership, transfers, and disposition, are recorded in digital files. If digital records are compromised either due to hacking, fraud, or lost credentials, the associated Bitcoin assets become irretrievable. For accounts in traditional banks, people can use their ID to retrieve their money over the counter, even if they forget their account details or passwords. However, if one's access to the Internet is cut off, money in cyberspace cannot be easily retrieved. Furthermore, even if one brings the case to the court, the final outcome will not be certain, because even courts may not be able to access the Bitcoin network. Even if a judge wants to sign a warrant to seize a ledger, no one knows to where the warrant should be sent. Again, this is partly due to the de-government design of cryptocurrencies.

7.2.6 *Quantum Computing Threats*

A premise of the cryptocurrency mechanism is that the encrypted hash function has zillions of possible values (2^{264}) so that it is almost impossible to decipher. Thus, safety is a key reason why people are willing to put their wealth in the decentralized cyberspace, rather than the banking system in the physical world. The above-mentioned premise, however, faces a threat given the recent development of quantum computing.

According to the Wall Street Journal, there has been a new Willow quantum computing chip which, when embodied in a quantum computer, can perform the calculation a million times faster than a regular computer.[18] While quantum computing technology is not yet fully developed, experts predict it could mature within a decade, and it may break Bitcoin's encryption, and cause losses of trillions of dollars. When this event is expected to happen, the blockchain and the Bitcoin will be in jeopardy. Of course, quantum computing can hack into traditional banking systems as well, but it is believed that cyberattacks are more serious for systems purely in cyberspace.

[18] https://www.wsj.com/tech/cybersecurity/a-looming-threat-to-bitcoin-the-risk-of-A-quantum-hack-24637e29.

7.3 Other Applications of Blockchains

In the above, we mentioned many doubts about Bitcoins raised by well-known economists, and also showed that it is unlikely that Bitcoins will play the role of replacing ordinary currencies in the future. However, these doubts about cryptocurrencies do not suggest that the blockchain technology is not useful. On the contrary, it is an area with many potential applications. The purpose of our discussion in this section is to help readers understand why China and the U.S. are competing in this area, and what kind of implications there are in international politics.

Recall that a blockchain involves several key elements: (1) there are many stakeholders who jointly form a P2P network; (2) there is some key information that needs to be shared among these peers in the network; and (3) information updating may be frequent and mistakes may occur, with peers hoping that the information they acquire is authentic, so that they will not make decisions based on wrong information. Given the above three features, peers in the blockchain network will want to have a mechanism that will regularly verify the information, but whether this mechanism is a "centralized one" or not may not be the key concern.

Whenever we face a scenario having the above-mentioned three elements, the blockchain technology may be of help. In fact, big companies such as IBM have already provided blockchain services of the IoT (Internet of Things), supply chain management, and transportation logistics. Many of these applications are for "private" blockchains, where they are implemented within a business. Of course, a private chain may well be "centralized"; for instance, a blockchain within a business must be a centralized one in the sense that it is under the control of the CEO. Some blockchains even enable the government to play the role of a peer, and it does not affect the function and benefit of the design. Below we discuss some of the well-known applications.

7.3.1 Autonomous-Driving Cars

Using autonomous-driving vehicles equipped with 5G and 6G (the 5th and 6th generations of telecommunications) as an example, we can understand how a modified version of the blockchain works. To implement self-driving, there must be networks of the IoT involved. The self-driving cars in question are equipped with many censors and cameras, which detect the environment surrounding the car and receive information sent by other moving vehicles nearby. It is referred to as the IoT because it is an internet connection of cars, not of individuals.

The local traffic authorities may also be included in the network, because they are better informed about recent possible accidents or bottlenecks nearby. These information updates may affect the best route calculation within each car. The police stations, hospitals, and insurance agencies are also involved, because in cases of accidents, computers on self-driving cars may want to know how many minutes are needed to wait for these agencies to come forward to the rescue. The information feedback is so diffuse and the verification and updating may be so frequent that the P2P network needs intime updating. In addition, a variety of information needs to be verified to avoid disturbances or attacks by malicious parties. When there are car accidents, the historical records preserved in the blockchain can be used for court rulings or for program improvement.

As Hampton (2016) noted, within a private blockchain there is no need for a "race" such as mining (proof of work), and there is no incentive to use power or to discover blocks faster than competitors. In this autonomous driving example, we note that the blockchain is nothing more than a cumbersome database with multiple users receiving and updating various pieces of information. Yesterday's traffic chain may well be deleted once we enter today, and hence the blockchain will not be very long.

7.3.2 Supply Chain Management

In 2008, there was a well-known Chinese milk scandal, which led to a significant food safety incident in China. This scandal concerned the production of infant milk powder, and a company referred to as the Sanlu Group included some ingredients that were adulterated with the chemical melamine. The melamine was used to increase the nitrogen content of diluted milk, making it appear to have a higher protein content in order to pass the quality control test. This chemical material would result in various forms of kidney damage to infants. The official report concluded that 300,000 children were identified as being affected by the contaminated milk, 54,000 of which were hospitalized, and at least six of them died.[19] Food security incidents also occur in other developing countries, where factories use cheap materials to manufacture poor-quality commodities, resulting in damage to public health.

A blockchain-based tracking system could offer a viable solution to enhance transparency in the food manufacturing industry. The imports, purchases, uses, and inventories are all recorded and hashed in ledgers. These ledgers can be viewed by all operators of nodes in the network, and hence are difficult to alter. Each manufacturer can only observe its own ledger, but all ledgers may be accessed by consumer protection agencies, or even the health authorities. Participation in this network may be voluntary, but this voluntary participation may be announced to the public, which increases the consumer's confidence in these volunteer producers, and therefore the corresponding product price of these participants may well rise. This constitutes an incentive for their participation. Again, the chain of records may be deleted, for instance, when concerns over materials imported long ago have disappeared.[20]

7.3.3 *Traceable Agricultural Products*

Many kinds of agricultural products have a long chain of traces, from the planting of seeds, through growing, harvesting, processing, packaging, transportation, distributing, and finally being bought and consumed by households. In order to improve consumer trust in such a long process, many farmers have proposed a "traceable certification system."

Livestock raised by various farmers can be traced; whether chickens are free-range raised can have verifiable records, and QR codes of products can easily be attached to various kinds of vegetables. As such, the life cycle footprints and sanitary conditions of these agricultural products can be recorded. Using blockchain technologies, these records can hardly be altered. Of course, government agencies may have to do various random checks to make sure that the records uploaded are authentic. Agricultural products using these traces will give rise to more consumer confidence, will be better received in the market, and will generate a higher profit

[19] See https://en.wikipedia.org/wiki/2008_Chinese_milk_scandal.

[20] Of course, one blind spot of this design is: when agent A records "I put in 50 gm of material X in the production process," it may well be the case that A actually put in 50gm of Y, which is much cheaper than X. In short, a blockchain can work only if the input data at all nodes are correct in the first place.

margin. Once again, these records can be updated after the products are consumed.

7.3.4 *Protecting the Rights of Digital Content*

Companies such as YouTube, Amazon, and Spotify provide digital content services to consumers. Sometimes a company will offer a limited number of items to be accessed for an unrestricted number of times, and sometimes the charge is based on the number of times the content is viewed or listened to. There is always the problem that the number of times the content is accessed is known only by the platform operator; the copyright owners have to trust such numbers which they cannot verify. Records that are difficult to verify can easily cause legal disputes.

This problem can be easily resolved using blockchain technology. If all marketing nodes join the blockchain, each viewing and listening, through whatever platforms, can be recorded and together form a record that cannot be altered. By the end of the year, the total royalty can be calculated with more confidence. Furthermore, the area and timing of footprints are also in the record, which provide the content creators with information about the popularity and trends of their products. In addition, the pattern of these footprints together with the marketing activities allows producers to know the impact of various promotion channels. An ideal system like this will provide more incentives for creating new and better digital content.

Other than the above applications, one can easily extend the discussion of blockchain applications to the health care system, financial industry, insurance, digital identification, real estate management, and so on. Broadly speaking, anything that needs an unalterable, verifiable, and chronologically traceable record for a network of many individuals or identities may find blockchain technology to be helpful.

7.4 Why Is China so Enthusiastic About the Blockchain?

As discussed in the opening section of this chapter, CCP Chairman Xi Jinping has publicly endorsed China's blockchain development initiative. We understand that China's blockchain development has two versions: one for users inside China and another for international developers.

Hung (2024) has argued that China's blockchain strategy largely sidelines cryptocurrencies and instead embraces a distinctly "Chinese-style blockchain" approach. Indeed, the idea of decentralization associated with cryptocurrency is intrinsically inconsistent with China's authoritarian regime.

According to Hung (2024), the Chinese government approaches the blockchain through the framework of "state techno-solutionism." The blockchain is just a technological tool to improve national competitiveness and modernize management. Under the doctrine of "the Party leads all," this pragmatic approach aligns itself with broader national goals, including what Chinese officials refer to as the "rejuvenation of the nation." Such a perspective stands in contrast to the Western blockchain argument of decentralizing and de-government. Because government (or party) control is a natural default, the Chinese approach places more emphasis on the chronological multiple recording, traceability, and unalterable side of the blockchain.

7.4.1 China's Domestic Deployment

According to various news releases on the Chinese government website, the country is integrating blockchain technology into various sectors. Among these, in 2024 China aims to leverage blockchain technology to enhance the efficiency of its foreign trade,[21] to foster social and economic development, to facilitate the digital trade sector,[22] and to modernize information infrastructure.[23] In addition, courts at all levels are exploring the use of blockchains to improve judicial processes. This integration is aligned with other advanced technologies such as 5G, artificial intelligence, the Internet of Things, and big data analytics. As one can see, many of these pragmatic applications are no longer consistent with the textbook definitions of blockchains.

21 https://english.www.gov.cn/news/202409/28/content_WS66f77ac3c6d0868f4e8eb58d.html.

22 https://english.www.gov.cn/news/202409/27/content_WS66f61866c6d0868f4e8eb512.html.

23 https://english.www.gov.cn/news/202409/04/content_WS66d83edbc6d0868f4e8ea979.html.

In a summary of blockchain technology prepared by Forbes,[24] in May 2023 China established a national blockchain research center with the goal of training at least 500,000 blockchain professionals for the country. With only 26,000 active blockchain developers worldwide in 2023,[25] China's target underscores both its ambition and the potential impracticality of the plan. In addition, in August 2023, Chinese officials unveiled a blockchain-powered data exchange platform at the Hangzhou Summit. This Data Exchange uses distributed ledger technology to enable enterprise IT data trading, providing a system for immutable and traceable transactions. Over 300 enterprises, including China's high-tech icon businesses, participated in its debut. In December 2023, China's Ministry of Public Security launched the RealDID project, a blockchain-based platform to verify the real-name identities of China's 1.4 billion citizens. The purpose of this system is to provide a platform where users can register and log in to websites using digital ID addresses and private keys, while keeping their real identities hidden from other users and businesses. The government of course reserves the ability to link these digital identities to real individuals when necessary.

Forbes also reported that the Ministry of Agriculture and Rural Affairs has issued guidelines encouraging social capital investment in key agricultural technology research and blockchain application promotion. According to Hung (2024), in 2020, Qingyuan, Guangdong province, introduced a blockchain-based system called "Persimmon Points." This system allows participants to earn points for positive actions and lose points for perceived negative behaviors, with the data transparently recorded on a public blockchain. This application appears to integrate the blockchain technology with the Chinese social credit system. Another example is the use of a blockchain and IoT devices to record and monitor the entire chicken production process, from breeding to sales, very similar to what we described in our previous discussion on traceable agricultural products.

From the above references, readers may be confused whether all the above-mentioned examples are truly related to blockchains. It appears to

[24] https://www.forbes.com/sites/digital-assets/2024/10/08/china-bets-on-massive-blockchain-infrastructure/.

[25] https://www.developerreport.com/.

be the case that some local officials just used the blockchain term to apply for the generous government funding.

7.4.2 *International Deployment in the BRI*

Internationally, on March 30, 2024, China launched its national key R&D program for a super scale blockchain infrastructure platform for the Belt and Road Initiative (BRI).

As is well-known, the BRI is one of the largest economic development projects in the twenty-first century, and the original focus was on the infrastructure of physical facilities. The blockchain project mentioned above can be viewed as a digital version of the BRI. This digital framework parallels the physical BRI corridors, serving as a foundation for advanced software-based services, including various blockchain applications. The integration of physical and digital elements positions the BRI as a comprehensive system of land, sea, space, and internet connectivity, potentially making countries in Central Asia more aligned with China's infrastructure deployments. Of course, this alignment has a lock-in effect: once a country is used to the Chinese blockchain system, it would be difficult for it to shift to another system. Furthermore, blockchain applications often correspond to various platforms, which collect all kinds of data. The accumulated big data generated from countries along the BRI corridors may also be useful in the future.

7.4.3 *Strategic Duality in the Financial Sector*

In the area of financial applications, China's approach to blockchain technology employs a dual-track approach to blockchain technology—one for domestic control and another for international influence. Within China, Beijing has skipped the global crypto networks, but has developed its own version of next-generation monetary technology which the CCP could firmly control. Meanwhile, China maintains a presence in global crypto markets by leveraging Hong Kong as a financial gateway.

As pointed out by Schreckinger,[26] this strategy enables China to "exert internal financial controls on the mainland while impeding capital flight to bet on the potential of global crypto networks to disrupt money and

[26] https://www.politico.com/newsletters/digital-future-daily/2023/06/26/chinas-move-to-control-the-blockchain-00103710.

finance." The author also noted that "Inside China, Beijing will be able to keep the world's biggest population and second-largest economy running on financial networks it designs and controls (and push trading partners to join them)—without giving up its ambitions to make China a player in the more unruly crypto networks used elsewhere."

7.4.4 *The U.S. Responses*

According to Coincub, as of 2023 China maintains a dominant position in blockchain patent filings, with 43,937 applications since 2009, accounting for 68% of all granted patents globally.[27] China's rapid advancement in blockchain technology has raised concerns in the U.S., leading to legislative action. According to a report by CoinDesk,[28] in November 2023, U.S. lawmakers introduced the CLARITY (Creating Legal Accountability for Rogue Innovators and Technology) Act, proposing to bar federal government officials from doing business with China-based blockchain firms and using China-based blockchains. The bill aims to prevent foreign access to national security intelligence and private information. The Act also directs U.S. agencies to develop a plan that addresses the risks associated with China's blockchain technologies.

Readers may find that the U.S. strategy in the case of blockchains is very much like how they have reacted to the cases of Chinese telecommunication facilities and TikTok. However, with regard to China's investment in and cooperation with BRI-related countries, there is not much that the U.S. can do. Many countries along the silk road are not democratic, and they welcome the infrastructural help from China, both in the physical space and in cyberspace. Just like the U.S. which has been forming a coalition with democratic countries (such as the Clean Network Initiative) to consolidate the digital infrastructure "on this side of the digital wall," China is making the same effort "on the other side of the wall," with more emphasis on various blockchain applications. The digital wall has not been formally seen, but both sides have started to do their landscaping and yardwork independently, possibly with the following

[27] https://coincub.com/ranking/blockchain-patent-report-2023/.

[28] https://www.coindesk.com/policy/2023/11/08/us-bill-proposes-outlawing-government-use-of-china-made-blockchains-and-tethers-usdt.

expectation in mind: once the wall is in shape some day, we can do well without having to rely on involvements from the other side of the wall.

7.5 Discussion and Remarks

As previously discussed, blockchain functions as a distributed ledger system that chronologically updates records. The key feature of the system is that records are difficult to alter and are viewable by multiple agents. Given this key feature, the degree to which these records are encrypted can be different. More importantly, the distinction between public and private blockchains plays a fundamental role.

In public blockchains with open access, security mechanisms are essential to prevent malicious actors who freely join the network but exploit the network in ways that contradict the intended purpose of the blockchain. In practice, the proof-of-work or proof-of-stake algorithms are designed to accomplish this task. For a private blockchain within a business or within a group of people with a common interest, the above-mentioned prevention concern is not important. There are also other compromises in the decentralization doctrine as they operate within restricted networks. Finally, in many instances, records do not have to be kept indefinitely. In essence, blockchains are not confined to Bitcoin's design; they encompass a wide range of architectural variations.

It is fair to say that a more rigorous record-keeping system such as a blockchain improves efficiency. This aligns with the CCP's emphasis: the control efficiency. In democratic societies, individuals are often reluctant to entrust their data to centralized servers without transparency and accountability. This, however, may be why China has been the leader in terms of blockchain development. After all, the blockchain can be described as a system where "the encrypted records control all," which is really consistent with "the Party leads all" doctrine of the CCP.

Some democratic countries (such as the UK) are considering the issuance of "digital money" (such as the digital pound) which, in order to increase their public acceptance, may be backed by the government as the traditional money. Meanwhile, the transaction ledgers of such digital money may be encrypted and decentralized, which makes it more like cryptocurrencies. Because these digital currencies are government-backed, they must be subject to state oversight.[29] Whether the above-mentioned design is feasible is still debatable. For instance, could the judicial system, through some due process, order the government to submit their oversight records? If not, then there is a government branch that overrides the judicial power, which may face a constitutional challenge. If yes, then it is still a variation of the centralized banking system. The core debate remains: Can a centrally governed banking system truly achieve decentralization solely through cryptographic mechanisms?

Finally, there appears to be a loophole regarding the idea of accumulating 1,000,000 Bitcoins in the U.S. Federal Reserve. For cryptocurrencies such as Bitcoins, whoever knows the decryption code actually "owns" the coins. This creates the incentive for people to steal the coin. Stealing tons of gold reserves and transporting them is extremely difficult, which we can only see in movies. However, stealing billions in cryptocurrency just involves changing a decryption code, which may be easy and tempting.

References

Bernholz, P. (2015). *Monetary Regimes and Inflation: History, Economic and Political Relationships* (2nd ed.). Springer.

Biais, B., Bisiere, C., Bouvard, M., Casamatta, C., & Menkveld, A. J. (2023). Equilibrium Bitcoin Pricing. *Journal of Finance, 78*(2), 961–1014.

Frey, B., & Schneider, F. (2001). Informal and Underground Economics. In N. J. Smelser & P. B. Baltes (Eds.), *International Encyclopedia of the Social and Behavioral Sciences*. Elsevier.

Hampton, N. (2016). Understanding the Blockchain Hype: Why Much of It Is Nothing More Than Snake Oil and Spin. *Computerworld, 5*, 45.

Hung, A.-C. (2024). The Curious Case of Blockchain in Rural China: Unravelling Power, Profit, and Surveillance. *Big Data & Society, 11*(2), 1–13.

Pankovska, E., Sai, A. R., Vranken, H., & Ransil, A. (2024). Electricity Consumption of Ethereum and Filecoin: Advances in Models and Estimates. In *Proceedings of the 39th ACM/SIGAPP Symposium on Applied Computing* (pp. 269–277). ACM Digital Library.

Shiller, R. J. (2019) *Narrative Economics: How Stories Go Viral and Drive Major Economic Events*. Princeton University Press.

[29] https://www.bankofengland.co.uk/the-digital-pound.

Teichmann, F. M. J., & Falker, M.-C. (2020a). Money Laundering via Cryptocurrencies—Potential Solutions from Liechtenstein. *Journal of Money Laundering Control., 24*(1), 91–101.

Teichmann, F., & Falker, M.-C. (2020b). Cryptocurrencies and Financial Crime: Solutions from Liechtenstein. *Journal of Money Laundering Control, 24*(4), 775–788.

Vranken, H. (2017). Sustainability of Bitcoin and Blockchain. *Current Opinion in Environmental Sustainability, 28*, 1–9.

CHAPTER 8

Difficult Regime Transition Across the Digital Wall

As for the term "technology neutrality," there are several different versions of interpretations, and the following two are related to our discussion. The first is documented in the European Union's Common Assessment Method for Standards and Specifications,[1] which states that regulations tied to a particular technology may quickly become obsolete and require further amendment, and that technology-specific regulations may lead to the society's dependence on specific manufacturers, developers, suppliers, or distributors of the technology or service in question. The implication is that the government should not pick and choose a particular technology, or set up rules corresponding to a particular technology. The second related interpretation puts more emphasis on individual rights; it states that technological neutrality refers to the freedom of individuals and organizations to choose the most appropriate

[1] See https://joinup.ec.europa.eu/collection/common-assessment-method-standards-and-specifications-camss/solution/elap/technology-neutrality.

Some of the content in this chapter is excerpted from a paper of mine (together with two other coauthors) which appeared in "Why does AI hinder democratization?" Proceedings of the National Academy of Sciences (2025), 122 (19), e2423266122.

C. Y. C. Chu, *An Emerging Digital Wall*,
https://doi.org/10.1007/978-981-95-3577-4_8

technology that is sufficient for their needs and requirements in relation to their respective development, acquisition, use, or commercialization.[2]

8.1 Are Technologies Really Neutral?

On the face of it, the term technology neutrality looks fair and innocent. An analogy is to think of technologies as tools, and the government should allow as many tools as possible to be available in the tool box for people to choose from. Nonetheless, the above discussion seems to be based on an implicit premise: that people's opportunities to choose tools are fair and equal. However, what if some of the technologies in question intrinsically favor some parties, so that individual choices are distorted right from the beginning? And what if the technology itself was invented or introduced by the government that decides the regulatory rules? In these cases, the above-mentioned arguments regarding technology neutrality appear to be irrelevant. This chapter discusses the intrinsic bias of some ICTs that may hinder the appearance and/or stability of democracy. Put differently, a seemingly neutral technology may actually help stabilize the authoritarian regime's control. Moreover, autocrats may even facilitate new technologies that strengthen their control.

An enlightening example was provided by Acemoglu and Johnson (2023): the invention of the cotton gin very much favored the cotton farm owners who hired slave labor. Although the technology was neutral in the sense that "everyone can use the cotton gin," in practice only farm owners would buy and use it. As a result, some of the slave labor's indoor factory work was replaced by the gin, and they would be further deprived by the owner by being forced to do tougher field work. In fact, the farm owners may even have wanted to acquire this technology, so that their profit might increase. The overall result of the introduction of the cotton gin technology was that the welfare of the slaves decreased, and the welfare of the farm owners increased.

Some recent discussions in political science address a similar question: Do ICT advancements facilitate democracy or stabilize autocracy? Does the recent rapid development of AI play any special role? The general opinion concerning the role of ICTs has taken an obvious turn in the past

[2] See https://www.greenchem-adblue.com/what-is-technology-neutrality/.

two decades. In this chapter we will study, both theoretically and empirically, the relationship between democratization and the development of ICTs/AI. We will attempt to explain recent political regime changes that reveal the fragility of democracy. We will argue that AI plays a very critical role in these changes, very much like the invention of the cotton gin. We begin with a description of the background to the worldwide democratic environment in the past two decades.

8.1.1 Early Enthusiasm After the Arab Spring

The conventional theory of democratization suggests that ICT advances would facilitate information plurality and broaden the space for democratic representation by decentralizing information systems and communication platforms, hence fostering in a new era of participatory democracy. These ICT technologies are expected to facilitate campaigning, networking, voting, information-seeking, and even rallying protests, thereby bolstering informational autonomy and the capability of checks and balances for citizens. Thus, this conventional view has suggested that in the future it would be less likely that autocrats would be able to maintain the same power that they had in the past (Iskander, 2011; Shirky, 2011).

The above optimism reached its peak in the early 2010s, as the Internet and social media facilitated the ouster of four of the world's longest-ruling dictators in countries in the Middle East—Egypt, Libya, Tunisia, and Yemen, being known as the Arab Spring movement. People enthusiastically placed great faith in the role of information technologies, such as websites, chat rooms, and media stories that contained numerous references to a "Facebook Revolution" or "YouTube Revolt." They believed that ICTs would facilitate political mobilization and lead to democracy.

The early empirical evidence seems to be consistent with this optimistic conjecture. According to Kendall-Taylor et al. (2020), between 1946 and 2000, before the prevalence of the Internet, most authoritarian regimes were ousted by coups rather than by protests. Between 2001 and 2017, however, coups unseated only 9% of the dictatorships, while many more were overturned by mass public movements.

Such a positive perception regarding the impact of ICTs, nevertheless, turns out to have been overly optimistic. In the past 15 years or so, many people have begun to think the opposite: ICTs are not neutral to all users; they intrinsically favor autocrats and may help them stabilize their control, and make democracy less likely to arise. Or, in a fragile democracy where the ruler tries to suppress the civil society forces, ICTs may successfully help the rulers and eventually enable them to turn into autocrats.

8.1.2 *Why Are ICTs Not Neutral to Users?*

There are two main reasons why advances in ICT have changed its role from facilitating democracy to stabilizing autocracy. First, anti-government groups are not the only ones who can use ICTs; autocracies may also take advantage of such advances in technology. They can use the Internet to screen information, to identify possibly disobedient citizens, to detect and shut down unfriendly websites, and even to preempt opposition rallies. In the domain of regulations, the autocrats can enact laws that restrict cyberspace anonymity, and allow the government to exercise cyber-assaults against opposition websites (perhaps under the disguise of national security threats), so as to achieve *ex ante* suppression against large-scale protests. Indeed, there is evidence to show that autocracies that use digital technologies to repress their citizens face a lower risk of protests than those that do not (Kendall-Taylor et al., 2020, p. 106).

When both civil society and the government can use ICTs as tools to confront each other, then which one has an intrinsic advantage over the other? It depends on which party benefits more from the technology advancement in question. In terms of economics, one would conjecture that a party can benefit more from the ICTs if that party has some endowment which is more *complementary* to ICT technology. This motivates our empirical and theoretical analysis which follows. Suppose that we interpret technologies as tools which can be used to help us. Then, as we will explain shortly, tool *availability* is simply not the determining factor for the decision as to whether someone would actually *use* such tools. Tools will be better and more frequently used by those who can benefit more from using them, and this is the key concept behind technology non-neutrality.

8.1.3 *The Critical Role of AI*

The second reason why the tide has turned in the past 15 years is related to the advancement of AI. AI has progressed significantly in the second decade of the twenty-first century, thanks to advances in computing power (which in turn has been assisted by the GPU, as described in

Chapter 3) and big data. After the triumph of AlphaGo over human players in 2016, some economists began to study AI's impact on the market economy, with the focus of attention being mostly on employment replacement (between software and humans), income inequality, and economic development.[3] Political scientists, by contrast, have focused on very different aspects. Feldstein (2019, p. 41) explicitly argues that AI is a *game-changer* for authoritarian rulers to shape discourses and crush the opposition. The reasons why AI has been argued to be such a good helper to the authoritarian ruler are indeed appealing and are described below.

According to Kendall-Taylor et al. (2020), in 1989 when the Berlin Wall fell, there were roughly 100,000 police employees in East Germany's Stasi, and somewhere around 500,000 to two million informants. East Germany had only 16 million people then. If we call Stasi employees and informants "spies," then roughly one spy was arranged for every seven citizens. This is an extremely high density of spy deployment; hence surveillance appears to have been rather inefficient for authoritarian rulers in the 1980s. In the digital era, however, by setting up databases of keywords and sensitive pictures, computer programs can screen millions of emails, web searches, social media communications, and e-commerce purchases. Furthermore, based on these rich data, AI can pick out possibly disobedient citizens. Indeed, aided by AI, computers are much more efficient in espionage than human spies.

Another cost of the traditional repression model is the problem of lacking trust: the more the authoritarian regime relies on police and soldiers, the more vulnerable the regime is to insurrection by these lackey soldiers (Feldstein, 2019, p. 42). By contrast, monitoring and surveillance by AI and ICTs is less costly and can reduce the risk of insurrection, thus improving monitoring efficiency. In short, computers and AI are much more *loyal* and trustworthy than soldiers. Note that in this case, ICTs help reduce the risk of authoritarian rulers, but not that of the citizens, because the latter do not face the risk of being insurrected.

[3] See Agrawal et al. (2019), Autor et al. (2022), and Korinek and Stiglitz (2017, 2021).

8.2 The Compounding Effect of Big Data

The power of AI and ICT is further amplified by the increasing prevalence of big data. In addition to traditional government-controlled personal data—such as tax returns, property registrations, (public) bank accounts, criminal records, and birth and death certificates—authoritarian regimes like China can also easily access an extensive range of digital information. This includes data from social media platforms (e.g., Weibo), search engines (e.g., Baidu), purchasing histories (e.g., Alibaba), and vast amounts of video footage collected through widespread surveillance cameras.[4] The scale of these datasets becomes even more alarming when individual genetic information is included. According to Tahir Hamut Izgil, DNA samples were indeed collected from Uyghurs in Xinjiang, raising concerns about their potential misuse.[5]

8.2.1 Lopsided Control Over Big Data

These vast datasets provide AI with abundant information to enhance screening and profiling efficiency. Feldstein (2019) and Kendall-Taylor et al. (2020) provide evidence that China has exported its AI-driven surveillance technologies to Cambodia, Russia, several African nations, Malaysia, and Singapore—many of which are participants in China's Belt and Road Initiative (BRI). On the one hand, being able to export the algorithm to other authoritarian or semi-authoritarian countries suggests that China's AI apps are very efficient for government control purposes. On the other hand, that the authoritarian or semi-authoritarian rulers are willing to spend money to procure such monitoring facilities suggests that they actually benefit from these imported technologies. As one can imagine, the regulatory rules will be set so that they are compatible with such imported technologies, and there is no technology neutrality from the beginning. As Applebaum (2024) pointed out, such a sharing of monitoring technologies has become prevalent among authoritarian countries in recent years.

[4] See, for instance, https://www.goethe.de/en/kul/ges/eu2/mue/21435440.html.

[5] See https://cn.nytimes.com/culture/20230802/uyghur-memoir-tahir-izgil/zh-hant/.

AI and ICTs further enable micro-targeting, allowing autocratic regimes to customize information dissemination for specific individuals. These targeted messages can be delivered through social media, messaging platforms, and other digital channels. Moreover, AI/ICT can generate deepfakes, including synthetic audio and video content that is nearly indistinguishable from authentic material. These two techniques together, as one can imagine, allow autocracies to influence people to either soften their willingness to oppose, discredit the opposition leaders, or undermine a planned social movement. These technology tools evidently favor the authoritarian ruler.

Moreover, in originally authoritarian countries or countries with a fragile democracy, most telecommunications facilities are operated by companies that are owned/controlled (or franchised with periodic review) by the state, and therefore the government has much easier access to data going through the Internet. This has been referred to as the data processing model of administrative control (see Cate et al., 2012).

8.2.2 *Digital Authoritarianism*

Furthermore, authoritarian governments frequently enforce data localization policies, mandating that all data and digital domains remain within national borders and that they be accessible to state authorities. In practice, this strategy is a fundamental component of national efforts to achieve cyber sovereignty and, in some cases, facilitate the development of digital authoritarianism (see Limbago, 2019; Sheppard et al., 2021).[6] As a result, data localization also gives authoritarian governments unique access to more personally identifiable data and makes it easier for them to block social forums that are deemed suspicious.

In authoritarian and fragile democratic nations, this disproportionate control over data incentivizes state actors to invest in supercomputing power and advanced AI/ICT applications for governance and surveillance purposes. By contrast, lacking access to big data undermines the usefulness of AI for civil society. As a result, AI/ICT, associated with big data, may favor the state and hinder the development of democracy, either by

[6] A recent policy brief by the Center for Strategic and International Studies (CSIS) defines digital authoritarianism as "the use of the internet and related digital technologies by leaders with authoritarian tendencies to decrease trust in public institutions, increase social and political control, and/or undermine civil liberties." See Sheppard et al. (2021).

making democracy less likely to arise from autocracy, or by easily pushing an originally fragile democracy toward autocracy.[7]

Of course, big data and technologies are not the only things that autocrats such as the CCP rely on to build the surveillance state. As Pei (2024) pointed out, China's vast labor-intensive spying infrastructure also plays a complementary role. This infrastructure constitutes a comprehensive network of eyes and ears, so that an authoritarian state can better survive.

In summary, the lopsided advantage of accessing big data makes it easier for an autocrat to procure ICT/AI facilities to exercise tighter political control, thereby making the regime switch from autocracy to democracy (i.e., democratization) less likely to happen. Using the terms adopted by Acemoglu and Robinson (2012), the *narrow corridor* becomes narrower.

8.3 The Data Advantage of the Chinese Government

According to deLisle and Yang (2022), nearly every major corporation in China, including technology companies, hosts a Chinese Communist Party (CCP) organization. These internal CCP committees serve not only as whistleblowers but also as policy enforcers. Whether foreign or domestic, companies operating in China must comply with these CCP organizations, ensuring that corporate policies align with party directives—even at the expense of commercial interests. In 2017, reports indicated that party organizations existed in nearly 70% of the 1.86 million privately owned companies in China. Over the past few years, the CCP's influence over private enterprises has expanded significantly.[8]

[7] Acemoglu (2021) has recently suggested that AI increases the ability of governments to closely monitor citizens' communications and stamp out political dissent, which may damage democracy's fundamental lifeblood, and is dubbed the "big brother" effect.

[8] Martina, M. (2017, August 24). Exclusive: In China, the Party's push for influence inside foreign firms stirs fears. See the connection of *Reuters*, https://www.reuters.com/article/us-china-congress-companies-idUSKCN1B40JU.

8.3.1 China's National Security Law: You Should Submit All Data When Asked

All Chinese companies are subject to the National Security Law as well as additional counter-espionage and intelligence laws. Of particular note, privacy is not explicitly protected under the Chinese Constitution, although certain provisions touch on related rights. For example, Article 39 protects individuals from illegal searches and seizures, while Article 40 safeguards the right to confidential correspondence. However, as Clarke (2003) points out, the Chinese Constitution is often regarded as "the least important document, in terms of binding force, in the entire Chinese legal system ... It is fair to say that the words of the constitution are essentially epiphenomenal," meaning that these constitutional provisions provide little real protection.

In addition to the inefficacy of constitutional protection, China has enacted many laws that aim to bring all tech giants into line. The most typical example is the National Security Law, which was enacted in 2015. Article 77 vaguely prescribes that citizens and organizations should report any clues, evidence, and information that may threaten national security to the authorities concerned. They should also "provide necessary support and assistance" to the national security authorities, police authorities, and military departments. Article 79 further requires that corporations should cooperate with the government and adopt security measures in accordance with the needs of national security. Both provisions empower the CCP to force tech companies into submitting their data. In terms of soliciting data, the CCP stands above the private sector.

8.3.2 China's Cybersecurity Law: You Are Always Monitored

In June 2017, China's Cybersecurity Law became effective. In terms of its scope of application, Article 5 of the Cybersecurity Law prescribes that the government shall adopt measures to monitor, prevent, and handle cybersecurity risks and threats from both inside and outside the national border. Article 57 further obligates network operators to stop the dissemination of information prohibited by laws and regulations, and report to the government when they discover such information. This article essentially allows the CCP to control the spread of information and intercept any data it deems disturbing and dangerous, not to mention that Article 49 requires network operators to cooperate with the government in conducting surveillance and investigations. In short, the Cybersecurity Law not only empowers the government, but also holds all operators jointly and severally responsible for monitoring and reporting.

In 2020, China drafted two more important laws to further facilitate its access to data stored by Chinese companies or by foreign companies based in China, i.e., the Personal Information Protection Law (enacted in 2021) and the Data Security Law (also enacted in 2021).[9]

8.3.3 *China's Data Security Law: You Are Under My Watch*

Article 2 of China's Data Security Law stipulates that the government will investigate and punish data activities that infringe upon national security, the public interest, or legitimate interests of citizens and organizations, even if they are outside China. In other words, China can extend its data governance regime beyond its territory and go after anyone whose data activities may threaten its national security. Article 41 further authorizes the authorities concerned to investigate data controllers when they find data activities that are potentially risky to security. More importantly, Article 32 stipulates that data controllers should submit their data and cooperate with the authorities concerned when the latter are investigating a crime or maintaining national security. We should note that this submission of data can be directly demanded by the investigation team, and does not go through any judicial system or judges. The above-mentioned provisions in fact give the CCP "the ability to regulate data controllers, whether they are in China or outside of China, so it has an extra-territorial effect."[10] As such, tech company owners who have interests or relatives in China will be intimidated by this law and be forced to submit the data to the CCP when the data allegedly raise national security concerns.

[9] For a general discussion on the two laws, see Data Guidance (2020, November). *China - Data Protection Overview*. https://www.dataguidance.com/notes/china-data-protection-overview. Shi, M. (2020, December 14). *China's Draft Privacy Law Both Builds On and Complicates Its Data Governance: The Personal Information Protection Law in China's data governance puzzle*. https://www.newamerica.org/cybersecurity-initiative/digichina/blog/chinas-draft-privacy-law-both-builds-on-and-complicates-its-data-governance/.

[10] Yang, M. (2020, October 12). China's Draft Data Security Law: Foreign Companies Caught in the Middle. *Voice of America*. https://www.voachinese.com/a/China-data-security-law-its-impact-on-foreign-companies-in-China-20201012/5618170.html.

Similarly, Article 3 (2) of the Personal Information Protection Law states that under three circumstances the Law is applicable outside China for the purpose of protecting the interests of data subjects in China. These three circumstances are: 1) when organizations provide products or services to individuals in China, 2) when organizations assess and analyze the behavior of individuals in China, and 3) when the protection of interests is in accordance with other statutes or regulations. Indeed, its scope of application is broader than the General Data Protection Regulation (GDPR) of the European Union, mainly because of circumstance 3), that is, foreign entities may be regulated by other Chinese laws and regulations.[11] We should further note that the Personal Information Protection Law also deals with cross-border transfers of personal data. Data processors need to meet the standard set by this Law or obtain the approval of the authorities concerned in advance, before they transfer their data to countries other than China.

In short, with long-arm controls, the data that the CCP can access from cyberspace actually cover the whole geographic space. As long as people or businesses are somehow connected to China, the related data can be retrieved by the CCP.

8.3.4 Authoritarian and Democratic Countries: The Fundamental Difference

Chinese people may not be satisfied with their privacy being violated by these Chinese tech giants. To appease this unrest, the Chinese government has at least to some extent started protecting Chinese netizens from commercial data collection. As mentioned above, China's Personal Information Protection Law took effect in 2021. However, the surveillance of the CCP has only increased rather than decreased in the past decade, and it is an unreasonable expectation that the CCP's surveillance will stop in the future because of the enactment of a law.

Here we should identify the differences between commercial surveillance and government surveillance. One important feature of China's

[11] Shi, M. (2020, December 14). "China's Draft Privacy Law Both Builds On and Complicates Its Data Governance: The Personal Information Protection Law in China's data governance puzzle," electronic version available at https://www.newamerica.org/cybersecurity-initiative/digichina/blog/chinas-draft-privacy-law-both-builds-on-and-complicates-its-data-governance/

privacy law is that it "build[s] consumer trust in a thriving digital economy but does not undermine the government's ability to maintain control."[12] In practice, when the government does not need the data, commercial surveillance will be restricted in order to facilitate economic development and build the CCP's reputation. When the state needs the data, the protection of privacy will surrender to governmental surveillance. In fact, because the boundary between private Chinese tech companies and the Chinese government/CCP is porous, the violation of privacy by tech companies in China should sometimes be attributed to the Chinese government.

Indeed, some researchers even go further to claim that "All Chinese tech companies have deep ties to the Chinese state security apparatus." (Australian Strategic Policy Institute, 2019). Given China's ambition to overtake the U.S. in AI and other leading-edge technologies, this is understandable because these tech companies have been selected and subsidized by the state, if not owned by the state, to be at the forefront of the development of high technologies. In return, these companies will assist the state in fulfilling its political and military agendas. This symbiotic model has been proved to be mutually beneficial to both the state and the few selected companies.

8.4 Institutional Differences and Macro Evidence

As discussed in Sect. 8.1, while ICT advancements initially facilitated democratization following the Arab Spring, recent evidence suggests a reversal of this trend. Figure 8.1 illustrates that although the number of AI/ICT patents granted worldwide (collected from the Global Patent Search System, GPSS) has steadily increased,[13] both the Democracy Index (published by the Economist Intelligence Unit, EIU) and the Political Rights Index (issued by Freedom House, FH) have declined over the observed period. Using the standard structural break test, we identify a break point around 2012–2013 for the EIU's Democracy Index and AI/ICT patent grants, while a break point for FH's Political Rights Index

[12] For more details, please see Sacks, S. (2019, February 14). *China's Privacy Conundrum*. https://www.newamerica.org/weekly/chinas-privacy-conundrum/.

[13] The number of AI/ICT published patents follows a similar trend.

and AI/ICT patents emerges in 2017.[14] As we will demonstrate, this structural shift is not coincidental.

8.4.1 The Macro Trend

Furthermore, the global average Democracy Index score in 2023 reached a historic low, dropping from 5.52 (out of 10) in 2006 (when the EIU began compiling the index) to 5.23. Among 167 countries, 108 experienced democratic regression, while only 59 saw improvements over the past 17 years. Similarly, Freedom House's Political Rights Index also fell to a record low in 2023, declining by 8.18% since 2006.

By measuring the degree of overall freedom, FH's Global Freedom Scores indicate that between 2006 and 2023, ten countries transitioned from a "free" to "partly free" status; they are Benin, the Dominican Republic, El Salvador, Hungary, India, Indonesia, Mexico, Peru, Senegal, and Ukraine. Eighteen countries transitioned from a "partly free" to "not free" status; they are Afghanistan, Bahrain, Burkina Faso, Burundi, Central African Republic, Congo (Brazzaville), Djibouti, Ethiopia, Gabon, Indian Kashmir, Jordan, Kyrgyzstan, Nicaragua, Thailand, Turkey, Uganda, Venezuela, and Yemen. One country (Mali) dramatically shifted from a "free" to "not free" status. These regime changes indicate the fragility of democracy, which motivates our exploration of the nexus between AI/ICT and democratic development in greater depth.

Democratic societies rely on the integration of high-quality information to support public decision-making. However, with the rise of the Internet and digital social media, disinformation campaigns have increasingly undermined this essential foundation of democracy. The U.S. intelligence community has concluded that Russia interfered in the 2016 U.S. presidential election by hacking the Clinton campaign headquarters and the Democratic National Committee, and employing troll armies to distribute false information on the Internet. If authoritarian rulers can infiltrate the campaign of another country, it is only natural to imagine how easily they can infiltrate their domestic civil society forces. In what follows, we will empirically investigate how this infiltration works.

[14] TO estimate the structural break year, we use the Supremum Wald test (e.g., Hansen, 1997) associated with an unknown break date in a regression with a constant and a time trend.

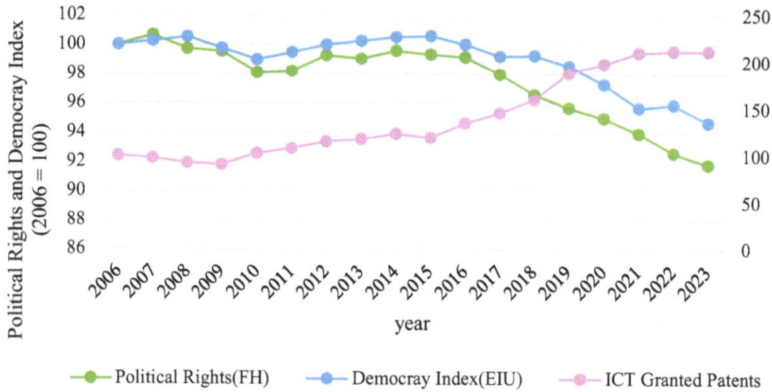

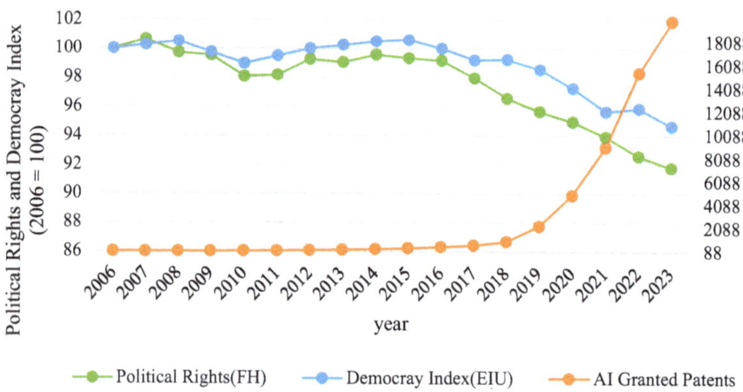

Fig. 8.1 Democracy/Political Rights and AI/ICT Granted Patents. *Notes* (1) The data for the Democracy Index and Political Rights are normalized so that 2006 = 100. The AI/ICT industry taxonomy is based on Eurostat Metadata. (2) The structural break test indicates that the structural break year for ICT granted patents and the EIU's Democracy Index and FH's Political Rights is 2012, while the structural break year for AI granted patents and these two democracy scores is 2017

8.4.2 Intuitive Structuring: The Role of Checks and Balances

We begin by outlining our empirical framework and explaining why governments in authoritarian and fragile democratic countries utilize AI/

ICT in ways that differ significantly from their counterparts in mature democratic regimes. We then derive testable hypotheses to check whether our conjecture is supported by empirical evidence.

Our empirical analysis is performed using the survey of the Digital Society Project (DSP) dataset (consisting of 164 countries). In Sect. 2.2 of the DSP dataset, there are three ICT measures of the Internet and social media, namely, cyber security (CS), content filtering (CF), and shut down (SD). As stressed by the DSP survey, independent of whether they actually do so *in practice*, CS, CF, and SD measure the technological *capacities* available to be adopted by actors (state rulers, or civil society groups).

Three Kinds of Capacities

The key differences between CS, CF, and SD need to be explained. CS functions to prevent external cyber threats, enhance the resilience of digital infrastructure, and safeguard internet users—including governments, citizens, and businesses—from malicious attacks.[15] CS is in general not individual-specific, because what or whom would be attacked cannot be predicted in advance.[16] By contrast, CF and SD are usually individual-specific, targeted at *internal* users or platforms. CF enables actors to pick out "harmful" information or "problematic" target individuals on the Internet and social media platforms.[17] SD enables the government, according to their target list, to take down social media posts and platform-specific user accounts from social media, and limit access to social media or even the Internet itself. Successful operations of CF and SD rely on the capability to identify the characteristics of targets (King et al., 2014).

The capability to identify and eliminate targets depends on (1) whether the user can access individual data and (2) whether the algorithm used

[15] See Cybersecurity and Infrastructure Security Agency (CISA), 2023–2025 Strategic Plan. CISA (2022).

[16] See C. Brookson et al., Definition of Cybersecurity-Gaps and Overlaps in Standardization. *European Network and Information Security Agency (ENISA)* (2016).

[17] See S. Gunitsky, The Great Online Convergence: Digital Authoritarianism Comes to Democracies. *War on the Rocks* (2020).

can analyze the acquired individual data.[18] Precisely targeting suspicious individuals and instantaneously taking down targets demands highly sophisticated AI algorithms and heavy computing resources. With large individual data, the marginal productivity of AI and ICT increases. This is the intrinsic complementarity between AI/ICT and the state ruler.

Capacity Procurement Pattern in Different Regimes

Although the intrinsic complementarity between AI/ICT and state power facilitates increased investment in CF and SD, some states may face obstacles in implementing such measures. This highlights a fundamental divergence in data governance between democratic and authoritarian regimes.[19] In democratic countries, the government's incentive to invest in CF and SD is hindered by various checks and balances, whereas in authoritarian or fragile democratic countries, these checks and balances are weak, or even nonexistent.

8.5 Country-Specific Micro Evidence

In authoritarian and fragile democratic nations, data regulations often grant governments exclusive access to individual data. This privileged access provides strong incentives for states to invest in content filtering (CF) and shutdown (SD) technologies to reinforce political stability—further strengthening the intrinsic complementarity between AI/ICT and state control. However, in democratic systems, institutional checks and balances significantly reduce the incentive for governments to invest in CF and SD, even if they possess the AI/ICT expertise necessary to operate them.

[18] For example, China's vast censorship apparatus has recently used a new technology (known as optical character recognition technology) on WeChat to root out banned words and images. With AI and large individual data, the new image censorship is very targeted and able to quickly take action if certain sensitive words, phrases, and images are contained. Details can be found in https://money.cnn.com/2018/03/01/technology/china-wechat-censorship-ai/index.html.

[19] More discussion can be found in https://nationalsecurity.gmu.edu/combating-digital-authoritarianism/, and https://www.csis.org/analysis/real-national-security-concerns-over-data-localization.

8.5.1 Deriving and Testing Hypotheses

Building on this analysis, our first hypothesis suggests that authoritarian and fragile democratic governments are more likely to prioritize investments in CF and SD technologies. Because CS is not individual-specific, there is no definite pattern in CS investments. As such, one may predict that advances in AI and ICT will drive autocratic and fragile democratic regimes to increase their CF and SD capacity, but not necessarily the capacity of CS. Table 8.1 summarizes our heuristic reasoning about the relationship between various ICT measures and political regimes.

To test this first hypothesis, we conduct a grouping for these 164 countries based on the democracy indices of FH (or the EIU) during 2006–2023. In light of the status quo effect, we use the 2006 democracy index (the beginning year of the sample period) to divide the countries into two quantile groups, in which group L is the less democratic one, consisting of countries whose democracy indices are in the lower 50%, while group H is the more democratic one, consisting of countries whose democracy indices are in the upper 50%. For both group L and group H in Fig. 8.2, there are 18 blue (red) points in each panel, where each point denotes a democracy (or political rights) index on the horizontal axis (country-specific demean) and an ICT capacity index on the vertical axis. L-group points are in blue and H-group points are in red, with points of earlier (later) years being lightly (densely) marked.

We can observe several patterns in Fig. 8.2. First, for governments in group L (authoritarian and fragile democratic countries), the technological capacities for CF and SD are much higher than those in group H (more democratic countries). Second, for group L countries, in the CF and SD panels, we observe an intriguing inverted-C turning, and the turning time is 2014 for the EIU democracy index and 2015 for the FH political rights index. This indicates that, for group L countries, these capacities increase first and then decrease with democracy scores, which is consistent with our discussion in Sect. 8.1. For group H countries, however, both the CF and SD indexes monotonically decrease with the democracy scores, and there is no inverted-C pattern.

Third, governments in group H own stronger technological capacities in CS, compared with group L countries. Overall, governments' technological capacities in CF and SD are *negatively* correlated with the democracy scores, but governments' technological capacities in CS

Table 8.1 Different adoptions of ICT measures in different countries—heuristics

Three ICT Measures(1)	*Individual Specificity?*(2)	*Big Data Helpful?*(3)	*State Advantage?*(4)	*Checks & Balances?*(5)	*More State Investment?*(6)	*Away from Narrow Corridor?*(7)
Cybersecurity	×	×	×	–	–	–
Shut Down	✓	✓	✓	Democrats ✓ Autocrats×	Democrats × Autocrats ✓	Democrats × Autocrats ✓
Content Filtering	✓	✓	✓	Democrats ✓ Autocrats×	Democrats × Autocrats ✓	Democrats × Autocrats ✓

Notes (1) The DSP dataset contains three ICT measures: cybersecurity (CS), shut down (SD), and content filtering (CF). (2) CS is to prevent outside attacks, which are less related to internal web users, whereas SD and CF are targeted at internal users or platforms, and the success of SD and CF is more related to the capability of identifying the characteristics of internal targets. (3) Because of (2), with the help of AI, individual big data can improve the effective operation of SD and CF. (4) States can usually access more individual data (from demographics, tax records, bank transactions, security cameras, property registrations, etc.) than civil society forces, which gives the state more of an incentive to invest in SD and CF. (5) In democratic countries, the above-mentioned incentive to invest in SD and CF may be hindered by various checks and balances, whereas in authoritarian or fragile democratic regimes, these checks and balances are weak. (6) (4) and (5) together predict that we should observe more state investments in SD and CF only in authoritarian or fragile democratic countries, but there is no definite pattern in CS investments. (7) Summarizing the above, the prediction is that ICT and AI will drive authoritarian and fragile democratic regimes away from the Narrow Corridor

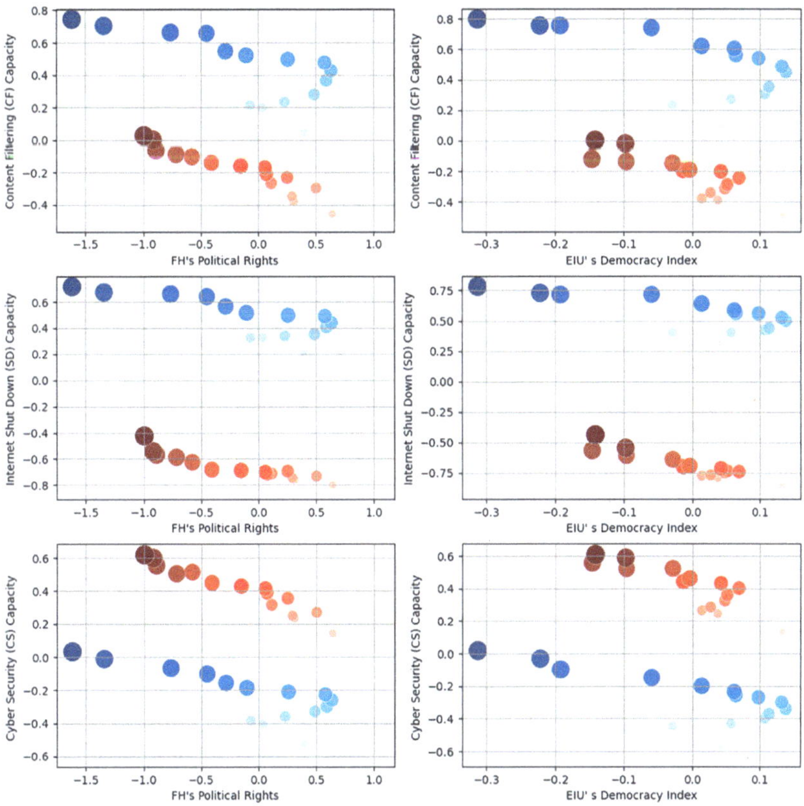

Fig. 8.2 States' Tech. Capacities for Low (Blue) and High (Red) Democracy Groups. *Notes* (1) Countries are grouped based on their 2006 democracy scores. Colors are shaded darker to represent more recent years. Democracy scores are centered by subtracting each country's mean, and the annual group means are calculated. Technological capability scores are simply averaged annually. (2) Governments in group L have stronger technological capacities for CF and SD, while governments in group H have stronger technological capacities for CS. (3) Group L exhibits an inverted-C relationship between the democracy scores and CF and SD capacities; CF and SD capacities have steadily increased, while the EIU democracy index started to decrease in 2014 and the FH political rights started to decrease in 2015. (4) Overall, governments' technological capacities for CF and SD are negatively correlated with the democracy scores, but governments' technological capacities for CS are positively correlated with the democracy scores

are *positively* correlated with the democracy scores.[20] These results are statistically significant and robust to alternative democracy indices in terms of FH's Political Rights and Global Freedom Score as well as the EIU's Democracy Index. The detailed regression results are provided in our Appendix (compiled toward the end of this book) regarding Data Descriptions and Supplementary Regressions.

8.5.2 From Capacity to Practices

Section 2.2 of the Digital Society Project (DSP) dataset focuses on Digital Media Freedom, providing empirical measurements of government-led censorship, content filtering, and internet shutdowns. These metrics reflect actual implementation practices. Six variables are related to the implementation *in practice*: Internet Filtering in Practice, Internet Shut Down in Practice, Social Media Shut Down in Practice, Social Media Alternatives, Social Media Monitoring, and Social Media Censorship in Practice (see the Appendix on Data Descriptions and Supplementary Regressions). Our second hypothesis is as follows. Because of the differences in checks and balances, the SD and IF capacity indexes are more likely to translate into practices for group L countries than for group H countries.

To shed light on this group-specific distinction, we examine the capacity-practice relationship for groups H and L, including the lagged effect. The Im-Pesaran-Shin panel unit-root test suggests that indices in some countries contain unit roots. To avoid the problem of panel spurious regression, we thus follow the standard statistical procedure (see Im et al., 2003). We take the first-order differences for all indices and then run regressions by applying the linear dynamic panel-data estimation, where country and year fixed effects have been taken into account. The regression model is

$$Z_{it} = \alpha_i + \mu_t^L + \mu_t^H + \gamma Z_{i(t-1)} + \gamma_x LG_i \times Z_{i(t-1)} + \sum\nolimits_{j=1}^{3} \beta_j^H HG_i \times X_{jit} + \sum\nolimits_{j=1}^{3} \beta_j^L LG_i \times X_{jit}$$

[20] The correlations between governments' technological capacities in CF and SD and FH's Political Rights (the EIU's Democracy Index) are respectively -0.345 (-0.284) and -0.519 (-0.499), while the correlation between governments' technological capacities in CS and FH's Political Rights (the EIU's Democracy Index) is 0.211 (0.313).

$$+\sum_{j=1}^{3}\delta_j^H HG_i \times X_{ji(t-1)} + \sum_{j=1}^{3}\delta_j^L LG_i \times X_{ji(t-1)} + e_{it},$$

where Z_{it} is government i's implementation practice in year t, X_{it} is government i's technological capacity in year t, and HG_i (LG_i) is a dummy variable that equals 1 if country i is in group H (group L). α_i measures the country fixed effect, and μ_t^H (μ_t^L) measures the year fixed effect for group H (group L).[21] The interaction terms of the group dummy variables are included in order to control for the autoregressive and lag distributed effects for different democratic groups. A standard method for estimating the linear dynamic panel-data regression is used to obtain the parameters (see Arellano & Bond, 1991). We also use high-order lagged independent variables as instrumental variables (IVs) to control for the endogeneity of X_{jit} caused by simultaneous effects.

Table 8.2 shows that stronger technological capacities in CF and SD enable governments to increase surveillance and censorship practices in less democratic countries (group L), and this positive relationship between governments' CF and SD capacities and their actual practices is statistically significant for all surveillance and censorship means. Literally, this means that "bad capacities always lead to bad activities" in group L countries. By contrast, as for more democratic countries (group H), the relationship is not statistically significant in most of the surveillance and censorship practices. For these group H countries, the fact that "bad capacities may not lead to bad activities" may reveal the function of checks and balances. Table 8.2 only shows the case where the democracy grouping is based on FH's Political Rights. The empirical findings that we obtain are also valid when the democracy grouping is based on either the FH's Global Freedom or the EIU's Democracy Index.

8.5.3 *From Monitoring Practices to the Drop in Democracy Indexes*

Finally, we run regressions to examine the effects of governments' surveillance and censorship practices on democracy, as measured by FH's Political Rights and Global Freedom as well as the EIU's Democracy Index. This regression facilitates in testing our third hypothesis: more surveillance and censorship lead to the deterioration of democracy. The

[21] The country fixed effect means that there are different constant terms for distinct countries. Similarly, the year fixed effect means that there are different constant terms for distinct years.

Table 8.2 Governments' technological capacities and their actual practices for various democracy groups

	Internet Filtering		*Internet Shut Down*		*Social Media Shut Down*		*Social Media Alternatives*		*Social Media Monitoring*		*Social Media Censorship*	
	Coeff	*Std*	*Coeff*	*Std*	*Coeff*	*Std*	*Coeff*	*Std*	*Coeff*	*Std*	*Coeff*	*Std*
Group L												
Internet Filtering Capacity	0.180***	(0.035)	0.164***	(0.038)	0.241***	(0.038)	0.068**	(0.026)	0.164***	(0.036)	0.136***	(0.033)
Internet Shut Down Capacity	0.155***	(0.038)	0.140***	(0.041)	0.138***	(0.041)	0.064*	(0.028)	0.279***	(0.039)	0.213***	(0.036)
Cyber Security Capacity	0.043	(0.050)	−0.060	(0.055)	−0.103 +	(0.054)	0.123***	(0.037)	0.049	(0.053)	0.069	(0.047)
Group H												
Internet Filtering Capacity	0.146***	(0.043)	0.027	(0.047)	0.077	(0.047)	0.027	(0.033)	0.078 +	(0.046)	0.182***	(0.041)
Internet Shut Down Capacity	0.018	(0.048)	0.075	(0.051)	0.126*	(0.051)	−0.021	(0.036)	0.102*	(0.050)	0.022	(0.045)

	Internet Filtering		*Internet Shut Down*		*Social Media Shut Down*		*Social Media Alternatives*		*Social Media Monitoring*		*Social Media Censorship*	
	Coeff	*Std*	*Coeff*	*Std*	*Coeff*	*Std*	*Coeff*	*Std*	*Coeff*	*Std*	*Coeff*	*Std*
Cyber Security Capacity	−0.014	(0.048)	0.026	(0.052)	−0.058	(0.051)	0.073*	(0.036)	−0.022	(0.050)	0.049	(0.045)
Constant	0.018	(0.014)	0.000	(0.015)	−0.001	(0.015)	0.009	(0.011)	0.003	(0.015)	−0.002	(0.013)

Notes (1) Standard errors are in parentheses: ***$p < 0.001$, **$p < 0.01$, *$p < 0.05$, and + $p < 0.1$. The total number of observations is $N = 2{,}296$. (2) All variables are first-differenced. The regression model is

$$Z_{it} = \alpha_i + \mu_t^L + \mu_t^H + \gamma Z_{i(t-1)} + \gamma_X LG_i \times Z_{i(t-1)} + \sum_{j=1}^{3} \beta_j^H HG_i \times X_{jit} + \sum_{j=1}^{3} \beta_j^L LG_i \times X_{jit}$$

$$+ \sum_{j=1}^{3} \delta_j^H HG_i \times X_{ji(t-1)} + \sum_{j=1}^{3} \delta_j^L LG_i \times X_{ji(t-1)} + e_{it},$$

where i is the index of the country, t is the index of the year, Z_{it} is the government's implementation practice, X_{jit} is the government's technological capacity and HG_i (LG_i) is a dummy variable that equals 1 if country i is in Group H (Group L), which is grouped according to the 2006 FH's Political Rights. α_i measures the country fixed effect, and μ_t^H (μ_t^L) measures the year fixed effect for Group H (Group L). The interaction terms of the group dummy variables are included in order to control for the auto-regression and lag distributed effects for different democratic groups. The Arellano-Bond method for the linear dynamic panel-data regression is used to estimate the parameters. We also use high-order lagged independent variables as IVs to control for the endogeneity of X_{jit} caused by simultaneous effects. (3) We only report the coefficients of the contemporary effects of X_{jit} for different democratic groups (β_j^L and β_j^H) for simplicity. The signs of δ_j^L and δ_j^H are consistent with β_j^L and β_j^H, while their magnitude and significance are less so. These statistically significant results are for the current variables of the governments' technological capacities, implying that governments' CF and SD capacities can immediately translate into their surveillance and censorship practices. (4) The above table indicate the positive effects of the government's technological capacities in CF and SD on their actual practices, which are statistically more significant for countries in group L than for those in group H.

regression model is

$$Y_{it} = \alpha_i + \mu_t + \gamma Y_{i(t-1)} + \sum_{j=1}^{5} \beta_j Z_{jit} + \sum_{j=1}^{5} \delta_j Z_{ji(t-1)} + e_{it},$$

where Y_{it} denotes FH's Global Freedom, FH's Political Rights, or the EIU's Democracy Index, and the variable z_{jit}, $j = 1, \ldots, 5$ represents the government's implementation practices.

Because the governments' surveillance and censorship practices will take time to affect democracy, Table 8.3 only reports the effects with a lag. Overall, these government implementations give rise to an unfavorable impact on democracy. The negative effects are particularly significant for those government implementations in internet filtering and shut down. The governments' surveillance and censorship practices on the Internet hurt democracy more than those in social media. Table 8.3 further indicates that the negative effects are mainly attributed to group L (authoritarian or fragile democratic countries). As for group H (democratic countries), the effects of the government implementations are almost statistically insignificant.

In summary, our findings align with the observations outlined in the previous sections, reinforcing the conclusion that AI/ICT investments in CF and SD are strongly associated with authoritarian regimes, whereas democratic systems mitigate their use through institutional checks and balances. In authoritarian or fragile democratic countries, democratic checks and balances are weak, allowing the state to have access to individual data and to improve the efficiency of surveillance and censorship. The state rulers in authoritarian or fragile democratic countries therefore have a strong incentive to invest in the capacity of CF and SD, and to use these tools in surveillance and censorship practices, which has finally led to the deterioration of democracy. By contrast, in democratic countries checks and balances may disturb all of the above three channels.

The availability of individual big data to rulers in authoritarian and fragile democratic countries may be the key reason why AI becomes a more worthwhile investment for these rulers. In economics terminology, the government's convenient access to big data means that the AI technology is intrinsically more complementary to the ruler than to other potential users in civil society groups. In the next section we theoretically analyze why this is the case.

Table 8.3 Effects of the Government's implementation practices on democracy

	FH's Global Freedom		*FH's Political Rights*		*EIU's Democracy Index*	
	Coeff	*Std*	*Coeff*	*Std*	*Coeff*	*Std*
Independent Lagged Variables (t–1)—All						
Internet Filtering	−2.521***	(0.372)	−1.492***	(0.245)	−0.113***	(0.033)
Internet Shut Down	−0.691 +	(0.353)	−0.473*	(0.232)	0.068*	(0.030)
Social Media Shut Down	−0.498	(0.350)	−0.109	(0.230)	−0.104***	(0.031)
Social Media Alternatives	−0.491	(0.430)	−0.128	(0.284)	0.044	(0.036)
Social Media Monitoring	−0.199	(0.336)	−0.151	(0.222)	0.006	(0.030)
Social Media Censorship	−0.610	(0.388)	−0.235	(0.256)	0.046	(0.034)
N	2296		2296		1804	
Independent Lagged Variables (t–1) — Group L						
Internet Filtering	−2.973***	(0.468)	−1.661***	(0.303)	−0.046	(0.049)
Internet Shut Down	−0.356	(0.401)	−0.337	(0.261)	0.115**	(0.039)
Social Media Shut Down	−0.585	(0.407)	0.020	(0.267)	−0.122**	(0.042)
Social Media Alternatives	−0.799	(0.515)	−0.231	(0.337)	0.052	(0.045)
Social Media Monitoring	−0.749 +	(0.449)	−0.482 +	(0.287)	0.003	(0.042)
Social Media Censorship	−0.527	(0.549)	−0.426	(0.348)	−0.055	(0.049)
Independent Lagged Variables (t–1) — Group H						
Internet Filtering	−0.695	(0.590)	−0.678 +	(0.399)	0.006	(0.049)
Internet Shut Down	−0.524	(0.683)	−0.304	(0.469)	−0.067	(0.055)
Social Media Shut Down	−0.288	(0.617)	−0.252	(0.413)	−0.133**	(0.046)
Social Media Alternatives	−0.140	(0.724)	0.309	(0.487)	−0.032	(0.061)
Social Media Monitoring	0.267	(0.489)	0.290	(0.337)	0.078 +	(0.042)
Social Media Censorship	−0.445	(0.518)	0.231	(0.355)	−0.001	(0.046)

8.6 Why Does AI Help Autocrats?—Theoretical Perspectives

In this section, we will provide some analytical arguments that support such empirical findings. In particular, we ask the following questions: Why do some ICTs usually benefit the autocrats instead of the civil society? And even if AI and ICT do benefit the autocrat, how do we arrive at the conclusion that a fragile democracy in question will be more likely to move toward a despotic regime, as shown by the empirical evidence in Fig. 8.1?

A concise analytical framework has been provided by Acemoglu and Robinson (2012, 2019, 2020). There they consider a framework where the state power interacts with the civil society power, and analyze when a democratic regime will arise, and when a despotic scenario will be the outcome. In this section, we will first briefly introduce the framework of Acemoglu and Robinson, and then ask how the introduction of AI and big data may change their initial results.

8.6.1 The "Narrow Corridor" Theory

Acemoglu and Robinson consider a society where the aggregate output (we can think of it as the GDP) is jointly produced by both the ruling group and the civil society force. If the state's ruling is too strong relative to the civil society force, then eventually we will observe a despotic result; and if the civil society force is too strong, then we will end up with anarchy. When the forces of the two sides are roughly equal, then both the joint production and the checks and balances are efficient, with the outcome being referred to by Acemoglu and Robinson as *an inclusive democracy*. The term "inclusive" is in contrast to the word "extractive," which was used by the two Nobel Laureates to describe an autocrat's intention to increase his own benefit, possibly at the expense of sacrificing some other benefits for the rest of the society.

Joint Output

Consider a subway system as an example of joint output. If state power is excessive and civil society lacks checks and balances, the outcome may resemble China's "social credit" system—where surveillance cameras monitor passengers and flag misbehavior. While such a system ensures operational order, it discourages citizen participation, reducing public feedback and innovation. There may be cameras everywhere which pick out individuals who "misbehave." The operation itself is in order, but citizens are afraid of providing suggestions for improvement, and hence useful feedback is lacking and the overall operation is not efficient. On the other hand, if the government is very weak but the civil society forces are too strong, then regulations and rules are often criticized, and they are not honored and respected by passengers. As a result, the overall outcome will not be efficient either.

Acemoglu and Robinson showed that only in the region where the forces of the government and the civil society are roughly equal and balanced can the society converge to an efficient equilibrium. As to the verb "converge," Acemoglu and Robinson meant that the forces of the government and the civil society both grow in a balanced way, and eventually stabilize. Because such a "roughly balanced" situation is rare in human history, they refer to this region as a "narrow" corridor. In short, we have three possible final equilibria: a despotic state, an anarchy, and an inclusive democracy.

Separate Investments

What determines which of these three outcomes prevails? This leads to the second element of Acemoglu and Robinson's model, which is that both the civil society and the government need to invest and gradually accumulate their respective forces. For example, the government may invest in subway cabin surveillance cameras and hence effectively know which cabin needs cleaning, which improves operational efficiency. The civil society forces may arouse social movements to encourage passenger feedback, which facilitates constructive suggestions and may also improve efficiency. In the above example, both "buying cameras" and "rallying social movements" are costly investment activities exercised by, respectively, the government and the civil society forces.

As Acemoglu and Robinson noted, however, there are usually *increasing returns* to the above investment. When the difference in forces between the government and the civil society is too big, the weak side will not want to invest, because the marginal return will be very low and insufficient to offset the costs, whereas the strong side will want to invest more because the marginal return is very high relative to the cost. Thus, an existing large difference between the government and the civil society forces may further enlarge the gap. In short, this increasing-return property may drive the result to a corner solution.

What Drives the Final Outcome?

As we mentioned above, once this increasing-return property is triggered, then we reach a state of no return: an originally strong government will become even stronger as time goes by, and will eventually become a despotic one; and an originally weak government will become weaker under the ever-rising pressure of the civil society forces, and finally reach a state of anarchy. The only corridor within which an inclusive democracy could arise is when the forces of the government and the civil society are roughly equal. This balanced-force situation will enable both sides to increase their investment, and hence both forces will steadily increase until healthy checks and balances are reached. This is the essence of the narrow corridor theory.

Our crucial question is as follows. In the digital era where advances in ICTs are rapid, what will happen to the prediction of Acemoglu and Robinson? Will the narrow corridor become narrower or wider? In particular, will the AI and big data facilitate the appearance of democracy or autocracy?

8.6.2 Which Side Will Benefit from AI?

As discussed earlier in this chapter, political scientists widely argue that AI disproportionately benefits autocrats. We believe that the key notion here is *complementarity*. In economics, the *substitutability* between two production factors X and Y can be measured by the elasticity of substitution: if we have a 1% increase in X, what is the percentage of Y that we can reduce in order to sustain the same output? The complementarity between two production factors is just the reverse of *substitutability*: The larger the substitution elasticity is, the smaller the complementarity index will be.

Indeed, a recent paper by Chu et al. (2025) suggests that whether AI would make the autocrat more stable hinges upon the complementarity between AI and government /civil society forces. More specifically, let the government force be denoted by s, the civil society checks and balances force be denoted by x, and the AI technology be denoted by a. Chu et al. (2025) have proved the following proposition: Suppose that a) s and a are complementary (i.e., a larger a increases the marginal productivity of s), and b) the complementarity between s and a is stronger than that between x and a (i.e., a is more complementary to government force s than it is to civil society force x). Then, the introduction of the AI technology will help reinforce the autocrat's control, and an inclusive democracy will be less likely to arise. In short, AI will make a fragile democracy more likely to converge to a despotic regime, or make an otherwise unstable autocrat more stable.[22]

If complementarity is the key, then we should ask: Is AI more complementary to the government force or to the civil society force? Our analysis in previous sections tells us that AI should be more complementary to the side that owns and possesses an abundance of big data: the larger the data sets, the more effectively that the computer can implement the generative learning and modification, and the more powerful the AI becomes. The key to this is that the government owns much bigger datasets than the civil society groups. In general, the government has the data for all records that need the authentication or verification of the public power. In countries that lack checks and balances, the government can further access the data of many social activities, as we discussed in previous sections. Evidently, the data owned by civil society forces can hardly be compared with that of the government, and therefore a is more complementary to s than it is to x.

This analysis helps explain why authoritarian regimes in the Middle East have resisted democratization over the past decade. Facing growing pressure from citizens and fearing loss of power, dictators have embraced new technologies, thereby enhancing their authoritarian controls. As a result, the Arab Spring eventually failed to flourish. As for China, big data provide ample information for AI and ICTs to improve the efficiency of government monitoring and surveillance. As such, newer and more advanced information technologies reinforce the centralized structure of control, rather than facilitating political participation and democracy.

[22] More specifically, Chu et al. (2025) showed that technology development has two conflicting effects. On the one hand, technological advances increase the marginal return on exerting effort for both the state and society. This not only enhances national output but also facilitates democratization, since technology leads the strengths of the state and society to grow in a parallel way. This is called the *output effect*. On the other hand, if information technology is more complementary to the strength of the state than to that of the society, it gives the state a stronger incentive to invest in its political capacity than the civil society. This asymmetry generates a detrimental effect on democratization. This is called the *relative productivity effect*. We also note that in the classic analysis of Acemoglu and Robinson, where the technology involved is a linear one, the relative productivity effect never arises.

8.7 A Long-Run Remark on Technical Neutrality

After the Arab Spring movements in the early 2010s, some social scientists were optimistic in predicting the trend of "democratization," meaning that ICTs may facilitate the transition from an authoritarian regime to a democratic one. In our previous discussion, we have shown that this is not going to happen: the fundamental complementarity between big data access and the productivity of AI has increased the intrinsic advantage of the autocrat. In the foreseeable future, we expect to witness fewer cases of successful democratization.

According to the Freedom House 2023 report, only Tunisia remains "partly free," while Egypt, Libya, and Yemen have regressed to "not free" status. The original optimism and the praise brought about by the Facebook or YouTube revolution after the Arab Spring have proved to be unfounded. After all, advances in AI/ICT are never "neutral."

Although we argued in the above analysis that AI favors the state rulers, it is possible that some time in the future we may witness an ICT advancement that favors the civilian. In Chapter 3 we mentioned the possibility that future LEOs may facilitate information autonomy, because private communications using LEOs may not be intercepted by government devices. Harari (2024) was also optimistic that ICT may hinder autocrats. The discussion in this chapter only focuses on one technology (AI) and one aspect (the complementarity between AI and big data). When the time span is extended, we may find new technologies that may nourish new perspectives.

References

Acemoglu, D. (2021). *Harms of AI*. NBER Working Paper 29247.

Acemoglu, D., & Robinson, J. A. (2012). *Why Nations Fail? The Origins of Power, Prosperity and Poverty*. Crown Business.

Acemoglu, D., & Robinson, J. A. (2019). *The Narrow Corridor: States, Societies, and the Fate of Liberty*. Penguin Press.

Acemoglu, D., & Robinson, J. A. (2020). The Political Agenda Effect and State Centralization. *Journal of Comparative Economics, 48*, 749–778.

Acemoglu, D., & Johnson, S. (2023). *Power and Progress: Our Thousand-Year Struggle Over Technology and Prosperity*. John Murray.

Agrawal, A., Gans, J., & Goldfarb, A. (2019). *The Economics of Artificial Intelligence: An Agenda*. The University of Chicago Press.

Applebaum, A. (2024). *Autocracy Inc.: The Dictators Who Want to Run the World*. Knopf.
Arellano, M., & Bond, S. (1991). Some Tests of Specification for Panel Data: Monte Carlo Evidence and an Application to Employment Equations. *Review of Economic Studies, 58*, 277–297.
Australian Strategic Policy Institute. (2019). *Mapping more of China's technology giants*.
Autor, D., Salomons, A., & Seegmiller, B. (2022). *New Frontiers: The Origin and Content of New Work, 1940–2018*. NBER Working Paper 30389.
Cate, F. H., Dempsey, J. X., & Rubinstein, I. S. (2012). Systematic Government Access to Private-Sector Data. *International Data Privacy Law, 2*, 195–199.
Chu, C. Y. C., Chang, J.-J., & Lin, C.-C. (2025). Why Does Artificial Intelligence Hinder Democratization? *Proceedings of the National Academy of Sciences* (2025), 122 (19), e 2423266122.
Clarke, D. C. (2003). Puzzling Observations in Chinese Law. In C. S. Hsu (Ed.), *Understanding China's Legal System* (pp. 93–121). NYU Press.
deLisle, J. & Yang, G. (Eds.) (2022). *The Party Leads All: The Evolving Role of the Chinese Communist Party*. Brookings Institution Press.
Feldstein, S. (2019). The Road to Digital Unfreedom: How Artificial Intelligence is Reshaping Repression. *Journal of Democracy, 30*, 40–52.
Hansen, B. E. (1997). Approximate Asymptotic p Values for Structural-Change Tests. *Journal of Business and Economic Statistics, 15*, 60–67.
Hariri, Y. N. (2024). *A Brief History of Information Networks from the Stone Age to AI*. Random House.
Im, K. S., Pesaran, M. H., & Shin, Y. (2003). Testing for Unit Roots in Heterogeneous Panels. *Journal of Econometrics, 115*, 53–74.
Iskander, E. (2011). Connecting the National and the Virtual: Can Facebook Activism Remain Relevant After Egypt's January 25 Uprising? *International Journal of Communication, 5*, 13–15.
Kendall-Taylor, A., Frantz, E., & Wright, J. (2020). The Digital Dictators: How Technology Strengthens Autocracy. *Foreign Affairs, 99*, 103–115.
King, G., Pan, J., & Roberts, M. E. (2014). Reverse-Engineering Censorship in China: Randomized Experimentation and Participant Observation. *Science, 345*, 1251722.
Korinek, A., & Stiglitz, J. (2017). *Artificial Intelligence and Its Implications for Income Distribution and Unemployment*. NBER Working Paper No. 24174.
Korinek, A., & Stiglitz, J. E. (2021). *Artificial Intelligence, Globalization, and Strategies for Economic Development*. NBER Working Paper No. 28453.
Limbago, A. L. (2019). *Combating Digital Authoritarianism: U.S. Alternative Needed to Counter Data Localization and Government Control*. The National Security Institute.

Pei, M. (2024). *The Sentinel State: Surveillance and the Survival of Dictatorship in China*. Harvard University Press.

Sheppard, L.R., Yayboke, E., & Ramos, C. G. (2021). *The Real National Security Concerns over Data Localization*. Center for Strategic and International Studies.

Shirky, C. (2011). The Political Power of Social Media: Technology, the Public Sphere, and Political Change. *Foreign Affairs, 90*, 28–41.

CHAPTER 9

Penetrating Through the Digital Wall

In Chapter 2, we listed several aspects of Chinese aggressions, including the BRI, AIIB, and reclaiming land in the South China Sea. These are all activities in the physical space. In this chapter, we will investigate aggressions in the form of penetrating targets of other countries through cyberspace. These aggressions occur in both directions; the penetrating side may be China, and may also involve other democratic countries (such as the U.S.). Other than penetrating cases, we will also discuss institutional issues.

As depicted in historical accounts, we know that in ancient conflicts intelligence warfare was important. Both sides in a war often wanted to use bows and arrows to shoot down messenger pigeons, to intercept the information being delivered, to decipher the encrypted codes of the message, to send misleading messages to confuse the enemy, to spread rumors in the opponents' backyard, or to send noisy signals to the enemy's camp. These intelligence warfare strategies are still valid today, except that most of them are exercised through communications in cyberspace. In addition, the intelligence warfare in the twenty-first century is more versatile than sending pigeons and carrying notes; we will discuss all varieties as we proceed.

C. Y. C. Chu, *An Emerging Digital Wall*,
https://doi.org/10.1007/978-981-95-3577-4_9

9.1 Espionage Tensions Between China and the U.S

In March 2023, the Center for Strategic and International Studies (CSIS), a U.S.-based research organization, published a report entitled "A Survey of Reported Chinese Espionage, 2000 to the Present," in which the authors summarized 224 reported instances of Chinese espionage. The summary does not include the cases where the targeted U.S. firms are located in China, nor the more than 1200 cases of IP theft lawsuits where the litigation side involves a U.S. company.[1]

Regarding these numbers, CSIS highlighted four key findings: (1) Among these 224 cases, 69% were reported after Xi Jinping took office in 2012. This indicates that the espionage became more active under Xi's rule. (2) Chinese espionage incidents far outnumber those by Russia or other countries. This suggests that China has become the #1 hypothetical enemy of the U.S. (3) Internet hacking is China's most preferred methods in recent years: there were 104 incidents in the 2013–2023 period. (4) 54% of the summarized incidents sought to acquire commercial technologies, 29% of the incidents sought to acquire military technologies, and 17% sought to acquire information on individuals, including U.S. citizens or politicians.

Among the above-mentioned espionage incidents that were launched through cyberattacks, the targets varied greatly, including U.S. government agencies (the FBI, NSA, CISA, DOD, NASA, the White House, the State Department, Navy War College, Department of Homeland Security, National Laboratories, Department of Commerce, NATO, etc.), private firms (GM, FORD, NetLogics, Boeing, Motorola, Dupont, Google, Dow, AMSC, Monsanto, United Airlines, GSK, Moody's, Bayer, etc.), media (the New York Times, Wall Street Journal, Washington Post, Bloomberg, etc.), election campaign headquarters, and many other platforms that collect extensive user data.

According to the CSIS report, among such incidents, 49% directly involved Chinese military or government employees, and 41% were Chinese citizens. Regarding the latter, because much of the cyber espionage involves sophisticated skills (such as breaking the firewall protection, locating the storage place of sensitive data, etc.), it was suspected

[1] See https://www.csis.org/programs/strategic-technologies-program/survey-chinese-espionage-united-states-2000.

that some government forces were behind the "civilian" activities, but the evidence was not sufficient to accuse the Chinese government. Finally, these incidents are summarized by CSIS researchers from various publicly accessible reports, and do not include undisclosed cases or those resolved through alternative channels (such as court settlements). These CSIS summaries give us a sobering picture of the seriousness of cyberspace espionage.

Stealing business or government secrets is just one kind of internet aggression targeted at foreign entities. These penetrations have specific targets and purposes, and their economic or political values are very clear. However, there is another kind of penetration, with less obvious direct benefits: collecting the big data of foreign countries. This kind of behavior may appear innocuous, and its true value may remain unclear. The collected big data may be used either by foreign businesses or by the foreign government in critical moments. A typical example is that a foreign country can use such big data to disseminate targeted information to citizens before an election, in an attempt to influence the outcome, on which there will be more discussion later in this chapter.

9.2 Key Features of Cyberattacks

Let us start by introducing some basic terms in cyberattacks.

9.2.1 Types of Malware

Worms and viruses are the most common cybersecurity threats, whereas malware is a general term that includes all software designed to do harm. A *virus* can be spread from one computer to another, but activation requires an additional user action. For example, a virus can be embedded inside a spreadsheet, and if one downloads and opens it, one's computer will be infected. As for a *worm*, it can both run and spread itself to other computers, and without requiring any user intervention. Because a worm has the ability to automatically propagate itself, one can get a worm in one's computer just because it is connected to the same network as another infected device. For example, the thing sent out by Robert Morris Jr. in 1988 (which we mentioned in Chapter 1) was a worm.

Building upon the above two classifications, Shapiro (2023) introduced two more sophisticated malwares: "vorm"—a malware that requires both Internet transmission and user action—and "wirus"—a malware that can self-activate without such transmission. These very much include all malwares that we are about to discuss.

9.2.2 *How Is Malware Activated and Stopped?*

We understand that all computer *programs* and *data* are written in 0s and 1s, which match with the transistors' off and on switches. This is called the *duality principle* of the 0–1 digits. The key to a malware is to use this duality principle to trick the computer: to let the computer believe that it is reading some innocent data in the form of 0s and 1s, while actually it changes the program or activates some destructive tasks. For example, a malware can overflow a computer's buffer space, and let the computer network perform endless meaningless computations, before finally becoming paralyzed.

Usually, we know that our computer is infected when it looks paralyzed. The way to find the malware is to check the related codes and detect places where some irregularities appear. However, this is the treatment after infection; in general, there are no perfectly safe ways to prevent our computers from being infected. Worse still, sometimes the malware is in hibernation mode (perhaps because the environment is not ready for the attack), and users cannot even find any irregularity even by scrutiny. In general, the various types of antivirus software need to be endlessly updated, and sometimes the antivirus dosages are written by individuals who themselves spread the virus. Users' caution can decrease the probability of infection, but we are human and we always make mistakes, no matter how careful we are. In short, cybersecurity is analogous to crime prevention: it is a matter of trade-offs between *ex ante* caution and *ex post* harm, and there is no perfectly secure network, just as zero-crime is an unrealistic target.

9.2.3 *Where Do Cyberattacks Come From?*

We know some famous cyberattack cases already: the Russian attack on Hillary Clinton's campaign headquarters; the Chinese cyber espionage directed at the U.S. which we mentioned at the beginning of this chapter; and the New York Times' report that the U.S. and Israel had used a malware named Stuxnet to dismantle Iran's nuclear weapon program of Iran.[2] These were massive attacks launched by major powers.

Other than Russia, China, and the U.S., there are also many smaller countries that can launch equally effective cyberattacks. Sanger (2018) mentioned that North Korea attacked U.S. facilities; and Shapiro (2023) also referred to Bulgaria as a major camp for writing computer malware in the 1990s. In terms of GDPs in 2023, Bulgaria was just ranked 67th in the world, and North Korea was ranked 137th, so neither of them is a superpower. In short, through cyberattacks, even an individual with minimal resources can bring down a massive institution.

This is indeed a key feature of cyberattacks. The knowledge needed to write a malware is not sophisticated, and sometimes a successful penetration depends on luck, such as the negligence of a few employees on the target side.[3] In the physical space, a poor country's deployment of thousands of soldiers can hardly invade a big country, but the deployment of merely several hundred hackers may end up with a success in terms of cyberattacks. Moreover, since it is very difficult to identify the exact names of foreign hackers, not to mention bringing the case to prosecution, there is almost no effective deterrence for such attacks. In fact, cyberattacks are seldom identified, and penalizing attackers is even less likely. All these factors together clearly indicate that the writing of malware and computer hacking have nothing to do with economic capabilities.

9.2.4 Why Is It "The Perfect Weapon"?

"The Perfect Weapon" was the title of Sanger's book (2018). Other than the fact that cyberattacks can be carried out by countries with relatively weak economic capability, there are several other reasons why they may be a preferred weapon when compared to conventional military tools such as bombs and tanks. The idea may be better understood by describing the famous case of Stuxnet, where a malware was claimed (by a New York Times reporter) to have infiltrated an Iranian plant, located at Natanz,

[2] https://archive.nytimes.com/www.nytimes.com/interactive/2012/06/01/world/middleeast/how-a-secret-cyberwar-program-worked.html?hp.

[3] For instance, according to Shapiro (2023), the Fancy Bear of Russia simply sent a message to staff at the Clinton headquarters: "Your account has been hacked, please reset your password." Somehow a negligent staff member bit the hook, and the whole network was compromised.

in which it was alleged that the Iranians were trying to build a nuclear bomb.

The Natanz cyberattack operation was reported to be jointly implemented by the U.S. and the Israeli military, likely in the year 2010. In the initial stage, a beacon program was introduced into the plant's computer system, possibly by a negligent worker. Through this beacon, the U.S. and Israel knew the process of the plant's operation. This was important, because it gives the attacking side sufficient time to come up with a perfect plan. Next, a spyware was transmitted into the plant and took control of its operations. This spyware could alter the electrical current and voltage that were sent to the centrifuge. This made the centrifuge spin either too slowly or too fast. Because of these unstable currents, the centrifuges experienced severe vibrations and eventually exploded. At the same time, the malware had also taken over the interior monitoring system, so that the serious shakes of the centrifuge would not generate any warning signals on the monitoring screen. As such, the internal workers in Stuxnet did not even notice this irregularity, until the centrifuge exploded and the rescue was already in vain.

According to Sanger (2018), if this cyberattack had not been executed, then eventually Israel might have resorted to a serious air strike to destroy the plant, which would have led to counterattacks by the Iranian military. These strikes and counterstrikes could lead to unpredictable geopolitical consequences. All physical space wars have irreversible and observable damage and casualties, whereas a cyberattack like that by Stuxnet does not have any observable impacts. This made it difficult for the Iranian side to justify any counterattacks. In addition, it was even more difficult to prove that this incident was executed by Israel and the U.S. Because there was no smoking gun, there was little aftermath in international politics. Indeed, if there were no New York Times reports, we might never know that such an incident took place.

9.2.5 The Case of Russia Attacking Ukraine

Another famous incident was when Russia targeted Ukraine's electricity system. In the 2010s. Russia had successfully infiltrated the Ukraine network several times and had occasionally started to test the attack before the final attack was launched.

The first test occurred in February–March 2014, coinciding with Russian troop movements in Crimea. By that time, the Ukrainian communication centers had been raided and their fiber optic cables tampered with, and hence the connection between the peninsula and mainland Ukraine was compromised. Later, on March 13, 2014, three days before the referendum on the status of Crimea, Russia launched an eight-minute-long DDoS cyberattack aimed at disturbing Ukrainian computer networks and communications.[4] That attack was believed to be to divert public attention from the presence of Russian troops in Crimea.

Then, in 2015, several waves of cyberattacks ensued. The first wave was to upload a malware which targeted specific individuals working in different energy companies in order to retrieve administrator credentials and gain access to the energy networks. During the second wave of the attack, the Russian hackers activated a destructive KillDisk malware, capable of wiping out portions of computer hard drives and preventing the systems from rebooting, ultimately leading to the power outages. That attack indeed resulted in power outages for nearly 225,000 consumers in Western Ukraine. However, that outage lasted only a few hours, because the purpose of the attack was just to perform a test.[5]

Finally, on one winter night in 2016, Ukrainians experienced the first known blackout caused by a malicious malware designed to autonomously attack the power grid. One-fifth of Kyiv's citizens were plunged into darkness as attackers used the malware to target the power grid of Kyiv. In 2017, Russia also launched attacks on the Ukrainian financial system and computer networks (Sanger, 2018, Chapter 7). Sanger has described how Ukraine was a testing ground for Russian hackers; they just attacked, checked the Ukrainian responses, modified the malware, and attacked again after a while. The petri dish just helped improve the efficiency of the Russian attacks.

Six years later, in the early months of the Russian invasion of Ukraine in 2022, there was also an attack that attempted to combine kinetic and

[4] A denial-of-service attack (DoS attack) is a cyberattack in which the perpetrator seeks to make a machine or network resource unavailable to its intended users. The first D of DDoS refers to some "distributed" attacks, which are launched from multiple sources. See also https://www.europarl.europa.eu/RegData/etudes/BRIE/2022/733549/EPRS_BRI(2022)733549_EN.pdf.

[5] See https://cyberlaw.ccdcoe.org/wiki/Power_grid_cyberattack_in_Ukraine_(2015).

cyber operations to take down Ukraine's power grid, which might have compromised part of the Ukrainian defense capability.

9.3 Cyberattacks: Institutional Differences

Now that we are aware of several famous cyberattacks over the past two decades, in regard to the possible launching of such attacks, there are several institutional differences between democratic countries and authoritarian regimes. We must understand these differences before we design and evaluate policy options.

9.3.1 Attackers: Private Entities or the Government

In cyberspace interactions, we can classify attackers into two types: the government (G) and private entities (PEs), including individuals and businesses. Similarly, we can also classify targets into two types: G and PE. The PE-to-PE penetrations are common, and the targeted party may pursue civil suits against the attacker. Usually, these cases do not involve aspects of international politics. The G-to-G attacks or infiltrations are also common forms of espionage, which are treated as normal (though not welcomed) in international practice.

After 911, the U.S. increased its telephone and cyberspace monitoring, which covered many civilians and even alliance leaders, as revealed by the Snowden documents.[6] These are typical G-to-PE cyber penetrations. However, for democratic regimes, this widespread G-to-PE monitoring (without court orders) is treated as an exception rather than a routine. Leaders in democratic countries must often apologize for such activities once uncovered, and sometimes such monitoring would be ruled as illegal by various levels of courts.

Here we see the first institutional difference: governments of democratic countries cannot penetrate private entities without a court order. If the target of hacking is a foreign private entity, say a private firm, the democratic government cannot share the hacked information with domestic competitors to increase their ability to compete against the foreign firm. In authoritarian countries, as one can see from the CSIS reports, most of the cyberattacks or hacks were executed by the Chinese

[6] See https://en.wikipedia.org/wiki/Edward_Snowden.

cyber army, and the sole purpose was to transfer the business secrets of the companies being hacked to their domestic firms, to increase the latter's competition capability. In a sense, the CCP is effectively assisting Chinese domestic private entities in obtaining business secrets of foreign competitors.

This is actually not surprising, once we understand the common practices of state-owned enterprises (SOEs) in Communist countries. Under a Leninist regime, even for superficially private companies, the party controls them all and treats them as a unified entity. In short, in Communist countries such as China and Russia, the distinction between government and private enterprises is blurred. As a result, the PE and G are very much the same.

As the former U.S. FBI Director James Comey pointed out in an interview with ABC News, the U.S. conducted surveillance for national security purposes but never shared information with U.S. businesses, which would give them an unfair competitive edge.[7] In fact, in any democratic countries, even if the government does steal some competitive know-how and wants to share it with some particular private businesses, it may have trouble sharing this information in a legal way without violating related rules of "misuse of public power for private profit." In short, the distinction between private businesses and the government in democratic countries is very clear, and that is very different from the practice in authoritarian countries.

9.3.2 *Firewalls: With or Without Internet Blocking*

As regards the cyberspace interactions, the second major institutional difference between democratic countries and authoritarian ones is the existence of internet blocks in the latter group of countries. The typical example is the "Great Firewall" (GFW) of China. According to the Freedom House 2023 report, the GFW is the world's most sophisticated internet censorship apparatus.[8] Content that contains criticism of individuals, policies, or events that are considered harmful to the one-party

[7] See https://www.voanews.com/a/chinas-alleged-cyber-spying-could-cost-us-billions-/1919757.html.

[8] See https://freedomhouse.org/country/china/freedom-net/2023#A.

system is blocked, resulting in Chinese users having access only to a highly controlled, monitored, and manipulated version of foreign information.

According to GreatFire.org—an anticensorship group that tracks filtering in China—as of March 2025, at least 175 of the 1,000 most heavily visited websites and social media platforms in the world were also blocked, and roughly 8,000 websites were blocked in China.[9] Many international news outlets and their Chinese-language websites are blocked, such as those of the *New York Times*, *Reuters*, the *Wall Street Journal*, the *Australian Broadcasting Corporation*, and the *British Broadcasting Corporation*. Websites of independent Chinese-language news services from Taiwan, Hong Kong, and the Chinese diaspora (such as the *Liberty Times* in Taiwan), *Initium* in Singapore, and the *China Digital Times* in the U.S., were also blocked at the time of writing.

Most international social media and messaging platforms are blocked, including *Facebook*, *WhatsApp*, *Twitter*, *Instagram*, *Signal*, *Clubhouse*, *YouTube*, *Telegram*, *Snapchat*, *Line*, and *Pinterest*. The popular discussion forum *Reddit* was blocked, and all languages of *Wikipedia* were blocked. A number of Google services (including *Maps*, *Translate*, *Calendar*, *Docs*, *Drive*, *Scholar*, and *Analytics*) were also blocked. Given this GFW, Chinese users can only access foreign websites if they use a VPN (virtual private network) to "bypass the firewall." However, that is illegal, and the government's monitoring of such activities has become increasingly strict since 2017.[10]

Given the GFW of China, if the U.S. cyber army attempts to send or collect information from Chinese individuals or private enterprises, it is extremely difficult, if not impossible, to do so. On the other hand, since democratic societies such as the U.S. do not have internet blocks, the Chinese government or its citizens can freely send information to or collect information from U.S. citizens. For example, Russia can mobilize millions of its citizens or hackers to send messages to U.S. social media, influence public opinion, and hopefully achieve its goal, just as in the case of the 2016 U.S. Presidential election. As for the U.S., however, since it cannot directly access the Russian or Chinese citizens because of internet blocking, such influence remains out of reach for the U.S.

[9] See also The Complete List of Blocked Websites in China & How to Access Them.

[10] Bloomberg News China Tells Carriers to Block Access to Personal VPNs by February. This can be retrieved from https://www.bloomberg.com/news/articles/2017-07-10/china-is-said-to-order-carriers-to-bar-personal-vpns-by-february, dated July 1, 2017.

Similarly, if the U.S. were to use a spyware to gather information from the Kremlin, such information could hardly be spread in Russia. Simply put, G-to-PE penetrations into authoritarian countries are extremely difficult, if not impossible.

9.3.3 *Institutional Impediment: Is Setting Up Platforms in China Allowed?*

Another disadvantage of the democratic countries is that they may not be allowed to establish platforms in authoritarian countries. Because all Western platforms such as search engines, social media, and e-commerce sites, are either blocked or censored in authoritarian countries such as China, very few Chinese use foreign platforms to search, interact, or shop. Indeed, Chinese can connect to foreign websites through VPNs, but since it is illegal, they would do this only occasionally. As a result, U.S. businesses can hardly use these platforms to collect information from Chinese citizens. This makes the PE-to-PE penetration into authoritarian countries difficult, or at least very inefficient.

On the other hand, there are many U.S. citizens who buy products from Alibaba, use TikTok, and drive vehicles equipped with GPS provided by Big Dipper, and hence these Chinese companies can collect information from U.S. citizens. Can the Chinese government retrieve information from these platforms? This leads us to the third institutional difference between democratic countries and the authoritarian regimes.[11]

9.3.4 *Can the Government Retrieve Private Information?*

As we have discussed in Chapter 8, the Chinese government has enacted various laws to compel Chinese tech companies to submit their data to the government. Although there is a "national security" premise, because of the vagueness of the wording, an authoritarian government can always interpret these laws in a favorable manner to retrieve the information it desires. Could a democratic government do the same? It is not that easy.

[11] This may change in the future. In April 2024, the U.S. President signed a law forcing TikTok to "sell or exit" within 270 days, which we have discussed in Chapter 5. See https://www.reuters.com/legal/us-appeals-court-upholds-tiktok-law-forcing-its-sale-2024-12-06/.

A famous case was that in February 2016 when Apple faced the United States District Court for the Central District of California. The Federal Bureau of Investigation (FBI) wanted Apple to create and electronically sign new software that would enable the FBI to unlock a work-issued iPhone 5C it recovered from one of the shooters in a December 2015 attack (in San Bernardino, California) in which 14 people died and 22 were injured. The two attackers later died in a shootout with police, having first destroyed their personal phones. Another work phone of a shooter was later recovered intact but was locked with a four-digit passcode and was set to erase all its data after ten failed password attempts (a common anti-theft measure on smartphones). Apple said "No" to the court order. Incidentally, the U.S. government withdrew the request afterward.[12]

In 2018, about 4000 Google employees signed a petition calling for a clear company policy, stating that neither Google nor its contractors should ever develop warfare technology. A handful of employees also resigned in protest, while some others were openly advocating that the company terminate the Maven contract. Google's work with the Defense Department on the Maven program uses artificial intelligence to interpret video images and could be used to improve the targeting of drone strikes, with the help of the Google work force. Many of the company's top AI researchers, in particular, worried that the contract was the first step toward using the primeval technology in advanced weapons.[13]

The above two incidents clearly show that the internet platform and device firms in democratic countries operate with considerable independence from government control—and are generally unwilling to cooperate with government demands. In cases where the U.S. government needs the help of private tech companies to infiltrate or plant a malware in some terminal devices, it is likely that many tech companies will decline. This refusal may earn market respect, which in turn may increase their market acceptance and hence their profit. However, if a Chinese tech company declines the CCP's request, the boss should be prepared to be prosecuted and go to jail.

[12] See https://en.wikipedia.org/wiki/Apple%E2%80%93FBI_encryption_dispute.

[13] See https://www.nytimes.com/2018/06/01/technology/google-pentagon-project-maven.html.

9.3.5 No Engagement Rules: Constraints or Freedom?

The final feature of cyberattacks that we should note here is the lack of clear rules of engagement. All physical wars are visibly evident, and there are well-known rules of engagement such as the Geneva Convention.[14] Most cyberattacks do not result in explosions or casualties, so the public may not know about the attacks. Even if the U.S.-Israel joint effort of destroying the nuclear facility at Natanz was as effective as that of bombing the plant, it did not create an appearance of an attack. Furthermore, because the external signs of cyberattacks may be faint, the side being attacked may be uncertain whether an attack has occurred, as long as there is no *New York Times* report.

In addition, neither does the attacking side want to admit the attack, just like the long period of time that Ukraine was kept in the dark in the Russia/Ukraine attacking case. That is, the longer that Ukraine did not know about the cyberattack, the more that Russia could do to modify its tactics, and the more effective that its subsequent attacks could be. Sanger (2018) even suspected that the U.S. had infiltrated the computer system of North Korea to disrupt and delay its missile launches for quite some years. However, once the target knows that it has been attacked, it will overhaul its entire network system, rendering the originally planted malware useless.

Because such cyberattacks are often covert, their launching procedure is often not clearly specified. In addition, because most countries do not have explicit engagement protocols and the attacks leave no physical traces, it is difficult to have any international rules that can be negotiated among major countries.

Perhaps the only exception was the U.S.-China Cyber Agreement, signed in September 2015, when President Xi Jinping of China and U.S. President Barack Obama met. According to this Agreement, in principle the U.S. and China agreed, among other things, to (1) provide timely responses to requests for information and assistance concerning malicious cyber activities, (2) refrain from conducting or knowingly supporting cyber-enabled theft of intellectual property, (3) pursue efforts to further identify and promote appropriate norms of state behavior in cyberspace within the international community, and (4) establish a high-level joint

[14] See https://www.icrc.org/en/document/ihl-rules-of-war-FAQ-Geneva-Conventions.

dialogue mechanism for combating cybercrime and addressing related issues.

In this agreement, the most substantive part was item 2). Although there is no specific objective attached to the verb "refrain," it certainly implies the government refraining from facilitating or directing private entities to implement cyberattacks. Indeed, the CSIS report that we introduced at the beginning of this chapter also showed that there was a sharp drop in China's espionage in 2016, one year after the Agreement was signed. However, the attacking incidents soon rebounded and eventually reached a new record high.

In May 2019, the European Council established a sanctioning framework which allows the EU to impose targeted restrictive measures to deter and respond to cyberattacks which constitute an external threat to the EU or its member states.

This framework allows the EU to impose sanctions on persons or entities that are responsible for cyberattacks or attempted cyberattacks, who provide financial, technical or material support for such attacks or who are involved in other aspects of such attacks.[15] As one can see, this framework has not mentioned two things: (1) If the attacks have a foreign government in the background, what could the EU do? and (2) Could the EU respond with counterattacks, if the attacking side is identified? In short, the engagement rules are not at all clear.

9.3.6 D-Day versus Everyday

It is also important to note the features of cyberspace attacks and defenses. Before the D-day of a physical war, we can often identify massive movements of soldiers, cars, tanks, and supplies. Given that these large-scale pre-D-day preparations are observable and the sites can be predicted, the defending side can practice various drills and be ready for such an attack. However, for massive cyberspace attacks, not much *ex ante* preparation can be observed, and D-day arrives without warning or alert.

From the above discussion, we also know that for wars in cyberspace, the importance of D-day is diminished. A cyberspace D-day defense could be successful only if the entities in question have good everyday defense. The success of the U.S./Israel coalition's attack on the Iranian nuclear

[15] See https://www.consilium.europa.eu/en/policies/cybersecurity/#sanctions.

facility on D-day was solely because Iran was not good at its everyday defense. If Iran had been sufficiently careful, then the initial beacon malware could not have been implanted, and there would have been no D-day attacks. The blurring of the boundary between D-day and every day is another reason why there are no cyberspace engagement rules.

In a world without engagement rules, it is usually the democratic countries that push for clear rules. The 2015 joint agreement between the U.S. and China was indeed pushed by the U.S. side. This is intuitive: democratic countries are governed by laws, and they always want to maintain a legal framework that clearly defines boundaries. However, for Leninist authoritarian countries, boundaries are usually defined by the Politburo, and vague rules are acceptable, and sometimes even welcomed.

9.4 Stealing Business Secrets

According to a well-known quote by former FBI Director James Comey in 2014, there are two types of American companies: those that have been hacked and those that do not yet know it.[16] Let us review a couple of cases that were revealed in the news.

The first case is from a BBC report in January 2023.[17] According to a Department of Justice (DOJ) indictment, a U.S. citizen Mr. Zheng hid confidential files (stolen from his employers, General Electric, GE) in the binary code of a digital photograph of a sunset, which Mr. Zheng then mailed to himself. It was a technique known as steganography, which involves hiding a data file within another data file. Mr. Zheng had utilized this technique on several other occasions to steal sensitive files from GE.

The information that Mr. Zheng stole was related to the design and manufacture of gas and steam turbines, including turbine blades and turbine seals, estimated to be worth millions of dollars. These business secrets were then sent to his accomplice in China, and ultimately would benefit the Chinese government and other China-based companies and research institutes.

[16] See https://www.independent.co.uk/news/business/news/fbi-s-james-comey-accuses-china-of-hacking-into-every-major-american-company-9777587.html.

[17] See https://www.bbc.com/news/world-asia-china-64206950.

Another more recent case occurred in March 2024. A federal grand jury indicted Linwei Ding,[18] who allegedly stole proprietary AI-related information from Google. According to the indictment, Mr. Ding is a national of the People's Republic of China and a resident of California, who transferred sensitive Google trade secrets and other confidential information from Google's network to his personal account while secretly affiliating himself with PRC-based companies in the AI industry.

While Mr. Ding was employed as a software engineer at Google, he was secretly working to enrich himself and two companies based in the People's Republic of China. The U.S. Justice Department alleged that Mr. Ding had stolen over 500 confidential files containing AI trade secrets from Google, while covertly working for China-based companies seeking an edge in the AI technology race.

According to the above-mentioned BBC report, it is a struggle for China to gain technological know-how to empower its industries and to challenge the incumbent power of the U.S. This national aggression on the side of China became more serious after Xi took power and announced the *Made in China 2025* initiative in 2015. The theft of trade secrets is attractive because it allows a country to "leapfrog up global value chains relatively quickly - and without the costs, both in terms of time and money, of relying completely on indigenous capabilities," as Nick Marro of the Economist Intelligence Unit told the BBC. This is consistent with what FBI director Christopher Wray said in 2022 that China aimed to "pilfer" the intellectual property of Western companies so that it could speed up its own industrial development and eventually dominate key industries. Wray warned that it was snooping on companies everywhere "from big cities to small towns - from Fortune 100s to start-ups, folks that focus on everything from aviation, to AI, to pharma."[19]

9.4.1 Stealing Secrets Through Joint Ventures

China has also gained expertise by compelling foreign companies to transfer technology under joint venture agreements in exchange for access to the Chinese market. This scenario often plays out in China between a

[18] See https://www.justice.gov/opa/pr/chinese-national-residing-california-arrested-theft-artificial-intelligence-related-trade.

[19] See https://www.bloomberg.com/news/articles/2022-07-07/china-is-trying-to-ransack-western-companies-fbi-head-warns.

foreign company (which has engaged in foreign direct investment) and a local cooperative firm. However, since most business secrets are stored in computers, the theft of these secrets often involves cyber intrusions. The following reviews show how it works.

In China, international technology transfer usually occurs through foreign direct investment (FDI), which can take on at least six different forms, including an equity joint venture (JV), a contractual JV, a Wholly Foreign-owned Enterprise (WFOE), and others (Lovely & Huang, 2018). However, not all business sectors are open to every form of FDI in China. To protect its own industries, China has prohibited WFOEs from competing with local companies in certain sectors of its market. For example, the Catalogue of Industries for Guiding Foreign Investment 2017, published by the Chinese government, requires that foreign companies find a Chinese partner and form a JV in order to invest in designated industries. While this list has been revised periodically in order to meet the needs of China's economic development strategies, the purpose of the policy is clear: in order to enter some sectors of the Chinese market, foreign companies are often compelled to form a joint venture with a local partner.

By using the above JV regulation as leverage, Chinese companies have gained significant bargaining power over foreign companies and could leverage it during negotiations and collaborations. It has been observed that in some business sectors, such as the automotive, aviation, and high-speed rail businesses (Carbaugh & Wassell, 2019), foreign companies have been subject to forced technology transfer (FTT).[20]

9.4.2 *Difficulties in Filing Complaints in China*

Sometimes, even though some business secrets belong to the foreign company, it is very easy for Chinese partners to breach secured areas

[20] In addition, Chinese laws often prescribe that the local partners in JVs formed in this way must control no less than 50% of the shares. Under such JVs, the IP rights or the know-how are practically used in the production process and can be seen by partners, which makes it difficult to prevent the leakage of technologies. As such, technologies possessed by foreign companies may not remain secret to the Chinese partners (Lee, 2020; Prud'homme & Zhang, 2019). This strategy has become the typical "market for technology" format, meaning that China has opened up the largest and fastest-growing market to the world in exchange for technology transfer from or sharing by foreign companies. See also Branstetter (2018).

of "their own computer systems" and retrieve them. In cases when the infringed foreign companies believed that they have evidence to prove the IP theft, they often face significant obstacles in the Chinese legal system. The following is a typical example.

In 2018, DuPont suspected its former Chinese partner of infringing its IP.[21] Because the infringement happened in China, DuPont attempted to resolve the dispute through arbitration in China. During the arbitration process, the Chinese authorities launched an antitrust investigation against DuPont and raided its Shanghai office. The antitrust authorities reportedly told DuPont to drop its IP infringement case in order to resolve the antitrust investigation.[22] This DuPont example illustrates that, given the legal practices in China, any infringement of patents taking place in China may be resolved in an unfair manner.

The above-mentioned stealing of business secrets might not have been a serious issue when China was in the stage without technology infrastructure.[23] Nowadays, however, China has not only become the world's second-largest economy, but it has also become a formidable contender in many cutting-edge technology sectors, as revealed in the ambition of the *Made in China 2025* initiative. People may not mind the petty theft in *Les Misérables*, but they do mind the theft of intellectual property from a major competitor challenging the global leader.

9.5 Internet Platforms: Domestic vs. International Aspects

In the Internet era, perhaps the most important channels for collecting big data are platforms. This is another means of penetrating cyberspace. As for the regulation of such platforms, there have been several economists who have criticized the distortion brought about by the advertising-driven internet platform, with a notable example being Nobel Laureate Paul Romer. We will first review Romer's argument, and

[21] See https://foreignaffairs.house.gov/wp-content/uploads/2020/02/Egregious-Cases-of-Chinese-Theft-of-American-Intellectual-Property.pdf.

[22] See https://foreignaffairs.house.gov/wp-content/uploads/2020/02/Egregious-Cases-of-Chinese-Theft-of-American-Intellectual-Property.pdf.

[23] "China is on the Path to Global Technology Dominance." *South China Morning Post*. https://www.scmp.com/business/global-economy/article/2081771/be-afraid-china-path-global-technology-dominance.

then highlight the differences between regulating platforms operated by domestic versus foreign companies. Romer's point is as follows.[24]

9.5.1 Domestic and Economic Perspectives of Internet Platforms

As regards the various internet platforms, Romer stressed the distortion caused by monopolies and the problems associated with the advertisement-based revenue model. In traditional demand-supply market economies, consumers buy products and pay the suppliers. Consumers' willingness to pay may be higher (or lower) if they find the products more (or less) satisfactory. Knowing this, the suppliers will try hard to improve their product quality. This feedback mechanism (from satisfied consumers to product suppliers), according to Romer, has vanished on most internet platforms.

In the case of the search engine Google, for instance, people use it for free and do not pay Google anything. Instead, Google generates its revenue from advertising firms. We, the consumers of the search engine, have therefore lost the mechanism for rewarding Google in cases where its search service is good. Furthermore, Google has the incentive to provide advertisements in an order matching the firms' willingness to pay Google: the firms that can afford more in terms of advertisement expenses obtain priority recommendations, and this priority has nothing to do with the consumer's satisfaction regarding the product quality or the Google service. As a result, Google users are presented with recommendations that do not necessarily reflect product quality, which is what they truly care about. In a sense, consumers are inappropriately penetrated by Google according to Google's interest.

Worse still, consumers do not have the ability to choose not to use Google, mainly because the search engine business is very much monopolized. As pointed out by Shapiro and Varian (2009), the property of the "network economy" enables most platforms to have increasing returns from the demand side, and thus the platform market is highly resistant to new competitors.

As for the above-mentioned problems, Romer mentioned two solutions: one is to empower consumers to refuse to allow their data to be collected or used. This is similar to the European Union's General Data

[24] See https://news.uchicago.edu/story/nobel-laureate-paul-romer-how-curb-big-techs-power.

Protection Regulation (GDPR), which we will discuss shortly. Another approach is taxation: governments could impose taxes on advertising revenue, and the tax rate can even be progressive. A progressive tax rate can discourage the expansion of a growing platform, diminish its inherent increasing returns, and thereby curb the appearance of platform monopolies.

9.5.2 *International and Political Perspectives*

Romer's proposal is perfectly reasonable in a closed economy, but it faces challenges in an open international economy. Again, let us take the search engine as an example. Under the WTO rules, the U.S. should allow foreign search engine companies to operate in the U.S. and compete with Google. However, for foreign companies, there are some problems with the feasibility of Romer's proposals.

For illustration purposes, suppose China's Baidu company is the other search engine company that does business in the U.S. The first issue has to do with when U.S. consumers refuse Baidu's data collection request. Can we trust Baidu to really comply? Knowing that all high-tech companies are led by the Party (CCP), one can hardly be convinced that the company would comply with a U.S. consumers' disclaimer, rather than a direct order from the CCP. In addition, the data collected by Baidu are not used only for advertisements, but may also be used by the CCP. The national security concern is that one day in the future, the CCP may use such data and send sensitive information to affect the U.S. election or disturb the society in some other ways. If Facebook had sold its data to Cambridge,[25] it would not at all be surprising for Baidu to let the CCP use the data collected from U.S. customers. Because Baidu is a foreign company, it is difficult for the U.S. to exercise regulatory authority over it. If even a high-profile grill by the U.S. Senate cannot make much progress in the case of TikTok,[26] how can the case of Baidu be different?

There is also the concern associated with the imposition of a tax on international companies. Suppose 80% of Baidu's users are in China, 15% in the EU, and only 5% in the U.S. If the U.S. imposes a tax on Baidu's

[25] See https://www.bbc.com/news/topics/c81zyn0888lt.

[26] See https://www.npr.org/2023/03/23/1165579717/tiktok-congress-hearing-shou-zi-chew-project-texas.

100 million in total annual advertising revenue, what should be the appropriate tax base for the U.S. tax authorities? Are the user bases equivalent to the advertisement viewer bases? To make the story more complicated, because China has internet blocks, most if not all U.S. advertisements on Baidu may not be seen by Chinese users. Then, how should the tax bases be recalculated? A more comprehensive discussion can be found in Kothenburger (2022) and Harari (2024).

9.5.3 *Difficulties in Regulating International Firms*

Conceptually, providing internet service itself is the start of internet penetration. If a foreign company were to offer more efficient telecommunications services in the U.S., it would be more welcomed by U.S. citizens, and thus be in a better position to collect data from them. Furthermore, if U.S. domestic platforms also use the service provided by a foreign telecommunications company, the data on this platform may also be retrievable by the foreign telecommunications provider.

In addition, from the U.S. domestic perspective, it is perfectly reasonable to forbid the integration of various arms of the telecommunications industry. However, if a foreign company has already accomplished horizontal and vertical integration before entering the U.S. market, what can the government do to prevent this unfair competition which may lead to undue telecommunications penetration?

This above example illustrates the complexity involved in regulating internet-related international businesses. As long as the telecommunications or platform services are something regarding which the U.S. and EU are committed to openness under the WTO accession protocols, attempts by foreign corporations to enter the market have to be dealt with. We have provided more discussion on this in Chapter 6.

9.6 Regulating Foreign Platforms

If the regulation of foreign companies is so difficult as described above, and if foreign internet or platform companies can easily give rise to national security concerns, what could democratic countries do? Under the current U.S. legal structure, one possible solution is to turn to the Committee on Foreign Investment of the U.S. (CFIUS). In Chapter 5, we have discussed the possibility of revising the legal framework.

As regards the sectors having access to sensitive secrets or information, different countries might have different categories when defining sensitivity. If we take the U.S. as an example, CFIUS of the U.S. has classified sensitive personal data as a strategic asset under the federal regulations since October 15, 2020. In the past, CFIUS had already blocked the acquisition of MoneyGram International (which was a U.S. money transfer provider) by Ant Financial (which was a Chinese financial technology company and Alibaba subsidiary, at that time controlled by Jack Ma) "reportedly due to concerns that Ant Financial may provide the Chinese government access to Americans' financial data through MoneyGram."[27] The new rule vests greater power in CFIUS to exercise the authority "to suspend, modify or prohibit foreign investments in the U.S." or "to force divestitures for completed transactions" whenever there is a risk to national security, such as a risk arising from the access to sensitive data, including location, biometric, health, and financial information.

Arguably, CFIUS is an either-0-or-1 regulator, and a denial would imply a total segregation of internet platform services. More care and caution should be exercised when considering this option. Moreover, CFIUS reviews are conducted on a case-by-case basis and may not sufficiently account for deeper and broader aspects. To counter the possible penetration by foreign platforms, one possibility proposed by Sitaraman (2022) is to treat these platforms as "public utilities" and impose a new set of regulations on these industries. More regulation possibilities have been discussed in Chapter 5.

9.6.1 The Impact of GDPR on Data Collection

The General Data Protection Regulation (GDPR) of the European Union is probably the most influential law in this regard. The following paragraphs only briefly introduce some pivotal provisions that are closely related to this chapter. The GDPR is now the overarching law in Europe, aiming to protect the right to privacy and to facilitate the movement of

[27] "CFIUS Rule Puts National Security Spotlight on Investments that Result in Foreign Access to Sensitive Personal Data," https://cdp.cooley.com/cfius-rule-puts-national-security-spotlight-on-investments-that-result-in-foreign-access-to-sensitive-personal-data/?utm_source=Mondaq&utm_medium=syndication&utm_campaign=LinkedIn-integration.

data throughout the EU. The GDPR was enacted in 2016 and took effect on May 25, 2018. Before that, the basic framework was set out in the Data Protection Directive (95/46/EC), which had been in effect since 1995.

One of the GDPR's core purposes is to strengthen the right to consent and restrict the processing of personal data, including the right of natural persons to be forgotten. Specifically, Article 7 of the GDPR explicitly protects the conditions of consent, which, according to Article 4 (11), should be "freely given, specific, informed, and unambiguous." Furthermore, Article 4 (4) describes "profiling" as "any form of automated processing of personal data consisting of the use of personal data to evaluate certain aspects relating to a natural person." A data controller should stop profiling when the data subjects oppose such actions. More importantly, even though the data subjects may have consented at some point in the past, they always possess the right to erasure. Article 17 of the GDPR clearly grants data subjects the right to erase their personal data when the data are no longer necessary, when the data have been illegally processed, and when the data subjects withdraw their consent, among other things.

It is worth noting that, according to Article 3 of the GDPR, the territorial scope of the GDPR extends beyond European borders despite the fact that it is a European law. Under some circumstances, it applies to the processing of personal data outside the EU. For example, non-EU organizations (such as Alibaba) that provide services involving personal data in the EU will be subject to the GDPR, at least in theory. According to Recital 23 of the GDPR,[28] therefore, a house in Yunnan that advertises in the EU via Airbnb, uses European languages on its website, and accepts euros, may be subject to this provision if it hosts any EU residents. Nevertheless, to our knowledge no multinational corporations have been fined because of this provision. The true deterrent effect of the GDPR's long-arm jurisdiction remains to be verified in the future.

The above discussion, however, leads to the following question. Again, let us use Baidu as an example. Suppose Baidu, Alibaba, and Tencent all have users in the EU, and they all exercise the right to be forgotten based on GDPR Article 4 (11). How could the EU be sure whether these forgotten rights are honored, given the doctrine that "the Party leads all?" Furthermore, even if all these companies claim that they comply with

[28] Recital 23, EU GDPR, https://www.privacy-regulation.eu/en/r23.htm.

GDPR Article 4 (4) in their profiling, how can they legally respond to the CCP's data requests based on the various National Security regulations in China?

The key here is that any regulation needs a mechanism of verifiability in order to guarantee compliance. Through various institutional designs, a democratic country can make sure of this compliance domestically; but for foreign companies, verification is very difficult. Without an independent third party, whether Baidu or TikTok has shared or will share data with the CCP is never verifiable.

9.6.2 Possible Malicious Use of Big Data by Foreign Countries

We mentioned the "Fancy Bear" case in Chapter 1 and described how the Russian hackers successfully infiltrated the Hillary Clinton campaign headquarters, stole information, diffused information in social media, and possibly affected the election result. However, in this case, because the Russian hackers did not have any big datasets for U.S. citizens, their interference in the U.S. election was limited.

Now suppose that Russia had collected extensive big data on U.S. citizens. These data might have been records of individuals purchasing from e-commerce platforms, searching, social media, e-payments, or GPS. Then the Russian cyber army could have used such big data to do profiling, and then penetrate the U.S. more efficiently. In particular, they could have done what Google or Facebook has been doing, that is, sending distinct information to different individuals that mostly fits their profiles and appetites.

For example, suppose that Mr. A bought large-grained dog food regularly and also bought a dog mattress with a golden retriever picture on it. Then, AI should be able to infer that Mr. A likely owns a couple of golden retrievers and is very fond of them. A couple of days before the election, the Russian cyber army can use AI to create several deep-fake videos where a particular candidate expresses an annoying view about dogs, and then send these videos to Mr. A and other dog-lovers. Similarly, other deep-fake videos could be created and sent to other people, based on their respective profiling. Because it is just the day before the election when voters receive these videos, and because 10,000 individuals receive 10,000 different personalized messages, it is very difficult to make

10,000 clarifications. Evidently, this is a more dangerous form of penetration than the Fancy Bear hacking. As long as there are 1% or 2% of voters who are affected, then a close election may be easily turned around.

The above example illustrates another type of infiltration, which is different from website hacking or business secret stealing. Hacking or stealing usually involves clear targets, and the targets can defend themselves by improving their cybersecurity. Big data collection and profiling lack pre-defined targets, but we all know that one day the big data may somehow be useful. This kind of infiltration, indeed, may be difficult to defend.

9.7 In a Nutshell: The Perfect Weapon Needs Curbs

In the previous sections we have primarily discussed the attacks in cyberspace, including hacking, stealing business secrets, and collecting information, and the attacking side appears to consist predominantly of authoritarian countries such as China, Russia, and North Korea. However, it is important to emphasize that this does not imply any moral high ground in the democratic camp. Several controversial cases have also emerged in democratic countries.

Perhaps the most well-known case is the one exposed by Edward J. Snowden. Snowden was a former National Security Agency (NSA) intelligence contractor of the U.S. government. In 2013, he leaked classified documents revealing the existence of a global surveillance program. This program covered the surveillance of U.S. citizens as well as numerous political leaders from American allied nations, including German Chancellor Angela Merkel. Much of this surveillance was handled by the NSA and the Five Eyes intelligence alliance with the cooperation of telecommunications companies and European governments. Snowden was later indicted for espionage by the U.S. government, and subsequently sought political asylum in Russia. The Snowden incident later prompted a critical discussion about national security and individual privacy. Even though some of the surveillance did have legal warrants signed by judges, the ethical and legal justification of such large-scale monitoring remains highly contentious.

The Stuxnet attack (allegedly jointly sponsored by Israel and the U.S., according to the New York Times) which we discussed at the beginning of this chapter is also a matter of controversy. Even though the strategic target was a nuclear facility allegedly developing weapons in violation of the UN Treaty, the cyberattacks were never approved by the UN. In principle, this attack was not very different from the one exercised by Russian cyberattacks against Ukraine during the 2014–2017 period. As with other cyberattacks, the Stuxnet operation raises ethical and legal concerns regarding the legitimacy of such actions in international relations.

There is, however, a crucial difference between the democratic camp and the authoritarian countries, namely, the checks and balances. Regarding the Snowden case, persistent scrutiny from independent media and public dissatisfaction compelled the U.S. government to reassess its surveillance practices and, in some cases, even issue apologies (notably to Chancellor Merkel). This is unlikely to happen in any authoritarian regimes. In particular, in a country where "the Party leads all," there would be no independent media, and the excellent reports by the *New York Times* would never surface.

In our previous discussion, we also raised the question as to who can authorize a cyberattack against another country. In the case of Russia attacking Ukraine's power grid, there may be collateral damage, such as whether this power outage will stop the water purification operation so that many Ukrainian civilians may become sick. Will the power outage affect nearby hospitals? And how many civilians in Kyiv would not be able to survive the cold winter without electricity? These are legitimate questions only in democratic countries, where the power to launch a cyberattack may need to have some institutional rules, and such a power must be accompanied by making the person who ordered the attack responsible for it, in case something goes wrong. Again, this discussion would not be possible in a Leninist autocrat regime.

As of 2024, the United States Cyber Command operates with a force of approximately 16,500 personnel (soldiers, civilians, and contractors) under the United States Cyber Command.[29] As for China, according to Fedasiuk (2021), the number is nearly 20 million, many of whom are "volunteers." The large number of volunteers often play the role of "framing the public opinion," either domestically or internationally in foreign platforms. This boils down to the basic and ideal criterion that

[29] See https://www.arcyber.army.mil/About/About-Army-Cyber/.

differentiates the democratic and authoritarian regimes: in an authoritarian state, information is to be controlled and led, whereas in democratic societies, information is meant to be shared and critically examined.

References

Branstetter, Lee G. (2018) China's Forced Technology Transfer Problem—And What to Do About It. Peterson Institute for International Economics.

Carbaugh, B., & Wassell, C. (2019). Forced Technology Transfer and China. *Economic Affairs, 39*(3), 306–319.

Fedasiuk, R. (2021). A Different Kind of Army: The Militarization of China's Internet Trolls. *China Brief, 21*(7). https://jamestown.org/program/a-different-kind-of-army-the-militarization-of-chinas-internet-trolls/

Harari, Y. N. (2024). *Nexus: A Brief History of Information Networks from the Stone Age to AI*. Penguin Random House.

Kothenburger, M. (2022). Taxation of Digital Platforms. In S. Cnossen & B. Jacobs (Eds.), *Tax by Design for the Netherlands*. Oxford University Press.

Lee, J. (2020). Forced Technology Transfer in the Case of China. *Boston University Journal of Science and Technology Law, 26*(2), 324–352.

Lovely, M. E., & Huang, Z. (2018). Foreign Direct Investment in China's High technology Manufacturing Industries. *China & World Economy, 26*(5), 104–126.

Prud'homme, D., & Zhang, T. (2019) *China's Intellectual Property Regime for Innovation: Risks to Business and National Development*. Springer Nature Switzerland AG.

Sanger, D. E. (2018). *The Perfect Weapon: War, Sabotage and Fear in the Cyber Age*. Owl Publishing House.

Shapiro, C., & Varian, H. (2009) *Information Rules: A Strategic Guide to the Network Economy*. Harvard Business School Press.

Shapiro, S. J. (2023). *Fancy Bear Goes Phishing: The Big History of the Information Age, in Five Extraordinary Hacks*. Penguin.

Sitaraman, G. (2022). The Regulation of Foreign Platforms. *Stanford Law Review, 74*, 1073–1152.

CHAPTER 10

Sensitivity of International Digital Coalitions

We mentioned in previous chapters the formation of two digital camps, one led by the U.S. and the other led by China. We should note that the member composition as well as the consolidation in each camp are time-variant: at any point of time a country can decide whether or not to join the coalition, as well as the degree of its involvement. As in the case of the export control coalition discussed in Chapter 4, each country may be faced with a difficult choice. For instance, as far as profits are concerned, the Dutch company ASML and the German company Zeiss may not want to join the chip-manufacturing export control initiated by the U.S. However, these companies are in the coalition mainly because of the criminal penalties contained within the U.S. export control law ECRA. In other words, firms in democratic countries may be dragged or coerced into being part of a coalition.

The above-mentioned coalition effort, in general, may serve as a carrot (favoring participation) or a stick (being ready to punish non-participation). Perhaps the most famous carrot was the Marshall Plan for the European Recovery after WWII. More recent examples of carrots include China's BRI in 2013 and the U.S. CHIPS and Science Act in 2022. However, these are rare examples; in international politics, we seldom observe a country providing generous subsidies to foreign companies to persuade them to cooperate. In most cases, we observe the stick approach: blunt diplomatic pressure or coercion.

C. Y. C. Chu, *An Emerging Digital Wall*,
https://doi.org/10.1007/978-981-95-3577-4_10

One can imagine that the country being squeezed or coerced may have a grudge against the coercing side. When there are many countries feeling the same way, their respective reactions may be correlated. The resulting dynamics of international politics may affect the digital coalition. This chapter aims to examine European countries' reactions to China's diplomatic aggressions in recent years. As to Europe's responses to the U.S. pressure placed on it by Trump since early 2025, we will defer the discussion to a later section.

10.1 Literature on Cross-Country Political Interactions

As described in the previous chapters, in the past 30 years, China has been aggressive in various dimensions, including the reclamation of islands in the South China Sea, cyberspace penetration into foreign countries, the worldwide establishment of the Confucius Institutes, and the initiation of the AIIB and BRI, etc. The goal of these actions is to establish a multi-polar international order, challenging or even replacing the unipolar order primarily backed by the U.S. Wolf warrior diplomacy can be regarded as the diplomatic counterpart of the above-mentioned aggressions: it intends to exhibit an uncompromising and deservedly official gesture against any foreign challenges to China's policies. As pointed out by Smith (2021), this gesture is believed to be consistent with China's "Major Country Diplomacy."

Of course, aggressions and uncompromising gestures often elicit responses. Were there no such aggressions by China, the U.S.'s proposal of a Clean Network Initiative (CNI) in 2020, a coalition targeted at blocking internet facilities manufactured by China,[1] would not have been successful. When the aggressions have many receiving targets, Cavalieri (2019) has pointed out that the Internet may generate an "amplification effect," where the coerced targets that would otherwise remain silent are encouraged by the availability of the Internet to speak out.

While most forms of aggression lack sufficient empirical evidence for analysis, international backlashes against China's wolf warrior diplomacy are well-documented by various media, thereby facilitating our analysis in this chapter. We will show that the backlashes by European countries

[1] See https://2017-2021.state.gov/the-clean-network/.

follow a pattern similar to the literature on coordinated moves, which has been a focus of recent studies. We also note that the coordinated moves in international politics in the internet era are different from those studied in the literature, and therefore deserve particular attention.

10.1.1 Political Movements and Information Cascades

There have been numerous studies on traditional political movements, both domestic and international. Before introducing the analysis of backlashes to wolf warrior diplomacy, for the purposes of comparison we first examine the social dynamics in Eastern Europe after the fall of the Berlin Wall in 1989 and the disintegration of the Soviet Union at the beginning of the 1990s.

The movements in Eastern Europe were often described by political scientists as a classic example of an *information cascade*. By that time, many countries in Eastern Europe had declared independence and abandoned their communist regimes. As pointed out by Kuran (1991), the change took place very quickly and was beyond anyone's expectations.

The traditional theory of social movements or riots in political interactions, such as the theory of relative deprivation (Gurr, 2015), the theory of political opportunity (Tilly, 1978), and the theory of exit, voice, and loyalty (Hirschman, 1970) provided good *static* explanations regarding why and when a riot may arise. These static theories, however, did not account for the decision interdependence among potential participants and thus failed to fully explain the rapidly evolving political *dynamics* in Eastern Europe between the late 1980s and early 1990s. The theory of information cascades provides us with a framework that complements the traditional static theories and gives us a better understanding of the drastic political changes that took place in Eastern Europe 35 years ago.[2]

The social movements in the modern internet era, however, are still different from the Eastern European experience 30 years ago. The first difference we observe is that the social movements in Eastern Europe around 1990 did not have the factor of a "power difference." In the case of social movements in the Internet era, as documented in Chi et al. (2024), it is usually the one who has a power or reputation closer to the

[2] An information cascade is a phenomenon described in behavioral economics in which a number of people make the same decision in a sequential fashion. A classic analysis can be found in Bikhchandani et al. (1992).

perpetrator who acts first, and is then followed by victims with less power or reputation. In essence, the Internet lowers the cost of information and searching, so that individual information (such as their "power" index) becomes available. When victims know the power difference between themselves and the perpetrator, they can make more accurate decisions regarding whether to join the movement or not.

In the case of the riots or gatherings in Eastern Europe, however, the personal identities of thousands (or even millions) of movement participants could hardly be ascertained. In Granovetter (1978), the earlier participants of social movements were called "radicals," and the later participants were called "conservatives." These two simplified stereotypes are perhaps the only information we have to label potential participants in the Eastern European movement, and all others are ones with unknown characteristics. Indeed, without much information about the participants, it is difficult to apply the theory of information cascades to predict the momentum and direction of political movements.

10.1.2 Empirical Evidence of Participating Political Movements

As for the social movements that have so far taken place in the twenty-first century, there have been several empirical studies in the past decade, but all have very different foci. Bursztyn et al. (2021) examined participation determinants in Hong Kong's Umbrella Revolution. Their study found that an individual's likelihood of participation depended on the proportion of his or her social network that was incentivized to participate. Barbera and Jackson (2020) also theoretically emphasized how mass protests serve as signals for subsequent revolts. Cantoni et al. (2022) provided survey evidence on how individual economic preferences determine the participation decision and the dynamics of protest movements. We note that the above-mentioned recent discussion has focused on area-specific political movements; very little discussion has been about international interactions.

10.2 Features of Social Movements in the Internet Era

We begin the discussion in this section with a review of the key features of the #MeToo movement in the internet era, which is arguably the typical social movement in the past decade. After this review, we will identify the salience of the dynamics of international politics under wolf warrior diplomacy. It turns out that the dynamics in response to diplomatic aggressions cannot be fully explained by traditional theories of political movements and instead require an understanding of mechanisms similar to those observed in the #MeToo movement. We will then pursue an empirical analysis in subsequent sections.

10.2.1 Features of the #MeToo Movement

The recent literature has revealed several features of the #MeToo movement, which we will summarize here. The first feature of #MeToo is that whether an individual is willing to join the movement and identify the perpetrator of the harassment depends on how many others have already done so (Cheng & Hsiaw, 2022). In general, the probability of a victim being willing to voice his or her concerns increases with the previously accumulated accusations. This is called the *demonstration effect*. The second feature of the #MeToo movement is the power difference: the larger the power difference between the perpetrator and the victim, the less likely it is that the latter will dare to speak out against the former. This is referred to as the *power difference effect*.

The third feature of the #MeToo movement is the speed of information updates. In the typical dynamic model of information cascades adopted by economists and political scientists, individuals can only observe the action (e.g., participating in a social movement or not), and they have to infer the background information that is behind this action. More often than not, one cannot even observe individual actions, but can only perceive the proportion of people who adopt certain actions. For instance, Hong Kong citizens observed that roughly 30% of the citizens participated in the anti-extradition protests on various occasions in 2019, but they do not know much about individual participants.

In the case of #MeToo, thanks to the prevalence of the Internet, almost all concerns of victims were posted through Twitter, Facebook, and other social media, which have an extremely fast speed of transmission. Furthermore, even in cases where a victim accepts an interview by a traditional paper medium, its detailed content can soon be posted on an internet platform and then shared by millions of viewers. Such revealed content often contains detailed information, allowing the Internet to accelerate and amplify the momentum of previous accusations.

10.2.2 Reduction in Coordination Cost

In addition, as shown in Cheng and Hsiaw (2022) and Lee and Suen (2020), the key difficulty for any victim of a harassment to speak up is that an individual victim would feel alone and susceptible, compared to the scenario where a group of victims act in a coordinated way. In game theory terminology, #MeToo can be viewed as a "coordination game." In traditional political protests against an autocrat, substantive coordination is very costly because potential protesters are afraid of being detected and identified. However, in recent years, the Internet has significantly reduced the coordination cost. The messages can be efficiently spread through the Internet, and voicing out is like podcasting the experience which, even though unpleasant, is less scary than participating in a riot.

In Chapter 8 we mentioned the case of the Arab Spring, and that movement was understood as an example of instantaneous coordination using the Internet. Domestic coordination may indeed be interfered with by autocrats' internet monitoring and interceptions, as is illustrated in Chapter 8, but international coordination is free of that threat. Thus, when there are several weak countries being bullied simultaneously by the same foreign country, then we expect that news exposure through the Internet may facilitate some kind of implicit international coordination and magnify the weak sides' reactions. We are going to verify this in our later discussion.

10.2.3 Amplified Public Decisions

We also observe that, in Eastern Europe around 1990, people joined in the demonstrations because they wanted to see changes, such as demanding more democratic elections, overthrowing the incumbent ruler, aborting the socialist regime, or restoring their country's independence. However, sometimes voicing out *per se* may be the only direct objective; participants may simply want the outside world to know the essence of the rulers and the unreasonableness of the regimes. In this sense, we can say that participating in the movement is a cry for dignity. Indeed, we observe a similar psychology among #MeToo victims. Many accusations in the #MeToo movements refer to incidents that occurred many years ago. In spite of a legal procedure sometimes providing victims with pecuniary compensation, since evidence might vanish and memories might become blurred for cases that took place a long time ago, the victims have a very low probability of prevailing in court trials. As such, the main factor that affects a #MeToo victim's decision as to whether or not to voice out is also her (or his) cry for dignity.

If we consider the reactions of countries where diplomatic aggressions occurred, we may find a factor that strengthens the amplification effect of the Internet. Incidents involving the #MeToo harassment mostly took place in private spheres and were originally unknown to those outside. As such, the victims' decisions as to whether to speak out were basically private ones. For countries being bullied in a diplomatic scenario, however, very often the incident was already known to the public and media. Therefore, the government's decision as to whether to summon China's ambassador to raise a formal protest was actually a public decision.

As one can imagine, private decisions do not face public pressure, and the previous decisions of other victims are just a piece of information for decision-making. In the arena of international politics, however, because the decision is essentially a public one, the fact that "other countries have had tough responses" puts pressure on the politicians who are considering their own decisions. The demonstration effect will therefore be much stronger, especially when the decision-making politicians face election pressure. For public officials, their response represents a cry for dignity for their country, and they simply cannot hesitate. As we will show shortly, this conjecture can also be tested empirically.

10.3 Wolf Warrior Diplomacy and Its Centrifugal Impacts

China's wolf warrior diplomacy, according to search engine results and various anecdotal accounts, refers to a style of *coercive* diplomacy, which is in contrast to the traditional diplomatic practices of cooperative rhetoric and the avoidance of controversy. The original intention may just be to express dissatisfaction, but an overreaction often makes it look like an coercion.

The country being *coerced* certainly has the feeling of being bullied, and its decision as to whether or not to protest against this coercion is similar to that of voicing out in the #MeToo scenario. Moreover, the relative power between the coercing side and the side being bullied also matters, and one would expect that larger and more powerful countries, such as the U.S., would be more likely to initiate their confrontation with China, and only then be followed by smaller countries or the ones that are more dependent on China for their imports and exports. This kind of demonstration effect may exist even in smaller geographic areas: for instance, if Sweden is the most powerful country in the Nordic area, we may expect to see Sweden taking a tough stance before other Nordic countries decide to do the same.

Several articles explore the evolution of China's diplomacy toward that of a wolf warrior and its effectiveness. Dai and Luqiu (2022) underscored Xi Jinping's leadership that strategically prioritizes a "fighting spirit" compared to previous diplomatic approaches. Yuan (2023) emphasized shifts in leadership, surging nationalism, heightened concerns about external threats, and a readiness to employ economic repression as the main factors that result in wolf warrior diplomacy. The evidence on the success of the wolf warrior diplomacy, particularly in relation to social media, is mixed. Mattingly and Sundquist (2023) conducted an experiment that randomly exposed Indian citizens to authentic Twitter messages from Chinese diplomats. They found that while messages highlighting aid and friendship can enhance public perceptions of China, aggressive rhetoric from "wolf warrior" diplomats, particularly when aimed at the U.S., proved to be ineffective and may have had adverse effects. By contrast, Guo and Qin (2024) showed that wolf warrior tweets increased readership on Twitter and audience engagement, as measured by the number of retweets.

The most well-known example of bullying, arguably, was the ban on salmon exports to China after the Nobel Peace prize was awarded to Liu Xiaobo (then a jailed dissident, who later died in 2017) in 2010. According to the CNBC news, Norway's market share of salmon exported to China plummeted from 92% in 2010 to just 29% in the first half of 2013.[3] Kolstad (2020) uses a synthetic control approach and estimates that the counterfactual Norwegian fish and total exports to China in the absence of the sanction would have been 10% to 14% higher than the actual values in the period from 2011 to 2013.

This above-mentioned trade shock then generated spillover effects via financial intermediation where banks exposed to the salmon industry cut lending to non-salmon firms and households by 3% to 6% (Cao

[3] See the report by Milne, R. (2013). *Norway sees Liu Xiaobo's Nobel Prize Hurt Salmon Exports to China*. CNBC. https://www.cnbc.com/2013/08/15/norway-sees-liu-xiaobos-nobel-prizehurt-salmon-exports-to-china.html.

et al., 2023). In 2013, following the electoral defeat of Norway's center-left government, the newly elected conservative government pledged to strengthen relations with China. In December 2016, China and Norway declared their intention to restore and normalize diplomatic relations.[4] This bullying in the form of a retaliatory trade embargo continued for 7 years, and was finally over in 2018.[5]

In the first half of the 2010s, because Norway was the only country to which China wielded its power, it could only maintain a low profile and be silent. As more and more wolf warrior practices were inflicted on other countries, the atmosphere began to change. U.S. policymakers, once willing to balance potential conflict against commercial gains from cooperation with China, were increasingly considering the prospect of long-term tensions with China without ruling it out (Campbell & Ratner, 2018). After 2016 when Donald Trump was elected President (his first term), the U.S. took the initiative to retaliate, in various forms, against China. Based on a term used by Granovetter (1978), the U.S. played the role of a "radical," which caused other smaller countries to speak out, these actions taking the form of hundreds of protests and ambassador summons.

In November 2019, former Chinese Ambassador to Sweden, Congyou Gui, made a controversial remark during an interview with Swedish PEN. Referring to the decision to award Minhai Gui the Tucholsky Prize—an honor given to writers or journalists who have faced persecution, threats, or exile and demonstrated a strong commitment to defending freedom of expression—Congyou Gui stated "We treat our friends with fine wine, but for our enemies, we have shotguns." This statement sparked an immediate backlash, with all eight major Swedish political parties condemning his threats.[6]

Another notable example is related to the tensions between the French government and Chinese Ambassador to France, Shaye Lu. Lu was the

[4] "Norway and China Restore Ties, 6 Years After Nobel Prize Dispute" by Sowell Chan, see https://www.nytimes.com/2016/12/19/world/europe/chinanorway-nobel-liu-xiaobo.html.

[5] See Huang, E., & Steger, I. (2017). *Norway Wants China to Forget about the Human Rights Thing and Eat Salmon Instead*. Quartz. https://qz.com/1000541/norway-wantschina-to-forget-about-the-human-rights-thing-and-eat-salmon-instead.

[6] See https://thediplomat.com/2019/12/china-tries-to-put-sweden-on-ice/, by Olsson, J. (2019). China Tries to Put Sweden on Ice. *The Diplomat*.

first Chinese diplomat to openly endorse China's "self-defensive" diplomacy and proudly embrace the title of wolf warrior.[7] In April 2020, Lu shared tweets from the embassy supporting Beijing's handling of the COVID-19 pandemic while criticizing the West's approach. In March 2021, he tweeted in response to "insults and threats" following new economic sanctions imposed on China for its treatment of the Uyghur minority. These actions provoked a backlash, as revealed by the rare incident where the French government summoned Lu multiple times in response to his public statements.[8]

Finally, we draw readers' attention to the so-called Bondaz effect. This was a case that came to light in March 2021 when Antoine Bondaz, a French researcher, intervened against the pressure exerted by Lu Shaye on Twitter to dissuade French senators from traveling to Taiwan. In response, Bondaz was then described by the Chinese embassy as a "small-time thug," "mad hyena" and an "ideological troll." China's *Global Times* internationalized the affair by publishing several articles in English supporting the ambassador and again attacking Antoine Bondaz.[9]

In three days, Antoine Bondaz gained more than 3,000 followers on Twitter, and gave numerous interviews to the press, radio, and television. Evidently, this affair weakened the Chinese embassy's partnerships and stirred up diplomatic tensions between China and France. It was part of a sequence from March 15 to 22, 2021, with disastrous consequences for China's public image in France. This case was an example of wolf warrior diplomacy's perverse effect of this strategy of influence, and of the embassy having drawn attention to the work of Antoine Bondaz by wanting to discredit him.

With the above examples and comments in mind, the following sections provide empirical evidence on the dynamics of countries' decisions in response to wolf warrior diplomacy and analyze the internet factors that shape these responses.

[7] See https://www.globaltimes.cn/page/202106/1226499.shtml, by Zhao, Y. (2021). Chinese Envoy Proud of 'wolf warrior' Title to Safeguard National Interest, as China Presents Respectable Image. *Global Times*.

[8] For references, see https://www.france24.com/en/asia-pacific/20210323-france-summons-chineseambassador-over-unacceptable-tweets.

[9] See Charon, P., & Vilmer, J. B. J. (2012, September 12). *Les opérations d'influence chinoises*. IRSEM. ISBN 978-2-11-155493-1.

10.4 The Change in Atmosphere in Europe: Empirical Evidence

To analyze country-level responses to wolf warrior diplomacy, we manually compiled a dataset covering international relations between China and specific countries during the period of wolf warrior diplomacy (from January 2017 to December 2023). Our dataset includes 44 European countries, grouped into several regions: Nordic, Eastern, Western, Southern, and Southeastern Europe. The news reports are summarized from Google search using three keywords: (1) the European country in question, (2) China, and (3) year. For each search, we exhaust all items popping up throughout all pages.

10.4.1 Data Compilation

The news articles were categorized based on their content as negative or positive, resulting in 564 negative and 603 positive pieces. In addition, we compiled country-level panel data on GDP, the amount of imports from China, and the amount of exports to China as indicators of country size and relative power in international politics.

The news articles covered a range of topics, including politics, economics, cultural activities, and education. An example of negative coverage was a Reuters article on December 21, 2023, reporting that Belgian Prime Minister Alexandre de Croo described China as "sometimes very hostile" in response to allegations that Beijing had recruited a member of the far-right Vlaams Belang party as an intelligence agent.[10] On the positive side, Bloomberg reported on November 23, 2022, that the Netherlands had resisted U.S. pressure to expand the ban on chip equipment sales to China, prioritizing its own economic interests.[11]

To measure the dynamic change in the relationship between a given country and China, we define a "friendly index" for each country as the number of positive news articles minus the number of negative news articles over a specified time period. The annual friendly index across 44 countries from 2017 to 2023 ranges from − 26 to + 15, with

[10] See https://www.reuters.com/world/europe/belgian-pm-sees-china-hostile-countryafter-espionage-allegations-2023-12-20/.

[11] See https://www.bloomberg.com/news/articles/2022-11-22/dutch-resistus-call-to-ban-more-chip-equipment-sales-to-china.

Lithuania having 26 negative interactions with China in 2021 and Serbia having 15 positive interactions with China in 2015. A spike in the annual numbers means that there was a very positive or very negative event in that year. The aggregate friendly index across the data period from 2017 to 2023 ranges from − 49 (Sweden) to + 36 (Luxembourg). The aggregate number reveals the long-term relationship between China and the country in question.

10.4.2 General Pattern of European Attitudes

Figure 10.1 plots the friendly index across countries and years. The upper left panel shows a significant variation in the overall relationships with China across countries. Specifically, countries in Northern Europe tend to have a more negative relationship with China, while countries in Southern, Eastern, and Southeast Europe generally have a more positive relationship with China.

Another crucial observation is the chronological dynamics of these relationships. In 2017, most European countries exhibited either positive or neutral relations with China. However, by 2020, a significant fraction of countries experienced multiple conflicts within a single year, especially in Northern Europe. These conflicts then "propagated" to other regions, such as Eastern Europe, in 2023. This pattern supports the demonstration argument that collective actions by neighboring countries are positively associated with individual countries' responses to China's wolf warrior diplomacy.

10.4.3 Matching Our Data with Pew Surveys

To validate whether the friendly Index that we compiled using the frequency of news articles is consistent with the big picture summarized in other surveys, we compared our compiled dataset with the widely cited survey data collected by the Pew Research Center. Specifically, we created a similar index using annual Pew Survey Data from 2017 to 2023.[12] We focused on a survey question asking respondents: "Please tell me if

[12] The data include surveys conducted in Spring 2017, Spring 2018, Spring 2019, Summer 2020, Spring 2021, Spring 2022, and Spring 2023. While two rounds of surveys were conducted in 2020, one in summer and the other in the fall, the latter did not include questions regarding public opinion about China.

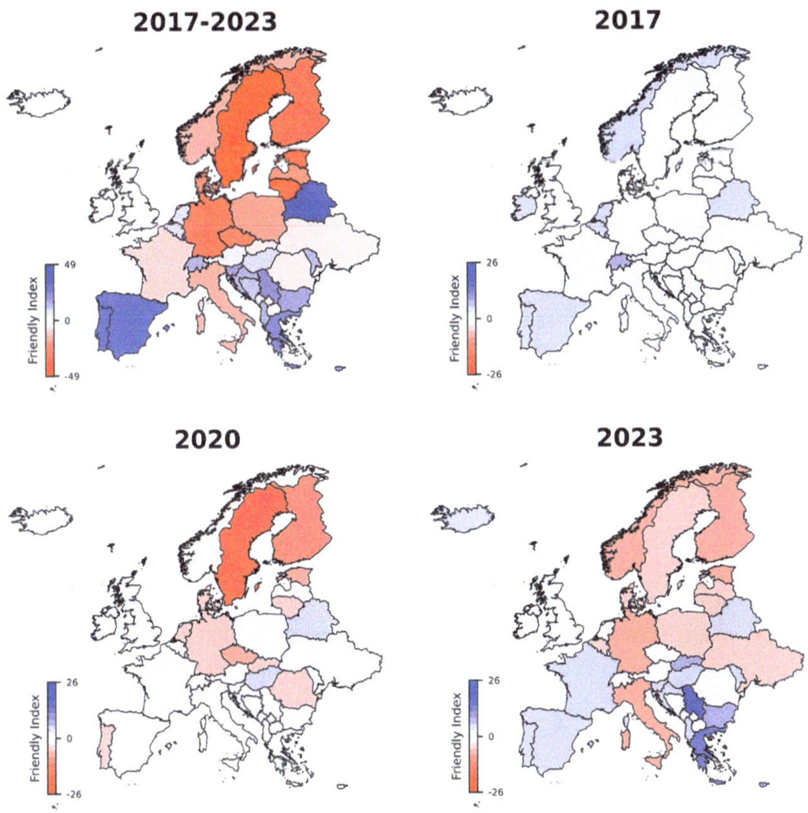

Fig. 10.1 Friendly index across European countries. *Notes* The Friendly index is calculated as the annual sum of news articles on positive interactions with China minus those on negative interactions for each selected European country. The upper left panel displays the total friendly index for the years 2017 to 2023. The data forms a balanced panel consisting of 44 countries, including Albania, Andorra, Austria, Belarus, Belgium, Bosnia and Herzegovina, Bulgaria, China, Croatia, Cyprus, Czechia, Denmark, Estonia, Finland, France, Germany, Greece, Hungary, Iceland, Ireland, Italy, Kosovo, Latvia, Liechtenstein, Lithuania, Luxembourg, Malta, Moldova, Monaco, Montenegro, the Netherlands, North Macedonia, Norway, Poland, Portugal, Romania, San Marino, Serbia, Slovak Republic, Slovenia, Spain, Sweden, Switzerland, and Ukraine

you have a very favorable, somewhat favorable, somewhat unfavorable, or very unfavorable opinion of China." Respondents could choose from the following answers: "Very favorable," "Somewhat favorable," "Somewhat unfavorable," "Very unfavorable," "Don't know (DO NOT READ)," and "Refused (DO NOT READ)." For the purpose of our analysis, we excluded responses that fell into the "Don't know" and "Refused" categories, resulting in a sample of 170,001 respondents from 48 countries worldwide.

Next, we quantified the first four response types by assigning scores of + 2, + 1, – 1, and – 2, respectively. We then calculated the average score for each year and country, denoting this as the "Pew Index." Fig. 10.2 compares the Friendly Index and the Pew Index across both time and cross-sectional dimensions. The left panel shows the annual comparison of the Friendly Index with the average Pew Index by country for each year. Both indices capture the decline in public opinion regarding China since 2020, followed by a subsequent recovery. We conjecture that the major background factor for the drop in China's public figure after 2020 was the global spread of COVID-19, which was believed to be related to China's early concealment of information.

The right panel compares the two indices across countries included in both datasets. For each year, we calculated an average country-level index

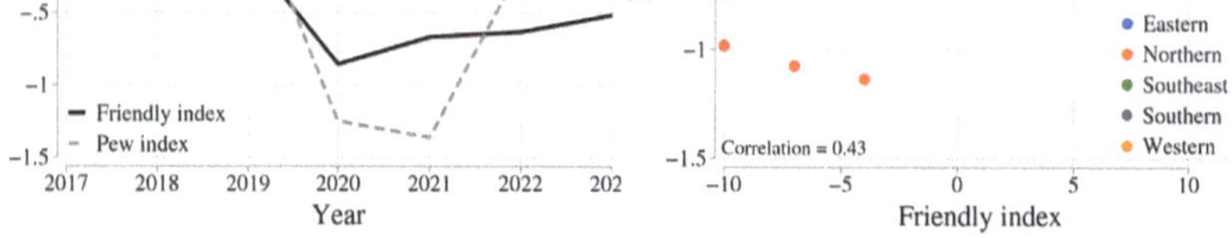

Fig. 10.2 Comparing the Friendly index with Pew survey data. *Notes* The left panel compares the time series of the aggregate Friendly Index with the Pew Index, averaged across all countries by year. The right panel compares the country-year data of the Friendly Index and the Pew Index, excluding 2021, as the Pew survey did not reveal country-specific information for that year

for six European regions. The two indices are quantitatively similar, with a significant positive correlation (=0.43). Moreover, the similarity persists at the regional level, as the indices for different regions tend to cluster. Of particular note, for both indices, countries in Northern Europe exhibit the most negative attitudes toward China.

To sum up, the Friendly Index we compiled effectively captures country-level dynamics comparable to those observed in the survey data by the Pew Research Center. We now proceed with the empirical analysis utilizing the Friendly Index, mainly because the Pew surveys do not have monthly data.

10.4.4 Statistical Setting

Our primary objective is to examine the determinants of countries' decisions to adopt a negative stance toward China. Specifically, we investigate whether a country's decision in international politics is influenced by the decisions of other nations. In addition, we assess whether the power difference between China and the country in question affects the likelihood of that country taking a negative stance against China.

Our baseline specification is given by

$$UF_{it} = \alpha_0 + \alpha_1 UF_{\sim i \in A, t-1} + \alpha_2 ReGDP_{i,t-1} + \beta X_{i,t-1} + F_{i \in A} + F_t \tag{10.1}$$

where UF_{it} is a dummy variable indicating whether country i engages in negative interactions with China. $UF_{it} = 1$ if at least one negative news article was released in month t, and $UF_{it} = 0$ otherwise. The monthly dummy UF_{it} is created by aggregating daily news article statistics. We use a monthly index to avoid possible repetitive-counting of events that were reported multiple times within a short time frame.

The term $UF_{\sim i \in A, t-1}$ in (10.1) represents the lagged number of countries, excluding country i, located in region A $\in$ {Nordic, Eastern, Western, Southern, Southeast Europe} that engaged in negative interactions with China during period-(t−1). This variable represents the demonstration effect of previous instances of voicing out. To avoid simultaneity bias, this variable has a one-month lag. $ReGDP_{i,t-1}$ is defined as the ratio of country i's nominal GDP relative to China's nominal GDP. This ratio serves as a proxy for the power gap between the two countries. $F_{i \in A}$ and F_t represent the region and time fixed effect, respectively.

In Eq. (10.1) we control for additional factors represented by the vector $X_{i,t-1}$, which includes the time elapsed since the first Confucius Institute was established in country i (Confucius_{it-1}), which serves as a proxy for China's efforts to enhance its image through financial and cultural investments.[13] Other control variables include country i's imports from China ($\text{Import}^{c}_{i,t}$) and from all countries ($\text{Import}^{w}_{i,t}$), as well as its exports to China ($\text{Export}^{c}_{i,t}$) and to all countries ($\text{Export}^{w}_{i,t}$). Finally, we incorporate dummy variables for industry-specific export dependence, $\text{ExDep}^{50}_{i,t}$ (or $\text{ExDep}^{30}_{i,t}$), which equals one if at least one industry within the 50 (or 30) classified sectors in country i exports more than half of its products to China. These measures of export dependence are more relevant, as country i's relationship with China can have a significant impact on certain industries in country i.

10.4.5 Estimation Results

Table 10.1 presents the empirical results. Model I directly examines the two fundamental factors influencing individual decisions: (1) the number of countries that have already made the same decision in previous periods, and (2) the power difference between the individual country and China. Model II incorporates additional control variables and the region fixed effect, with Northern European countries serving as the reference group. Model III further accounts for the time fixed effect, while Models IV through VII explore different measures of exports to China.

Several key observations emerge. First, the coefficient of $UF_{\sim i\in A,t-1}$ in the first row supports the argument that a country is more likely to adopt a negative stance toward China when other countries have already done so. Specifically, for each additional neighboring country that takes an unfriendly stance toward China, the likelihood of another country following increases by 0.6% to 2.7%. More importantly, the coefficient of $ReGDP_{i,t-1}$ indicates that more powerful countries are more likely to take a negative position against China. A 1% increase in relative GDP raises the probability of a country adopting a negative relationship with China by approximately 0.5%.

[13] "The Rise, Decline, and Possible Resurrection of China's Confucius Institutes," The Diplomat, https://thediplomat.com/2024/08/the-risedecline-and-possible-resurrection-of-chinas-confucius-institutes/, by Si-yuan Li and Kenneth King.

Table 10.1 Countries' negative responses to wolf warrior diplomacy

	I	*II*	*III*	*IV*	*V*	*VI*	*VII*
$UF_{\sim i \in A,t-1}$	0.027***	0.027***	0.006	0.027***	0.006	0.027***	0.006
	(13.89)	(9.61)	(1.22)	(9.52)	(1.17)	(9.53)	(1.16)
$ReGDP_{i,t-1}$	0.761***	0.465**	0.504***	0.467**	0.503***	0.472**	0.508***
	(7.34)	(2.51)	(2.78)	(2.53)	(2.77)	(2.55)	(2.79)
$Confucius_{i,t-1}$		−0.002	−0.005*	−0.002	−0.005*	−0.002	−0.005*
		(−0.61)	(−1.81)	(−0.58)	(−1.82)	(−0.63)	(−1.88)
$Import_{i,t-1}^{W}$		−0.010	0.007	−0.016	0.004	−0.012	0.007
		(−0.36)	(0.24)	(−0.56)	(0.15)	(−0.44)	(0.24)
$ImportCi,t{-}1$		−0.006	−0.013	−0.002	−0.011	−0.003	−0.012
		(−0.38)	(−0.86)	(−0.11)	(−0.74)	(−0.22)	(−0.82)
$Export_{i,t-1}^{W}$		0.020	0.024	0.027	0.024	0.027	0.024
		(0.95)	(1.14)	(1.44)	(1.29)	(1.40)	(1.27)
$Export_{Ci,t}$		0.006	0.001				
		(0.75)	(0.07)				
$ExportDep50_{i,t}$				−0.009	−0.006		
				(−0.56)	(−0.34)		
$ExportDep30_{i,t}$						0.004	0.004
						(0.29)	(0.29)
Eastern		−0.109***	−0.071***	−0.116***	−0.073***	−0.114***	−0.071***
		(−4.98)	(−3.05)	(−5.42)	(−3.22)	(−5.28)	(−3.13)
Southeast		−0.192***	−0.219***	−0.199***	−0.220***	−0.198***	−0.219***
		(−8.70)	(−9.97)	(−9.54)	(−10.60)	(−9.45)	(−10.53)
Southern		−0.155***	−0.194***	−0.161***	−0.195***	−0.159***	−0.194***
		(−5.60)	(−7.03)	(−5.99)	(−7.29)	(−5.93)	(−7.25)
Western		−0.168***	−0.144***	−0.166***	−0.143***	−0.167***	−0.143***
		(−6.14)	(−5.23)	(−6.08)	(−5.20)	(−6.11)	(−5.22)
Region FE		v	v	v	v	v	v
Year-month FE			v		v		v
N	3524	3026	3026	3032	3032	3032	3032
$R2$	0.069	0.119	0.189	0.118	0.188	0.117	0.188
Adj. R^2	0.068	0.116	0.163	0.114	0.162	0.114	0.162

Note t statistics are in parentheses.*p < 0.1, **p < 0.05, and ***p < 0.01. *Data sources* UN Comtrade and World Bank

Furthermore, the negative coefficient on Confucius_{it-1} suggests that countries are less likely to oppose China the longer they are exposed to its influence through Confucius Institutes. However, this effect is not consistently statistically significant across all specifications. Lastly, we observe significant regional variations after controlling for country-specific trade measures. Consistent with the pattern shown in Fig. 10.1, countries in Northern Europe tend to have more strained relations with China, while countries in Southeast Europe on average maintain better relations with China.

10.4.6 Eliminating Endogeneity Concerns

One potential concern with specification (10.1) is the endogeneity problem, which may arise from omitted factors that jointly influence both a country's current relationship with China and its neighboring countries' past relationships with China. A potential candidate for such a factor is a common shock to international relations with China, such as debates over the narrative of COVID-19. Such a shock could simultaneously affect multiple countries' stances toward China over an extended period. We have addressed this identification concern, and the results demonstrate that the two key factors—the number of countries that have engaged in negative relationships with China and the power difference—remain statistically significant, and the results are consistent with Table 10.1. Technical details are skipped here.

10.5 Consequential Changes in Digital Coalition Camps

A recent study by Cavalieri (2019) showed that victims' responses in the #MeToo movement may have an "amplification" effect, similar to the demonstration effect that we mention in this Chapter. However, in international politics, this amplification may even be stronger: victims of harassment can quietly decide whether or not to voice out, whereas the coercive moves by wolf warrior diplomats are all observed by the citizens of the country. In democratic regimes, this usually gives rise to huge political pressures if the politician does not take tough action. In this sense, the amplification effect may be even stronger in international politics than in ordinary harassments of individuals.

10.5.1 Capturing the Impact of Domestic Political Pressure

To capture this special amplification effect faced by politicians, we manually collected data on major elections and analyzed whether a country is more likely to adopt a negative stance against China following the decisions of neighboring countries, particularly when there are upcoming elections. We documented 87 major elections, including presidential, parliamentary, and federal elections. Out of the 44 European countries, 42 experienced at least one major election during the sample period. The country with the highest number of elections was Bulgaria, with six major elections between 2017 and 2023.

We then ran the following regression:

$$\begin{aligned} UF_{it} &= \alpha_0 + \alpha_1 UF_{\sim i\in A,t-1} + \alpha_2 ReGDP_{i,t-1} \\ &\quad + \alpha_3 Amp_{i,t} + \beta X_{i,t-1} + F_{i\in A} + F_t + \epsilon_{i,t} \end{aligned} \tag{10.2}$$

where $Amp_{i,t} = Election_{i,t} \times UF_{\sim i\in A,t-1} \times Stance_{i,t-1}$. $Election_{i,t}$ is a dummy variable that takes a value of one if an election is scheduled for a given month, and serves as a proxy for political pressure. $Stance_{i,t-1}$ is a dummy variable representing the existing stance against China, which takes a value of one if the cumulative number of positive interactions minus negative interactions between country i and China is two standard deviations below the mean. $Stance_{i,t-1}$ serves as a proxy for negative public opinion in country i toward China. Therefore, $\alpha_3 > 0$ suggests the presence of an amplification effect, where politicians facing electoral pressure are more likely to adopt a negative stance toward China following the decisions of neighboring countries, especially when public opinion is already quite negative. $X_{i,t-1}$ is the vector defined in specification (10.1), with the addition of $Election_{i,t}$.

Table 10.2 confirms the amplification effect in international politics, as α_3 is significantly positive across all specifications. For each additional neighboring country that adopts an unfriendly stance toward China, the likelihood of another country undergoing elections taking a negative stance increases by 5.6% to 7.1%, compared with countries not holding elections. However, elections alone tend to reduce the probability of country i taking a negative stance toward China, as politicians may seek to minimize uncertainty. Importantly, the two fundamental effects— the demonstration effect and the power difference effect— captured by α_1 and α_2, respectively, remain statistically significant.

10.5.2 *The Snowball Effect and the Changing Digital Coalition*

The discussion in the previous two sections signifies the possibility of rapid change in international digital coalitions. Diplomatic bullies, once toughly

Table 10.2 Amplification effects under wolf warrior diplomacy

	I	*II*	*III*	*IV*	*V*	*VI*	*VII*
$UF_{\sim i\in A,t-1}$	0.026***	0.027***	0.006	0.027***	0.006	0.027***	0.006
	(13.92)	(9.56)	(1.20)	(9.46)	(1.15)	(9.47)	(1.14)
$ReGDP_{i,t-1}$	0.738***	0.462**	0.502***	0.465**	0.501***	0.470**	0.506***
	(7.07)	(2.50)	(2.77)	(2.51)	(2.76)	(2.54)	(2.78)
$Am_{i,t}$	0.071**	0.061*	0.056*	0.061*	0.056*	0.061*	0.056*
	(2.18)	(1.82)	(1.68)	(1.81)	(1.68)	(1.83)	(1.69)
$Election_{i,t}$	−0.049	−0.051	−0.053	−0.049	−0.052	−0.050	−0.053
	(−1.41)	(−1.33)	(−1.40)	(−1.29)	(−1.38)	(−1.31)	(−−1.40)
$Confucius_{i,t-1}$		−0.002	−0.005*	−0.002	−0.005*	−0.002	−0.005*
		(−0.60)	(−1.79)	(−0.58)	(−1.81)	(−0.62)	(−1.86)
$Import^{W}_{i,t-1}$		−0.009	0.007	−0.015	0.005	−0.011	0.008
		(−0.33)	(0.27)	(−0.52)	(0.19)	(−0.41)	(0.27)
$Import^{C}\, i,t-1$		−0.006	−0.013	−0.002	−0.011	−0.003	−0.012
		(−0.39)	(−0.86)	(−0.12)	(−0.75)	(−0.23)	(−0.84)
$Export^{W}_{i,t-1}$		0.019	0.023	0.027	0.024	0.026	0.023
		(0.92)	(1.11)	(1.42)	(1.27)	(1.38)	(1.24)
$ExportC_{i,t}$		0.006	0.001				
		(0.77)	(0.09)				
$ExDep50_{i,t}$				−0.008	−0.004		
				(−0.49)	(−0.28)		
$ExDep30_{i,t}$						0.005	0.004
						(0.35)	(0.34)
Eastern		−0.109***	−0.071***	−0.116***	−0.073***	−0.114***	−0.071***
		(−4.98)	(−3.05)	(−5.42)	(−3.22)	(−5.27)	(−3.13)
Southeast		−0.191***	−0.217***	−0.198***	−0.219***	−0.197***	−0.218***
		(−8.65)	(−9.92)	(−9.49)	(−10.55)	(−9.40)	(−10.47)
Southern		−0.154***	−0.193***	- 0.160***	−0.194***	−0.159***	−0.193***
		(−5.58)	(−7.01)	(−5.97)	(−7.28)	(−5.91)	(−7.24)
Western		−0.168***	−0.143***	−0.166***	−0.142***	−0.167***	−0.143***
		(−6.12)	(−5.22)	(−6.06)	(−5.18)	(−6.09)	(−5.20)
Region FE		V	V	V	V	V	V
Year-month FE			V		V		V
N	3452	3026	3026	3032	3032	3032	3032
R^2	0.072	0.120	0.190	0.119	0.189	0.119	0.189
Adj. R^2	0.071	0.116	0.164	0.115	0.163	0.115	0.163

Note t statistics are in parentheses. *$p < 0.1$, **$p < 0.05$, and ***$p < 0.01$. *Data sources* UN Comtrade and World Bank

responded to by one country, may easily be confronted by other countries echoing and mimicking that country. For those countries that have forthcoming elections, the politicians will also face more pressure and will have to respond toughly. This snowball effect may escalate to facilitate a breakdown of the original coalition. This may be what happened at the beginning of the 2020s.

From the above discussion, we note that, other than the earlier incident of boycotting Norwegian salmon, most wolf warrior conflicts happened after the late 2010s. These incidents seriously damaged China's image in Europe, thereby allowing the U.S. to lobby for its CNI in 2020. Before the U.S. lobbying took place, most European countries had already decided to adopt the 5G facilities manufactured by Huawei, a Chinese telecommunications giant.

In 2020, the U.S. issued warnings about the risks of reliance on Chinese telecommunications equipment. According to U.S. Under Secretary Krach in late 2020, "when we looked at this six months ago it looked like Huawei was unstoppable. It looked like they were going to run the table in Europe and everywhere else."[14] At a February 18, 2020 press conference in London, Huawei's president of carrier business Ryan Ding even announced that "We have 91 commercial 5G contracts worldwide, including 47 from Europe."[15] Following the U.S. government's campaign to reduce international reliance on Chinese-made telecommunications equipment, Huawei's deals outside of China decreased from 91 to 12.

Evidently, the U.S. CNI successfully turned around the coalition and made many European countries decide not to procure Huawei facilities. This example shows the tricky sensitivity of a digital coalition, which is just a part of the overall atmosphere of international politics.

10.6 Discussion and the Developments After 2025

In this chapter, we have examined the similarities between European countries' backlashes against China's diplomatic aggressions during the period between January 2017 and December 2023. Our motivation is

[14] See https://en.wikipedia.org/wiki/The_Clean_Network#Impact_on_Huawei_and_similar_companies.

[15] See "Huawei claims over 90 contracts for 5G, leading Ericsson". *Nikkei Asia*.

intuitive: a country's decision regarding how to respond to coercive diplomacy such as that of a wolf warrior is similar to the response of an individual who is bullied or harassed. We show that the demonstration effect and the power difference effect, which are typical features of the #MeToo movement, also exist in the backlashes of the European countries. In addition, we find that there is also the "amplification effect" in the internet era.

10.6.1 *China's Recent Modifications*

Recent research has shown that wolf warrior diplomacy has been declining, and China's diplomacy is entering a period of adjustment. This is reflected by the fact that some typical proponents of wolf warrior diplomacy have been transferred to relatively low-profile departments within the Ministry of Foreign Affairs or are facing retirement.

CCP Chairman Xi Jinping recently "stressed adopting a narrative tone that reflects openness and confidence, yet conveys modesty and humility, in a bid to shape a reliable, admirable and respectable image of China."[16] These moves appear to be an attempt to tone down China's confrontational diplomatic gestures and soften Chinese foreign policies. Beijing does not want its foreign policies to jeopardize its economic relations with the West, particularly during times of domestic economic slowdown. It will take some time to see how Beijing is adjusting its foreign policies; if the adjustment is substantive and comprehensive, wolf warrior diplomacy may only have been a temporary phenomenon.

10.6.2 *The Tide Turned Again After 2025*

After the January 2025 commencement of his second term as U.S. President, Donald Trump may have changed the scenario of international politics. Both Trump's humiliation of Ukraine's President Zelensky in the White House, the Nazi gesture by Elon Musk, and the severe "reciprocal" tariff on the EU have tremendously damaged the image of the U.S. among European citizens.[17] If Europeans have to choose between

[16] See https://thediplomat.com/2023/09/the-rise-and-fall-of-chinas-wolf-warrior-diplomacy/.

[17] See the Financial Times' report Zelensky's humiliation in the White House, and the New York Times report What Elon Musk's Salute Was All About—The New York Times.

the world's two superpowers, the U.S. vs. China, their decisions may be different before and after January 2025.

Indeed, from the viewpoint of a European country, the reason why it may want to stand out and oppose one superpower may be because the other superpower signifies similar democratic values and more humanistic respect. If, however, the U.S. exhibits a tendency to humiliate the Ukrainian President, then that European country's attitude toward China may be different. At the time of writing, we have not been able to collect sufficient data to check our conjectural changes after 2025. More research along these lines can be conducted in the future.

References

Barbera, S., & Jackson, M. O. (2020). A Model of Protests, Revolution, and Information. *Quarterly Journal of Political Science, 15*(3), 297–335.

Bikhchandani, S., Hirshleifer, D., & Welch, I. (1992). A Theory of Fads, Fashion, Custom, and Cultural Change as Informational Cascades. *Journal of Political Economy, 100*(5), 992–1026.

Bursztyn, L., Cantoni, D., Yang, D. Y., Yuchtman, N., & Jane Zhang, Y. (2021). Persistent Political Engagement: Social Interactions and the Dynamics of Protest Movements. *American Economic Review: Insights, 3*(2), 233–250.

Campbell, K. M., & Ratner, E. (2018). The China Reckoning: How Beijing Defied American Expectations. *Foreign Affairs, 97*, 60.

Cantoni, D., Heizlsperger, L. J., Yang, D. Y., Yuchtman, N., & Zhang, Y. J. (2022). The Fundamental Determinants of Protest Participation: Evidence from Hong Kong's Antiauthoritarian Movement. *Journal of Public Economics, 211*, 104667.

Cao, J., Dinger, V., Juelsrud, R. E., & Liaudinskas, K. (2023). *Trade Conflicts and Credit Supply Spillovers: Evidence from The Nobel Peace Prize Trade Shock.* Norges Bank Working Paper.

Cavalieri, S. (2019). On Amplification: Extralegal Acts of Feminist Resistance in the #MeToo Era. *Wisconsin Law Review, 6*, 1489–1549.

Cheng, I.-H., & Hsiaw, A. (2022). Reporting Sexual Misconduct in the #Me Too Era. *American Economic Journal-Microeconomics, 14*(2), 761–803.

Chi, C. C., Chu, C. Y. C., & Hsieh, C. S. (2024). *The Dynamics of #MeToo—Theory and Empirical Analyses.* Mimeo.

Dai, Y., & Luqiu, L. R. (2022). Wolf Warriors and Diplomacy in the New Era. *China Review, 22*(2), 253–283.

Granovetter, M. (1978). Threshold Models of Collective Behavior. *American Journal of Sociology, 83*(6), 1420–1443.

Guo, L., & Qin, Q. (2024). Wolf Warrior Spreads Superior: The Narrative and Effectiveness of Chinese Public Diplomacy Behaviors on Twitter. https://link.springer.com/article/10.1007/s11366-024-09889-z

Gurr, T. R. (2015). *Why Men Rebel*. Routledge.

Hirschman, A. O. (1970). *Exit, Voice, and Loyalty: Responses to Decline in Firms, Organizations, and States*. Harvard University Press.

Kolstad, I. (2020). Too Big to Fault? Effects of the 2010 Nobel Peace Prize on Norwegian Exports to China and Foreign Policy. *International Political Science Review, 41*(2), 207–223.

Kuran, T. (1991). Now Out of Never: The Element of Surprise in the East European Revolution of 1989. *World Politics, 44*(1), 7–48.

Lee, F. X., & Suen, W. (2020). Credibility of crime allegations. *American Economic Journal: Microeconomics, 12*(1), 220–259.

Mattingly, D. C., & Sundquist, J. (2023). When Does Public Diplomacy Work? Evidence from China's "Wolf Warrior" Diplomats. *Political Science Research and Methods, 11*, 921–929.

Smith, S. N. (2021). China's 'Major Country Diplomacy': Legitimation and Foreign Policy Change. *Foreign Policy Analysis, 17*(2), orab002. https://doi.org/10.1093/fpa/orab002

Tilly, C. (1978). *From Mobilization to Revolution*. McGraw Hill.

Yuan, S. (2023). Tracing China's Diplomatic Transition to Wolf Warrior Diplomacy and Its Implications. *Humanities and Social Sciences Communications, 10*(1), 1–9.

CHAPTER 11

Conclusions: The Digital Wall as a Self-Fulfilling Expectation

The *Containment* strategy proposed by George Kennan facilitated the formation of NATO in 1949. We understand that *Containment* referred to a military coalition among many Western European countries to jointly confront the then aggression of the Soviet Union. The confrontational line of *containment* was clearly along geopolitical country borders. Countries in the same coalition camp were military "friends" with goods and services traded frequently, while those in the other camp were considered enemies—or at least opponents. During the Cold War period, there was hardly any trade between NATO and the Warsaw Pact. We can imagine that there was a *military wall* between NATO and the Warsaw Pact which blocked the interactions between the two camps.

In the past several decades, there have also been some FTAs (free trade agreements) among various countries. The FTAs form many *tariff walls*. Despite there being the MFN (most favored nation) clause for WTO members, this FTA exception is allowed, given that certain conditions are met.[1] For instance, the USMCA and CPTPP are both tariff walls, and on both sides of each tariff wall there are coalitions of trade terms. Again, on the same side of the tariff wall, countries are friends with more

[1] The conditions for goods are listed in GATT Article 24, and those for services are listed in GATS Article 5. Various details can be found on the WTO website.

C. Y. C. Chu, *An Emerging Digital Wall*,
https://doi.org/10.1007/978-981-95-3577-4_11

extensive economic integration, and correspondingly a more refined division of labor is exercised. Members on different sides of the tariff wall are more loosely tied economically.

The cyberspace confrontation between China and the U.S. over the past 20 years has facilitated the appearance of a cyberspace wall or a digital wall,[2] and we have discussed various dimensions of this wall in previous chapters. The construction of this new wall is not yet completed, and so far, no one knows its exact specifications. However, from our previous discussion we can describe the policies that helped form the digital wall, and what the digital wall may look like when it is finished. Before doing that, let us first describe the salience of this digital wall.

11.1 The Importance of Trust in Cyberspace

The emergence of cyberspace has two distinctive characteristics that were previously absent in human history. The first is that, partly thanks to Moore's Law, many digital industries have experienced exponential growth for several decades. This rapid pace of growth would be impossible in the physical world characterized by atoms. Because some areas of the digital industries serve dual (military and commercial) purposes, the competition driven by military uses is particularly severe. This led to the *Made-in-China-2025* initiative and the U.S.'s ECRA legislation, both of which are the backbones of the recent *technology decoupling*.

In regard to the decoupling of platforms, data collection, and infrastructure facilities such as base stations and undersea cables, the background causes are more complicated, but perhaps we can summarize all of them into one: the lack of trust. This point may need further explanation.

In the digital world today, there may at times not be any "critical information" in existence; rather, information is often abstracted from "big data." Once the big data are compiled, critical information can be generated with the help of artificial intelligence. As a result, efficient and comprehensive data collection has become a fundamental necessity.

[2] In accordance with the content of this book, this wall should be referred to as a "cyberspace wall," although it may appear a little awkward to use the physical world term "wall" to describe a barrier that exists only in the digital world. In this chapter, we use the terms "digital wall" and "cyberspace wall" interchangeably.

11.1.1 Resisting Cyberattacks: Forming Trustworthy Coalitions.

A method widely used to conduct this massive collection of information is to deploy satellite cameras to capture millions of pictures, or to establish a regular data-collecting mechanism in critical infrastructure devices to extract and transmit data from every corner of the world. The above-mentioned mechanism may consist of various platforms or spywares embedded in infrastructure devices or facilities. These facilities include cellphones or other mobile devices, backbone undersea optic-fiber cables, LEO and GEO satellites up in the sky, inland telecommunications base stations, and computer servers.

We understand that the malicious chips or spywares can be remotely switched on or off, and hence they are difficult to detect. Moreover, other than engaging in regular information monitoring, in critical moments spyware may also play the role of intercepting, disturbing, or even paralyzing critical facilities. Because of these daily risks of monitoring and data collection, the parties confronting each other may wish to have their own trustworthy infrastructure, simply to avoid the paranoid daily caution, prevention, and inspection.

However, since infrastructure facilities are expensive, it is impossible for each country to have its own facilities, and instead we may expect to observe some form of group coalitions of infrastructures, such as several countries with mutual trust sharing the same facilities. In recent years, we can at least see two such coalitions: one is formed by liberal democratic countries (the U.S., Japan, Australia, Canada, the U.K., etc.), and the other consists of authoritarian ones (China, Russia, North Korea, etc.). This facilitates the coalition of trustworthy infrastructures.

11.1.2 How Is Trust in Cyberspace Earned?

The digital age has also introduced an unprecedented expansion of virtual networks. Notable examples include SWIFT and the various applications of the blockchain. If we take the blockchain as an example, because all the blockchain calculations are performed by the computer and each may take several hours to complete, few individuals truly comprehend the intricate processes occurring behind the scenes. All we have is our trust in the computation taking place behind the scenes. We therefore hope and believe that the computers and programs associated with the blockchain are trustworthy. If two countries do not trust each other, then it would be difficult for them to share a digital network with respect to which they both have trust. This facilitates forming a coalition of trustworthy application networks.

Generally speaking, trust is built on a system with public monitoring and verification. Evidently, this is unlikely to happen between democratic and authoritarian countries.

11.2 Cyberspace Confrontation: Strategy Classification

We have mentioned various aspects of China-U.S. interactions in previous chapters, and these interactions can now be categorized into distinct strategic approaches.

11.2.1 U.S.: Technology Access Denial.

The foundation of the digital wall is largely shaped by U.S. legislation in the form of the Export Control Reform Act (ECRA) and the Entity List. When applied together, these restrictive measures create a stringent technological blockade preventing critical technologies from being transferred to "the other side of the wall." These technology restrictions are not uniform, but are limited to technologies that are directly related to military use or dual use (military and civilian). As a result, technologies that are closer to the military end will be more affected by the decoupling, whereas commodities in other sectors (such as toy manufacturing) will be traded as usual.

The export controls are not limited to physical items and also include software, patents, and talents. As such, the digital wall is not only concerned with the commodity dimension, but may also be extended to talents, technology designs, and specifications. These restrictions will be pertinent to many kinds of infrastructure and end device products.

11.2.2 China: Rare Earth Export Controls.

In 2025, China implemented its first export restriction on rare earth elements (REEs) against the U.S. Because REEs are used in many high-tech products such as permanent magnet motors, computer hard disks, electric cars, MRI machines, etc., China's export controls on REEs are a very powerful weapon against the U.S.' export controls. Before the U.S.-led coalition countries improve their ability to extract and purify REEs, such export controls will further decouple many related manufacturing practices.

11.2.3 U.S.: Data Collection Denial.

The second pillar of the U.S. digital strategy focuses on preventing data collection by authoritarian states—a measure particularly critical for democratic nations due to the following concerns.

As we mentioned, many internet platforms collect users' data gradually and quietly. After several years of data collection, the platforms will have a huge dataset. For democratic countries, to effectively prevent the possibility of D-day penetration, the only way is to deny the everyday data collection, and very often the conclusion is to ban the operation of platforms owned or controlled by adversary foreign states. This is essentially the TikTok case that we discussed in Chapter 5.

11.2.4 China: Foreign Data Denial by the Great Firewall.

Authoritarian regimes, on the other hand, do not have to worry about data collection denial, mainly because foreign companies are not allowed to operate platforms in authoritarian countries. Furthermore, because authoritarian regimes often have internet blocking and censoring, it is very easy for them to cut off any D-day attack from democratic governments. Thus, foreign data denial becomes a default status for China.

11.2.5 Both Sides: Infrastructure and Application Coalitions.

Although the digital wall remains a work in progress, it always pays to form coalitions on each respective side of the wall. For democratic regimes, such coalitions emphasize the threats posed by backdoor malware embedded in facilities constructed by firms in authoritarian countries. The coalition often refers to the hardware in the telecommunications infrastructure, such as the clean network initiative (CNI) led by the U.S. The U.S. usually has to persuade allies to compromise some business interests in exchange for mutual trust and network security.

The landscaping on the other side of the wall is designed to promote various network-related applications, especially in developing countries, where the authoritarian leader such as China exerts influence. The embedded technologies behind these applications do not have to be frontier ones; the point is to establish compact network ties between members on the same side of the wall, so as to create a lock-in effect. In the case where the digital wall is in good shape in the future, a more comprehensive application coalition will improve the convenience enjoyed by coalition members.

11.2.6 Both Sides: Consolidating the Fortress.

Both democratic and authoritarian leaders would like to have a stable or at least resilient regime, ensuring that external cyber intrusions remain unsuccessful. For democratic regimes, the stability very often hinges upon democracy itself, and therefore their focus is to eliminate antagonistic measures that may compromise the democratic values and operations (such as tampering with the election result). Thus, there have been regulations to deal with disinformation and efforts made to establish mechanisms to verify unknown sources of information.

On the authoritarian side of the wall, the firmness of the fortress hinges upon the effectiveness of internet blocking, the frequent checks of keywords, the immediate shutting down of problematic websites, the identification of disobedient citizens, and the implementation of some form of social credit system. Authoritarian regimes have been very successful in developing technologies fulfilling these needs and have exported such technologies and shared them with like-minded countries.

11.2.7 Both Sides: Screening Foreign Direct Investments.

Knowing that foreign direct investment (FDI) is a possible means of penetration, the scrutiny by CIFIUS in the U.S. and similar mechanisms in other countries have become tougher. Any investments that could possibly compromise national security may not be approved. On China's side, they have from the outset been critical when reviewing foreign investments in ICTs, and the cyberspace tensions with the U.S. have also made the review more stringent.

11.2.8 Both Sides: Routine Penetrations.

With these strategic deployments in place, both democratic and authoritarian camps are preparing for a bifurcated digital landscape, despite the fact that the digital wall remains incomplete. However, regardless of how thick, high, and wide the digital wall is, both sides still attempt to penetrate it, just as we described in Chapter 9.

Regarding such penetrations, again, the democratic regimes are more constrained, because they have less regulation on information flow, and hence are more susceptible to outside attacks. Furthermore, authoritarian governments often help their private entities to spy on the private companies of foreign countries, and then share this information with their domestic firms. This is less likely to happen in democratic regimes.

11.2.9 Retaliation by Internet Blocking?

In Chapter 6 we pointed out that China's internet blocking has created asymmetric market access, which has given China the advantage in e-commerce, and has created unfair trade between China and the democratic countries. Although Taobao is also an internet platform, it may be difficult to force it to exit the U.S. market, as was the case with TikTok, mainly because banning Taobao would affect many U.S. consumers' purchasing practices, and the policy impact would be too large.

In fact, among all cyberspace conflicts, "internet blocking" remains one of the least feasible countermeasures for democratic countries to consider. Even though China's GFW has resulted in unfair market access, there is not much the democratic countries can do in retaliation. Perhaps the only possible countermeasure is to impose tariffs on all imports from China, including e-commerce. This, however, will necessitate many tedious customs checks, because most e-commerce shipping is not distinguishable from regular mailed parcels.

11.3 Cyberspace Containment?

As discussed earlier, on both sides of a digital wall, we observe infrastructure-sharing coalitions, interdependent manufacturing supply chains, and unrestricted movement of hardware and software. This coalition permits limited exceptions to information localization and relaxed restrictions on technology transfers within the same coalition. At the same time, there will be many regulations regarding the movement of cyberspace-related technologies and resources to the other side of the wall. What can we say about the future of the digital wall?

11.3.1 A Self-Fulfilling Expectation?

Symbolically, during the Cold War the NATO and the Warsaw Pact countries were divided by the Berlin Wall. In the digital era, if there is a wall that divides the world, it will be the digital wall. The formation and the lock-in effect of the coalition are what makes the multi-pole system more likely to emerge. As Applebaum (2024) noted, following Russia's removal from the SWIFT financial network after its 2022 invasion of Ukraine, China intervened to mitigate the economic impact on Moscow. If China and Russia establish a parallel system, such as the CIPS (Cross-Border Interbank Payment System), future Western financial sanctions are likely to have a far more limited effect.

The occasional espionage cases that have been prosecuted and gone public in the U.S. in fact strengthen the democratic camp's concerns over the future stealing and leaking of confidential information. The U.S. therefore further enforces the strategy of technology denial. In addition, occasional boycotting moves, such as banning Russia from using SWIFT, have reinforced the need for authoritarian regimes to form an alternative system, such as the CIPS, because they expect and fear further boycotting in the future. Finally, there is also the expectation that there may be multiple systems in the future that also facilitate the network refinement within each system. The Berlin Wall in the physical space needed to be built to appear, whereas the digital wall in cyberspace needs to be "incubated" to be realized. To sum up, the expectation that there may be multiple systems in the future is self-fulfilling: both democratic and authoritarian regimes fear it, prepare for it, and facilitate it.

11.3.2 Disturbing Turbulence.

Of course, on each side of the digital wall there are also disturbing factors that affect the coherence of the coalition. In April 2025, U.S. President Trump announced heavy tariffs on future imports from almost all countries around the world. In spite of China facing a high tariff, other democratic countries such as the EU, the UK, Australia, and Japan are all included.[3] This has resulted in serious global backlashes.

As we mentioned in Chapter 4, the U.S.'s implementation of export controls needs the cooperation of many companies in European countries, such as ASML of the Netherlands and Zeiss of Germany. In cases where moves by the U.S. incur serious dissatisfaction from allies, the effectiveness of the export controls will be affected. In general, all countries have different interests, and they are a centrifugal force of the coalition. Any one member emphasizing too much of its own interests will affect the sustainability of the coalition.

11.3.3 What Can We Say About the Final Curtain?

During the containment period, no one knew how the Cold War was going to end. The fall of the Berlin wall and the disintegration of the Soviet Union happened so quickly that it was beyond most people's expectations, as pointed out by Kuran (1991).

Could a rapid geopolitical shift similar to the Cold War's conclusion occur in cyberspace? This scenario seems unlikely. Unlike military assets—such as NATO aircraft and tanks, which can be withdrawn within days—cyberspace infrastructures are deeply embedded in daily operations and not easily dismantled. Cyberspace facilities are used in daily business, and all citizens have to be familiar with how they adapt themselves to the networks. These kinds of adaptations are like addictions and have a natural lock-in effect. When people in separate camps have adapted themselves to their respective systems and applications, it will be difficult to "tear down this digital wall."[4]

References

Applebaum, Anne (2024) *Autocracy, Inc.: The Dictators Who Want to Run the World*. Knopf.

[3] https://www.cnbc.com/2025/04/02/trump-reciprocal-tariffs-countries-chart-imports-united-states.html

[4] For the famous speech by President Reagan, see https://www.gilderlehrman.org/history-resources/spotlight-primary-source/reagan-speech-tear-down-wall-1987?gad_source=1&gclid=CjwKCAiA74G9BhAEEiwA8kNfpaJfgsYiHE5viSuxdeuhbdjt8RMsFLobtpazf8InMJVvebD_7v8BbxoCKsQQAvD_BwE

Kuran, T. (1991). Now out of never: The element of surprise in the east European revolution of 1989. *World Politics, 44*(1), 7–48.

Technical Appendices

Appendix for Chapter 6

A Model of E-Commerce and International Trade

In the modeling section of Chapter 6, we introduce a general equilibrium quantitative model of international trade that effectively integrates both conventional brick-and-mortar and e-commerce sectors within the broader framework of international market dynamics. Our model is a variation of Krugman (1979), which incorporates a market structure of monopolistic competition, firm heterogeneity, and trade. Here we present the detailed structure.

Model Framework

We construct our model to analyze an international trade setting consisting of two countries, China and the U.S. Each country is indexed by i or n (where $i, n = 1, 2$), and within each country, production is categorized into two distinct modes, indexed by m. These modes are denoted as $m \in \mathbb{M} \equiv \{b, e\}$, where b represents brick-and-mortar producers and e represents e-commerce producers.

Production and Labor Allocation

In each country i, the labor force, denoted as L_i, constitutes the primary input for production activities. This labor endowment is distributed across the various producers in both the brick-and-mortar and e-commerce sectors, and we assume that labor is freely mobile across modes of production within a country, but immobile across countries. The total number of producers in mode m within country i is represented by M_i^m.

C. Y. C. Chu, *An Emerging Digital Wall*,
https://doi.org/10.1007/978-981-95-3577-4

Consumer Preferences and the Utility Function

In this model, consumers from each country i derive utility from a wide range of differentiated products indexed by ω where $\omega \in \Omega$. The set Ω represents the total variety of products available in the market. The utility function for consumers in each country i is specified by the constant elasticity of substitution (CES) form:

$$U_i = \left(\int_{\omega \in \Omega} [q_i(\omega)]^{\frac{\sigma-1}{\sigma}} d\omega \right)^{\frac{\sigma}{1-\sigma}}$$

Here, $q_i(\omega)$ denotes the quantity of product ω consumed in country i, and σ represents the elasticity of substitution between different products.

Market Structure and Product Diversity

Each producer, regardless of mode, offers a unique product to the market. The aggregate market diversity is represented by the total number of product varieties available across all countries and production modes, which is mathematically expressed as:

$$\Omega = \sum_{i=1}^{2} \sum_{m \in \{b,e\}} M_i^m$$

This measure of product variety covers different production modes as well as both domestic and foreign production sites.

Aggregate Price Index

The price index for each country i reflects the cost to consumers of purchasing the basket of goods, incorporating all available varieties ω. The price index in each country i aggregates these prices across all domestically produced and imported varieties, across different modes of production, and is written as:

$$P_i = \left(\int_{\omega \in \Omega} [p_i(\omega)]^{1-\sigma} d\omega \right)^{\frac{1}{1-\sigma}}$$

Production Costs and Modes

Production in each country i can be undertaken in either of the two modes – brick-and-mortar (b) or e-commerce (e). The marginal cost of producing a specific variety ω by a producer in mode m in country i is given by:

$$c^{m,i}(\omega) = \frac{w_i}{z_i^m(\omega)A_i^m}$$

Here, w_i represents the wage rate in country i, A_i^m signifies the productivity of producers in mode m specific to country i, and $z_i^m(\omega)$ is a productivity shock for producing variety ω in mode m, drawn from a Pareto distribution:

$$\Pr\left(z_i^m(\omega) < z\right) = 1 - z^{-\theta}.$$

This distribution introduces heterogeneity in productivity levels across producers and products, reflecting real-world discrepancies in production efficiencies.

Iceberg Trade Costs

Transporting goods between countries involves additional costs, modeled here as iceberg trade costs. These costs depend on the mode of production and the specific origin and destination countries. The cost of delivering product ω from country i in mode m to country n is expressed as:

$$c_n^{m,i}(\omega) = c^{m,i}(\omega)d_n^{m,i}$$

where $d_n^{m,i}$ represents the trade cost factor for shipping goods from country i to country n using production mode m. These iceberg costs imply that only a fraction of the shipped goods arrives at the destination.

Components of Trade Frictions

In our setting, we incorporate geographical, mode-specific, and institutional barriers that influence trade flows and pricing structures. The formula for calculating these trade frictions between country i and country n for goods produced in mode m is assumed to be multiplicative:

$$d_n^{m,i} = \left(1 + \tau_n^i\right) \times \left(1 + s_n^m\right) \times \left(1 + t_n^{m,i}\right).$$

In the above expression, the representation of trade frictions between countries incorporates three primary components.

Firstly, τ_n^i represents the geographic trade friction, which includes factors such as physical distance, transportation costs, and other geographic constraints between countries i and n. Second, s_n^m represents production-mode-specific friction. For example, in the context of e-commerce, this might include longer or shorter delivery times or the associated waiting costs, which differ from those encountered in traditional brick-and-mortar transactions. Third,

$t_n^{m,i}$ captures institutional barriers, which are regulatory and policy-driven constraints imposed by country n on imports from country i depending on the mode of production m. These include regulations, red tape, and other non-tariff barriers; in particular, internet blocking may be a trade friction for the e-commerce mode.

Pricing and Consumer Demand

From the utility specification we can derive the demand for a particular product variety ω within country i which is captured by the following relationship:

$$p_i(\omega)q_i(\omega) = \left[\frac{p_i(\omega)}{P_i}\right]^{1-\sigma} E_i$$

Here, $p_i(\omega)$ is the price of product ω in country i, P_i is the aggregate price level (or price index), $q_i(\omega)$ is the quantity demanded, E_i is the total expenditure of country i, and σ is the elasticity of substitution between products. The derivation is standard in microeconomics.

Given the model's assumption of monopolistic competition where each firm sets prices above marginal costs with constant markups, the price of a product variety ω from country i sold in country n using production mode m can be formulated as:

$$p_n^{m,i}(\omega) = \frac{\sigma}{\sigma-1}c_n^{m,i}(\omega) = \frac{\sigma}{\sigma-1}\frac{w_i d_n^{m,i}}{z^{m,i}(\omega)A^{m,i}}$$

In this equation, $c_n^{m,i}(\omega)$ is the marginal cost of delivering variety ω produced using mode m from country i to country m, w_i is the wage rate in country i, $d_n^{m,i}$ is the composite trade friction parameter, $z^{m,i}(\omega)$ represents a productivity shock for a particular variety, and $A^{m,i}$ denotes the aggregate technology parameter using production mode m in country i.

International Trade

It can be shown that in consumers' optimization, the probability that a consumer in country n purchases from a producer in country i operating under mode m (either brick-and-mortar or e-commerce) is given by the following expression:

$$\pi_n^{m,i} = \frac{M^{m,i}\left(d_n^{m,i}\right)^{1-\sigma}\left(A^{m,i}\right)^{\sigma-1}(w_i)^{1-\sigma}}{\sum_{m'\in\{b,e\}}\sum_{i'=1}^{N} M^{m',i'}\left(d_n^{m',i'}\right)^{1-\sigma}\left(A^{m',i'}\right)^{\sigma-1}(w_{i'})^{1-\sigma}}$$

This formulation reflects the influence of both the number of producers $M^{m,i}$ in each mode and country, and various trade frictions $d_n^{m,i}$ along with country and mode-specific productivity $A^{m,i}$, and the wage levels w_i.

Furthermore, the aggregate price index for country i, which reflects the overall cost of living and influences consumer expenditure decisions, is determined by:

$$P_i = \left(\left[\frac{\sigma}{\sigma-1}\right]\left[\frac{\theta}{\theta+1-\sigma}\right]\sum_{n=1}^{N}\sum_{m\in\mathbb{M}}\left[M^{m,n}\left(d_i^{m,n}\frac{w_n}{A^{m,n}}\right)^{1-\sigma}\right]\right)^{\frac{1}{1-\sigma}}$$

This formulation integrates the effects of trade frictions $d_i^{m,n}$, wage rates w_n, and productivity factors $A^{m,n}$ across all trade partners and production modes.

Market Clearing Conditions

The equilibrium in the labor and product markets of each country is determined by a set of market clearing conditions. In country i, the total household expenditure W_i consists of the sum of labor compensation and the firm profits:

$$W_i = w_i L_i + \Pi_i$$

Here, $w_i L_i$ represents the total labor compensation in country i, where w_i is the wage rate and L_i is the labor supply. Π_i denotes the profit generated by firms in country i. Under the assumption of constant markups dictated by the monopolistic competition model, total expenditure is proportional to total labor compensation, adhering to the relationship:

$$W_i = \frac{\sigma}{\sigma-1} w_i L_i$$

This equation implies that total household expenditure is a markup over labor compensation, where σ is the markup factor derived from the degree of product differentiation and market power of firms.

In addition, the labor market clearing condition ensures that the total demand for labor equals the available labor supply. This is expressed by the equation:

$$w_i L_i = \sum_{m\in\mathbb{M}} \sum_{n\in\mathbb{N}}\left(\frac{\sigma-1}{\sigma}\right)\pi_n^{m,i} W_i$$

In this formulation, the right-hand side accumulates the labor demand across all production modes m and from all countries n that participate in the market. $\pi_n^{m,i}$ represents the proportion of total expenditures from country n on goods produced using mode m by country i, reflecting the interconnectedness of the global economy. This condition ensures that all the labor provided in the market is employed in the production processes across different sectors and countries, maintaining a balance between labor supply and demand.

Welfare

Welfare in each country i is evaluated by real income. The welfare or utility function U_i for consumers in country i is defined as:

$$U_i = \left(\frac{w_i L_i + \Pi_i}{L_i}\right) / P_i$$

Here, $w_i L_i$ represents the total wages paid to the labor force, and Π_i denotes the total profits generated by firms. The ratio $(w_i L_i + \Pi_i)/L_i$ simplifies to the average income per labor unit, which when divided by the price index, P_i, gives the real income per capita.

Given the model's assumption of constant markups and monopolistic competition, we can further simplify the expression for real income in equilibrium:

$$U_i = \left(\frac{\sigma}{1-\sigma}\right)\left(\frac{w_i}{P_i}\right)$$

Equilibrium Conditions in terms of Relative Changes

The related literature has developed a relative change approach, or *hat algebra*, which allows for the dynamic assessment of equilibrium conditions in response to economic policies or other shocks. Here we will expand on the equilibrium conditions rewritten in terms of relative changes, and explain how this approach enhances the model's analytical capabilities.

In this extended framework, the equilibrium conditions are reformulated in terms of relative changes, defined as $\hat{x} = x'/x$. The equilibrium conditions can be expressed as follows:

Relative Change in Trade Shares:

$$\hat{\pi}_n^{m,i} = \frac{\hat{M}_n^{m,i}\left(\hat{d}_n^{m,i}\right)^{1-\sigma}\left(\hat{A}^{m,i}\right)^{\sigma-1}(\hat{w}_i)^{1-\sigma}}{\sum_{m' \in \mathbb{M}} \sum_{i' \in \mathbb{N}} \pi_n^{m',i'} \hat{M}_n^{m',i'}\left(\hat{d}_n^{m',i'}\right)^{1-\sigma}\left(\hat{A}^{m',i'}\right)^{\sigma-1}(\hat{w}_{i'})^{1-\sigma}}.$$

This formula adjusts the share of the market that each firm holds based on relative changes in the number of firms allowed in the market, trade costs, productivity, and wages.

Relative Change in Labor Market Clearing

$$\left(\widehat{w}_i \widehat{L}_i\right) \times (w_i L_i) = \sum_{m \in \mathbb{M}} \sum_{n \in \mathbb{N}} \pi_n^{m,i} \widehat{\pi}_n^{m,i} \times \left[\left(\widehat{w}_n \widehat{L}_n\right) \times (w_n L_n)\right]$$

This condition ensures that the labor market remains in equilibrium, reflecting changes in wages and labor supply across all regions and sectors.

Relative Change in the Price Index

$$\widehat{P}_n = \left(\sum_{m \in \mathbb{M}} \sum_{i \in \mathbb{N}} \pi_n^{m,i} \widehat{M}_n^{m,i} \left[\frac{\widehat{d}_n^{m,i} \widehat{w}_i}{\widehat{A}^{m,i}}\right]^{1-\sigma}\right)^{\frac{1}{1-\sigma}}$$

The change in the price index reflects adjustments in market dynamics, capturing the overall impact of changes in trade costs, wages, and productivity on consumer prices.

Relative Change in Welfare

$$\widehat{U}_i = \frac{\widehat{w}_i}{\widehat{P}_i}$$

This condition assesses the impact of economic changes on individual welfare, especially in relation to how variations in wages relative to prices affect real income.

The hat-algebra method offers two significant advantages in quantitative analysis. First, it simplifies the analytical process by eliminating the need to recompute base-year values for key variables such as productivity $A^{m,i}$, market access parameters $M_n^{m,i}$, and trade frictions $d_n^{m,i}$. Second, the method facilitates counterfactual analysis, making it possible to explore hypothetical scenarios by applying relative changes directly to actual data.

Bringing the Model to Data

To apply our theoretical analysis to empirical assessment, we focus on China and the U.S., two dominant players in global trade and e-commerce. To conduct robust counterfactuals, we require specific economic data moments that capture the economic interactions between these countries under different trade modes. Essential data points include the $\pi_n^{m,i}$, which represent the expenditure shares of each country on different countries and modes, accounting for a total of eight distinct moments such as brick-and-mortar and e-commerce in both directions (from China to the U.S. and from the U.S. to China). In addition, $w_i L_i$ captures the total compensation or GDP within each country, providing insights into overall economic size and labor compensation.

To calculate these data moments, we first need to amalgamate various sources. Key datasets include global e-commerce revenue by country for 2022, retail e-commerce sales projections in the U.S. from 2014 to 2025, and revenue statistics for the U.S. e-commerce industry extending to 2027. For China, we utilize data on the proportion of e-commerce in total retail sales from 2014 to 2022 and forecasts for the B2B cross-border e-commerce market size through 2025. Furthermore, we consider the distribution of domestic and cross-border e-commerce revenues by country for 2023. Complementing these e-commerce-specific datasets, the OECD input-output table from 2018 provides the foundational economic variables that help in understanding cross-country economic flows and incomes. We also double-check our data with the numbers in statistica.com, and find that they are compatible.

Specifying the Institutional Trade Barriers

Given the above setting, the Great Firewall institutional barrier, GFW^i_{CHN}, is assumed to be:

$$GFW^i_{CHN} = a \cdot \frac{[\text{wait time}]^i_{\text{CHN}}}{S\left([\text{wait time}]^i_{\text{CHN}}\right)}$$

where a is a positive scaling constant, $[\text{wait time}]^i_{\text{CHN}}$ is the waiting time for China to access a country-i website, and $S\left([\text{wait time}]^i_{\text{CHN}}\right)$ is the retention rate as a function of wait time. The above setting assumes that GFW^i_{CHN} is increasing in $[\text{wait time}]^i_{\text{CHN}}$ (because longer waiting times discourage users from staying on the site), and decreasing in retention rate $S\left([\text{wait time}]^i_{\text{CHN}}\right)$ (because a larger retention rate means people do not care about waiting).

Recall our citation of a Google report in Sect. 6.1 that "53% of visits are abandoned if a platform site takes more than 3 seconds." Assuming that the decay in visiting follows an exponential distribution, then the above information roughly suggests that the half-life of decay is 3 seconds. If we let the number of visitors be N_t, we then have $1/2 \approx (N_t/N_0) = e^{-\lambda t}$. From this relationship we can solve $\lambda \approx (\ln 2)/3$.

We normalize $GFW^{\text{CHN}}_{\text{CHN}} = 1$, which means that for Chinese users accessing domestic websites, the index is set as a reference point. From Chu and Lee (2020), the average waiting time for Chinese internet users to visit Chinese websites is 0.87 seconds, and the average waiting time for Chinese users to visit U.S. websites is 14.57 seconds. Because $GFW^{\text{CHN}}_{\text{CHN}}$ is normalized to be 1, we have

$$1 = \frac{a \times 0.87}{S(0.87)},$$

which implies that $a = S(0.87)/0.87$. Plugging this expression for a and the waiting time for accessing U.S. websites of 14.57 seconds into the GFW formulation yields the Great Firewall Index for the U.S.:

$$GFW^{\text{USA}}_{\text{CHN}} = \frac{14.57}{0.87} \exp\lambda(14.57 \quad 0.87) = 396.7$$

Later we will use this number in our calculation.

To incorporate the effects of the Great Firewall of China (GFW), we assume that the institutional barrier China imposes on U.S. e-commerce follows the formulation:

$$T^{e,\text{USA}}_{\text{CHN}} = \log\left(GFW^{\text{USA}}_{\text{CHN}}\right) \times s^{e}_{\text{CHN}} + 1\,.$$

Recall that s^{e}_{CHN} represents the pre-existing e-commerce barrier in China. This assumption indicates that the institutional burden is proportional to the extent of the Great Firewall Index ($GFW^{\text{USA}}_{\text{CHN}}$) as well as the friction specific to e-commerce in China. If the waiting time for Chinese internet users to visit U.S. websites were exactly the same as for visiting Chinese websites, meaning $GFW^{\text{USA}}_{\text{CHN}} = GFW^{\text{CHN}}_{\text{CHN}} = 1$, then our formulation would imply that $T^{e,\text{USA}}_{\text{CHN}} = 1$. This would suggest that China does not impose any additional institutional barriers on U.S. e-commerce, as there would be no differential in accessibility between domestic and foreign websites. However, given that $GFW^{\text{USA}}_{\text{CHN}} = 396.7$, the institutional burden translates to:

$$T^{e,\text{USA}}_{\text{CHN}} = \log(396.7) \times (P^{e}_{\text{CHN}} - 1) = 2.636.$$

This value of 1.636 (=2.636-1) is analogous to China imposing a 163.6% tariff on all U.S. e-commerce. This implies a substantial barrier to market entry for U.S. e-commerce platforms, making it significantly more expensive and less competitive for them to operate in China.

Quantitative Experiments

Our analysis examines the economic and welfare impacts of removing Chinese institutional barriers on foreign e-commerce. This study will shed light on the potential for increased market access and the associated shifts in trade dynamics, consumer welfare, and economic efficiency.

Eliminating Chinese Institutional Barriers to Foreign E-commerce

In our counterfactual analysis of removing institutional frictions on foreign e-commerce in China, we establish a series of assumptions designed to frame the economic interactions between the U.S. and China within a simplified yet rigorous analytical context. First of all, the analysis is confined to these two nations, which are represented by CHN (China) and U.S. (United States), effectively comprising the entire analytical world, denoted as $\mathbb{N} = \{\text{CHN}, \text{U.S.}\}$.

Secondly, we assume symmetry in geographical barriers, indicating that the obstacles to trade in terms of distance, transportation costs, and related geographic factors are identical in both directions, such that $\tau_n^i = \tau_i^n$. This simplifies the model by avoiding the need to account for differing impacts of geography based on the direction of trade.

In addition, we standardize productivity across different modes of production, assigning a uniform productivity level A_i^m to both brick-and-mortar and e-commerce sectors within each country. This assumption helps to isolate the effects of other variables by eliminating productivity differences as a confounding factor.

The model also stipulates that there are no mode-specific frictions for brick-and-mortar products in either country ($s_i^b = 0$), and no country imposes institutional burdens on its own domestic production ($t_i^{m,i} = 0$). In the context of international frictions, the model assumes that the U.S., as a democratic country, does not impose any institutional burdens on imports regardless of their origin or mode of production ($t_{\text{USA}=0}^{m,i}$). Conversely, China does not apply institutional burdens to brick-and-mortar imports, which could be reflective of broader trade policies that traditionally favor these more conventional forms of commerce ($t_{\text{CHN}}^{b,i} = 0$).

The mode-specific frictions for e-commerce in China are derived using the equilibrium condition which relates the market shares of e-commerce to brick-and-mortar based on observed data:

$$\frac{\pi_{i,\text{data}}^{e,i}}{\pi_{i,\text{data}}^{b,i}} = \left(1 + s_i^e\right)^{-(\sigma-1)}.$$

From the data, the calculated specific friction for e-commerce in China (s_{CHN}^e) is found to be 0.2787.

Incorporating the Great Firewall (GFW)

In the counterfactual scenario, we remove the calculated frictions, aiming to illustrate the potential changes in trade flows and market dynamics if China were to eliminate its institutional barriers against U.S. e-commerce. Firstly, we assume constant productivity across all modes of production, denoted by $\widehat{A}^{m,i} = 1$, ensuring that any changes observed in the economic equilibrium are attributable solely to variations in institutional trade barriers rather than shifts in productivity levels. In addition, the labor forces in both countries are kept stable, with $\widehat{L}_i = 1$, to remove any effects from fluctuations in employment or labor market conditions. The central part of our analysis involves adjusting the trade frictions to simulate the removal of institutional barriers to e-commerce. To be specific, by eliminating the trade barrier imposed by the GFW, we mean that, after the change, the per-click waiting time for Chinese to access the U.S. is also 0.87 seconds, the same as the waiting time for U.S. citizens to connect with China's website. This adjustment effectively normalizes trade conditions for e-commerce, mirroring an environment of more open data flow.

Using these assumptions, we recalculate the necessary equilibrium wage adjustments ($\widehat{w}_i$) that would maintain all model equilibrium conditions in this scenario of reduced trade frictions. The results are as shown in the main text of Chapter 6.

References

Krugman, P. R. (1979). Increasing Returns, Monopolistic Competition, and International Trade. *Journal of International Economics, 9*(4), 469–479.

Appendices for Chapter 8

Appendix 8.1: Data Description and Variable Construction

The data utilized in Chapter 8 are integrated from multiple sources to ensure comprehensive coverage. For the democracy indicators, the Freedom Index is obtained from the Freedom House (FH) annual global report, and the Democracy Index is from the *Economist* Intelligence Unit (EIU). FH measures the degree of freedom by two indices: Political Rights (PR) and Civil Liberties (CL); the overall score is presented as Global Freedom (GF). These indicators are country-year panel data.

For the government's actions or implementations, the indicators are obtained from the Digital Society Project (DSP). The Digital Society expert survey features 37 variables, grouped topically into five sections, namely, Sect. 2.1 to Sect. 2.5. For our analytical purposes, we focus on Sect. 2.2 Digital Media Freedom, which consists of 2.2.1 Government Internet Filtering Capacity, 2.2.2 Government Internet Filtering in Practice, 2.2.3 Government Internet Shut Down Capacity, 2.2.4 Government Internet Shut Down in Practice, 2.2.5 Government Social Media Shut Down in Practice, 2.2.6 Government Social Media Alternatives, 2.2.7 Government Social Media Monitoring, 2.2.8 Government Social Media Censorship in Practice, 2.2.9 Government Cyber Security Capacity, and 2.2.10 Political Parties Cyber Security Capacity.

There are four technological *capacities* variables (2.2.1, 2.2.3, 2.2.9, and 2.2.10). Independent of whether it actually does so in practice, 2.2.1 measures the extent of the government's technical capacity to censor information (text, audio, images, or video) on the Internet by filtering (blocking access to certain websites) if it decides to; 2.2.3 measures the extent of the government's capacity to actively shut down domestic access to the Internet if it decides to; and 2.2.9 measures whether the government has sufficient technologically skilled staff and resources to mitigate harm from cyber-security threats. Instead, 2.2.10 measures the cyber-security technological ability of the main political parties, which is not related to our study. We thus abstract it from the analysis. The other six variables (2.2.2, 2.2.4, 2.2.5-2.2.8) are related to the government's implementation *in practice*. We compile these variables with the normalization that higher values indicate more frequent government enforcement in practice.

The DSP is a country-year dataset from 2000 to 2024. In 1972, Freedom House (FH) introduced its annual *Comparative Study of Freedom* indices. Since then, FH has provided PR, CL, and GF annually. The EIU began compiling its index in 2006. Data for 2007 and 2009 are missing, and the latest version at the time of writing is from 2023 (as of Aug. 12, 2024). To reconcile the data between DSP and FH and the EIU, we then consider 161 countries during 2006-2023 in our empirical analysis (there are only 164 countries with complete data for DSP 2.2.1 ~ 2.2.9 and FH during 2006-2023). Brief summary statistics are provided in Table 8A.1.

Table 8A.1 Summary statistics

	Mean	*Std*	*Min*	*Max*
Democracy Index				
FH's Political Rights (N = 2,952)	22.59	13.14	−3	40
Global Freedom (N = 2,952)	57.12	29.45	−1	100
EIU Democracy (N = 2,624)	5.45	2.25	0.26	9.93
Digital Society Project's Sect. 2.2 (N = 2,952)				
2.2.1 Internet Filtering Capacity	0.08	1.24	−3.12	2.92
2.2.2 Internet Filtering in Practice	−0.47	1.55	−2.69	3.70
2.2.3 Internet Shut Down Capacity	−0.09	1.30	−3.26	2.50
2.2.4 Internet Shut Down in Practice	−0.61	1.29	−2.08	4.07
2.2.5 Social Media Shut Down in Practice	−0.63	1.31	−2.06	3.83
2.2.6 Social Media Alternatives	−0.22	1.30	−2.28	4.66
2.2.7 Social Media Monitoring	−0.17	1.45	−2.90	3.66
2.2.8 Social Media Censorship in Practice	−0.41	1.40	−2.38	4.80
2.2.9 Cyber Security Capacity	−0.01	1.30	−3.56	3.54

Appendix 8.2: Panel Unit-Root Test and Regression Analysis

We use the Im-Pesaran-Shin (IPS) test for unit roots in panel data. Year dummy variables are considered in the test to control for cross-sectional dependence, and the Akaike Information Criterion (AIC) is used to select the lags (the maximum potential lag is set to 3) for augmented Dickey-Fuller (ADF) type tests. The test results suggest that the indices in some countries contain unit roots. Thus, we take the first differences for the indices to mitigate the risk of spurious regression and the first-differenced variables are found to be stationary. The results are similar when we divide the countries into two or four groups based on FH's Political Rights, FH's Global Freedom, or the EIU's Democracy Index. Table 8A.2 presents our basic results.

As for the regression analysis, the Arellano-Bond linear dynamic panel-data estimation is applied. We first examine the relationship between governments' technological capacities and their implementation practices; the results are

Table 8A.2 Unit-root test

	Original IPS	*Difference of First Order IPS*
Democracy Index		
FH's Political Rights	0.699	0.000***
FH's Global Freedom	0.213	0.000***
EIU's Democracy Index	0.782	0.000***
Digital Society Project's Sect. 2.2		
2.2.1 Internet Filtering Capacity	0.100	0.000***
2.2.2 Internet Filtering in Practice	1.000	0.000***
2.2.3 Internet Shut Down Capacity	1.000	0.000***
2.2.4 Internet Shut Down in Practice	0.999	0.000***
2.2.5 Social Media Shut Down in Practice	1.000	0.000***
2.2.6 Social Media Alternatives	1.000	0.000***
2.2.7 Social Media Monitoring	0.968	0.000***
2.2.8 Social Media Censorship in Practice	1.000	0.000***
2.2.9 Cyber Security Capacity	0.998	0.000***

presented in Table 8.2 in the main text. Our regression model is given by:

$$Z_{it} = \alpha_i + \mu_t^L + \mu_t^H + \gamma Z_{i(t-1)} + \gamma_x LG_i \times Z_{i(t-1)} + \sum_{j=1}^{3} \beta_j^H HG_i \times X_{jit}$$
$$+ \sum_{j=1}^{3} \beta_j^L LG_i \times X_{jit}$$
$$+ \sum_{j=1}^{3} \delta_j^H HG_i \times X_{ji(t-1)}$$
$$+ \sum_{j=1}^{3} \delta_j^L LG_i \times X_{ji(t-1)} + e_{it}$$

where Z_{it} is the government's implementation practice, X_{jit} is the government's technological capacity, and t denotes time. The term HG_i (LG_i) is a dummy variable that equals 1 (0) if country i is in Group H (Group L); countries are grouped based on the 2006 FH's Political Rights. α_i measures the country fixed effect and μ_t^H (μ_t^H) measures the year fixed effect for Group H (Group L) countries.

To control for the auto-regression and lagged distributed effects for different democratic groups, the interaction terms of the group dummy variables and $Z_{i(t-1)}$ and $X_{ji(t-1)}$ are included. We then use the Arellano-Bond method for linear dynamic panel-data regressions to estimate the parameters, as shown in Table 8.2 in the main text. Here, explanatory variables are set to be predetermined and the second- and third-period lagged dependent variables and the second to the fourth lagged explanatory variables are used as the instrumental variables (IVs). Our results are qualitatively robust and quantitatively similar when we add the fourth-period lagged dependent variable to the IV list.

Next, we examine the effects of governments' implementation practices on democracy. The regression model we use is

$$Y_{it} = \alpha_i + \mu_t + \gamma Y_{i(t-1)} + \sum_{j=1}^{5} \beta_j Z_{jit} + \sum_{j=1}^{5} \delta_j Z_{ji(t-1)} + e_{it},$$

where Y_{it} is FH's Global Freedom, FH's Political Rights, or the EIU's Democracy Index and the Z_{jt}, j = 1,…,5 are the governments' implementation practices. α_i measures the country fixed effect and μ_t measures the year fixed effect. The total number of observations for the regression of the EIU's Democracy Index is 1,449 because the original index is missing in 2007 and 2009. The results are presented in Table 8.3 of the main text.

Appendix 8.3: Supplementary Analytical Results

This Appendix presents a comprehensive theoretical model analyzing the impact of AI/ICT on democratization, helping to explain the underlying reasons behind our empirical findings. We begin by incorporating AI/ICT into a standard model developed by Acemoglu and Robinson (2019a, b), and then explain how the technology changes the equilibrium dynamics.

Analytical Structure

In the standard model of state/society interactions, the dynamics are categorized into three equilibrium regimes, as shown in Fig. 8A.1. When the power balance between the state and society is highly asymmetrical, one side fully dominates the other, leading to an extreme outcome, either a despotic or a weak state. If the powers of the state and the society are roughly balanced, then ongoing competition makes both sides stronger over time, which leads to an *inclusive state* of democracy. The dynamics that lead to the inclusive state of democracy are braced by two boundary arms (B_u and B_l in Fig. 8A.1), and a democratic equilibrium attainable only under specific initial conditions, which is why Acemoglu and Robinson (2019b) have called it *the narrow corridor*. Our empirical findings suggest that in less democratic countries, governments tend to intensify surveillance and censorship of their citizens. To account for this fact, the theoretical analysis that follows will focus on the upper boundary of inclusive democracy, where a fragile democracy is at risk.

The State-Civil Society Interactions

The aggregate output of the nation is produced by the joint effort of the state (s_t) and the civil society (x_t): $f(s_t, x_t)$, where f is the aggregate production function. Both s_t and x_t are normalized to the [0,1] range so that Fig. A8 looks compact. The gross investment of s_t is written as $i_{s,t} = \dot{s_t} + \delta$, where the dot describes an instantaneous increase, and δ is a constant depreciation rate. Similarly, the gross investment of x_t is written as $i_{x,t} = \dot{x_t} + \delta$. The investment costs are respectively denoted as $C_s\left(i_{s,t}\right)$ and $C_x\left(i_{x,t}\right)$. Given s_t and x_t, the expected output shares to be received by the state and the civil society are respectively $H(s_t - x_t)$ and $H(x_t - s_t)$, where $H(.)$ represents a stochastic distribution function.

For simplicity, the time subscript for all variables is omitted in our following presentation unless necessary for clarity. Given any x, the state maximizes its net expected return:

$$\Pi_s = H(s - x)f - C_s(i_s),$$

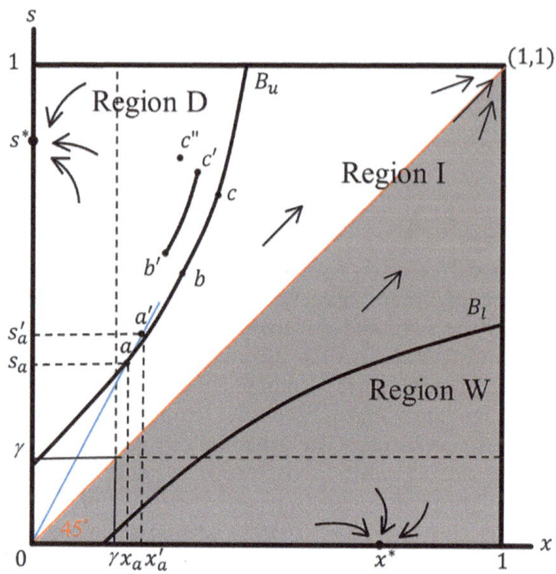

Fig. 8A.1 Technology Changes and the Upper Boundary of the Corridor *Notes* (1) The shape of corridor boundaries: Beyond $s > \gamma$ and $x > \gamma$, the northwest triangle must have tangential slopes larger than 1 that bend upward. (2) How technologies affect B_u: Before technology increases, an initial point a on the upper boundary will move $a \to b \to c$. After technology increases, the dynamics change to $a \to b' \to c''$. Some points originally in Region I will now fall into Region D. (3) We only analyze the scenario for authoritarian or fragile democratic regimes, and therefore ignore the southeast triangle (gray area), where a state of anarchy is the focus

and given any s, the civil society maximizes its net expected return:

$$\Pi_x = H(x - s)f - C_x(i_x).$$

The final distribution of the output is determined by the usual Nash solution.

The Reward Probability Distribution

The distribution function H is assumed to capture the following properties: (i) when x and s are close, both the state and the society are motivated to exert more effort, and (ii) when x and s are far apart, neither the state nor the society is willing to exert effort. For analytical tractability, we follow Acemoglu and Robinson and propose the following:

Assumption 1 (A1): *The reward probability distribution follows the raised cosine function:*

$$H(s-x) = \frac{1}{2}\left[1 + \frac{(s-x)-\mu}{\sigma} + \frac{1}{\pi}\sin\left(\frac{(s-x)-\mu}{\sigma}\pi\right)\right].$$

The standard raised cosine distribution is characterized by zero mean ($\mu = 0$) and unit variance ($\sigma = 1$). It is easy to verify the following properties for this cumulative distribution function (CDF): (i) $H(s-x) + H(x-s) = 1$; (ii) $H(0) = 1/2$; and (iii) $H(s-x)$ is increasing in its argument.[1] Although a particular functional setting appears restrictive, since our later analysis only hinges upon local properties, our results hold for any functional specifications that can be locally approximated by the functional form specified here. Properties (i) and (iii) are quite standard; the key property needed for our analysis is (ii), which specifies the symmetry between the state and the civil society.

The Investment Cost Function

To capture the increasing returns property of political investment, Acemoglu and Robinson argue that there is a threshold such that, whenever one side does not invest enough so that its state variable falls below the threshold, it then becomes more difficult to restore the momentum. For analytical tractability, Acemoglu and Robinson assume that the threshold level of s is γ_s such that, if $s < \gamma_s$, then there is an additional cost for the investment of s. Similarly, with a threshold level γ_x for x, there is an additional cost for the investment of x if $x < \gamma_x$. Accordingly, the following is assumed by Acemoglu and Robinson:

Assumption 2 (A2): *The investment cost functions for the state and the society are*

$$C_s(i_s) = c_0 \cdot i_s^2 + \max\{\gamma - s; 0\}i_s,$$

and

$$C_x(i_x) = c_0 \cdot i_x^2 + \max\{\gamma - x; 0\}i_x,$$

where c_0 is the cost parameter of investments.

Note that although the thresholds γ_s and γ_x are theoretically different, these parameters will appear only in areas where the effort levels are limited. Within

[1] The corresponding probability density function (PDF) is $h(s-x) = \{1 + \cos[((s-x)-\mu)\pi]\}/2$, which indicates that the PDF is symmetric around zero with $h(0) = 1$ *and* $h(s-x) = h(x-s)$.

the democracy corridor, these threshold parameters eventually disappear, when both the state and the civil society make sufficient investments. For the time being, we assume that $\gamma_s = \gamma_x = \gamma$.

The Production Function

We now introduce information technology in the model and arrive at the major difference between our specification and that in Acemoglu and Robinson's analysis. As already mentioned in the main text of Chapter 8, AI and ICTs are likely to benefit the ruling elites more than the civil society. To capture this asymmetry, we adopt the production function of Krusell et al. (2000). To be specific, we propose:

Assumption 3 (A3): *The production function is given by*

$$f = \phi_0 + \left[\alpha x^{\varepsilon} + (1-\alpha)(s^{\upsilon} + T^{\upsilon})^{\frac{\varepsilon}{\nu}}\right]^{\frac{1}{\varepsilon}} with \varepsilon,\ \upsilon \in [-\infty,\ 1]. \tag{A1}$$

where ϕ_0 *is a baseline productivity level,* $s(x)$ *is the share accruing to the state elite (civil society),* α *is the* relative weight of civil society in production, *and* T *is the AI/ICT. Thus, the elasticity of substitution between* s *and* T *is*

$$E_{sT} = -\frac{\partial \ln(T/s)}{\partial \ln(f_s/f_T)} = \frac{1}{1-\upsilon},$$

and that between x *and* T *is*

$$E_{xT} = -\frac{\partial \ln(T/x)}{\partial \ln(f_x/f_T)} = \frac{1}{1-\varepsilon}.$$

In Assumption 3, if the substitution elasticity is less (larger) than 1, i.e., $\nu < 0$ or $\varepsilon < 0$ ($0 < \nu < 1$ or $0 < \varepsilon < 1$), technology and state power are complements (substitutes) to each other. In the extreme case where $\nu \to 1$ ($\varepsilon \to 1$), $s(x)$ and T are perfect substitutes, and the production f reduces to a linear function: $f = \phi_0 + \alpha x + (1-\alpha)(s + T)$, which is the specification of Acemoglu and Robinson (2019a). In this case, technology favors neither the state nor society. If technology is more complementary to the ruling elites' capacity than to the civil society's capacity, we then have $\varepsilon > \nu$.

As the baseline case, we assume that $T = 0$ initially, which specifies the degenerated case that the original technology does not have any complementary relationship with s or x. Thus, we examine the marginal impact of an increase in T from this original state.

To rule out some trivial solutions, we need a regularity condition as follows:

Assumption 4 (A4): *When s and x are close* ($s \approx x$),

$$h(0)\phi_0 - \gamma_s \geq c_s{\prime}(\delta) \text{ and } h(0)\phi_0 - \gamma_x \geq c_x{\prime}(\delta). \quad \text{(A2)}$$

This regularity condition guarantees that near the point where s and x are equal (so that $s - x \approx x - s \approx 0$, which is the argument in $h(.)$), there are sufficient incentives for both sides to increase their investments (gross investment is larger than the depreciation). This assumption is made partly to exclude the possibility of $(s, x) = (0,0)$ being a trivial stable steady state. Intuitively, Assumption 4 implies that the state and society are willing to invest in their political powers (positive values of s and x) in the initial stage $(s, x) = (0,0)$.

A Phase Diagram Illustration

Figure A8 presents a phase diagram that illustrates the impact of AI advancements. This illustration is primarily heuristic, while a more technical analysis can be found in Chu et al. (2025). Below, we provide a concise description of the key concepts.

As in our setup given in the previous section, let s be the government's force, and x be the civil society's force. s and x jointly produce total output, $f(s, x) = y$, which is to be divided between s and x. Both s and x are normalized in the range [0,1], so that our figure looks compact. In this [0,1]X[0,1] box, the area is separated into three parts: D, W and I, where D denotes despotism, W denotes weak state, and I refers to the inclusive state (or narrow corridor). They will be explained one by one below.

The D area is where the government's force is very strong so that, because of the increasing returns property, the return to accumulating the x (s) force is low (high). As a result, the s force continues to grow, whereas the x force shrinks, eventually leading to a corner solution where $(s,x) = (s^*,0)$. The W area is where the x force is very strong so that, due to the increasing returns property, the return to accumulating s (x) is low (high). As a result, the x force continues to grow, whereas the s force diminishes, eventually leading to a corner solution $(s,x) = (0, x^*)$. In Fig. A8, the arrows indicate the dynamics, and show how the state variables (s,x) eventually move toward either corner $(s^*,0)$ or $(0, x^*)$.

In the I area, s and x are close to each other. As a result, both s and x are willing to invest, which causes both s and x to grow, eventually achieving an inclusive democracy with healthy checks and balances. Note that only starting points within the narrow corridor (area I) would converge to an inclusive democracy.

Now consider that there is a technology advancement a. When a is more complementary to s than it is to x, then the s force accumulation will be more rewarding and hence encouraged by this change in technology, enlarging the marginal return on accumulation s. Because the x force is less complementary to a and hence less encouraged, x's accumulation will increase less than it originally did. In Fig. A8, this shift causes all directional flows in the northwest quadrant of the [0,1]X[0,1] to drift leftward. Consequently, points that were previously within the inclusive democracy region (I) may now fall outside the corridor, demonstrating that AI advancements effectively "narrow" the democratic space.

What does it mean to say that the narrow corridor becomes narrower? It may not affect a solid and healthy democratic state such as the UK or Belgium or Canada. For these countries, the dynamics were originally in the I region before the technology change, and will still be in the I area after the technology change. However, for fragile democratic regimes, which were originally in the neighborhood of the upper arm of the I region, the technology change may shake them out of the I region.

This might be what happened in some African countries after the Arab Spring. Even though Egypt, Tunisia, Libya and Yemen became democratic after the Arab Spring, their democratic institutions were weak, and their democracy was really fragile. As long as the rulers realized that they could use AI/ICTs to suppress opposing civil society forces, they would find that the government's investment in ICT facilities would be rewarding.

Comparative Dynamic Analysis

It is impossible to solve the closed-form boundaries of the narrow corridor. However, we can still perform analytical comparative dynamics with respect to technology changes. We first derive the optimal trajectories. The two sets of parties (state and society) optimize the resources devoted to investment in political strength. The state chooses s to satisfy the first-order condition

$$h(s-x)f + H(s-x)f_s = 2c_0 i_s + \max\{\gamma - s; 0\},$$

yielding the optimal investment:

$$i_s = \frac{1}{2c_0}\left[h(s-x)f + H(s-x)f_s - \max\{\gamma - s; 0\}\right].$$

Because net investment is $i_s - \delta$, we obtain the following law of motion function:

$$\dot{s} = \max\left\{\frac{1}{2c_0}\left[h(s-x)f + H(s-x)f_s - \max\{\gamma - s, 0\}\right], 0\right\} - \delta.$$

Similarly, for the civil society, the law of motion for x is

$$\dot{x} = \max\left\{\frac{1}{2c_0}\left[h(x-s)f + H(x-s)f_x - \max\{\gamma - x, 0\}\right], 0\right\} - \delta.$$

The above two equations will jointly determine the dynamic trajectories in the phase diagram. We now look at the slope of $\theta \equiv ds/dx$ along such trajectories. Since

$$\theta = \frac{ds}{dx} = \frac{\left(\frac{ds}{dt}\right)}{\frac{dx}{dt}} = \frac{\dot{s}}{\dot{x}},$$

we have

$$\theta = \frac{max\left\{\frac{1}{2c_0}\left[h(s-x)f + H(s-x)f_s - max\{\gamma - s, 0\}\right], 0\right\} - \delta}{max\left\{\frac{1}{2c_0}\left[h(x-s)f + H(x-s)f_x - max\{\gamma - x, 0\}\right], 0\right\} - \delta}. \tag{A3}$$

In Fig. A8, θ is the slope of the tangent at each point of any trajectory in the phase diagram.

Three Regions and Three Steady States

Under Assumptions A1-A4, there are two characteristic roots with negative real parts in the dynamic system in terms of two pre-determined state variables s and x, producing three stable steady states. As shown in Fig. A8, the three steady states consist of one in the despotism region (Region D) with $x^* = 0$, one in the weak-state region with $s^* = 0$ (Region W), and one in the inclusive democracy region with $x^* = s^* = 1$ (Region I).[2]

The two boundaries separating the three regions in Fig. A8, one upper and one lower, are denoted respectively as B_u and B_l. Because we are interested in technology changes that threaten fragile democracies, we focus on the upper boundary B_u- the one separating Region I and Region D. Note that the upper boundary must be above the 45° line; otherwise, $x = s = 1$ could not be a stable steady state.

Analytical Propositions

First, we assume that initially $T = 0$ in (A1), and then the production function has the traditional CES form. This implies that at the *status quo*, technology is input-neutral and does not favor any party. For the sake of clarity, we first

[2] See Acemoglu and Robinson (2019a) for a detailed proof.

focus on the increasing returns region ($(s, x) > (\gamma, \gamma)$), and then deal with cases where the levels of state variables s and/or x may be below the threshold γ.

Under A1-A4, we can show that when technology T increases from the original state $T = 0$, $\frac{d\theta}{dT}$ will have two effects[3]: The first is the relative productivity effect, and the second is the output effect. The *output effect* indicates that as technology improves, national output increases. Expecting a bigger pie to be shared, the marginal return of exerting investment increases for both the state ruler and the civil society force. This is favorable to democratization since technology leads the strengths of the state and society to grow in a balanced way. In Fig. A8, the output effect makes the slope θ decrease as T increases. This makes the nation less likely to enter the despotic region. The output effect therefore expands the democracy corridor.

Conversely, $d\theta/dT$ is positive in response to a rise in T, and hence the tangent slopes of the trajectories in the region above the 45°-line increase. The condition $\varepsilon > \nu$ means that the technology in question is more complementary to the strength of the state than to that of the society, i.e.,$E_{sT} < E_{xT}$. Given $\varepsilon > \nu$, an increase in T increases the marginal product of s more than that of x, inducing the state to exert greater effort. Thus, AI and ICT favor the state, increasing the government's investment in powers and raising the efficiency of surveillance and censorship. This result helps us explain why the governments in authoritarian and fragile democratic countries have quite intensive procurement of information technology equipment in Internet filtering and shut down, as shown in our empirical results in the main text.

Note that in the special case where $\varepsilon = \nu = 1$, the production function reduces to a linear one, i.e., $f = \phi_0 + \alpha x + (1 - \alpha)(s + T)$, meaning that the information technology favors neither party in the production of national output. In this case, the relative productivity effect vanishes. Because only the output effect remains, technological advances unambiguously make the slope of the tangent θ smaller, thereby expanding the democracy corridor.

Summarizing the above, we have the following proposition:

Proposition A1: Suppose that the state variables (s, x) *are above their threshold values of increasing returns. (i) If AI/ICT* does not exhibit asymmetric complementarity *in the production of national output (e.g., under a linear production function), an improvement in AI/ICT* strictly reduces *the slope of* θ ($d\theta/dT < 0$) *in the area above the* 45° *line. This makes the motion dynamics less likely to reach the despotic region and hence widens the democracy corridor. (ii) If AI and ICT are more complementary*

[3] The technical derivation can be found in Chu et al. (2025).

to the state's effort than to that of the civil society, then the relative productivity effect generates the reverse effect, which tends to narrow the democracy corridor.

Clearly, if $\varepsilon > \nu$, then the relative productivity effect and the output effect are in conflict with each other. The following analysis will show that, as long as $\varepsilon > \nu$ (the technology is more complementary to the strength of the state than to that of the society) and $\nu < 0$ (the technology and the resource input of the state are gross complements), then the relative productivity effect always dominates the output effect, and enhanced technology always narrows the democracy corridor. The condition $\nu < 0$ (i.e., $E_{sT} < 1$) captures the interplay between the state and the technology. The state can use the new AI/ICT technologies to improve production efficiency and increase national output. The state can also use AI/ICT to strengthen its political power, which consolidates the authoritarian regime. To sum up, we can also establish the following proposition:

Proposition A2: Consider the state variables to be above the 45° *line* ($s > x$). *If (i) technology T is a gross complement to the state's effort* s ($\nu < 0$) *and (ii) the complementarity between s and T is greater than that between x and T* ($\varepsilon > \nu$), *then* $d\theta / dT > 0$. *An advance in technology from* $T = 0$ *will* always make the inclusive corridor narrower *for all points in the region where* $x > \gamma$ *and* $s > \gamma$.

Proposition A2 provides a theoretical foundation to support our empirical findings. In an authoritarian or fragile democratic country ($s > x$ at the *status quo*), AI advances that welcome the input of big data favor the state ($\nu < 0$ and $\varepsilon > \nu$), which enables it to achieve ultimate control by increasing the surveillance and censorship of citizens (increasing s more than x). As a result, the relative productivity effect dominates the output effect, making the inclusive corridor narrower.[4] In response to an improvement in AI/ICT, the increase in θ makes the trajectory dynamics turn counter-clockwise, which is a momentum that may turn an originally fragile democracy into a despotic regime. AI and ICT are therefore unfavorable to democracy, as shown in our empirical results. Moreover, we also know that when the technology in question is more complementary to the state than to the society ($\varepsilon > \nu$), the momentum is stronger. This is because asymmetric elasticities reinforce the relative productivity effect, making the fragile democracy less stable.

Thus far, we have discussed the political competition between the state and society in the case where $x > \gamma$ and $s > \gamma$. From Assumption A2, it is

[4] Note that the result of Proposition A1 holds true, regardless of whether x *and* T are complements or substitutes.

possible that the state variables initially lie below their respective thresholds. For these cases, there must exist a point of time t^* such that$\forall t > t^*$, $s_t > \gamma$ and$x_t > \gamma$. Hence, our propositions above can apply after time t^*.

Robustness

Finally, our analysis also applies to any general production function which can be locally approximated by a generalized CES production function. Because we only need local properties to generate our results, our analysis can also be applied to a general output share distribution that fulfills the local properties of the raised cosine function.

References

Acemoglu, D., & Robinson, J. A. (2019a). *The Emergence of Weak, Despotic and Inclusive States*. Working Paper.

Acemoglu, D., & Robinson, J. A. (2019b) *The Narrow Corridor: States, Societies, and the Fate of Liberty*. Penguin Press.

Chu, C. Y. C., Chang, J., & Lin, C. (2025). Why Does AI Hinder Democratization?. *Proceedings of the National Academy of Sciences, 122*(19), e2423266122 https://doi.org/10.1073/pnas.2423266122.

Krusell, P., Ohanian, L. E., Ríos-Rull, J. S., & Violante, G. L. (2000). Capital-Skill Complementarity and Inequality: A Macroeconomic Analysis. *Econometrica, 68*, 1029–1053.

FSC
www.fsc.org
MIX
Papier | Fördert gute Waldnutzung
FSC® C083411

Kolibri 360 GmbH
Ferdinand-Jühlke-Straße 7
99095 Erfurt, Deutschland
produktsicherheit@kolibri360.de